International Marine Environmental Law

International Environmental Law and Policy Series

VOLUME 64

In the decade that has passed since this influential series was established under the general editorship of Stanley Johnson, international environmental law has truly come of age. The Rio process – the series of international negotiations leading to the 1992 United Nations Conference on Environment and Development in Rio de Janeiro – gave rise not only to crucial multilateral treaties on Climate Change and Conservation of Biological Diversity but also to the Rio Declaration on Environment and Development, which sets out basic principles for the future development of the subject. There is now an extensive network of multilateral environmental treaties in place, and an increasing recognition of basic principles, such as 'the polluter pays' and the precautionary principle, which have already been examined in this series.

The aim of the Editors, supported by their distinguished Editorial Board, is to publish works of the highest calibre which will serve not only to advance the subject itself, but also to consolidate the analytical thinking underpinning new and established issues of international environmental law and policy.

The recent titles published in this series are listed at the end of this volume.

International Marine Environmental Law

Institutions, Implementation and Innovations

Edited by

Andree Kirchner

GAUSS Institute for Environmental Protection
and Safety in Shipping

KLUWER LAW INTERNATIONAL
THE HAGUE / NEW YORK / LONDON

A C.I.P. Catalogue record for this book is available from the Library of Congress.

ISBN 90-411-2066-1

Published by
Kluwer Law International,
P.O. Box 85889, 2508 CN The Hague, The Netherlands
sales@kluwerlaw.com
http://www.kluwerlaw.com

Sold and distributed in North, Central and South America by
Aspen Publishers, Inc.
7201 McKinney Circle, Frederick, MD 21704, USA

Sold and distributed in all other countries
by Turpin Distribution Services Limited
Blackhorse Road, Letchworth, Herts.,
SG6 1HN, United Kingdom

Printed on acid-free paper

Printed and bound in Great Britain by Antony Rowe Limited

in memoriam

Elisabeth Mann Borgese
1918–2002

"Und was ist hinter dem Horizont?"

Contents

Series Editors' Preface

The protection of the marine environment was one of the first areas to be addressed comprehensively by international treaty law. As Dr. Kirchner points out, the initial impetus for the development of an international law regime to address marine environmental protection is often attributed to the publicity surrounding the major oil spill from the 1967 wreck of the Liberian-registered oil tanker the *Torrey Canyon* on the Seven Stones off the coast of the United Kingdom while en route to Milford Haven. Since then we have seen the development of a significant corpus of treaty law, including the overarching framework of the 1982 Law of the Sea Convention, which provides a number of important and innovative legal mechanisms for marine environmental protection.

The papers in this book demonstrate vividly the extent and the variety of the legal response while at the same time reminding us that there is still a great deal to be done. This response includes the large number of international legal and political instruments that have been developed in the last thirty years but also their implementation through national, regional and UN organizations, notably important new UN institutions such as the International Tribunal for the Law of the Sea (ITLOS) and the International Sea Bed Authority (ISA). The international regulatory framework (including the compensation regime) has clearly reduced vessel source pollution and this framework now extends to the use of toxic anti-fouling paints and soon to ballast water discharges. Farsighted and pro-active regulations for deep-sea bed mining are also in place even before it has become economically viable. In addition we see national and regional regimes for a wide range of marine activities including the establishment of protected areas and regulation of aquaculture.

We are pleased to include this volume in the Series. It includes papers by a number of distinguished authors addressing issues that continue to be important and are still highly topical in the wake of the 2002 Johannesburg World Summit on Sustainable Development.

David Freestone
Washington, D.C.

Dan Bodansky
Athens, Georgia

Preface

In April 2002, the GAUSS Institute for Environmental Protection and Safety in Shipping in Bremen, Germany, with the encouragement and support of the Free Hanseatic City of Bremen, the European Commission (DG Environment) and the International Maritime Organization (IMO), hosted the International Conference on Marine Environmental Law (ICMEL).

Maritime quality, environmental protection, safety and health are ethical matters which require sustainable efforts to raise knowledge and consciousness and in-depth consideration of human and creature dignity. *Inter alia*, social and cultural, economical and ecological aspects plus the legal framework are determining factors. Therefore the challenges of maritime and marine issues need a widespread, holistic approach rather than a sectoral view.

With this in mind and to mark the Fifth Anniversary of the Institute, we the GAUSS chose to broaden its series of conferences in the field of marine environmental protection and safety in shipping to marine environmental law. We developed this Conference into a forum for the exchange of views on common values and shared visions. Aptly, this edited collection is dedicated to "a common and differentiated approach to the protection of the marine environment". It is an effort to capture that vision and those common values in contemporary law-making as well as its implementation and enforcement.

Marine environmental law was introduced for the first time at the United Nations Conference on the Human Environment (UNCHE), held in Stockholm in 1972. This marked the birth of an environmental consciousness of the international community. In its Thirtieth Anniversary year we are also celebrating the twentieth anniversary of the United Nations Convention on the Law of the Sea (UNCLOS). Combined with earlier IMO work these conferences form the foundation on which we base marine environmental law today.

I would like to thank both the speakers and the participants from 27 countries for their role in ensuring the success of the Conference and for their contributions to this book. Moreover, I should express once again my gratitude to our sponsors and supporters. Finally, I would like to thank our staff members and the editor, Andree Kirchner, for their work in managing ICMEL.

Hans Gerd Knoop
Director
GAUSS Institute

List of Contributors

Mr. David Heywood Anderson, LL.M. (LSE)
Judge
International Tribunal for the Law of the Sea (ITLOS)
Hamburg (Germany)

Dr. Awni Behnam
Senior Adviser to the Secretary-General
United Nations Conference on Trade and Development (UNCTAD)
Geneva (Switzerland)

Dr. Agustín Blanco-Bazán
Senior Deputy Director and the Head of the Legal Office
International Maritime Organization (IMO)
London (United Kingdom)

Mr. Bela Hieronymus Buck
Ph.D. Candidate
Foundation Alfred Wegener Institute for Polar and Marine Research
Bremerhaven (Germany)

Mr. Aref Fakhry, LL.M. (Montreal), M.M.M. (Dalhousie)
Lecturer
IMO International Maritime Law Institute (IMLI)
Msida (Malta)

Dr. Thomas Höfer
Federal Institute for Risk Assessment
Berlin (Germany)

Professor Dr. Zou Keyuan
Senior Research Fellow
East Asian Institute
National University of Singapore

Dr. Andree Kirchner, LL.M. (Stockholm)
Advisor for International Law
GAUSS Institute
Bremen (Germany)

Ms. Gesche Krause
Ph.D. Candidate
Systems Ecology Department
University of Stockholm (Sweden)

Ms. Louise Angélique de La Fayette
Principal Legal Officer
Division for Ocean Affairs and the Law of the Sea
United Nations
New York (United States)

Professor Dr. Rainer Lagoni, LL.M.
Director
Law of the Sea and Maritime Law Institute
University of Hamburg (Germany)

Mr. Michael W. Lodge, M.Sc. (LSE)
Chief of the Office of Legal Affairs
International Seabed Authority (ISA)
Kingston (Jamaica)

Professor Dr. Moira McConnell
Professor of Law
Dalhousie University
Nova Scotia (Canada)

Professor Dr. Thomas A. Mensah, LL.M. (Yale)
Judge

International Tribunal for the Law of the Sea (ITLOS)
Hamburg (Germany)

Dr. Lutz Mez
Otto-Suhr-Institute for Political Science
Free University Berlin (FFU)
Berlin (Germany)

Professor Dr. Dr. h.c. mult. Harald Rosenthal
Professor
Institute for Marine Science
University of Kiel (Germany)

Dr. Iwona Rummel-Bulska
Senior Legal Adviser
World Meteorological Organisation (WMO)
Geneva (Switzerland)

Dott. Lorenzo Schiano di Pepe,
LL.M. (London), LL.M. (Georgetown)
Doctoral Candidate
University of Milano (Italy)

Professor Dr. Victor Smetacek
Head of the Department Pelagic Ecosystems
Foundation Alfred Wegener Institute for Polar and Marine Research
Bremerhaven (Germany)

Professor Dr. Hjalmar Thiel
Emeritus Professor
University of Hamburg (Germany)

GAUSS Institute for Environmental Protection and Safety in Shipping Bremen

The GAUSS Institute was founded in 1996 as a non-profit-making limited liability company in the Hanseatic City of Bremen. Its supervisory board includes representatives from the Senator for Education and Science, the Senator for Economics and Ports and the Senator for Constructions and Environment as well as the Universities of Applied Sciences in Bremen and Bremerhaven. The research advisory board consists of experts drawn both from science and practice, from associations and of individuals bearing political and economic responsibilities.

The GAUSS Institute has no own profit-making interests. Its funds may only be used for aims in accordance with the shareholders' agreement.

Since its foundation the GAUSS Institute has initiated, carried out, co-ordinated and supervised different research and development projects in the fields of safety in shipping and protection of the marine environment. Moreover, the GAUSS Institute's activities focus on advanced maritime education and training measures along with consulting services for companies, public authorities and other institutions. The co-operation with other maritime institutes and institutions as well as the establishment and supervision of technical bodies and task forces complement the range of assignments of the GAUSS Institute.

Projects were carried out with a wide range of customers, including the European Commission, the German Federal Ministry for Environment and its German Federal Environment Agency, the German Federal Ministry for Transport and the German Federal Ministry for Education and Research, and the Bremen Federal State Government, as well as shipping companies all over the world. Among the co-operation partners of the GAUSS Institute are the International Standardization Organization (ISO), the Nautical Institute, the Green Award Bureau, companies of the shipping industry, the German Federal Association of Sea and Harbour Pilots, several classification societies, and the Institute of Shipping Economics and Logistics (ISL) in Bremen.

Presently, members of the GAUSS Institute are master mariners or marine engineers as well as from other marine-related backgrounds. Senior members of the GAUSS Institute have long-lasting experience in their fields, including close relationships to the International Maritime Organization (IMO), the World Maritime University (WMU), the Nautical Institute, the International Maritime Lecturers Association (IMLA), the German Nautical Association (DNV), and other international and regional bodies.

The GAUSS Institute characterises itself as a point for communication, exchange of information and transfer of questions related to the marine environment and maritime safety. By linking research with and utilizing/applying its results with the interests and needs of the maritime community the GAUSS Institute actively contributes to the protection of the marine environment and to safety in shipping.

Further information may be found at <www.gauss.org>

International Marine Environmental Law: Editorial Introduction

*Andree Kirchner**

To defend and improve the human environment for present and future generations has become an imperative goal for mankind – a goal to be pursued together with, and in harmony with, the established and fundamental goals of peace and of worldwide economic and social development.[1]

This proclamation by the participating States at the United Nations Conference on the Human Environment (UNCHE), held in Stockholm (Sweden) in 1972, marks the beginning of international environmental law as a new field within international law. This is true even though international agreements and customs indirectly touching environmental protection go even back to the late eighteenth century.[2] But it was not until the late 1960s, following the *Torrey Canyon* disaster in March 1967, which involved the contamination of large areas of coastline by oil, that the international community was forced to react substantially. Until then only rudimentary instruments to protect the marine environment were in place.[3] In the following years several conventions were adopted in order to protect the marine environment from oil pollution.[4] It was still too early to recognize the true importance of the marine environment.

Only a few months after the disaster, on 1 Novermber 1967, Ambassador *Arvid Pardo*, "the Father of the Law of the Sea", delivered his prophetic speech at the United Nations General Assembly in which he urged delegates to consider the resources of

* Dr. Andree Kirchner, LL. M. (Stockholm) is the Advisor for International Law to the GAUSS Institute and was the Project Manager for the International Conference on Marine Environmental Law (ICMEL). Contact: kirchner@gauss.org. He is also a lecturer for international law at the universities of Bremen and Dresden (Germany) and at the IMO International Maritime Law Institute in Msida (Malta).

1 Declaration of the United Nations Conference on the Human Environment, 16 June 1972 [UN Doc. A/CONF.48/14/REV.1], para. 6.

2 Treaty of Amity Commerce and Navigation (Jay Treaty), 19 November 1794 [CTS, Vol. 52, p. 243].

3 Namely, the International Convention for the Prevention of Pollution of the Sea by Oil, 12 May 1954 [327 UNTS 3] and the Convention on the High Seas, 29 April 1958 [450 UNTS 82].

4 For example the Agreement for Co-operation in Dealing with Pollution of the North Sea by Oil, 9 June 1969; the International Convention Relating to Intervention on the High Seas in Cases of Oil Pollution Casualties, 29 November 1969 [ILM, Vol. 9 (1970), S. 25] and the International Convention on Civil Liability for Oil Pollution Damage, 29 November 1969 [973 UNTS 3].

A. Kirchner (ed.), International Maritime Environmental Law, 1–7.

the oceans beyond national jurisdiction as "the common heritage of mankind". His quest to protect the oceans from arbitrary appropriation, and his call for a regime to efficiently administer their resources, created the necessary momentum and provided "the unique opportunity to lay solid foundations for a peaceful and increasingly prosperous future for all peoples". He was much ahead of his time. But his approach marked the beginning of the negotiation process at the United Nations Conferences on the Law of the Sea starting in 1969. It is thanks to Ambassador *Tommy Koh*'s, President of UNCLOS III, dedication that the United Nations Convention on the Law of the Sea (UNCLOS),[5] "the Constitution for the Oceans", the most far-reaching treaty ever negotiated under United Nations auspices, was adopted in 1982 and has since then fostered the maintenance of peace and security.

In the years 1972/73 two major international conventions were adopted to protect the marine environment.[6] The goal of these Conventions, adopted under the auspices of the International Maritime Organization (IMO), is to protect the global marine environment from pollution by ships. Moreover, the year 1972 was a major benchmark for the further development of a general environmental consciousness. As mentioned above, the UNCHE formulated a new approach to the human environment and stated the common conviction, that

> States have [...] the responsibility to ensure that activities within their jurisdiction or control do not cause damage to the environment of other States or of areas beyond the limits of national jurisdiction.[7]

UNCHE also proposed a new UN Agency, the United Nations Environment Programme (UNEP). UNEP actively further developed marine environmental law with its Regional Seas Programme. These conventions apply the same principles for the maritime regions, often including norms contained in global conventions.

The protection and the sustainable use of the marine environment came to the top of the agenda at the United Nations Conference on Environment and Development (UNCED) in Rio de Janeiro (Brazil), in June 1992, and will also be a key element at the World Summit on Sustainable Development (WSSD) in Johannesburg (South Africa), in September 2002. This was due to the approach taken at the Rio Summit to redefine environment and its close interrelation to sustainable development. The oceans and seas are of major importance for the earth's ecosystem and for providing the vital resources for food security and for sustaining economic prosperity and the well-being of present and future generations.[8]

---

5 United Nations Convention for the Law of the Sea, 10 December 1982 [ILM, Vol. 21 (1982), S. 1261].

6 Namely, the Convention on the Prevention of Marine Pollution by Dumping of Wastes and Other Matter, 29 December 1972 [ILM, Vol. 11 (1972), S. 1294] and the International Convention for the Prevention of Pollution from Ships (MARPOL), 2 November 1973 [ILM, Vol. 12 (1973), S. 1319], amended by the Protocol of 1978 Relating to the International Convention for the Prevention of Pollution from Ships, 1973, 17 February 1978 [ILM, Vol. 17 (1978), S. 546]; cf. IMO/LC.2/Circ.380.

7 Stockholm Declaration, Principle 21.

8 UN General Assembly Resolution 54/33, Results of the review by the Commission on Sustainable Development of the sectoral theme of "Oceans and seas": international coordination and cooperation, 18 January 2000.

This book discusses some controversial legal aspects of the marine environment in the context of UNCLOS, as a framework for national, regional and global action in the marine sector.[9] It is based on contributions made at the International Conference on Marine Environmental Law (ICMEL), held in Bremen (Germany), in April 2002. The purpose of this book is to faithfully report the scientific expertise, legal acumen and policy wisdom presented by the speakers and participants at the Conference.

The book identifies major aspects of the status quo and possible future development of marine environmental law. Among the key issues covered are implementation and enforcement of environmental conventions; the avoidance, prevention and settlement of disputes; and liability and compensation for environmental damage. There are also included several articles which discuss the role of main institutions in this field within the UN system. The following institutions are represented by authors of this book:

- International Maritime Organization (IMO)
- International Maritime Law Institute (IMO/IMLI)
- International Seabed Authority (ISA)
- International Tribunal for the Law of the Sea (ITLOS)
- United Nations Environment Programme (UNEP)
- United Nations Conference on Trade and Development (UNCTAD)
- World Maritime University (IMO/WMU)
- World Meteorological Organization (WMO)

The Conference was divided into four themes relating to the protection of the marine environment. The first part dealt mainly with the institutionalization with regard to UNCLOS. The second part covered some issues related to implementation and the third part related to enforcement of international marine environmental law. Finally, the fourth part mentioned a few legal aspects of the marine industry.

Professor Dr. *Thomas Mensah*, Judge and former President of the International Tribunal for the Law of the Sea (ITLOS) in Hamburg (Germany), introduces the overall topic in his "Protection and Preservation of the Marine Environment". During the negotiation process of UNCLOS the settlement of disputes was included as Part XV of the Convention. Following these provisions of UNCLOS ITLOS was established.[10] Five years ago, at a meeting on 14 February 1997, ITLOS formed the Chamber for Marine Environment Disputes as a standing special chamber of the Tribunal.[11]

Judge *David Anderson* of ITLOS in "The Role of ITLOS as a Means of Dispute Settlement under UNCLOS" gives an insight to the work of the Tribunal. He argues that governments take care to negotiate settlements rather than to litigate. He clearly states that courts do not choose their own cases. He wants the Tribunal to be accorded the central, supervising role in the interpretation and application of the Convention. He refers to the Convention's preamble which notes that the problems of ocean space are inter-related and need to be considered as a whole.

9 United Nations Conference on Environment and Development, Agenda 21, chapter 17.

10 UNCLOS, Annex VI.

11 ITLOS, Resolution on the Chamber for Marine Environment Disputes, 8 October 1999; Judge *Anderson* and Judge *Mensah* are both members of the "Environment Chamber".

This factor led to the adoption of a single Convention. Finally, he assumes that it should also lead in time to the wider acceptance of the Tribunal as the principal "guardian" of the Convention.

Dr. *Agustín Blanco-Bazán*, the Head of the Legal Office and Deputy Director of the Legal Affairs and External Relations Division at IMO in London (United Kingdom), in "The Environmental UNCLOS and the Work of IMO in the Field of Prevention of Pollution from Vessels" describes IMO's basic features as the UN maritime agency. He refers to the general legal framework of the interface between UNCLOS and IMO treaties. Additionally he deals with the subject of special mandatory measures for certain areas and addresses the topic of emergencies at sea and the operation of the International Convention on Oil Pollution Preparedness, Response and Co-operation (OPRC) in conformity with UNCLOS. Finally, he refers to recent treaty law developments in the field of environmental protection.

With regard to the close interrelation of problems of ocean space, Mr. *Michael W. Lodge*, the Chief of the Office of Legal Affairs at the International Seabed Authority (ISA) in Kingston (Jamaica), in "Environmental Regulation of Deep Seabed Mining" gives an introduction into the establishment and work of the International Seabed Authority. After the adoption of the Agreement on 28 July 1994 relating to the implementation of Part XI of UNCLOS, the seabed and ocean floor, and the subsoil thereof, beyond the limits of national jurisdiction ("The Area") is considered as common heritage of mankind and enjoys a special protection from all activities.[12] He explains legal instruments with regard to deep seabed mining and the need for cooperation and the exchange of views in order to enable ISA to respond in an appropriate and timely manner to seabed mining activities as they progress.

Dr. *Iwona Rummel-Bulska*, Senior Advisor at the World Meteorological Organization (WMO) in Geneva (Switzerland), in "Law of the Sea and Meteorological and Oceanographic observations from Ocean Areas" explains the role and importance of the system of meteorological and oceanographic observations at sea. She continues with the protection of marine meteorological and oceanographic observations in the context of the negotiation process leading to UNCLOS. Finally, she mentions the role and activities of the newly established Joint WMO/IOC Technical Commission for Oceanography and Marine Meteorology.

Following the conviction expressed by the General Assembly "of the need, building on existing arrangements, for an integrated approach to all legal, economic, social, environmental and other relevant aspects of oceans and seas and the need to improve coordination and cooperation at both intergovernmental and inter-agency levels",[13] Professor Dr. *Moira McConnell* from the World Maritime University (WMU) in Malmö (Sweden) and from the Dalhousie Law School in Halifax (Canada) in "Inter-Agency Collaboration or Inter-Agency Competition – A Challenge for the UN System" considers the question of the relationship amongst UN organisations concerned with marine environmental protection. She examines the development of an ecosystem worldwide and Integrated Management as

12 UN GA Res. 2749 (XXV), 17 December 1970.
13 UN GA Res. 54/33 (2000), preamble, para. 7.

a response. Additionally, she mentions international environmental governance and problems related to the implementation of an integrated approach.

In the light of the rights and obligations arising from UNCLOS and the increasing needs of States, especially developing States, for advise and assistance in the implementation of the Convention, Mr. *Aref Fakhry* from the IMO International Maritime Law Institute (IMLI) in Msida (Malta) in "Capacity-Building in International Marine Environmental Law: Perspectives of Developing Countries" identifies in the first part the Achievements of international marine environmental law in developing countries, e.g. raising environmental awareness, technical cooperation and raising of environmental standards: a measured assessment. In the second part he explains the failures of international marine environmental law in developing countries, e.g. lack of faith in international standards, lack of knowledge, globalization, etc. The developing States, however, can only benefit fully from the legal regime for the seas and oceans if they develop and if they strengthen their capabilities.[14]

Dr. *Thomas Höfer* from the German Federal Institute for Risk Assessment in Berlin (Germany) and Dr. *Lutz Mez* from the Free University of Berlin (Germany) in their paper on the "Effectiveness of International Environmental Protection Treaties on the Sea Transport of Mineral Oil and Proposals for Policy Revision" examine the effectiveness of international treaties and regulations concerning environmental protection during sea transport of mineral oil. They determine that the problems surrounding flags of convenience and the limitations in authority and competence of IMO impede more effective policy instruments for marine environmental protection. They conclude with policy proposals to fortify environmentally conscious coastal states within the political regime by reducing the influence of flags of convenience, and to convert of IMO to a specialized organization of the UN system for marine environmental protection and maritime affairs.

In reference to the rethinking of traditional principles in the law of the sea since the late 1960s and to a new legal order for ocean space, Dr. *Awni Behnam*, Senior Advisor to the Secretary-General of the United Nations Conference for Trade and Development (UNCTAD) in Geneva (Switzerland) and member of the Governing Board of the International Ocean Institute (IOI) in Gzira (Malta), in "Ending Flag State Control?" challenges flag State control as a viable proposition and refers to global governance of the oceans. He elaborates certain needs to be addressed by the international community. He closes his paper with a suggestion to establish a single international registry for ships.

Dott. *Lorenzo Schiano di Pepe* from the University of Milano (Italy) gives an overview over Port State Control as an instrument to ensure compliance with international obligations relating to the protection of the marine environment in "Port State Control as an Instrument to Ensure Compliance with International Marine Environmental Obligations". He also explains the features of PSC as a compliance tool. Additionally, he elaborates on recent developments, e.g. the EU Directive 2001/106/EC.

To develop a practical response to the need for protecting coastal and marine waters, the international community has to resolve issues of governance of marine areas. Professor Dr. *Rainer Lagoni*, Director of the Law of the Sea and

14 UN GA Res. 56/12 (2001), para. II.

Maritime Law Institute at the University of Hamburg (Germany), in "Marine Protected Areas in the Exclusive Economic Zone" discusses the legal prerequisites for the designation of marine protected areas with regard to the exclusive economic zone. He explains the implications or affects on international lawful uses of the sea. He concludes with a statement concerning the importance of the designation of marine protected areas for the implementation of Part XII of UNCLOS.

Professor Dr. *Hjalmar Thiel* in "Approaches to Marine Protected Areas on the High Seas" identifies use and environmental impacts with regard to deep-sea resources. He explains approaches for the establishment of biodiversity, species and community protection in the deep sea. The General Assembly stressed in its Resolution 56/12 (2001) "that marine science, by improving knowledge, through sustained research efforts and the evaluation of monitoring results, and applying such knowledge to management and decision making, is important for [...] conserving the world's marine environment and resources, helping to understand, predict, mitigate the effects of and respond to natural events, and promoting the sustainable development of the oceans and seas".[15] In this line he develops the idea of and proposes unique science priority areas (USPAs).

Professor Dr. *Zou Keyuan* from the National University of Singapore in "Management of Marine Nature Reserves in East Asia: The Case of the People's Republic of China" gives an introduction to the adoption of laws and regulations in the field of marine nature reserves from a more national perspective. He continues with an overview of the implementation and monitoring of such instruments. In a second part he gives practical examples in China. Moreover, he discusses the implications of international law to national legislation and enforcement concerning the management of marine nature reserves in China. He touches on UNCLOS, the Convention on Biological Diversity, the Convention on Wetlands of International Importance Especially as Waterfowl Habitat, the Convention for the Protection of the World Cultural and Natural Heritage, MARPOL 73/78 and other treaties. Finally, he shows prospects of the Chinese policy, e.g. the China Ocean Agenda 21.

The joint paper by four authors, Mr. *Bela H. Buck* from the Foundation Alfred Wegener Institute for Polar and Marine Research, Bremerhaven (Germany), Ms. *Gesche Krause* from the University of Stockholm (Sweden), Professor Dr. Dr. h.c. mult. *Harald Rosenthal* from the University of Kiel (Germany) and Professor Dr. *Victor Smetacek*, Head of the Department on Pelagic Ecosystems at the Foundation Alfred Wegener Institute, on "Aquaculture and Environmental Regulations: The German Situation within the North Sea", provides a short summary of the current legislative framework existent on international, national and regional levels. The authors highlight the question of decision-making in the coastal zone within an integrated coastal zone management (ICZM) approach. They propose a scheme for further development and the establishment of an independent regulatory/advisory body, which encompasses all spatial levels. They close with a call for integrative action in Germany for the further promotion of aquaculture development by endorsing the idea of ICZM in order to sustain its economic potential as an alternative livelihood for coastal communities.

---

15 UN GA Res. 56/12 (2001), para. 15 and VIII.

Ms. *Louise Angélique de La Fayette*, Principal Legal Officer at the Division for Ocean Affairs and the Law of the Sea of the United Nations, New York (United States), in "Compensation for Environmental Damage in Maritime Liability Regimes" distinguishes between damage through the environment and damage to the environment. She gives an example by referring to the U.S. Regime for Compensation for Natural Resource Damage. Finally, she provides an outlook on recent developments.

The views presented in this book will indeed further the development of an international dialogue to facilitate a more effective protection of the marine environment.

The International Conference on Marine Environmental Law (ICMEL) was initiated as a process to discuss critically the importance of the further development of marine environmental law. It has shown in the past that oceans are the inspiration for the beginning of changes of the legal, economic and social order. Many principles in international law have their roots particularly in the law of the sea.[16] Also in our time, the oceans have proven to provoke new approaches. When thinking about *Pardo*'s ideas about the common heritage principle and the ideas discussed *inter alia* at ICMEL one might assume an emerging legal order for the high seas in the next decades.

In this context, the presentations and the discussions at ICMEL compiled in this book may, as an external effect, prompt *inter alia* the members of the United Nations Open-ended Informal Consultative Process on the Law of the Sea[17] (UNICPOLOS) to discuss and spread such ideas. They may also contribute to the evaluation of and to possible future amendments of UNCLOS from the year 2004 onwards.[18]

Finally, I would like to mention that this book is dedicated to the memory of the fascinating and powerful lifework of Professor Dr. *Elisabeth Mann Borgese* from Dalhousie University in Halifax (Canada), Founding Member of the Club of Rome in Hamburg (Germany) and Founding Member of the International Ocean Institute in Gzira (Malta). She kindly intended to speak at ICMEL on "Ending of Flag State Control?" before she died in St. Moritz (Switzerland) in February 2002. The international marine community has lost a recognised voice and a strong supporter of ocean affairs and a unique personality.

Moreover, I would like to express my gratitude to Professor Dr. *Moira McConnell* for her very kind interest in and support of ICMEL, ever since the first discussions in 2000. Additionally, I am very grateful for her most generous and personal advice on the preparation of this publication.

There is a companion website, specially created to work alongside the texts. A selected bibliography, documents, conventions and links connected to the contents of the book are included to provide an updated and comprehensive resource for the reader: www.andreekirchner.de/imel

---

16 Hugo Grotius, *De mari libero,* 1609 and *De iure belli ac pacis libri tres*, 1625.

17 UN GA Res. 54/33 (2000), para. 2.

18 Amendments to the United Nations Convention for the Law of the Sea according to Art. 312 UNCLOS.

Protection and Preservation of the Marine Environment and the Dispute Settlement Regime in the United Nations Convention on the Law of the Sea

*Thomas A. Mensah**

The 1982 United Nations Convention on the Law of the Sea designates a number of judicial bodies to which it assigns responsibility for the settlement of disputes under the Convention. These bodies are listed in Article 287 of the Convention and constitute what are referred to as "compulsory procedures entailing binding decisions" under Section 2 of Part XV of the Convention.[1] Pursuant to the Convention, the courts and tribunals referred to in Article 287 of the Convention have jurisdiction to adjudicate over disputes that may arise concerning the interpretation or application of the Convention, and the decisions they render in those disputes are binding on the parties involved.[2] Accordingly, these courts and tribunal have an important role in the implementation of the Convention's provisions, including the provisions that relate to the protection and preservation of the marine environment. Specifically, the courts and tribunals may be called upon to settle disputes between States Parties, or involving States Parties and other entities, regarding the interpretation or application of such provisions. For example, Article 297 of the Convention provides that a dispute may be submitted to the competent court or arbitral tribunal by a State Party against another State Party when "it is alleged that a coastal State

* Professor Dr. *Thomas A. Mensah*, LL.M. (Yale) has been a judge of the International Tribunal for the Law of the Sea (ITLOS), Hamburg (Germany) since 1996. He was the first president of the tribunal from 1996–1999. Judge Mensah served *inter alia* as Assistant Secretary-General and Legal Counsel to the International Maritime Organization (IMO) from 1968–1990. Contact: mensah@itlos.org.

The views expressed in this paper are attributable solely to the author.

1 The procedures, as enumerated in paragraph 1 of Article 287 of the Convention, are (a) the International Tribunal for the Law of the Sea established in accordance with Annex VI (to the Convention); (b) the International Court of Justice; as provided for in Section 2 of Part XV of the Convention; (c) an arbitral tribunal constituted in accordance with Annex VII; and (d) a special arbitral tribunal constituted in accordance with Annex VIII for one or more of the categories of disputes specified therein.

2 Article 288 of the Convention states that "a court or tribunal referred to in Article 287 shall have jurisdiction over any dispute concerning the interpretation or application of this Convention which is submitted to it in accordance this Part"; and Article 296 provides that "any decision rendered by a court or tribunal having jurisdiction under this section shall be final and shall be complied with by all the parties to the dispute".

A. Kirchner (ed.), International Maritime Environmental Law, 9–18.

has acted in contravention of specified international rules and standards for the protection or preservation of the marine environment which are applicable to the coastal state and which have been established by this Convention or through a competent international organization or diplomatic conference in accordance with this Convention".[3] The jurisdiction of a court or tribunal in such a case is not subject to any of the limitations on jurisdiction specified in Article 297 or the optional exceptions to jurisdiction available to States Parties under Article 298 of the Convention.[4] Thus, where all the States involved in a dispute are subject to the jurisdiction of a particular court or tribunal under Article 287 of the Convention, that court or tribunal will be competent to deal with such a dispute if it concerns the interpretation or application of any provisions of the Convention relating to the marine environment, as provided in the Convention.[5]

THE PROVISIONS OF THE CONVENTION RELATING TO THE ENVIRONMENT

The provisions of the Convention on the marine environment are not just the articles in Part XII of the Convention, but also include articles in the other Parts and Annexes to the extent that they concern activities that can have an impact on the quality of the marine environment. Among these are the articles which give rights and powers to coastal states to take measures for the prevention of pollution of the marine environment, or which set conditions and limitations on the exercise of such rights and powers. Disputes concerning the interpretation or application of any of these provisions may be brought before one or other of the courts or tribunals designated in Article 287 of the Convention. Special reference may be made in this regard to the following provisions:

1. Article 19 on innocent passage states that an "act of wilful and serious pollution" in the territorial sea is one of the acts that may be considered as "prejudicial to the peace and good order or security of the coastal state" and which will, therefore, deprive a ship of the rights of innocent passage in the territorial sea of the state concerned.[6]
2. Article 21, paragraph 2, sets limitations on the laws and regulations which a coastal state may adopt for, *inter alia*, the prevention, control and reduction of pollution of the marine environment. The paragraph states that such laws and regulations "shall

3 Article 297, paragraph 1(c).

4 Article 297, entitled "limitations on the applicability of section 2", provides that a State Party "shall not be obliged to accept the submission (of certain categories of disputes) to any of the courts or tribunals designated in Part XV of the Convention. And Article 298 gives to each State Party the discretion to declare in writing that "it does not accept any one or more (of the courts or tribunals) provided for in Section 2 (of Part XV of the Convention)".

5 The various sources of pollution of the marine environment are listed in Article 194 of the Convention.

6 Paragraph 1 of Article 19 states that passage is innocent so long as it is "not prejudicial to the peace, good order or security of the coastal state"; and paragraph 2 of the article states that "passage of a foreign ship shall be considered to be prejudicial to the peace, good order or security of the coastal State if, in the territorial sea, it engages in ... any act of wilful and serious pollution contrary to this Convention".

not apply to the design, construction, manning or equipment of foreign ships unless they are giving effect to generally accepted international rules or standards".

3. Article 56 gives jurisdiction to the coastal state in the exclusive economic zone with regard to the protection and preservation of the marine environment, including the power to enforce national and international regulations for the prevention, reduction and control of pollution from vessels.
4. Article 60 specifies the rights and obligations of the coastal state regarding the construction of artificial islands, installations and structures in the exclusive economic zone, including the removal of abandoned or disused installations. and the establishment of safety zones around such installations, taking into account applicable international standards.

Provisions relating to the protection and preservation of the marine environment are also to be found in Parts XI and Parts XIII of the Convention. For example, Article 145 in Part XI specifies measures that need to be taken to protect the marine environment from harmful effects from activities in the International Seabed Area. In Part XIII, Article 240(d) stipulates that marine scientific research "shall be conducted in compliance with relevant regulations adopted in conformity with this Convention, including those for the protection and preservation of the marine environment". And Article 263, paragraph 3, provides that "states and competent international organizations shall be responsible and liable... for damage caused by pollution of the marine environment arising out of marine scientific research undertaken by them or on their behalf".

POTENTIAL DISPUTES UNDER PART XII

The substantive articles in Part XII of the Convention present many areas of potential disputes between States Parties to the Convention. For example, disputes could arise where it is alleged that a coastal state has exceeded the powers given to it by the Convention to take measures for environmental protection against a foreign vessel; or that a coastal state has failed to comply with the applicable "safeguards" specified in the Convention when taking measures against a foreign vessel. The safeguards include the measures that should be taken to facilitate the hearing of witnesses and evidence submitted by other States or the competent international organization in proceedings (Article 233); the specification that powers of enforcement against foreign vessels may only be exercised by officials and identifiable government ships and craft (Article 224); the duty of the coastal State to avoid adverse consequences to the vessel or the marine environment (Article 225); the obligation on the coastal or port State to avoid unnecessary delay to a vessel (Article 226, paragraph 1); the requirement that "further physical investigation", beyond the examination of the certificates, records or other documents which the vessel is required to carry, may be undertaken only in certain clearly defined circumstances;[7]

7 Further "physical investigations" may only be undertaken if the examination reveals that "there are clear grounds for believing that the condition of the vessel or its equipment does not correspond substantially with the particulars of those documents"; or that "the contents of such documents are not sufficient to confirm or verify a suspected violation"; or that "the vessel is not carrying valid certificates and records": Article 226, paragraph (a) sub-paragraphs i–iii.

the duty of the detaining state to release a vessel promptly "subject to reasonable procedures such as bonding or other appropriate financial security" (Article 226, paragraph 1(b)); the obligation of the enforcing State not to discriminate in form or in fact against the vessels of any other State (Article 227); the duty of a coastal State to suspend proceedings to impose penalties in respect of violations in favour of measures taken or to be taken by the flag State (Article 228); the requirement that only monetary penalties may be imposed with respect to violations committed by foreign vessels outside or inside the territorial sea, except in cases of wilful and serious acts of pollution in the territorial sea (Article 230); and the obligation on the coastal State to notify the flag State and other States concerned of measures taken against a foreign vessel (Article 231).

These safeguards apply, *mutatis mutandis*, to enforcement measures taken by a State bordering a strait used for international navigation against a vessel which has committed a violation of laws and regulations if the violation causes major damage to the marine environment of the strait (Article 233).

Disputes under Part XII of the Convention may also arise concerning whether a State has legitimately exercised the right under Article 234 to adopt or enforce non-discriminatory laws and regulations to prevention, reduce or control marine pollution in ice-covered areas within the limits of the exclusive economic zone. In particular, there may be controversy over whether the laws or regulations adopted by the coastal state satisfy the requirement that they should have "due regard to navigation and the protection and preservation of the marine environment based on the best available scientific evidence".

The dispute settlement regime of the Convention can also play a major role in relation to the issue of liability and compensation for damage to the marine environment. One or other of the courts and tribunals referred to in Article 287 of the Convention may be required to deal with questions of liability and compensation for damage resulting from the exercise by a coastal or port state of powers under the Convention. Pursuant to Article 232 of the Convention, a State "shall be liable for damage or loss attributable to it arising form measures taken (pursuant to the relevant provisions of the Convention) when the measures are unlawful or exceed those reasonably required in the light of available information". The article further provides that states are obliged to "provide recourse in their courts for actions in respect of such damage or loss". A dispute as to whether or not a coastal or port State has complied with this provision, and the determination of any loss or damage resulting from proven non-compliance, will fall within the competence of one or other of the judicial bodies, if the states involved in the dispute have accepted its jurisdiction under Article 287 of the Convention.

A court or tribunal may also be called upon to adjudicate in disputes relating to Article 236 of the Convention. This concerns the extent to which the provisions of the Convention on the protection and preservation of the marine environment may be applied to warships, naval auxiliaries, other vessels or aircraft "owned or operated by a State and used, for the time being, only on government non-commercial service"). Although Article 236 states that the provisions of the Convention do not apply to such vessels, it nevertheless requires each State Party to "ensure, by the adoption of appropriate measures not impairing operations or operational capabilities of such vessels or aircraft owned or operated by it, that such vessels or aircraft act in a manner consistent, so far as is reasonable and practicable, with this

Convention". And Article 31 of the Convention states that "the flag State shall bear international responsibility for any loss or damage to the coastal State resulting from the non-compliance by a warship or other government ship operated for non-commercial purposes with the laws and regulations of the coastal State concerning the passage through the territorial sea or with the provisions of this Convention or other rules of international law". Where a coastal State claims that it has suffered loss or damage to the marine environment as a result of the failure by another State Party to comply with this provision, or where a flag State Party alleges that the coastal State has improperly applied the provisions of the Convention to a warship or other appropriate governmental vessel or craft, the dispute may be submitted to one of the procedures for dispute settlement provided for in the Convention, to the extent that the parties in the dispute either have chosen that procedure or are otherwise subject to its jurisdiction in accordance with the Convention.

POTENTIAL DISPUTES UNDER OTHER PARTS OF THE CONVENTION

As indicated above, disputes affecting the protection and preservation of the marine environment may also arise in the application of the provisions of Part XIII of the Convention on Marine Scientific Research. The relevant articles include Article 240(d) regarding the obligation on the part of States and international organizations to ensure that marine scientific research conducted by them or on their behalf complies with relevant regulations for the protection and preservation of the marine environment, and Article 263 which declares that States and international organizations shall be responsible and liable, pursuant to Article 235, for damage caused by pollution of the marine environment arising out of scientific research undertaken by them or on their behalf".[8]

Allegations of non-compliance with provisions of the Convention may also be brought before a court or tribunal under Article 292 of the Convention in connection with applications for the "prompt release" of arrested vessels and their crews upon the posting of reasonable bond or other security. The provisions of the Convention that may be invoked to request the prompt release of a ship or its crew include those relating to the protection of the marine environment from vessels. The Convention gives the right to coastal and port states to arrest or detain foreign vessels for violations of, *inter alia*, laws and regulations for the protection and preservation of the marine environment. For example, Article 220, paragraph 6, empowers a coastal state to institute proceedings against a vessel, "including detention of the vessel in accordance with its laws" if there is "clear objective evidence" that the vessel has, in the exclusive economic zone of the state, committed a violation of applicable international or national rules and standards for the prevention, reduction and control of pollution from vessels, and if such violation has caused "major damage or threat of major damage to the coastline or related interests" of the state. Similarly, Article 226, paragraph 1, gives to a port state the right to undertake physical inspection" of

8 Paragraph 3.

a foreign vessel where the conditions stated therein are satisfied.[9] In each case, however, the coastal state is obliged promptly to release the ship, "subject to reasonable procedures such bonding and other appropriate security".[10] Article 292 of the Convention gives to the flag State of an arrested ship the right to apply to a competent court or tribunal for the release of the ship if the detaining State fails to release the ship upon the posting of the requisite bond or other appropriate security. In the absence of an agreement between the states involved in the dispute to bring the matter to a particular court, such an application may be brought before the International Tribunal for the Law of the Sea. Indeed, in such a situation, the International Tribunal for the Law of the Sea is competent to deal with the request for the prompt release of the ship or its crew even if neither the arresting State nor the flag State of the ship has accepted the jurisdiction of the Tribunal under Article 287 of the Convention.

A dispute alleging non-compliance with the Convention may also be brought before one or other of the procedures for the settlement of disputes specified in Article 287 of the Convention to challenge measures taken by a coastal state under Article 111 of the Convention to deal with an alleged violation of laws and regulations for the protection and preservation of the marine environment. As provided in paragraph 8 of that article, a ship may be entitled to compensation for any loss or damage if the ship is stopped or arrested outside the territorial sea "in circumstances that do not justify the exercise of the right of hot pursuit". Where a flag state alleges that a ship flying its flag has been arrested as a result of "hot pursuit" that was not justified in the circumstances, it may bring an application for compensation in under the dispute settlement regime of the Convention.

DISPUTES SUBJECT TO THE JURISDICTION OF THE SEABED DISPUTES CHAMBER

Under Part XI of the Convention, the Seabed Disputes Chamber of the International Tribunal for the Law the Sea has special competence over disputes concerning the prevention of pollution or other forms of degradation of the marine environment of the Area arising from activities undertaken in the Area. Pursuant to Article 187, the Seabed Disputes Chamber has jurisdiction over, *inter alia*, disputes concerning the interpretation or application of (Part XI) and disputes concerning "acts or omissions of the Authority or a State Party alleged to be in violation of (Part XI) or the Annexes relating thereto or of rules, regulations and procedures of the Authority adopted in accordance thereto" or "acts of the Authority alleged to be in excess of jurisdiction or a misuse of power". Thus the Chamber is competent to deal with disputes concerning the interpretation or application of any provisions of Part XI which relate to the protection and preservation of the marine environment. In this regard special reference may be made to Article 145 which empowers the Authority to adopt appropriate rules, regulations and procedures "to ensure effective protection of the marine

9 See note 8 above.
10 As provided in Article 220, paragraph 7; and Article 226, paragraph 1 (c).

environment from harmful effects which may arise from (activities in the Area)"; and to Article 17 of Annex III to the Convention which requires the Authority to adopt and uniformly apply rules, regulations and procedures on, *inter alia*, "mining standards and practices, including those relating to operational safety, conservation of the resources and the protection of the marine environment".[11] Disputes could arise on the legitimacy or otherwise of the rules, regulations and procedures adopted by the Authority for the protection or preservation of the marine environment, especially in cases where it is alleged that the rules, regulations or procedures in question are "in excess of jurisdiction or constitute a misuse of power".

Paragraph (e) of Article 187 also endows the Seabed Disputes Chamber with jurisdiction in disputes between the Authority and a State Party, a state enterprise or a natural or juridical person … "where it is alleged that the Authority has incurred liability, as provided in Annex III, Article 22". This refers to the provision of article 22 of Annex III which states that the Authority shall have "responsibility or liability for any damage arising out of wrongful acts in the exercise of its powers and functions …". The article imposes a similar "responsibility or liability" on a contractor "for any damage arising out of wrongful acts in the conduct of its operations …". Where the damage alleged to have been caused by the Authority or a contractor includes damage to the marine environment, it will be for the Seabed Disputes Chamber to determine whether any responsibility or liability exists and, if so, the compensation to be paid, having regard to the circumstances of the particular case.

In cases where disputes arise in relation to these articles or other provisions in Part XI, the Seabed Disputes Chamber is the competent body to give the interpretation required for their effective application. Indeed, except where the parties have agreed to settle the dispute by another procedure of their choice, the jurisdiction of the Chamber in such cases is mandatory, regardless of the choice of dispute settlement procedure that may have been made under Article 287 by any States Parties involved in the dispute.

THE ROLE OF COURTS AND TRIBUNALS IN THE PRESCRIPTION OF PROVISIONAL MEASURES

The role of the dispute settlement mechanisms of the Convention in the protection and preservation of the marine environment is further amplified by the jurisdiction given to the courts and tribunal to prescribe provisional measures in cases involving possible damage to the marine environment. By virtue of Article 290 of the Convention, a court or tribunal referred to in Article 287 has the power to prescribe provisional measures, pending final judgment in cases duly submitted to it. Under that article provisional measures may be prescribed not only to preserve the rights of the parties but also to "prevent serious harm to the marine environment". This means that any of the courts or tribunals may, if it considers that the circumstances of a particular case so warrant, prescribe provisional measures either partly or solely to "prevent serious damage to the marine environment". In accordance with

11 Paragraph 1(b)(xii).

the Convention, any provisional measures prescribed by the Tribunal in such a case are binding on the parties to the dispute, unless and until the measures are revoked or modified by the arbitral tribunal to which the merits of the dispute are being submitted.[12]

In addition to the general jurisdiction given to the courts and tribunals listed in Article 287, paragraph 5 of Article 290 of the Convention gives to the International Tribunal for the Law of the Sea a special "residual" jurisdiction to prescribe provisional measures in a dispute even when the substantive merits of the dispute are not being submitted to the Tribunal. The jurisdiction applies where the parties to a dispute have agreed to submit the dispute to an arbitral tribunal to be constituted pursuant to Annex VII to the Convention. The paragraph provides that, pending the constitution of such an arbitral tribunal, the International Tribunal for the Law of the Sea or, as appropriate, the Seabed Disputes Chamber of the Tribunal, may prescribe provisional measures in the case, if it considers that "*prima facie* the tribunal which is to constituted would have jurisdiction and the urgency of the situation so requires". There is, however, a condition precedent for the exercise of this jurisdiction by the Tribunal. The Tribunal is competent to deal with the request for the prescription of provisional measures only if the parties in the case have failed to agree on another court or tribunal to deal with the request "within two weeks from the date of the request for provisional measures". When this condition is fulfilled the Tribunal is competent to prescribe provisional measures, if it requested to do so by one of the parties to the dispute. Upon such a request, the Tribunal has the power to prescribe the provisional measures that it considers to be appropriate in the circumstances. The measures prescribed may be those needed to, *inter alia*, prevent "serious damage to the marine environment". The jurisdiction of the Tribunal in such cases is "compulsory" in the sense that it does not depend on the choice of dispute settlement procedure that may have been made under Article 287 by the states involved in the dispute. This means that a State Party which has not chosen the Tribunal as its preferred procedure for the settlement of disputes is, nevertheless, entitled to bring a request for provisional measures to the Tribunal under paragraph 5 of Article 290 of the Convention. By the same token any State Party in the dispute is obliged to accept the jurisdiction of the Tribunal, even if it has not accepted the jurisdiction of the Tribunal under Article 287. And, as stated earlier, the provisional measures prescribed by the Tribunal will be binding on the parties to the dispute.[13]

SPECIAL ARRANGEMENTS FOR ENVIRONMENTAL DISPUTES IN THE INTERNATIONAL TRIBUNAL FOR THE LAW OF THE SEA

As one of the judicial bodies within the dispute settlement regime of the Convention, the International Tribunal for the Law of the Sea has taken note of the special role assigned to it in connection with the implementation of the Convention's provisions

---

12 Paragraph 6 of Article 290 of the Convention states that "the parties to the dispute shall comply promptly with any provisional measures prescribed under this article".

13 See note 13.

for the protection and preservation of the marine environment; and it has made special provision and established appropriate arrangements to enable it to discharge that role. Of the two special chambers that have been established for "particular categories of cases", one is for marine environment disputes. The Chamber for Marine Environment Disputes is composed of seven judges, and is "available to deal with disputes which the parties may agree to submit to it relating to the protection and preservation of the marine environment".[14] This means that States Parties to the Convention on the Law of the Sea, and parties to other agreements related to the purposes of the Convention, may utilize a smaller body for settling their marine environmental disputes, if they do not wish to use the full bench of the Tribunal for such disputes. This may be particularly useful where a dispute needs to be dealt with more expeditiously in order to prevent serious damage to the marine environment that might otherwise occur if more extended proceedings, requiring the participation of all twenty-one judges of the Tribunal, were used.

Another procedure for using the Tribunal without recourse to the full bench is available under Article 15 of the Statute of the Tribunal. Paragraph 2 of Article 15 provides that the Tribunal shall form "a chamber for dealing with a particular dispute submitted to it the parties so request". Such a chamber may consist of three or more members, and its composition is to be determined by the Tribunal "with the approval of the parties". Thus, in addition to the Chamber on Marine Environment Disputes, the parties in a dispute concerning the protection and preservation of the marine environment may, if they so desire, have their dispute dealt with by a smaller chamber whose composition will be determined with their agreement. This is another way in which the Tribunal can be especially "user-friendly" in cases relating to the protection and preservation of the marine environment.

CONCLUDING REMARKS

The dispute settlement regime of the United Nations Convention on the Law of the Sea is intended to play an important role in the interpretation and application of the Convention's provisions on the protection and preservation of the marine environment where disputes arise regarding the application of those provisions. In the majority of cases, the jurisdiction of the various courts and tribunals will depend on the agreement of the parties involved in the dispute; but there are situations in which the parties to a dispute may be obliged to accept the jurisdiction of a court or tribunal which they have not accepted beforehand. For example, the International Tribunal for the Law of the Sea, and the Seabed Disputes Chamber of the Tribunal, have jurisdiction in a number of cases, regardless of the choice of procedure that may have been made by one or all of the parties involved in the dispute. The Tribunal has put in place arrangements that are intended to make it attractive and convenient for parties involved in disputes regarding the interpretation or application of any provisions of the Convention on the Law of the Sea relating to the

---

14 The mandate of the Chamber established in 1996 is given in Yearbook of the International Tribunal for the Law of the Sea, 1996–1997, page 26.

protection and preservation of the marine environment. It is to be hoped that States and other entities will make greater use of the Tribunal, or the other courts and tribunals designated by the Convention. This will help to promote the objective in the provision of the Convention which states that disputes concerning the interpretation or application of its provisions shall be "by peaceful means in accordance with Article 2, paragraph 3, of the Charter of the United Nations".[15]

15 Article 279 of the Convention.

The Role of ITLOS as a Means of Dispute Settlement under UNCLOS

*David H. Anderson**

The International Tribunal for the Law of the Sea ("the Tribunal") is a permanent international judicial body,[1] set up in 1996 in the Free and Hanseatic City of Hamburg. Since that time, it has adopted its Rules and established its internal judicial practice.[2] It has adopted the policy, included in its Rules, of seeking to administer justice in accordance with the applicable rules of law and without any unnecessary expense or delay.[3] In 2000, it moved into its permanent premises overlooking the River Elbe, along which many sea-going ships pass every day. The excellent facilities, generously provided by the German authorities, give a solid basis for the work of the Tribunal. I trust you will all have an early opportunity to visit its premises.

The role of the Tribunal is to act as one of the means of dispute settlement under the United Nations Convention on the Law of the Sea ("the Convention"). The Tribunal is an autonomous international organisation which provides services to the States Parties, now totalling 138, or 70% of the international community. So far, the Tribunal has registered ten cases and it has given eight reasoned judgments and Orders. In many ways, the Tribunal complements the International Court of Justice ("the Court") as far as the law of the sea is concerned. The members of the Tribunal have high regard for the Court and have followed its practice, procedures and jurisprudence in large measure.[4]

---

* Mr. *David Heywood Anderson*, LL.M. (LSE) has been a judge of the International Tribunal for the Law of the Sea (ITLOS), Hamburg (Germany) since 1996. Contact: anderson@itlos.org.
The views expressed in this paper are attributable solely to the author.

1 For a general survey, see G. Eiriksson, *The International Tribunal for the Law of the Sea*, 2000. For a collection of essays by judges, see P. Chandrasekhara Rao and R. Khan (eds.), *The International Tribunal for the Law of the Sea*, 2001. For annual surveys of the work of the Tribunal, see the Tribunal's Annual Yearbooks, as well as articles by Sh. Rosenne and Vaughan Lowe in the International Journal of Marine and Coastal Law. Full information about the Tribunal is available on its website www.itlos.org.

2 *International Tribunal for the Law of the Sea: Basic Texts* 1998.

3 This policy is analysed in M. Evans (ed.), *Remedies in International Law*, 1998, chapter 4, at p. 79.

4 The Statute and Rules of the Tribunal were based on those of the Court, but with modifications. Professor Oxman has noted over 50 citations of decisions of the Court in the work of the Tribunal in his comments to the panel on the Horizontal Growth of International Courts and Tribunals at the 96th Annual Meeting of the American Society of International Law, Washington DC, on 16 March 2002.

A. Kirchner (ed.), International Maritime Environmental Law, 19–29.

The role of the Tribunal under the scheme of the Convention is conditioned by two main factors. First, the terms of the Convention, which both shape the constitution of the Tribunal and determine the scope of its jurisdiction. Second, the decisions of the States Parties to the Convention in submitting or not submitting disputes to the Tribunal. I will examine these two factors in turn, giving some personal impressions as a former negotiator and now interpreter of the Convention.

I. THE TRIBUNAL AND THE TERMS OF THE LOS CONVENTION

The general scheme for the settlement of disputes in Part XV of the Convention is both comprehensive and multi-faceted. It includes provisions for exchanges of views and conciliation, as well as for recourse to binding procedures such as judicial settlement and arbitration. The overall scheme is soundly based and the procedures not involving binding decisions are valuable. For example, recourse to conciliation, through the good offices of a neutral third party, may often produce worthwhile results for the parties.[5]

With regard to binding procedures, article 286 provides that:

> Subject to section 3, any dispute concerning the interpretation and application of this Convention shall, where no settlement has been reached by recourse to section 1, be submitted at the request of any party to the dispute to the court or tribunal having jurisdiction under this section.

The basic rule is one of compulsory jurisdiction. True, there are qualifications by virtue of the cross-references to sections 3 and 1.[6] Part XV, like the rest of the Convention, bears the marks of compromise. Dispute settlement was part of a wider "package deal", designed to lend stability to balances between opposed interests such as those of flag states and coastal states. Clear rules were not regarded as sufficient by themselves: some under-pinning or an overall structure involving binding, compulsory dispute settlement was also required.[7] In practice, the possibility of compulsory, binding litigation is likely to affect the course of prior negotiations between the two sides, ensuring that each side listens carefully to the words of the other.[8]

Whilst there was general acceptance of the advantages of having compulsory, binding procedures, there was less agreement over the forum. Some delegations preferred the Court, which had decided many important issues to do with the

---

5 A good example is provided by the Conciliation Commission set up by the governments of Iceland and Norway to address the question of delimitation of the EEZs between Iceland and Jan Mayen. See Charney and Alexander (Eds.), *International Maritime Boundaries*, Vol. II, p. 1755.

6 For example, article 297 sets out qualifications and article 298 permits some optional exceptions, all of which were needed in order to reach a consensus in the negotiations.

7 Stevenson and Oxman, 69 AJIL (1975) 1; see also the Comments by Professor Oxman to the panel on the Horizontal Growth of International Courts and Tribunals at the 96th Annual Meeting of the American Society of International Law, Washington DC, on 16 March 2002.

8 Governments are more likely to negotiate in a meaningful way if the alternative of litigation is a real one, apparent to both of them. This is one of the main advantages of dispute settlement provisions. Actual litigation is often a last resort and carries obvious risks for the parties.

customary law of the sea. Others supported the creation of a new permanent tribunal which would be given an overview of the operation of the entire Convention and a central role in its interpretation and application. This is one of the benefits of permanent courts over *ad hoc* courts. The need for a special tribunal for deep seabed mining disputes, involving mining consortia, was widely recognised. A third group of delegations considered that pre-formed tribunals were less satisfactory than *ad hoc* tribunals whose members were hand-picked by the parties for the particular dispute. The result was the Montreux formula in article 287, allowing for the choice of forum. This was another part of the price paid in order to secure consensus on binding, compulsory procedures for the settlement of disputes. The default rule, that is to say, the rule applicable where different or no choices had been made by the parties to a dispute, kept changing. At Montreux, Ambassador Riphagen's proposal was that the choice of the defendant should apply. Later, it was to be the new tribunal which was to have the default role. Finally, it became arbitration. This latter was a significant change for the Tribunal.

From the standpoint of upholding the rule of law in international relations, the overall arrangements in the Convention are far superior to the Optional Protocol attached to the Geneva Conventions of 1958. However, the arrangements remain very much a compromise, and one which may have pleased few delegations. The role given to the Tribunal retained only small elements of the central overview which should have been one of the benefits of having a permanent body. In other words, the role of the Tribunal was shaped very much by the outcome of the negotiations, as contained in the text of article 287.

The Organisation of the Tribunal

With 21 elected members, the Tribunal is a large judicial body. The judges enjoy a positive collegial spirit. This facilitates their work. All the judges enjoy the challenges presented by creating a new judicial organisation and tackling the cases submitted to it by the parties. The last decision was unanimous and in those cases in which there have been majority decisions the judges have never divided along East/West or North/South lines. There have been a good number of separate opinions, but this is normal in the case of a permanent international tribunal.[9]

The Tribunal has several types of chamber, including one of five members for Summary Jurisdiction. The Tribunal's members also make up the 11-member Seabed Disputes Chamber provided for in Part XI of the Convention. This Chamber has exclusive and compulsory jurisdiction over mining disputes arising in the international seabed area. To date, no case has been submitted to the Chamber, probably on account of the low level of activity to do with deep seabed mining and the consequential absence of disputes. The Tribunal has exercised its power to create standing Chambers by establishing two Chambers of seven members each, one for fisheries

9 For a survey of the voting patterns and separate opinions, see the present writer's article in M. Nordquist and J. Norton Moore (Eds.), *Current Marine Environmental Issues and the International Tribunal for the Law of the Sea*, 2001, p. 63.

disputes and the other for environmental disputes. The Chamber on Environmental Disputes is presided over by Judge Yankov, who was the Chairman of the Third Committee at the Conference which prepared Part XII of the Convention. I am pleased to serve under him in this Chamber. The Chambers give States the option of a smaller and perhaps quicker body for hearing urgent applications over such matters as fish quotas or oil-spills. The Chamber could hear cases brought under Part XII, including all the different forms of pollution: land-based sources, discharges from ships contrary to MARPOL, the dumping of wastes contrary to the standards contained in the London Convention, pollution caused by oil and gas installations on the continental shelf, and atmospheric pollution. So far, no litigant has submitted a dispute to either the fisheries or the environmental chamber.

In addition to the two standing chambers, the Tribunal may also establish *ad hoc* Chambers in consultation with the parties in order to hear a particular dispute. For instance, the Tribunal made an Order constituting an *ad hoc* Chamber of five members in the Swordfish Stocks Case between Chile and the European Community. In all other cases heard so far, the full Tribunal of 21 has sat.

Jurisdiction

The jurisdiction of the Tribunal is laid down in the Convention, including Parts XI and XV, plus Annex VI. The Tribunal has jurisdiction over disputes concerning the interpretation and application of the Convention which are submitted to it under the terms of Part XV and over disputes concerning international agreements related to the Convention which are submitted in accordance with the terms of those agreements. An example of a related agreement is the Agreement on the Implementation of the provisions on Straddling Fish Stocks and Highly Migratory Fish Stocks, which has entered into force recently and which provides for the settlement of disputes relating to its provisions and those of regional and sub-regional fisheries agreements.[10] Another possible example would be an agreement among a group of States to submit a question for an Advisory Opinion. The Rules of the Tribunal make provision for this possibility in Rule 138.

Potentially, the Tribunal, including the Seabed Disputes Chamber, has jurisdiction *ratione personae* over disputes concerning the States Parties, other entities such as mining consortia and the International Seabed Authority. The European Community is counted as a State Party, in accordance with Annex IX of the Convention. The EC, to the exclusion of the member states, is a party to the case with Chile concerning Swordfish Stocks in the SE Pacific Ocean.[11]

In Paragraph 10 of Resolution 56/12 of 2001, the UN General Assembly noted *"with satisfaction the continued contribution of the International Tribunal for the Law of the Sea to the peaceful settlement of disputes in accordance with Part XV of*

10 The Protocol to the London (Dumping) Convention of 1996 and the recent UNESCO Convention on the Protection of the Underwater Cultural Heritage may also be mentioned in regard to article 288.

11 As required by Annex IX to the Convention, the EC made a declaration upon becoming a party, specifying the matters governed by the Convention in respect of which it exercised competence.

the Convention". The General Assembly underlined the Tribunal's *"important role and authority concerning the interpretation and application of the Convention ... "* Probing a little deeper, however, some more specific attitudes emerge. In making choices under article 287 of the Convention, only 16 States Parties have made the Tribunal their first choice and only 9 have named the Court. In contrast, the remaining 113 States Parties, over 80% of the total, have chosen, in effect, arbitration by silence.[12] To date, no case has been submitted to the Tribunal or the Court under the mechanism in article 287, whereas three compulsory arbitrations have commenced under Annex VII.[13] Thus, the role of the Tribunal is also being shaped by the actions of the States Parties in implementing article 287.

II. ENVIRONMENTAL AND SHIPPING ASPECTS OF THE TRIBUNAL'S CASELAW

So far, the Registrar has entered 10 cases on the Tribunal's list. There were some environmental aspects present in most of the cases, whether directly or indirectly. In addition, the Tribunal has had to consider some questions which will be of general interest to the shipping industry. My brief survey will concentrate on some impressions of the environmental and shipping aspects of these cases, without attempting full surveys.

1. The Saiga (No. 2) Case and the question of bunkering in the EEZ

The Saiga, a tanker, was seized 70 miles offshore, just beyond the southern limit of the EEZ claimed by Guinea in its legislation. The vessel was taken under arrest to Conakry where the Master was charged with customs offences in that he had supplied bunkers to three fishing vessels at places just beyond the outer limit of the territorial sea of Guinea. When considering the merits of the case, the Tribunal rejected the Respondent's argument that it was entitled to apply Guinean customs law in an extensive customs surveillance area beyond the territorial sea.[14] Guinea did not assert its fisheries or environmental jurisdiction. In a future case, the Tribunal may have to consider whether or not a coastal state is entitled to regulate bunkering and other similar activities in support of fishing vessels as part of its regulatory jurisdiction over fishing in the EEZ in accordance with article 62 of the Convention. Many coastal states have enacted legislation imposing a system of licences or permits for bunkering and other operations in support of authorised fishing vessels whilst they are fishing in the EEZ.

---

12 Information taken from the website www.un.org/ in March 2002.

13 These were the Saiga Case (later referred to the Tribunal by agreement between the parties), the Southern Bluefin Tuna Case (the arbitral tribunal later found it was without jurisdiction) and the MOX Plant Case (an arbitration is pending).

14 Saiga (No 2) Case, Reports 1999 10, at 54, paragraph 127. For comment, see L. de La Fayette, "ITLOS and the Saga of the Saiga: Peaceful Settlement of a Law of the Sea Dispute", 15 IJMCL (2000) 355.

2. The Saiga (No. 2) Case and arrest at sea

The Saiga was seized by the customs and naval officers of Guinea who opened fire with machine guns on the vessel. On the basis of written evidence, especially the ship's logbook, and oral testimony before the Tribunal of the Master and the arresting officers, the Tribunal decided that the respondent had stopped and arrested the vessel in circumstances which did not justify the exercise of the right of hot pursuit in accordance with article 111 of the Convention. The procedures for exercising the right of visit and search, as defined in article 110, had not been followed correctly. Unnecessary force had been used to arrest the vessel. Here, the Tribunal paid regard to the "I'm Alone" and "Red Crusader" Cases, as well as to article 22(1) (f) of the Straddling Stocks Agreement. The Tribunal found that the arresting officers had used excessive force and endangered human life, contrary to customary international law, both before and after boarding the vessel.[15] Compensation was awarded to two persons on board the ship injured by bullets and to the owners for damage to the vessel. This was one of the most important findings in the case.

3. Prompt Release of detained fishing vessels and reefers

Three applications have been made under article 292 for the prompt release of fishing vessels detained pending trial. In these cases, environmental factors have arisen indirectly. In both the Camouco[16] and Monte Confurco[17] Cases, the vessels had been apprehended in the EEZs around the *Isles Crozet* and Kerguelen on suspicion of fishing for Patagonian Toothfish at times not contemplated by the coastal state nor by the conservation measures adopted by the Commission for the Conservation of Antarctic Marine Living Resources. In each case, the French fishery protection officers escorted the vessel to Reunion for trial before the competent court. Early release, pending trial, against the deposit of cash as *caution* was available, but the cash was not paid by the operators who applied instead for release under article 292. The Tribunal has heard these applications without delay. The Tribunal took account of the gravity of the alleged offences, the penalties imposable, the value of the vessel and its contents and the amount of the security ordered by the detaining state. The Tribunal ordered release and fixed an amount for each bond, in the form of a bank guarantee, that was lower than the *caution* fixed by the court in Reunion for release. In dissenting, I expressed the view that in considering whether the coastal state had breached its duty to allow prompt release against a reasonable bond (as required by article 73(2)), greater regard should be paid to the wider duty of the coastal state under Part V of the Convention to conserve the stocks in its EEZ. This duty means that a coastal state needs to enforce its laws effectively by maintaining patrols, by boarding vessels and by prosecuting those suspected of fisheries offences. Legislatures have laid down high maximum penalties upon conviction. The courts may need the power to impose deterrent penalties and, in my view, this may be a relevant factor in fixing the size of the "reasonable" bond.

15 Saiga (No. 2) Case, Reports 1999 10, at 63, paragraph 158.
16 Reports 2000 10.
17 Reports 2000 86.

In the third instance of an application for the release of a fishing vessel from detention in Reunion, the Grand Prince Case,[18] the Tribunal found that it lacked jurisdiction. Had the Tribunal considered the merits of the application for prompt release, it would have had to consider the question of whether the release of a vessel could be ordered under article 292 at a time when the vessel had been confiscated by order of a court in the coastal state as a penalty imposed upon conviction for fisheries offences in the EEZ.

In the case of the Chaisiri Reefer No. 2, the parties reached agreement, settling their differences, just before the date set for the hearing. The detained vessel was allowed to sail and the proceedings were discontinued. Had the Tribunal been called upon to give a decision, one of the issues would have been whether the provisions about prompt release in articles 73(2) and 292 of the Convention applied to a transport vessel which, when detained, was engaged in transporting fish that had been caught by other vessels in the EEZ of the coastal state. Logistical support for fish catching vessels raises issues similar to bunkering, as in the Saiga case.

4. The Southern Bluefin Tuna Cases

These two cases, which were the subject of a joined hearing and a single Order, had clearer environmental dimensions. The two applicants, Australia and New Zealand, began arbitrations under article 287 and Annex VII of the Convention concerning a Japanese experimental fishing programme for Southern Bluefin Tuna. They also submitted applications to the Tribunal under article 290(5) of the Convention for provisional measures, pending the constitution of the arbitral tribunal. Such measures are binding under the terms of the Convention. The applicants sought an order putting an end to the experimental fishing programme and the capping of Japan's total annual catch. In certain defined circumstances, the Tribunal has the power to order provisional measures *"to preserve the respective rights of the parties to the dispute or to prevent serious harm to the marine environment, pending a final decision"* by the arbitral tribunal.

After considering extensive written arguments and hearing the parties, the Tribunal decided that it did have jurisdiction to prescribe provisional measures. In the course of its reasoning, the Tribunal stated that:

> The conservation of the living resources of the sea is an element in the protection and preservation of the marine environment.[19]

In this finding, the Tribunal made a link between conservation of fish stocks and the protection of the marine environment. In other words, the Tribunal made the link between Parts V and VII of the Convention, concerning fishing in the EEZ and on the high seas, on the one hand, and Part XII concerning the protection and preservation of the marine environment, on the other. Here was a dispute about fishing to which considerations to do with the protection of the environment were applied.

---

18 Reports 2001 17.
19 Reports 1999 280, at 295, paragraph 70.

A second important question was that of the precautionary principle or approach. Australia and New Zealand requested the Tribunal to order the parties "to act consistently with the precautionary principle in fishing" southern bluefin tuna. The Tribunal did not accede to this request in the form it was presented. However, the Tribunal did state that:

> the parties should ... act with prudence and caution to ensure that effective conservation measures are taken to prevent serious harm to the stock of southern bluefin tuna.[20]

It should be recalled that the Tribunal was considering an urgent request for provisional measures, not the merits of the dispute. Caution is inherent, in a sense, in the entire notion of *"mesures conservatoires"*, to quote the French title of article 290.[21] In the circumstances, it was not appropriate or necessary for the Tribunal to make any finding as to the status of the precautionary principle in international law.

Environmental considerations, in particular the poor state of the stock of southern bluefin tuna, were very much in mind in ordering the provisional measures. The parties were in agreement that the stock was severely depleted and there were serious grounds for biological concern. The picture painted of the southern bluefin tuna was that of a most valuable species, very much reduced in total numbers, slow to reach maturity, and widely dispersed across the southern Indian Ocean and the Tasman Sea. The collective management of this species, entrusted by the three parties to the Commission for the Conservation of Southern Bluefin Tuna, appeared to have broken down. No decisions were being taken in the Commission, and this at a time when new entrants were coming into the fishery, producing unpredictable results. Notwithstanding the experimental catches by commercial fishing vessels in what would normally have been a time of little fishing, all three parties indicated in response to a question from the Tribunal that they intended to open their respective fishing seasons on 1 September 1999, and to do so on the usual basis.[22] The prospect at that point was one of increasing annual catches of a species which was agreed by everyone concerned to be at its lowest ever levels. Faced with that prospect, the Tribunal decided to impose provisional measures on *all three* parties, not just Japan. These measures were, first, capping their respective annual catches; second, calling for renewed and closer cooperation amongst the three parties; and third calling for improved relations with third states and entities entering the fishery to the end that the latter would join in the collective efforts at conservation and management. In this context, I would note that the issues were not seen primarily as ones between a distant water fishing state and two coastal states. The state of origin of the stock was Indonesia, a coastal state increasing its catch, and part of the problem concerned third states and entities. The issues were seen as being ones to do with a breakdown of cooperation in a regional fisheries arrangement involving a highly migratory species.

The parties reported to the Tribunal on the steps taken to implement the measures. As with all other cases, the Tribunal's measures were fully complied with.[23]

---

20 Reports 1999 280, at 296, paragraph 77.

21 A point made by Judge Treves in paragraph 9 of his separate opinion.

22 Ibid., paragraph 75.

23 Particularly noteworthy was the decision of the Court of Appeals in St. Denis, Reunion, that the decision of the Tribunal in the Camouco case was binding upon French Courts since France is a party to the Convention: Judgment No. 266/2000 of 21 March 2000.

Subsequently, the dispute was settled by agreement among the parties. The Commission has re-started its work and membership has increased. All concerned appear to have benefited, including the bluefin tuna.[24]

5. Swordfish Case

The case concerning the conservation and sustainable exploitation of swordfish stocks in the south-eastern Pacific Ocean was submitted to a chamber of the Tribunal by means of an agreement between Chile and the European Community.[25] Both sides have made claims against the other concerning the exploitation and management of this stock. The proceedings have been suspended at the request of the parties and it would not be appropriate to go into the details of the claims. The case shows the type of issues on which the Tribunal, or in this case an *ad hoc* Chamber, can play a role.

6. MOX Plant Case

This case was initiated by Ireland against the United Kingdom. Ireland sought from the Tribunal an order under article 290 of the Convention, pending the constitution of an *ad hoc* arbitral tribunal under annex VII of the Convention. The measures requested were that the UK should suspend the authorisation of a new plant on the Sellafield site in Cumbria and should ensure that there were no associated movements of radioactive materials in waters under British sovereignty or jurisdiction. Like Australia and New Zealand in the SBT Case, Ireland invoked the precautionary principle, contending that the burden lay on the UK to show that no harm would result from discharges into the Irish Sea and other consequences of the operation of the MOX Plant. After placing on record some assurances by the UK, the Tribunal decided that the urgency of the situation was not such as to require the prescription of measures as requested in the short time before the constitution of the *ad hoc* body. In the circumstances, no findings were made concerning the status or applicability of the precautionary principle. At the same time, the Tribunal did state that "prudence and caution require that Ireland and the United Kingdom cooperate in exchanging information concerning risks or effects of the operation of the MOX Plant..." The Order called for consultations to exchange information on possible consequences, to monitor risks or effects, and to devise measures, as appropriate, to prevent pollution of the marine environment.[26] The parties reported to the Registrar of the Tribunal that such consultations had taken place. The arbitration under annex VII to the Convention is proceeding.

---

24 See the remarks of W. Mansfield (Counsel to New Zealand) to a SEAPOL Conference on 21 March 2001, as well as in a letter to the Editor of the American Journal of International Law: 95 AJIL (2001) 624.

25 The latter could not appear as a party to a case before the International Court of Justice, in view of the terms of its Statute.

26 Reports 2001 95, at 110, paragraph 89.

7. Issues to do with the registration and management of ships

Several cases have concerned ships flying a flag different from the nationality of the Master and the operating company.[27] In other words, the flags flown were what are often described as ones of "convenience".

In both the Saiga (No. 2) and Grand Prince Cases, the Tribunal considered the question of whether or not it had been established that the vessel was registered in the applicant state at all material times. In the former case, an objection to the admissibility of the claims based on an alleged absence of valid registration was rejected only after a lengthy analysis of the law and practice of St Vincent.[28] In the Grand Prince Case, after a lengthy review of the facts, including evidence of Belizean law and administrative practice, the Tribunal was not satisfied that Belize was the flag state of the vessel when the application for prompt release was submitted. Accordingly, the Tribunal decided it was without jurisdiction to entertain the application under article 292.[29]

In the Saiga Case, the Tribunal had also to consider an argument that the claim was inadmissible on the additional ground that there was no genuine link between the ship and St Vincent within the meaning of article 91 of the Convention. The Tribunal found that there was no legal basis for that argument. The genuine link test had to do with ensuring the effective administration and management of ships and not with the recognition of nationality by other states.[30] The Tribunal also found that, on the facts, Guinea had not shown there was no genuine link. The Attorney General of St Vincent took part in the case and evidence of management, surveys and Vincentian supervision was produced.[31] The finding could have been different on different facts.

In all these cases, the Tribunal has stressed the importance of flag states complying with their obligations under articles 91 and 94 of the Convention.

III. SUMMING UP

To sum up, numerous international maritime disputes are mentioned in the press. For example, Lloyd's List often refers to incidents, arrests and differences between governments which could potentially come before a court or tribunal under Part XV. Very few of them actually materialise as legal cases, which may simply show that governments take care to negotiate settlements rather than to litigate. Clearly, courts

27 This was the situation in the Saiga, Camouco, Monte Confurco and Grand Prince Cases. The Saiga was registered in St Vincent and the captain came from the Ukraine. The Camouco was flying the flag of Panama but the Master was Spanish. The Monte Confurco was flying the flag of the Seychelles when its Spanish Master was detained. The Grand Prince was flying the flag of Belize when its Spanish Master was apprehended. The operators appeared not to be based in the flag states.

28 Reports 1999 10, at 33 to 39, paragraphs 55 to 74.

29 Reports 2001 7, at 36 to 44, paragraphs 62 to 93.

30 Reports 1999 10, at 39 to 42, paragraphs 75 to 86.

31 Ibid., paragraph 87.

do not choose their own cases, nor would it be proper for them to solicit work. The Tribunal can play a role only when asked to do so by State Parties.[32]

As I have attempted to demonstrate, the role of the Tribunal today has been conditioned by two main factors: first, what the negotiators wished to give it during the Conference, as set out in the Convention; second, what the States Parties actually give it by choosing the Tribunal under article 287 or by submitting cases to it.

In the result, most of Tribunal's work so far has come from the two main areas of its compulsory jurisdiction, namely applications for the prompt release of vessels under article 292 and applications for interim measures of protection under article 290 pending the constitution of an arbitral tribunal under annex VII. Of the eight reasoned decisions, seven have been given in urgent proceedings. In addition, two cases have been submitted by agreement, namely the Saiga No. 2 (Merits) and the Swordfish Case. The ten cases have come from different seas and oceans and they have raised issues under several parts of the Convention.

Part XV may be leading to an increase in the sum total of international litigation. This may be explained by two factors. First, the number of applications for prompt release, a completely new procedure, based upon the novel provisions in article 292 and, second, the number of arbitrations commenced under Annex VII. This second factor may be more significant. A new phenomenon – compulsory arbitration under article 287 and Annex VII – may be emerging.

A third shaping factor is the role which the judges play. What have the judges made so far of the hand dealt them? The rules and working methods are designed to administer justice in accordance with the Convention without unnecessary expense or delay. The Tribunal has acquired a reputation for adopting new approaches, for hard work, and for prompt decisions. The Members of the Tribunal remain ready, willing and able to play their role in the settlement of disputes under the Convention and the related instruments. They remain available 365 days a year. I am confident that they will continue to try to handle cases efficiently, to deliberate intensively, and to reach correct and fully reasoned decisions.[33] I should like to think that the Tribunal will come to be accorded the central, supervising role in the interpretation and application of the Convention. As the Convention's preamble accurately notes, the problems of ocean space are inter-related and need to be considered as a whole. This factor led to the adoption of a single Convention. Perhaps it should also lead in time to the wider acceptance of the Tribunal as the principal "guardian" of the Convention.[34]

32 Or States Parties to other related Conventions such as the Straddling Stocks Agreement.

33 The judges are aware that the most common criticism advanced by commentators is the paucity of reasoning. This is often caused by the need to work quickly in urgent cases.

34 The role already played by the Seabed Disputes Chamber with regard to disputes arising under Part XI.

The Environmental UNCLOS and the Work of IMO in the Field of Prevention of Pollution from Vessels

*Agustín Blanco-Bazán**

INTRODUCTION AND SUMMARY

The relationship between the 1982 United Nations Conventions on the Law of the Sea (UNCLOS) and the treaties adopted by the International Maritime Organization (IMO) is highlighted here under a historical and legal perspective.

Part I contains a description of IMO's basic features as the UN maritime agency and information on the most relevant IMO treaties.

Part II refers to the general legal framework of the interface between UNCLOS and IMO treaties.

The main jurisdictional issues involving the application of MARPOL in the light of UNCLOS are addressed in Part III.

Part IV deals with the subject of special mandatory measures for certain areas.

Part V addresses the topic of emergencies at sea and the operation of the OPRC Convention in conformity with UNCLOS.

Part VI refers to recent treaty law developments in the field of environmental protection.

Annex 1 contains a MARPOL/UNCLOS cross reference table.

I. BASIC FACTS ON IMO'S MANDATE AND ITS TREATY-MAKING ACTIVITY

The Mandate of IMO

IMO is the sole agency of the United Nations entirely devoted to maritime affairs. Since the inception of its activities in 1958 IMO has elaborated a comprehensive set of treaty and non-treaty instruments aimed at enhancing *safety of commercial navigation* and the *prevention and control of marine pollution from vessels source.*

* Dr. *Agustín Blanco-Bazán* is a Senior Deputy Director and the Head of the Legal Office of the International Maritime Organization (IMO), London (United Kingdom). Contact: ablancob@imo.org.

The opinions expressed in this paper are those of the author and should not be construed as necessarily reflecting the views of the IMO or its Secretariat.

A. Kirchner (ed.), International Maritime Environmental Law, 31–47.

The term "maritime" applies to IMO in a restrictive sense. IMO is a maritime organization as long as *maritime* relates to *shipping*. This limitation is clearly reflected in article 1(a) of the treaty establishing the Organization.[1] In accordance with this provision, IMO comes into being in order *"to provide machinery for co-operation among Governments in the field of governmental regulation and practices relating to technical matters of all kinds affecting shipping engaged in international trade; to encourage and facilitate the general adoption of the highest practicable standards in matters concerning maritime safety, efficiency of navigation and prevention and control of marine pollution from ships"*.

In terms of prevention of marine pollution this limitation means a lot. It means that all IMO's environmental work aims at protecting the marine environment from a source that produces only 10 per cent of man-made marine pollution. The remaining 90 per cent is the result of land-based sources of pollution. This means that States should counteract sea pollution coming from their own coasts to complement IMO's work on the protection of the marine environment.

IMO treaty-making work in the field of marine pollution from ships has been particularly successful on account of the international nature of shipping: only through world-wide applicable international regulations can a conflict-free interaction between flag, coastal and port State jurisdiction be put in place in order to make possible the harmonious development of sea-borne international trade.

In the case of land-based sources of pollution, States are not ready to cede their sovereignty in such a way that national and municipal law are interfered with through regulations indicating what can or cannot be disposed of in the sea by every single factory along the coast. For this reason, de-neutralization of land-based sources of pollution cannot be regulated in the same way that the IMO conventions do in the case of shipping.

The different features of development of international law depending on whether it relates to prevention of marine pollution from ships or to land-based sources of pollution lead to important considerations of *jus aequum*: it seems unfair to impose upon the shipping industry extremely stringent global anti-pollution measures while enabling land-based interests to continue polluting the sea in a proportion of 9 to 1. The process of internationalization of law at the expenses of national sovereignty should perhaps also be intensified in the field of prevention of pollution from land-based sources.

Treaty-Making Activity

The usual classification of IMO treaties in safety and anti-pollution conventions should be approached bearing in mind the close interconnection of the safety and pollution risks these treaties aim to counteract. IMO safety conventions mainly regulate measures to prevent accidents endangering human life and goods at sea. However they include many regulations aimed at preventing marine pollution occurring as a result of these accidents.

1 Convention on the International Maritime Organization, adopted by the United Nations Maritime Conference in Geneva on 6 March 1948.

Among the most important treaties dealing mainly with safety of navigation, mention should be first made of the International Convention for the Safety of Life at Sea (SOLAS), 1974, and the International Convention on Standards for Training, Certification and Watchkeeping for Seafarers, 1978 (STCW 1978).

IMO environmental treaties exclusively regulate antipollution measures, irrespective of whether the introduction of polluting substances into the sea is the result of an accident involving a ship or from the operational discharges from vessels. The main treaties under consideration for the purposes of this paper are:

> International Convention for the Prevention of Pollution from Ships, 1973, as modified by the Protocol of 1978 relating thereto (MARPOL 73/78). It covers accidental and operational oil pollution as well as pollution by chemicals, goods in packaged form, sewage, garbage and air pollution;
>
> International Convention on Oil Pollution Preparedness, Response and Co-operation (OPRC), 1990. The Convention provides a global framework for international co-operation in combating major incidents or threats of marine pollution. A protocol to this convention (HNS Protocol) covers marine pollution by hazardous and noxious substances; and
>
> International Convention on the control of harmful anti-fouling systems on ships, 2001 (AFS 2001). This treaty prohibits the use of harmful organotins in anti-fouling paints used on ships and will establish a mechanism to prevent the potential future use of other harmful substances in anti-fouling systems.

The Marine Environment Protection Committee (MEPC) is IMO's senior technical body on marine pollution-related matters. MEPC has the mandate to introduce amendments to technical regulations contained in IMO antipollution treaties.

At present MEPC is developing a draft convention for the control and management of ships' ballast water and sediments in order to prevent the transfer of harmful aquatic organisms in ballast water. The draft is expected to be adopted at a diplomatic conference during late 2003.

Apart from elaborating treaties to counteract pollution from vessels source, IMO also has a mandate to elaborate international treaties for the prevention of marine pollution by dumping. For decades the Organization has been performing Secretariat responsibilities for the Convention on the Prevention of Marine Pollution by Dumping of Wastes and Other Matter (LDC), 1972, generally known as the London Convention. The Convention should be replaced by the 1996 Protocol to the London Convention (not yet in force).

IMO has also elaborated treaties on liability and compensation for pollution damage resulting from shipping accidents:

> Two IMO conventions regulate a liability and compensation regime for oil pollution damage from vessels source. The 1969 International Convention on Civil Liability for Oil Pollution Damage (CLC) provides limits of compensation to be paid by the shipowner. His liability is strict. CLC is complemented by the 1971 Convention establishing the International Fund for Compensation for Oil Pollution Damage (Fund 71) which regulates additional compensation available in cases where pollution damage exceeds the compensation available under CLC. The Fund for Compensation established by the Convention (IOPC Fund) receives contributions from cargo interests, mainly oil companies receiving crude oil by sea.
>
> The limits of liability in the two conventions were greatly increased through amendments adopted in 1992 and 2000.

Further amendments to the Fund Convention will be considered at a diplomatic conference in 2003 in order to increase compensation limits payable by the IOPC Fund.

The 1996 International Convention on Liability and Compensation for Damage in connection with the carriage of Hazardous and Noxious Substances by Sea (HNS Convention) regulates a liability and compensation regime for pollution and other damage involving hazardous and noxious substances (HNS).

The 2001 International Convention on Civil Liability for Bunker Oil Pollution Damage establishes a liability and compensation regime for pollution damage caused by spills of oil, when carried as fuel in ships' bunkers.

The Legal Committee of IMO has a mandate to amend liability conventions in order to update limits of compensation of IMO liability and compensation treaties.

II. GENERAL LEGAL FRAMEWORK OF THE INTERFACE BETWEEN UNCLOS AND IMO TREATIES

Following the entry into force of the 1982 United Nations Convention on the Law of the Sea (UNCLOS) the International Maritime Organization (IMO) published a comprehensive study the title "*Implications of the entry into force of the United Nations Convention on the Law of the Sea for the International Maritime Organization*".[2] In accordance with this study, UNCLOS is acknowledged to be an "umbrella convention" because most of its provisions, being of a general kind, can be implemented only through specific operative regulations in other international agreements. There is widespread and uncontested consensus that references in UNCLOS to generally accepted international shipping rules and standards on safety of navigation and prevention of marine pollution from vessel source means references to IMO rules and standards contained in global treaties and recommendations.

In order to understand the way in which public law of the sea provisions contained in UNCLOS are applied through IMO treaties, a key distinction should be made: UNCLOS references to IMO rules and standards are *jurisdictional* provisions. They regulate the basic features of flag, coastal and port State jurisdiction and the extent to which these types of jurisdiction should be exerted in order to effectively enforce IMO treaties. Obviously, this enforcement varies depending on three different kind of IMO treaties.

The first category comprises the only law of the sea treaties ever adopted at IMO, namely the 1969 *International Convention relating to Intervention on the High Seas in Cases of Oil Pollution Casualties* (known as *the Intervention Convention*) and the 1973 *Protocol relating to Intervention on the High Seas in Cases of Pollution by Substances other than Oil (the Intervention Protocol)*. These are essentially *law of the sea* treaties because they regulate globally and generically the rights of coastal States to act in their public capacity in order to prevent or reduce damage to marine areas over which they exert jurisdiction.

The second category includes *private law–maritime law* treaties, namely the conventions and protocols which regulate certain aspects of maritime commercial

2 LEG/MISC/2, dated 6 October 1997. An updated version is expected shortly.

activities undertaken by private persons, mainly shipowners. The most important treaties in this regard are those on liability of the shipowner for damage caused to third parties. The public law element in these treaties is restricted to the introduction of compulsory provisions on liability and compulsory insurance in order to guarantee fair compensation. The law of the sea element in these treaties is to be found in provisions relating to the application of the *polluter pays* principle in cases of pollution damage. Even if this principle operates within the context of private law compensation schemes, its implementation relates to environmental features involving public law interests such as compensation and restoration in connection with damage to the environment of coastal States.

A third category of IMO treaties regulate primarily the relationship between the shipowner and the Maritime Administration of the flag State in connection with the implementation of safety and anti-pollution rules and standards. The most important IMO safety and anti-pollution treaties are within this category. In legal terms they could be characterized as *maritime administrative law*, namely, a set of provisions which regulate the relationship between private persons (shipowner) and the Administration of the flag State as the public power imposing measures to ensure the application of navigational rules and standards. The law of the sea element governing this relationship is ever present. Several provisions in UNCLOS not only regulate the obligation for States to ensure that ships flying their flag apply IMO regulations, they also establish the jurisdictional framework for the enforcement of those regulations by coastal and port States.

IMO and the Right of Intervention of Coastal States

In the opinion of many, the 1969 IMO Intervention Convention has been made redundant by the provisions of UNCLOS regulating the extension and regime of the different sea zones and the right of intervention to avoid pollution in article 221. Nevertheless, this treaty and its 1973 Protocol are still in force and several States parties to UNCLOS have become party to them after the entry into force of UNCLOS. For this reason, it is important to establish what IMO Intervention treaties mean in terms of treaty law. An historical approach is here necessary.

The alternative of an IMO diplomatic conference adopting global regulations defining the rights and extension of the powers of the coastal State would be unthinkable today due to the existence of UNCLOS as the sole treaty defining the jurisdictional rights and obligations of the coastal State. The situation was different in 1969, when in the aftermath of the *Torrey Canyon* incident the international community was compelled to use treaty law to establish legal certainty regarding the rights of the coastal State to fight the novel risks posed by the ever-increasing size of tankers. The 1958 Convention on the Territorial Sea and Contiguous Zone regulated the status of both sea zones but not their extension, and a second conference convened in 1960 had equally failed in this regard. Customary law did not provide a solution because traditional rules which had been widely accepted until the end of the Second World War were being continuously contested by increasing unilateral State action leading to *de facto* extension of coastal state jurisdiction over the sea and sea bed. It was amid this chaotic situation that it was decided that action should be placed in the hands of the UN and in the safer hands of a UN specialized agency, where failures arising out of inconclusive political debates could be avoided.

The unfinished debates at the 1958 and 1960 Law of the Sea Conferences had important repercussions at the 1969 IMO Diplomatic Conference which adopted the Intervention Convention. In the view of some countries the convention should apply to all seas, without making distinctions between the territorial and the high seas since these areas *"had different meanings in different parts of the world… In the view of many countries… the territorial sea only extended for 3 miles; but in the view of other countries it extended to 12 or even 200 miles from the shore. If, therefore, the Convention mentioned only the high seas, there would be a doubt as to whether large areas, extending up to 200 miles from the coasts, were covered…"*.[3] Other countries felt that to apply the convention to territorial sea *"would mean limiting the sovereign rights of coastal States. For example, such States would have to enter into consultation with other States and actions would have to be decided not in local courts, but through consultation or arbitration. That would be a dangerous precedent…"*.[4]

How did IMO's treaty-making activities in the field of the law of the sea progress after the adoption of the Intervention Convention? In 1973 an ancillary treaty to the Convention was adopted, namely the 1973 Protocol relating to Intervention on the High Seas in Cases of Pollution by Substances other than Oil. However, it was precisely during the same year that the Third United Nations Conference on the Law of the Sea initiated the preparatory works which would lead to the adoption of UNCLOS in 1982. It was obvious that from then on, any jurisdictional issue relating to the powers of States over the oceans would be brought into the scope of the comprehensive codification of the law of sea undertaken by the Third Conference.

These historical developments explain why the only real extrapolation of scope between IMO treaties and UNCLOS is to be found in the IMO Intervention treaties on one side, and in article 221 (1) of UNCLOS. This provision recognizes the rights of States *"pursuant to international law, both customary and conventional to take and enforce measures beyond the territorial sea proportionate to the actual or threatened damage to protect their coastline or related interests, including fishing, from pollution or threat of pollution following upon a maritime casualty which may reasonably be expected to result in major harmful consequences"*.

This provision echoes the main features of the right of intervention regulated in article I (1) of the Intervention Convention: *"Parties to the present Convention may take such measures on the high seas as may be necessary to prevent, mitigate or eliminate grave and imminent danger to their coastline or related interests from pollution or threat or pollution of the sea by oil, following upon a maritime casualty or acts related to such a casualty, which may reasonably be expected to result in major harmful consequences."*

The degree to which these two public law regimes can coexist is a matter for serious consideration, particularly bearing in mind that they belong to historical periods

---

3 Statement by Germany, Official records of the International Legal Conference on Marine Pollution Damage, International Maritime Consultative Organization, London 1973, page 291.

4 idem, statement by Brazil, page 292.

with different notions of the meaning of "territorial sea" and "high seas". At the time of the adoption of the IMO intervention treaties the concept of Exclusive Economic Zone (EEZ) had not been developed and, as a consequence, the high seas started immediately beyond a territorial sea, the extension of which no international treaty dared to establish. After regulating this extension as up to 12 miles, UNCLOS refers to any sea zone *beyond the territorial sea* as the territorial scope for the intervention of the coastal State in accordance with article 221 (1). The conclusion is that UNCLOS creates uniformity and legal certainty as to the geographical features of the right of intervention defined in both IMO treaties. Both should be considered as regulating the right of intervention not only in the high seas but also in the EEZ.

During the 1969 Conference some States expressed the view that the existence of the right of intervention, as a derivative of the right of self-defence of states acknowledged under customary international law, did not need to be regulated in a public law treaty. An important further question was the convenience or otherwise of becoming party to a treaty which made the right of intervention conditional on the fulfilment of a process of consultation among States which also involved the intervention of an international agency such as IMO. To IMO's knowledge, the treaty has never been applied. There have been interventions beyond the territorial sea where states have followed some of its regulations regarding consultations. But IMO has *never* been involved in the way explicitly prescribed in the treaty.

UNCLOS's and IMO's Work in the Field of Liability and Compensation for Pollution Damage from Vessels Source

Aside from the Intervention Convention, the 1969 International Legal Conference on Marine Pollution Damage adopted a private law convention, the *International Convention on Civil Liability for Oil Pollution Damage, 1969* (CLC). The decision to do so was significantly polemical. Throughout the twentieth century, countries had met in Brussels to adopt private law treaties regulating commercial navigation at international conferences convened by the Government of Belgium. At these conferences States considered and adopted draft treaties elaborated by the Comité Maritime International (CMI), the leading international, non-governmental law association actively engaged in the preparation of legal instruments aimed at unifying international maritime law. The political decision to choose IMO as the forum for the preparatory works followed the trend initiated during the post-war era to transfer to UN bodies the power to elaborate and adopt treaties. It was nevertheless a novelty in the field of maritime law which was taken further with the adoption in 1971 of the *International Convention on the Establishment of an International Fund for Compensation for Oil Pollution Damage* (the *"Fund Convention"*).

The Fund Convention plays a complementary role to that of CLC by establishing an international fund, contributed by oil cargo interests, intended to provide additional compensation to that of the shipowner whenever this compensation proves to be insufficient. Important amendments to the CLC and the Fund Conventions introduced in 1992 and 2000 have ensured that limits of compensation for oil pollution damage are updated. A further increase of compensation limits is being proposed in a draft protocol to the Fund Convention to be considered at a Diplomatic Conference in 2003.

The CLC and the Fund Convention are the treaty precedents of article 235 (2) and (3) of UNCLOS:

> 2. States shall ensure that recourse is available in accordance with their legal systems for prompt and adequate compensation or other relief in respect of damage caused by pollution of the marine environment by natural or juridical persons under their jurisdiction.
>
> 3. With the objective of assuring prompt and adequate compensation in respect of all damage caused by pollution of the marine environment, States shall cooperate in the implementation of existing international law and the further development of international law relating to responsibility and liability for the assessment of and compensation for damage and the settlement of related disputes, as well as, where appropriate, development of criteria and procedures for payment of adequate compensation, such as compulsory insurance or compensation funds.

These provisions regulate obligations of States to cooperate in the enforcement of the *polluter pays* principle in the field of liability and compensation, and make concrete reference to mechanisms of enforcement such as compulsory insurance and compensation funds which, as we have seen, had already been regulated in the CLC and the Fund Convention at the time of elaboration of UNCLOS. These two compensation mechanisms, even if basically within the purview of private maritime law, have important implications in the protection of common interests normally protected by public law.

Since the adoption of UNCLOS two new treaties have been adopted at IMO providing for liability of compensation for pollution damage from vessels source:

- The 1996 International Convention on Liability and Compensation for Damage in Connection with the Carriage of Hazardous and Noxious Substances by Sea (the HNS Convention) applies not only to pollution risks in the territorial sea and EEZ, but also to death, injury and damage to property *irrespective of the place where they occur*.
- The 2001 International Convention on Civil Liability for Bunker Oil Pollution Damage extends IMO's treaty law work in the field of liability and compensation for pollution damage to cover damage caused by oil carried as fuel on ships.

UNCLOS and IMO Technical Treaties in the Field of Prevention of Marine Pollution

The environmental UNCLOS as a framework for the implementation of IMO antipollution measures already features in article 1. The important distinction between "pollution of the marine environment" and "dumping" contained in article 1 of UNCLOS is of key importance to understanding the subject matter of IMO environmental rules and standards. Both definitions should be read together with those contained in the two main treaties within IMO's mandate, namely MARPOL in the case of pollution from vessels source and the 1972 London Convention and the 1996 Protocol to that Convention in the case of dumping.

Other provisions of UNCLOS, such as the characterization of rights and obligations under flag State jurisdiction, become applicable to both safety and antipollution IMO rules. UNCLOS Part XII on protection and preservation of the marine environment is an entirely different matter: UNCLOS's role as an "umbrella convention" is greatly altered in Part XII, which includes provisions which are *per se* of an operative kind. These provisions, rather than formulating principles of a general kind only executable through further legislation, prescribe several rights and duties in a self-executing manner. As such, they should be *read and interpreted together* with MARPOL. For instance, the provisions on investigation of foreign vessels contained in article 226 of UNCLOS regulate the same subject matter of MARPOL article 5. Both articles indicate how certificates should be inspected, which measures should be taken when things are not in order, etc.

The following paragraphs highlight the way in which several provisions of UNCLOS, both outside and within Part XII, relate to the implementation of MARPOL as the comprehensive IMO treaty regulating the main features of the exercise of flag and port State jurisdiction in the implementation of IMO antipollution measures.

III. MAIN JURISDICTIONAL ISSUES INVOLVING THE APPLICATION OF MARPOL IN THE LIGHT OF UNCLOS

Flag State Jurisdiction

In a way similar to SOLAS and STCW, the *public law* characterization of MARPOL is clearly shown by the fact that it imposes rights and obligations upon a public authority, namely, the maritime administration of the flag State. In this regard an important distinction should be made: although the rules should be primarily implemented by the shipowner, MARPOL imposes the obligation to enforce these rules primarily upon the maritime administration. Governments of States Parties, through their maritime administrations, have a duty to ensure that shipowners under their flag comply with the rules and standards prescribed by the convention. The consequence is the establishment of a legal regime binding the shipowner to comply with the requirements imposed by the administration on the one hand, and binding the administration to comply with requirements imposed by international law on the other.

The fact that, as in any IMO treaty, implementation of MARPOL basically relies on flag State jurisdiction, makes of the requirement of a genuine link between the flag State and the ship regulated in UNCLOS, article 91 (1) a paramount proviso to establish the responsibility of the flag State's responsibility under international law to implement shipping antipollution measures. Unless there is a genuine link, the Administration cannot fulfil its obligations to effectively supervise enforcement of safety and antipollution regulations by ships flying its flag.

After establishing the fundamental principle of the genuine link, UNCLOS devotes an extensive article (94) to regulating basic duties of the flag States. Paragraphs 3 and 4 of this article should be read as references to regulations contained in the most important IMO conventions in matters of construction, equipment, seaworthiness, manning and training of crews, prevention of collisions, prevention, reduction and control of marine pollution, etc.

Port State Jurisdiction

Since provisions on the exercise of port State jurisdiction contained in UNCLOS Part XII should be read together with those of MARPOL, it is important to explain the way in which port State jurisdiction operates through both treaties.

In principle, port State jurisdiction is a concept of an essentially corrective kind and, as such, is necessarily linked to that of flag State jurisdiction: the exercise of port State jurisdiction aims to correct non-compliance or ineffective flag State enforcement of IMO regulations by foreign ships voluntarily in port.

In common with the main safety treaties SOLAS and STCW, MARPOL regulates the right of the port State to verify the contents of certificates issued by the flag State attesting compliance with their respective technical rules and standards. It also entitles the port State to inspect the ship if the certificates are not in order, or if there are clear grounds to believe that the condition of the ship or of its equipment does not correspond substantially with the particulars of the certificates, or if they are not properly maintained.

A significant difference between safety treaties and MARPOL is that the latter includes not only regulations relating to the inspection of ship's certificates (article 5) but also detailed procedural provisions on procedures by port States in the case of violations; it is well understood that in this case violations consist of illegal discharges of polluting substances. Unlike the case of safety incidents, which mainly concerned the welfare of persons and goods on board ships, pollution incidents affect interests *outside* the ship, be it those of the port State, the coastal State or even the wider context implied in a concept of the marine environment as a universal unity. It is bearing in mind this feature that the operation of a framework treaty such as UNCLOS should be coordinated with MARPOL rules in order to enforce antipollution provisions.

Of particular importance is the coordinated enforcement of both treaties in the case of inspections and institutions of proceedings:

Article 6 of MARPOL contains regulations on the detection of violations and procedures to be undertaken by port States. They include detailed requirements on co-operation between the administrations of the port and flag State following the detection of a violation to this Convention committed by a foreign ship. These provisions should be considered bearing in mind article 226(2) of UNCLOS. Resolution A.787(19) on procedures for port State control adopted by the IMO Assembly in 1995 contains comprehensive guidelines on port State inspections, identification of contraventions, detention and port and flag State reporting requirements. The guidelines include provisions on the detention of ships.

UNCLOS (article 231) provides that States shall promptly notify the flag State, particularly its diplomatic agents or consular officers and maritime authority, and any other State concerned, of enforcement measures taken against foreign ships. However, with respect to violations committed in the territorial sea, this obligation applies only to such measures as are taken in proceedings. The obligation of port authorities to notify the consul or diplomatic representative and the Administration of the ship concerned of any action against the ship is contained in article 5 (3) of MARPOL.

In accordance with article 223 of UNCLOS, States are obliged in the proceedings taken against a vessel to facilitate the admission of evidence submitted by, *inter alia*, the "competent international organization". States are also required to facilitate the attendance at such proceedings of official representatives of the "competent international organization". Such representatives shall have such rights and duties as may be provided under national law or international law. The appropriate bodies of IMO may find it necessary to consider the procedures and arrangements required to enable IMO to intervene in such proceedings, including the criteria for determining when such an intervention would be appropriate and the procedure for designating the "official representatives" of the Organization, as envisaged in UNCLOS.

UNCLOS regulates special suspension and restriction conditions on proceedings to impose penalties. In accordance with article 228(1), proceedings taken against a foreign ship for violations which occurred beyond the territorial sea of other States must be suspended if the flag State institutes proceedings within six months after the original proceedings were initiated. However, the requirement of suspension does not apply in cases of proceedings which relate to a case of major damage to the coastal State or when the flag State has repeatedly disregarded its obligations to enforce effectively the applicable international rules and standards in respect of violations committed by its vessels. The flag State which has taken proceedings is obliged in due course to "make available to the State previously instituting proceedings a full dossier of the case and the records of the proceedings, whenever the flag State has requested the suspension of proceedings in accordance with this article".

Coastal State Jurisdiction. Routeing Measures

IMO treaty instruments do not attempt to regulate the jurisdictional power of the coastal State, since this is a subject exclusively within the scope of UNCLOS. UNCLOS provides the enforcement framework for IMO instruments by establishing the degree to which coastal States may legitimately interfere with foreign ships in order to ensure compliance with IMO rules and standards.

However the general principle according to which IMO does not regulate coastal State jurisdiction is qualified by an exception in the case of measures which do not establish general features of coastal State jurisdiction but prescribe specific routeing measures to be implemented by coastal States. In other words, while the role of regulating coastal State jurisdiction at a *global* level (as in the case of the Intervention Convention) is no longer part of IMO's mandate, the so-called *approval role*, namely, the adoption of routeing provisions at the request of coastal States along *particular* sea zones adjacent to their coast, has been continuously expanded after receiving its initial legitimation in the Convention on the International Regulations for Preventing Collisions at Sea, 1972 (COL REG) in connection with the adoption of traffic separation schemes (TSS).

Article 211(1) of UNCLOS prescribes that States, acting through the competent international organization or general diplomatic conference, shall promote the adoption of routeing systems designed to minimize the threat of accidents which might cause pollution of the marine environment, including the coastline and related interests of coastal States. IMO is the competent international organization for developing guidelines and regulations on ships' routeing systems, and comments made under that chapter apply to the prevention of marine pollution. In this regard, mention should be made of new SOLAS regulation V/8, (a) and (j). According to paragraph (a), ships' routeing systems should also be established bearing in mind the need to protect the marine environment. Paragraph (j) requires that routeing systems comply with UNCLOS.

IMO General Provisions on Ships' Routeing (resolution A.572(14) adopted by the IMO Assembly in 1985) were amended in 1995 by the insertion of new paragraphs 3.6 and 3.7, which deal with routeing systems for the protection of environmentally sensitive areas. Paragraph 3.6 establishes the criteria to be taken into account when considering the adoption of a routeing system for the protection of the marine environment. Paragraph 3.7 sets limits for the adoption of routeing systems. In accordance with this paragraph IMO should not adopt a system that would impose unnecessary constraints on shipping, or establish an area to be avoided that would impede the passage of ships through an international strait.

IV. SPECIAL MANDATORY MEASURES FOR CERTAIN AREAS

An important issue relating IMO regulations to the environmental UNCLOS relates to the adoption of special mandatory measures for areas deserving the application of special mandatory measures restricting navigational activities on account of features which make them particularly vulnerable to pollution from vessels.

In accordance with article 211(6) of UNCLOS the coastal State may adopt special mandatory measures for the prevention of vessel-source pollution in certain clearly defined areas of its EEZ. To justify the adoption of such measures, evidence must indicate that the existing international rules and standards are inadequate for the special circumstances of the area concerned. The area must be clearly defined and the adoption of special measures must be required for recognized technical reasons in relation to the oceanographical and ecological conditions, as well as the utilization or the protection of the resources and the particular character of the traffic of the area concerned.

Article 211(6)(a) and (b) include specific conditions for the adoption of special mandatory measures:

- the coastal State should conduct appropriate consultations through the "competent international organization" (IMO) with other States concerned. It should also submit a communication to IMO for special mandatory measures, supported by scientific and technical evidence and information on reception facilities;
- IMO, within 12 months of receiving the communication, shall determine whether the conditions in the proposed area justify the adoption of special mandatory measures;
- following a decision by IMO, the coastal State may adopt laws and regulations implementing such international rules and standards or navigational practices as are made applicable, through the organization (IMO), for special areas. These laws shall not become applicable to foreign vessels until 15 months after the submission of the communication to the organization (IMO);
- the coastal State shall publish the limits of the area where the special mandatory measures are to be enforced.

In accordance with article 211(6)(c) the coastal State may enact for the same area additional laws and regulations on discharges or navigational practices. However, these laws and regulations shall not require foreign vessels to observe design, construction, manning or equipment standards other than those defined by generally accepted international rules and standards. If the coastal State intends to adopt additional laws and regulations it must notify the organization (IMO) thereof at the time it submits the communication referred to above. In accordance with article 220(8) of UNCLOS, the provisions on enforcement contained in article 220(3) to (7) also apply to the enforcement of national laws and regulations implementing special mandatory measures pursuant to article 211(a).

Special Areas and Particularly Sensitive Sea Areas (PSSA)

Special mandatory requirements for certain areas regarding the prevention of operational discharges of harmful substances are contained in Annexes I, II and V of MARPOL. The Convention defines certain sea areas as "special areas" in which, for technical reasons relating to their oceanographical and ecological condition and to their sea traffic, the adoption of special mandatory methods for the prevention of sea pollution is required. Under the Convention, these special areas are provided with a higher level of protection than other areas of the sea.

A Particularly Sensitive Sea Area (PSSA) is an area that needs special protection through action by IMO because of its significance for recognized ecological or socio-economic or scientific reasons and which may be vulnerable to damage by international maritime activities. The criteria for the identification of particularly sensitive sea areas and the criteria for the designation of special areas are not mutually exclusive. In many cases a PSSA may be identified within a Special Area and vice versa. Among the kind of special mandatory measures which may be adopted to protect a PSSA the Guidelines mention the adoption of specific routeing measures, including the possibility of declaring part or the whole of a PSSA to be an area to be avoided by ships. The adoption of routeing measures for PSSA should take into account the IMO General Provisions on Ships' Routeing (resolution A.572(14)), as amended. Other possible measures are compulsory pilotage schemes or vessel traffic management systems. The Guidelines indicate that a proposed PSSA may include a buffer zone, which would only be justified once it is demonstrated how it would contribute to the adequate protection of the core area identified as particularly sensitive.

Guidelines for the designation of Special Areas under MARPOL are formulated in resolution A.720(17) on guidelines for the designation of special areas and the identification of particularly sensitive sea areas adopted by the IMO Assembly in 1991. These guidelines were revised by resolution A.885(21) and again by resolution A.927 (22).

Four sea areas, namely the Great Barrier Reef off Australia, the Sabana-Camagüey archipelago off Cuba, the Florida Keys and the Malpelo Islands off the United States have been declared a PSSA by IMO. Two other areas have been agreed in principle, i.e., the sea area surrounding the Florida Keys and the sea area around the Malpelo Islands off Columbia. A declaration of these two areas as particularly sensitive sea areas is expected at MEPC 47 (2002).

Declaration of special areas and identification of PSSA involve restrictions to navigation and should be accordingly carried forward in a restrictive way: a balance must be established between freedom of navigation at a global level and the establishment of limitations to navigation through treaty and soft law provisions. This balance can only be achieved if these limitations are regulated solely on the basis of proven need to do so.

V. POLLUTION INCIDENTS AND EMERGENCIES AT SEA

In accordance with article 198 of UNCLOS, when a State becomes aware of cases in which the marine environment is in danger of being damaged or has been damaged by pollution, it must give immediate notification to other States likely to be affected by such damage and to the competent international organizations. Article 199 provides that the affected States shall co-operate with the competent international organizations, to the extent possible, in eliminating the effects of pollution and preventing or minimizing the damage. States are further required jointly to develop and promote contingency plans for responding to marine pollution incidents.

The OPRC provides a global framework for international co-operation in combating major oil pollution incidents or threats of marine pollution. In article 3(1)(a), OPRC establishes that each Party shall require that ships entitled to fly its flag have on board a shipboard oil pollution emergency plan. In accordance with article 5(1)(c) and 3, Parties are required to inform all States concerned and IMO in cases of major oil pollution incidents. Provisions concerning reports on incidents involving harmful substances are also contained in MARPOL, article 8 and Protocol I.

Article 7 of OPRC further develops the main principles of international co-operation in pollution response. Paragraph 3 provides that, in accordance with applicable international agreements, each Party shall take the necessary legal or administrative measures to facilitate the arrival and utilization in and departure from its territory of ships, aircraft and other modes of transport engaged in responding to an oil pollution incident or transporting personnel, cargoes, materials and equipment required to deal with such an incident.

Article 12 on institutional arrangements gives IMO important co-ordinating roles regarding the provision of information, education and training services, technical services and technical assistance.

The Marine Environment Protection Committee of IMO is at present considering the adoption of treaty regulations to extend the scope of the Convention to pollution incidents caused by harmful substances other than oil.

VI. RECENT TREATY LAW DEVELOPMENTS IN THE FIELD OF ENVIRONMENTAL PROTECTION

The recent adoption of the AFS Convention and the prospective adoption in 2003 of a treaty on prevention of marine pollution from harmful aquatic organisms in ballast water justifies the inclusion of basic information in this paper. Both initiatives reflect the continuous reassessment of the concept of pollution of the marine environment and the political will of IMO to counteract it by means of developing appropriate international regulations.

The AFS Convention

Anti-fouling paints are used to coat the bottoms of ships to prevent sealife such as algae and molluscs attaching themselves to the hull – thereby slowing down the ship and increasing fuel consumption.

In the early days of sailing ships, lime and later arsenic were used to coat ships' hulls, until the modern chemicals industry developed effective anti-fouling paints using metallic compounds.

These compounds slowly "leach" into the sea water, killing barnacles and other marine life that have attached to the ship. But studies have shown that these compounds persist in the water, killing sealife, harming the environment and possibly entering the food chain. The harmful environmental effects of organotin compounds were recognized by IMO in 1989.

The International Convention on the control of harmful anti-fouling systems on ships (AFS) adopted on 5 October 2001 defines "anti-fouling systems" as "a coating, paint, surface treatment, surface or device that is used on a ship to control or prevent attachment of unwanted organisms".

The Convention prohibits the use of harmful organotins in anti-fouling paints used on ships and will establish a mechanism to prevent the potential future use of other harmful substances in anti-fouling systems. Parties to the Convention are required to prohibit and/or restrict the use of harmful anti-fouling systems on ships flying their flag, as well as ships not entitled to fly their flag but which operate under their authority and all ships that enter a port, shipyard or offshore terminal of a Party.

Ships of 400 gross tonnage and above engaged in international voyages (excluding fixed or floating platforms, FSUs and FPSOs) will be required to undergo an initial survey before the ship is put into service or before the International Anti-fouling System Certificate is issued for the first time; and a survey when the anti-fouling systems are changed or replaced.

Ships of 24 metres or more in length but less than 400 gross tonnage engaged in international voyages (excluding fixed or floating platforms, FSUs and FPSOs) will have to carry a Declaration on Anti-fouling Systems signed by the owner or authorized agent. The Declaration will have to be accompanied by appropriate documentation such as a paint receipt or contractor invoice.

Anti-fouling systems to be prohibited or controlled will be listed in an annex (Annex 1) to the Convention, which will be updated as and when necessary.

The new convention will enter into force 12 months after 25 States representing 25% of the world's merchant shipping tonnage have ratified it.

Annex I attached to the Convention and adopted by the Conference states that by an effective date of 1 January 2003, all ships shall not apply or re-apply organotins compounds which act as biocides in anti-fouling systems.

By 1 January 2008 (effective date), ships either:

(1) shall not bear such compounds on their hulls or external parts or surfaces; or
(2) shall bear a coating that forms a barrier to such compounds leaching from the underlying non-compliant anti-fouling systems.

This applies to all ships (excluding fixed and floating platforms, floating storage units (FSUs), and Floating Production Storage and Offtake units (FPSOs)).

The Convention includes a clause in article 12 which states that a ship shall be entitled to compensation if it is unduly detained or delayed while undergoing inspection for possible violations of the Convention.

The Convention provides for the establishment of a "technical group", to include people with relevant expertise, to review proposals for other substances used in anti-fouling systems to be prohibited or restricted. Article 6 on Process for Proposing Amendments to controls on Anti-fouling systems sets out how the evaluation of an anti-fouling system should be carried out.

Ballast Water Management

The MEPC is working on developing draft new regulations for ballast water management to prevent the transfer of harmful aquatic organisms in ballast water. A new international convention "for the control and management of ships' ballast water and sediments" should be adopted in 2003.

It is estimated that about 10 billion tonnes of ballast water are transferred globally each year, potentially transferring from one location to another species of sealife that may prove ecologically harmful when released into a non-native environment.

The proposed new instrument is being developed on the basis of a two-tier approach.

Tier 1 includes requirements that would apply to all ships, including mandatory requirements for a Ballast Water and Sediments Management Plan, a Ballast Water Record Book and a requirement that new ships shall carry out ballast water and sediment management procedures to a given standard or range of standards. Existing ships would be required to carry out ballast water management procedures after a phase-in period, but these procedures may differ from those to be applied to new ships.

Tier 2 includes special requirements which may apply in certain areas and would include procedures and criteria for the designation of such areas in which additional controls may be applied to the discharge and/or uptake of ballast water. The text for Tier 2 remains to be developed.

The working group on ballast water management, which reports to the MEPC, has confirmed that ballast exchange on the high seas is the only widely used technique currently available to prevent the spread of unwanted aquatic organisms in ballast water and its use should continue to be accepted.

However, it has been stressed that this technique has a number of limitations. Because it is of variable efficiency in removing organisms, the percentage removed depends on the type of organism. The discharged water quality depends on the original quality of the water taken up. It also has geographical limits. Existing ships may be subject to operational constraints, but it was recognised that new ships may be designed to accommodate ballast exchange in a much wider range of circumstances.

The Working Group has concluded that development of alternative treatment technologies might produce techniques that were substantially more reliable and that ballast water exchange is an interim solution.

ANNEX: MARPOL/UNCLOS CROSS REFERENCE

Marpol Section	*UNCLOS Section*
1(1)	94, 211(2), 217
2(5)	94, 56(1) (b), 60, 80, 208
3(1)	208, 211(2)
4(2)	21(1), 56(1)(B), 211, 220, 228, 231
3(2)	2, 56, 77
3(3)	236
4(1)	214, 217
4(2)	21, 27(5), 42, 52, 54, 56(1)(b), 111, 211, 220, 223, 228, 231, 233, 234
4(3)	217 (6) and (7)
4(4)	217(8), 218, 220, 228, 230
5(1)	217(3)
5(2)	217(2),219,226
5(3)	25(5), 226,231
6(1)	211(3), 226(2), 217(5),218
6(2)	218, 220, 226, 231
6(3)	223,231
6(4)	217(6),
6(5)	218
7	226(1), 232
8	211(7)
9(3),	21, 27(5), 42, 52, 54, 56(1)(b), 91, 92, 94,111, 211, 217, 218, 220,223, 234 (for annex VI, see 212,222)
10	287, 288,297

Environmental Regulation of Deep Seabed Mining

*Michael W. Lodge**

I. INTRODUCTION

In July 2000, after three years of negotiation, the Authority approved a set of Regulations on Prospecting and Exploration for Polymetallic Nodules in the Area.[1] These are the first set of regulations to be issued by the Authority since its conception as the custodian of the "common heritage of mankind" more than 30 years ago. The significance of the Regulations lies primarily in the fact that they complete and give effect to the regime for the international seabed ("the Area")[2] set out in Part XI and Annex III of the 1982 United Nations Convention on the Law of the Sea[3] and the 1994 Agreement relating to the Implementation of Part XI.[4] More specifically, the approval of the Regulations paved the way for the issue by the Authority of the first 15-year contracts for exploration for polymetallic nodules in the Area.[5]

---

* Mr. *Michael W. Lodge*, M.Sc. (LSE) is the Chief, Office of Legal Affairs, International Seabed Authority (ISA), Kingston (Jamaica). Contact: mwlodge@isa.org.jm.
The views expressed in this article are those of the author and do not necessarily represent the views of the International Seabed Authority or its member States.

1 The official text of the Regulations was published as document ISBA/6/A/18, annex (13 July 2000). Reproduced in Selected Decisions 6, at 31 and in *The Law of the Sea: Compendium of Basic Documents*, International Seabed Authority/The Caribbean Law Publishing Company, 2001, p. 226 [hereinafter "the Regulations"].

2 The "Area" is defined in article 1, of the 1982 Convention, as the seabed and ocean floor and the subsoil thereof beyond the limit of national jurisdiction.

3 United Nations Convention on the Law of the Sea, 1982: A/CONF.62/122 and Corr. 1–11, ILM 21 (1982) 1261. *The Law of the Sea: Compendium of Basic Documents*, International Seabed Authority/The Caribbean Law Publishing Company, 2001, p. 1 [hereinafter the "1982 Convention"].

4 Agreement relating to the Implementation of the Part XI of the United Nations Convention on the Law of the Sea of 10 December 1982, A/RES/48/263, annex. Also reproduced in *The Law of the Sea: Compendium of Basic Documents*, International Seabed Authority/The Caribbean Law Publishing Company, 2001, p. 206 [hereinafter "the 1994 Agreement"].

5 Since the Regulations were approved, the Authority has signed 15-year contracts for exploration with all of the entities that had been registered under resolution II of the Third United Nations Conference on the Law of the Sea as pioneer investors; namely Yuzhmorgeologiya (Russian Federation), Interoceanmetal Joint Organization (Bulgaria, Cuba, Czech Republic, Poland, Russian Federation and Slovakia) and the Government of the Republic of Korea all on 29 March 2001, COMRA (China) on 22 May 2001, IFREMER/AFERNOD (France) and DORD (Japan) both on 20 June 2001, and India on 25 March 2002. See ISBA/7/C/4, Status of contracts for exploration issued in accordance with the Regulations for prospecting and exploration for polymetallic nodules in the Area.

A. Kirchner (ed.), International Maritime Environmental Law, 49–59.

Ironically, despite the enormous diplomatic efforts that have been made to resolve the concerns with respect to the regime contained in Part XI of the Convention, firstly through the adoption of the 1994 Agreement and subsequently through an evolutionary and cost-effective approach to the establishment of the International Seabed Authority, it is apparent that, nearly 20 years after the adoption of the 1982 Convention, seabed mining is further off than ever before. Commercial interest in deep seabed polymetallic nodules has dwindled to the point where commercial exploitation of these resources seems, at best, a remote possibility. In the present economic climate, none of the contractors and sponsoring States are actively pursuing exploration programmes aimed at future exploitation of these resources. On the other hand, the international community has recently expressed interest in exploring the potential for development of resources other than polymetallic nodules, including cobalt-rich ferromanganese crusts and seafloor massive sulphides[6] and there is growing concern over how best to manage potential risks to biodiversity and the marine environment both on the high seas and in the Area.

In these circumstances, the questions may well be asked about what the purpose is of environmental regulation of deep seabed mining and why the Authority has devoted so much time and effort over the past few years to the elaboration of a framework for environmental protection.

I believe the answer to these questions lies partly in the emphasis given in the 1982 Convention and the 1994 Agreement to the need to protect and preserve the marine environment and partly in the growing awareness of our lack of detailed knowledge of the deep sea environment. Deep seabed mining, when it eventually takes place, will consist of unprecedented commercial-scale mineral recovery operations in areas populated by unique biological communities, many of which, in the case of those associated with polymetallic sulphide deposits, were unknown to science before 1979 and remain only very poorly characterized to date. It is now known, for example, that the biodiversity of the deep seabed is greater than had hitherto been thought.[7] This extreme environment supports unique biological

6 In August 1998, during the resumed fourth session of the Authority, the delegation of the Russian Federation reminded the Assembly that, in addition to polymetallic nodules, other mineral resources existed in the Area, including hydrothermal polymetallic sulphides and cobalt-rich ferromanganese crusts, and requested the Authority to adopt rules, regulations and procedures for exploration for such resources (ISBA/4/A/18. Reproduced in Selected Decisions 4, at 64). In light of the request made by the delegation of the Russian Federation, the Authority convened, in June 2000, a workshop on the mineral resources of the Area in order to provide information on the occurrence, technical parameters, economic interest and potential resources contained in these mineral resources which would assist in drafting appropriate rules, regulations and procedures. At the seventh session, in 2001, the Secretariat produced a paper on considerations relating to the regulation of prospecting and exploration for hydrothermal polymetallic sulphides and cobalt-rich ferromanganese crusts (ISBA/7/C/2).

7 See Craig H. Allen, *Protecting the Oceanic Gardens of Eden: International Law Issues in Deep-Sea Vent Resource Conservation and Management*, Georgetown International Environmental Law Review, Vol XIII, Issue 3 (2001); Lyle Glowka, *The Deepest of Ironies: Genetic Resources, Marine Scientific Research and the Area*, Ocean Yearbook 12 (1996); Cyrill de Klemm, *Fisheries and Marine Biological Diversity*, in Hey (ed.) Developments in International Fisheries Law, Kluwer (1999).

communities which exist both in the sediments of the deep seabed and in association with hydrothermal vents located at the mid-ocean ridges. Heat tolerant microbes (thermophiles) associated with hydrothermal vents are of great interest to science and to industry. Analysis of their genetic material indicates that certain of these microbes are at the base of the tree of life and their study may elucidate the origin of life. Bioactive compounds found in these microbes are already employed in replicating DNA for forensic and medical applications (polymerase chain reaction) and for enhancing flow in deep oil wells. They also hold promise for use in high-temperature industrial processes, as well as in pharmaceuticals applicable to cancer and other diseases. The more we learn, however, the less we know.[8]

Clearly, any human activity in the Area, whether prospecting, exploration or exploitation, is likely to have some effect on the marine environment. Yet some such activities need to go ahead if there is to be any utilization of the resources of the Area in future. Deep seabed miners face particular challenges with respect to environmental issues because of the relatively undefined nature of the deposits to be mined and the systems to be used to mine them as well as the popular mystique with regard to the oceans and marine biodiversity. In these circumstances it is essential to begin the process of environmental regulation at an early stage with a view to ensuring that the critical decisions that will have to be made in the future are made on the basis of adequate scientific information, using consistent methods of analysis and environmental characterization, rather than on the basis of political considerations and public perceptions. In this regard, it is also noteworthy that the marine mining industry has itself taken steps to develop its own voluntary code for environmental management of marine mining.[9]

In this paper I shall attempt to describe the legal framework for the protection of the marine environment from the effects of deep seabed mining and to explain the approach that has been taken by the Authority to the regulation of such activities. I shall also say a few words about the potential problems associated with the implementation of the legal framework that has been created.

---

8 According to the International Seabed Authority's workshop on mineral resources of the Area held in June 2000, discoveries associated with sea-floor hot springs at polymetallic massive sulphide deposits included the fact that new species are found in every square metre of sediments sampled and that in each field that has been sampled, species have been found that are not found in other fields. The workshop found that the global hydrothermal vent fauna is one of the most unusually adapted assemblages of organisms found in the oceans, in terms of tolerance of extreme physico-chemical conditions and chemo-synthetic food sources, but that the biogeography of marine microbes has not been extensively studied. This degree of uniqueness, together with the fact that most vent species do not occur outside of the hydrothermal environment, and that many have restricted distributions along the global ridge system, are important issues to be considered in developing strategies and regulations for mining.

9 Code for Environmental Management of Marine Mining, adopted by the International Marine Minerals Society, 2 November 2001. Available at http://www.ngdc.noaa.gov/mgg/imms/codefeb2002.html. The Code draws on prior marine mining environmental statements, such as the Madang Guidelines of 1999, the Green Paper on Offshore Mining Policy developed by the Government of Papua New Guinea and the Code for Environmental Management adopted by the Minerals Council of Australia.

II. THE 1982 CONVENTION AND 1994 AGREEMENT

The existing legal framework for the protection of the marine environment from "activities in the Area"[10] is composed of a wide variety of provisions within the 1982 Convention, the 1994 Agreement and the Regulations. Some of these provisions specifically address protection of the environment, while others are more general but are also relevant to environmental protection. Within the 1982 Convention, important rights and duties are to be found not only within Part XI and the associated Annexes, but also within Part XII.

The provisions on the protection of the marine environment contained in Part XII of the Convention, which were developed in the light of the outcomes of the 1972 Stockholm Conference on the Human Environment, constitute the basic framework for the legal regime that establishes the obligations, powers and responsibilities of States with respect to the marine environment. Article 192 of the Convention establishes a basic obligation on all States to protect and preserve the marine environment. Part XII also describes the specific measures to be taken by States to prevent, reduce and control marine pollution as well as to ensure that activities under their jurisdiction or control do not cause pollution damage to other States and their environment, and that pollution does not spread beyond the areas where they exercise sovereign rights under the Convention. In relation to the Area, article 209 states that "[i]nternational rules, regulations and procedures shall be established in accordance with Part XI to prevent, reduce and control pollution of the marine environment from activities in the Area".

The Authority, which in accordance with article 157 of the Convention and the 1994 Agreement, is the organization through which States Parties to the Convention shall organize and control activities in the Area, has an important role to play in relation to the protection of the marine environment. This is made clear *inter alia* by article 145 of the Convention which states that "[n]ecessary measures shall be taken in accordance with this Convention with respect to activities in the Area to ensure effective protection for the marine environment from harmful effects which may arise from such activities". Article 145 goes on to require the Authority to adopt rules, regulations and procedures for, *inter alia*:

(a) the prevention, reduction and control of pollution and other hazards to the marine environment, including the coastline, and of interference with the ecological balance of the marine environment, particular attention being paid to the need for protection from harmful effects of such activities as drilling, dredging, excavation, disposal of waste, construction and operation or maintenance of installations, pipelines and other devices related to such activities;

(b) the protection and conservation of the natural resources of the Area and the prevention of damage to the flora and fauna of the marine environment.

---

10 Defined in article 1, paragraph 1(3), of the 1982 Convention as "all activities of exploration for, and exploitation of, the resources of the Area". Under article 1, paragraph 1(1), the "Area" means "the seabed and ocean floor and subsoil thereof beyond the limits of national jurisdiction". Under article 133, "resources" means "all solid, liquid or gaseous mineral resources *in situ* in the Area at or beneath the seabed, including polymetallic nodules".

A similar enabling provision appears in Annex III, which sets out the basic conditions of prospecting, exploration and exploitation, in article 17, paragraph 1(b)(xii). This requires the Authority to adopt rules, regulations and procedures on "mining standards and practices... including those relating to...protection of the marine environment".

In addition to those provisions, article 165, paragraph 2, of the Convention requires the Legal and Technical Commission[11] to *inter alia*: make recommendations to the Council on the protection of the marine environment; take into account assessments of environmental implications when formulating rules, regulations and procedures referred to in article 162, paragraph 2 (o), of the Convention; and make recommendations to the Council regarding the establishment of a monitoring programme.

The duties of the Authority under the Convention with respect to the marine environment were given added emphasis in the 1994 Agreement, which, *inter alia*, requires the Authority to give priority to the adoption of rules, regulations and procedures incorporating applicable standards for the protection and preservation of the marine environment[12] and requires that an application for approval of a plan of work for exploration is accompanied by an assessment of the potential environmental impacts of the proposed exploration activities and a description of a programme for oceanographic and baseline environmental studies.[13]

III. THE REGULATIONS

These various provisions of the Convention and the 1994 Agreement were given substance in the Regulations, approved by the Assembly in July 2000.

The Regulations are organized into nine parts, containing 40 regulations, and four annexes. The Regulations deal only with the prospecting and exploration phases, and are applicable only to polymetallic nodules. Part I of the Regulations consists of introductory material and definitions. Part II addresses prospecting. Part III deals with the process of applying for approval of a plan of work for exploration, including the content of the plan of work, the form of the application and the procedure for consideration of applications by the Legal and Technical Commission and the Council. Part IV describes the form and content of the contract for exploration. Parts I to IV are essentially an elaboration of Annex III of the Convention, which contains the basic conditions of prospecting, exploration and exploitation. Annex III itself expounds upon the provisions of article 153 of the Convention by describing the procedures by which States, state enterprises and other entities may

---

11 The Legal and Technical Commission is established under article 163 of the 1982 Convention as one of the organs of the Council. Its powers and functions are set out in article 165. Members of the Commission are elected by the Council and are expected to have appropriate qualifications such as those relevant to exploration for and exploitation and processing of mineral resources, oceanology, protection of the marine environment, or economic or legal matters relating to ocean mining and related fields of expertise.

12 1994 Agreement, annex, Section 1, paragraph 5(g).

13 1994 Agreement, annex, Section 1, paragraph 7.

apply for prospecting, exploration and exploitation in the international seabed area, the procedure for approval of plans of work and the basic legal and contractual conditions attached to such plans of work.

Part V of the Regulations deals with protection and preservation of the marine environment. It also contains detailed procedures for the exercise by the Council, pursuant to article 162, paragraph 2(w), of the Convention, of its power to issue emergency orders to prevent serious harm to the marine environment arising out of activities in the Area. Part VI deals with confidentiality of data and information. Part VII contains general procedures for the implementation of the Regulations. Part VIII deals with settlement of disputes and Part IX sets out the procedure to be followed should the prospector or contractor locate resources other than polymetallic nodules. Annexes 1 and 2 are the forms used to notify the Authority of the intention to engage in prospecting and to apply for approval for a plan of work for exploration. Annex 3 is the contract for exploration and Annex 4 contains the standard clauses of the contract for exploration.

The provisions relating to protection and preservation of the marine environment were among the most controversial to be addressed during the process of negotiation of the Regulations. Whilst, on the one hand, contractors and potential contractors strongly preferred an incremental approach to environmental regulation, with an emphasis on the need to gather more data during the exploration phase, other participants in the negotiations considered there was a need to take a precautionary approach to any activities from the outset. Ultimately, what is contained in the Regulations is somewhat of a mixture of the two approaches, which might be best described in the jargon used by the U.S. Council on Environmental Policy as the beginning of a process of "scoping" and "tiering".[14] "Scoping" simply involves an "early and open process for determining the scope of issues to be addressed and for identifying the significant issues related to a proposed action". It requires two basic steps: first, a definition of the proposed action which is detailed enough to permit meaningful environmental impact analysis; and second, an iterative and open review procedure that can identify and set priorities for the issues identified in the analysis. "Tiering" is the "coverage of general matters in broader environmental impact statements with subsequent richer statements of environmental analyses." The purpose is to allow decision-makers to "focus on the issues which are ripe for decision and exclude from consideration issues already decided or not yet ripe". Most importantly for the prospective seabed miners, tiering involves phasing of the resolution of environmental issues to be compatible with the schedule of activities contemplated in the proposed action.

Against this background, the scheme set out in the Regulations is broadly as follows. Firstly, as required by article 145 of the Convention, the Authority is under a duty to establish and keep under review environmental rules, regulations and procedures to ensure effective protection for the marine environment from harmful

---

14 Council on Environmental Quality, Guidelines for Environmental Impact Assessment (1979), Title 40, U.S. Code of Federal Regulation, cited in Charles L. Morgan, *Environmental Impact for Deepsea Mining*, Report of the Offshore Mineral Policy Workshop, Madang, Papua New Guinea, 1999 (SOPAC Miscellaneous Report 323).

effects which may arise from activities in the Area.[15] To this end, Regulation 1(5) provides that the Regulations may be supplemented by further rules, regulations and procedures, in particular on the protection and preservation of the marine environment.

Secondly, the Authority and sponsoring States are required to apply a precautionary approach, as reflected in Principle 15 of the Rio Declaration, to activities in the Area.[16] The Legal and Technical Commission is to make recommendations to the Council on the implementation of this requirement.[17]

Thirdly, the Regulations impose a duty on each contractor to "take necessary measures to prevent, reduce and control pollution and other hazards to the marine environment arising from its activities in the Area as far as reasonably possible using the best technology available to it".[18] To give effect to this general duty, every contract for exploration for polymetallic nodules shall require the contractor to gather environmental baseline data and to establish environmental baselines, utilizing the best available technology, against which to assess the likely effects of its programme of activities under the plan of work for exploration on the marine environment and a programme to monitor and report on such effects.[19] The contractor shall cooperate with the Authority and the sponsoring State or States in the establishment and implementation of such monitoring programmes.[20] The contractor shall report annually on the results of its environmental monitoring programmes and these reports are to be forwarded to the Legal and Technical Commission for its consideration pursuant to article 165 of the Convention.[21] Furthermore, when applying for approval of a plan of work for exploration, each applicant is required to provide, *inter alia*, a description of a programme for oceanographic and environmental baseline studies in accordance with the Regulations and any environmental rules, regulations and procedures

---

15 Regulation 31(1). See also the 1982 Convention, article 165, paragraphs 2(e), (f) and (h), Annex III, article 17, paragraph 1(b)(xii) and 17, paragraph 2(f); 1994 Agreement, annex, Section 1, paragraph 5(g).

16 Principle 15 of the Rio Declaration states as follows: "In order to protect the environment, the precautionary approach shall be widely applied by States according to their capabilities. Where there are threats of serious or irreversible damage, lack of full scientific certainty shall not be used as a reason for postponing cost-effective measures to prevent environmental degradation." U.N. Doc. A/CONF./151/26 (Vol. 1), located at http://www.un.org/documents/ga/conf151/aconf15126-1annex1.htm. The reference to the precautionary approach in the Regulations originated in a proposal submitted to the Council by the delegation of the Netherlands (ISBA/5/C/L.8).

17 No such recommendations have been made so far.

18 Regulation 31(3). This duty is said to exist pursuant to article 145 of the Convention and paragraph 2 of regulation 31, i.e. the application of a precautionary approach.

19 Regulation 31(4); Annex 4, Section 5.2. Under the 1994 Agreement, annex, Section 1, paragraph 7, each applicant for approval of a plan of work for exploration is required to submit a description of the programme for environmental baseline studies (See also Regulation 18(b) and Annex 2, paragraph 24(b)).

20 *Ibid.*

21 Regulation 31(5). The reference to article 165 is interesting because it implies that the Legal and Technical Commission may use the information obtained from contractors' reports not only for the purpose of monitoring compliance with the terms and conditions of the contract, but also for the broader purposes set out in article 165 of, *inter alia*, making broad recommendations on the protection of the marine environment (article 165, paragraph 2(e)) and formulating and keeping under review rules, regulations and procedures referred to in article 162, paragraph 2(o) (article 165, paragraphs 2(f) and (g)).

established by the Authority that would enable an assessment of the potential environmental impact of the proposed exploration activities, taking into account any recommendations issued by the Legal and Technical Commission, as well as a preliminary assessment of the possible impact of the proposed exploration activities on the marine environment.[22]

Recommendations for the Guidance of Contractors

To give practical effect to the above broad principles, the Regulations contain an important provision which enables the Legal and Technical Commission to issue from time to time recommendations of a technical or administrative nature for the guidance of contractors to assist them in the implementation of the rules, regulations and procedures.[23] The contractor is required to observe any such recommendations as far as reasonably practicable. On 10 July 2001, the Commission issued the first set of recommendations for the guidance of the contractors for the assessment of possible environmental impacts arising from exploration for polymetallic nodules in the Area.[24] Those recommendations describe the procedures to be followed in the acquisition of baseline data, and the monitoring to be performed during and after any activities in the exploration area with potential to cause serious harm to the environment. Their specific purposes are stated as follows:

(a) To define the biological, chemical, geological and physical components to be measured and the procedures to be followed by contractors to ensure effective protection for the marine environment from harmful effects which may arise from the contractors' activities in the Area;
(b) To facilitate reporting by contractors; and
(c) To provide guidance to potential contractors in preparing a plan of work for exploration for polymetallic nodules in conformity with the provisions of the Convention, the 1994 Agreement relating to the implementation of Part XI of the United Nations Convention on the Law of the Sea, and the Regulations.[25]

Given the technical nature of the recommendations and the limited understanding of the impact of exploration activities on the marine environment, the recommendations were issued along with an explanatory commentary and a glossary of technical terms.

It is important to note that the obligations placed upon contractors under the Regulations and standard clauses are progressive in nature. It is widely accepted that,

22 Regulation 18(b).
23 Regulation 38(1).
24 ISBA/7/LTC/1/Rev.1**, Recommendations for the guidance of the contractors for the assessment of possible environmental impacts arising from exploration for polymetallic nodules in the Area. The recommendations were based on a draft prepared by an expert workshop on the development of environmental guidelines convened by the Authority in 1998, taking into account the need for clear and common methods of environmental characterization based on established scientific principles. The draft guidelines were considered by the Legal and Technical Commission at its meetings in August 1999 and July 2000.
25 Ibid., paragraph 5.

during the initial phase of exploration, there would be little, if any, impact on the marine environment. Most exploration work is likely to be non-invasive, relying primarily on remote sensing and standard sampling techniques.[26] However, the standard clauses also recognize that a secondary phase of exploration begins with the commencement of testing of collecting systems and processing operations. At this time, the contractor will be required to submit a site-specific environmental impact assessment and a proposal for a monitoring programme to determine the effect on the marine environment of the equipment that will be used during the mining tests. This approach is reflected in the recommendations for guidance, which distinguish between two distinct phases of exploration: (a) environmental baseline studies; and (b) monitoring during and after testing of collecting systems and equipment.

The purpose of environmental baselines is to ensure that measures can be taken to evaluate the impact of exploration activities on the marine environment. The environmental baseline data to be collected consists of data on physical oceanography, chemical oceanography, sediment properties, biological communities, bioturbation and sedimentation. Although the actual technology that will be used for nodule collecting systems and equipment is not currently known and current knowledge of the deep-sea environment is insufficient to predict the real impacts of tests of such technology, the Legal and Technical Commission considered that the likely environmental disturbances, based on experience and knowledge gathered from previous activities carried out by registered pioneer investors and by the scientific community, may be forecast to some extent. The main impacts are expected to occur at the seafloor, with minor impact expected at the tailings-discharge depth. The nodule collector will disturb the semi-liquid sediment-surface layer and will create a near-bottom plume. It will also compress, break up and squeeze the harder underlying sediment layer. To predict the impacts of such activities it is therefore particularly necessary to target data collection towards the dose-response function for the sediment communities for a single deposition event; the chronic disturbance effect, i.e. the disturbance effect of multiple sediment depositions in a given area, which would yield information on how frequently a plume is produced in an area that yields a small amount of sedimentation, without having a negative impact upon the ecosystem; and the time scale of community recovery after a very intense disturbance.

IV. OUTSTANDING ISSUES

Although the Regulations do not go as far as some delegations participating in the negotiations would have liked, it is suggested that what is contained in Part V of the Regulations is in fact a very significant advance upon article 145 of the Convention and provides a firm basis for the elaboration of a comprehensive code of environmental regulation. It must be recognized, however, that there remain a number of provisions contained in Part XI, the 1994 Agreement, and the Regulations relating

26 It may be noted that the recommendations for guidance issued by the Legal and Technical Commission list, consistent with regulation 31(4), a number of activities which are deemed to have no potential for causing any adverse effect on the marine environment.

to protection of the marine environment which will require further elaboration if they are to become effective. These include the following:

(a) Criteria for identification of (i) areas which the Council disapproves for exploitation by contractors or the Enterprise in cases where substantial evidence indicates the risk of serious harm to the marine environment[27] and (ii) "impact reference zones" and "preservation reference zones".[28]
(b) Recommendations by the Committee to the Council on the application of the precautionary approach, as reflected in principle 15 of the Rio Declaration, to activities in the Area.[29]
(c) Criteria for determination of whether an effect from an activity in the Area represents, or is likely to represent, a significant adverse change in the marine environment.
(d) Guidelines for the assessment of the potential environmental impacts of proposed activities in the Area.[30]
(e) Guidelines for the description by the applicant of his proposed measures for the prevention, reduction and control of pollution and other hazards, as well as other possible impacts, to the marine environment, in light of the tests of reasonableness and best available technology.[31]
(f) Guidelines for (a) the description of the applicant's technical capability to respond to any incident or activity which causes serious harm to the marine environment[32] or (b) the content of his guarantee of technical capability to comply promptly with any emergency orders issued by the Council.[33]
(g) Guidelines on decommissioning.[34]

One of the areas in which there was particular difficulty in reaching agreement was on the question of liability for damage to the marine environment arising out of activities in the Area. While the Regulations follow the provisions of Annex III of the Convention and provide that the contractor shall be liable for the actual amount of any damage, including damage to the marine environment, arising out of its wrongful acts or omissions, a proposal was made during the negotiations in the Council to the effect that the contractor should be required to deposit an environmental guarantee prior to the phase of testing of collecting systems and processing operations in order to ensure compliance with emergency orders and the effective protection of the marine environment. While this proposal was considered to be premature for inclusion in the Regulations, the need to carry out future studies of

27 Convention, article 162, paragraph 2(x) and article 165, paragraph 2(l).
28 Regulation 31(7).
29 Regulation 31(2).
30 Convention, article 165, paragraph 2(d); 1994 Agreement, annex, Section 1, paragraph 7; Regulations, Regulation 18(c) and 31(4); Regulations, Annex 2, paragraph 24(c); Annex 4, Section 5.5(a)–(b). Section IV of the Recommendations for Guidance already identifies (a) categories of activity requiring or not requiring an environmental impact assessment and (b) types of activity information to be provided to the Authority.
31 Regulation 18(d); 31(4); Annex 2, paragraph 24(d); Annex 4, Section 5.1.
32 Regulation 12(7)(c); Annex 2, paragraph 23(c).
33 Regulation 32(7).
34 Convention, article 147; Regulations, Annex 4, Section 21.7. During negotiations on this issue, it was pointed out by some delegations that existing international rules and regulations already cover the use, removal and disposal of offshore installations, for example, the regulations of the International Maritime Organization.

appropriate instruments or arrangements which may be available for the purpose of establishing a mechanism for environmental guarantees was reflected in the decision of the Council adopting the draft regulations.[35] Even with respect to the provisions contained in the Regulations themselves, it is clear that there will be a need for more detailed consideration of how these principles might be applied in practice. This might involve, for example, the development of guidelines on acceptable heads of claim regarding damage to the marine environment for which liability may potentially arise[36]. and guidelines on levels of monetary penalties that may be imposed by the Council on contractors for damage to the marine environment.[37]

V. CONCLUSION

Since the adoption of the Regulations, the Authority has continued to adopt an incremental approach to environmental regulation based on the need to gain a better understanding of the marine environment before regulating the conduct of contractors. Opportunities have been provided to scientists and experts at workshops and meetings of the Authority to exchange views on the work that they are doing and to discuss with their peers some of the trials, tribulations and results of that work.

For example, in June 2001, the Authority organized an international workshop to review the status of environmental research currently being undertaken on the protection of the flora and fauna around deep seabed polymetallic nodules. The workshop developed a number of recommendations on the need to standardize the environmental data and information required by the Regulations and in particular highlighted the need for sampling designs for acquisition of environmental baseline data and for conducting monitoring tests and strategies for standardization of ongoing efforts in taxonomy, sample processing and field collection of data. A further workshop will be convened in August 2002. This workshop will build upon the results of previous workshops by examining the prospects for international collaboration in marine environmental research to enhance understanding of the deep sea environment, including its biodiversity. The workshop will review various proposals for research topics to be carried out through international cooperation in order to fill gaps in scientific knowledge that would enable better management of the environmental impacts of future deep seabed mining.

The outcomes of workshops and seminars such as the International Conference on Marine Environmental Law (ICMEL), as well as the cooperation of the marine mining industry and the contractors with the Authority, will provide the necessary basis for the Legal and Technical Commission to keep the present system of environmental regulation of deep seabed mining under review and to respond in an appropriate and timely manner to seabed mining activities as they progress.

35 ISBA/6/C/12. Reproduced in Selected Decisions 6, at 86.
36 Convention, Annex III, article 22; Regulation 30; Annex 4, Section 16.1.
37 Convention, Annex III, article 18, paragraph 2; Regulations, Annex 4, Section 21.5.

Law of the Sea and Meteorological and Oceanographic Observations from Ocean Areas

*Iwona Rummel-Bulska**

I. SYSTEM OF METEOROLOGICAL/OCEANOGRAPHIC OBSERVATIONS AT SEA, THEIR ROLE AND IMPORTANCE

The first formal international meteorological meeting to coordinate weather observing at sea took place as early as in 1853.

Since that time ships' meteorological observations have provided essential inputs to weather warnings and forecasts, which have become progressively more accurate. The need for improved knowledge of ocean weather and climate has been further reinforced by the threat of global warming and by the prospect that weather forecasts can be made on time-scales of months to years by using information on oceanic conditions.

The World Meteorological Organisation (WMO) and the Intergovernmental Oceanographic Commission (IOC) of UNESCO have been working with the maritime community to enhance voluntary observational programmes carried out by ships at sea.

WMO's World Weather Watch (WWW) coordinates round-the-clock monitoring to take the pulse of the weather over the oceans, drawing on meteorological observations from ships, drifting and moored buoys, oil rigs and orbiting satellites as well as from inland observing sites. Under the WMO Voluntary Observing Ships (VOS) Programme ships are recruited by National Meteorological Services to record and transmit meteorological observations, mainly air pressure, air temperature, sea surface temperature, wind and sea state.

Meteorological observations made by officers on board vessels participating in the programme are recorded in meteorological logbooks and coded in a standardized format for immediate transmission to shore. They are then routed around the world on WMO's Global Telecommunication System for use by meteorologists, ship routing services, radio and television broadcasts. Until recently voluntary

* Dr. *Iwona Rummel-Bulska* Senior is a Senior Legal Adviser of the World Meteorological Organisation (WMO), Geneva (Switzerland). She served at the United Nations Environment Programme (UNEP) from 1982–2000, most recently as the Executive Secretary of the Basel Convention and Head of Compliance and Enforcement of Environmental Conventions. Contact: Rummel_I@gateway.wmo.ch.

A. Kirchner (ed.), International Maritime Environmental Law, 61–67.

observing ships' reports were usually transmitted in Morse code to coastal radio stations but, with the implementation of the Global Maritime Distress and Safety System, most are now relayed via satellite communication or by voice radio.

Vessels participating in the voluntary observing ships Programme are usually classified into one of three major categories:

- "Selected Ships" carry out a complete programme of meteorological observations and utilize the full WMO SHIP code for relay of their reports.
- "Supplementary Ships" undertake a somewhat reduced observational programme and use an abbreviated code form.
- Any vessel travelling through a data-sparse region may be recruited into a third category, known as "Auxiliary Ships" and requested to supply limited observations.

Worldwide voluntary observing ships numbers reached a peak of about 7700 ships in 1984–85 but have declined since that time with just over 6700 vessels from 52 countries participating in early 2000. This decline reflects the continuing trend towards fewer but larger ships but has been balanced, to some extent, by the fact that vessels, in general, now spend reduced time in port. This fact, in addition to improved communication via satellite, has actually led to enhancements in both the quantity and the quality of meteorological reports from these vessels. Meteorological Officers in ports provide free training in weather observing and in the use of WMO codes. The Voluntary Observing System Programme operates at no direct costs to participating vessels. No communication charges are levied for the transmission of meteorological observations.

Observations from ships significantly complement information on weather system and ocean variables obtained from satellites. They supply information on variables and phenomena which can not, as yet, be accurately, reliably and consistently observed from space. They also continue to be used routinely in the preparation of weather forecasts, thus supplying a constant check on actual weather conditions, contributing directly to short-range prediction and providing important inputs to numerical weather prediction models.

Historical records of these observations of oceanic conditions is registered in the Marine Climatological Summaries Scheme which was established by WMO in 1963.In addition, historical marine meteorological observations recorded in ships' logbooks since the nineteenth century form one of the longest continuous climate records in existence and are essential to the assessment of natural and anthropological climate changes.

During the last two decades, concern regarding the potential impacts of global warming has intensified efforts to understand the functioning of the global climate system. In addressing this challenge, the Second World Climate Conference (Geneva, 1990) identified the need for a comprehensive ocean observing system as a vital component of the Global Climate Observing System. Subsequently, in 1998, the Conference of the Parties (COP) to the United Nations Framework Convention on Climate change called on the world's Governments to enhance substantially systematic monitoring and data collection activities over and within oceans. This requirement for enhanced operational ocean monitoring was based on the decision 14/CP.4 of the 1998 COP entitled "Research and systematic observation". The operational system comprises a large variety of remote-sensing (both satellite and ground based) and in-situ observing platforms, the latter increasingly to include unmanned free-floating buoys and sub-surface floats. The system is coordinated internationally through the new Joint WMO/IOC Technical Commission for Oceanography and Marine Meteorology, an intergovernmental technical body, and is implemented taking into account joint programmes such as the Global Ocean Observing System and the Global Climate Observing System.

The provision of specialized services, the development of long-range forecasts and climate change research require oceanic observations with increased accuracy and coverage.

In 1988, WMO initiated the Voluntary Special Observing Project – North Atlantic, to address these latter aspects. This three-year study of the effects on ship observations of different instrumentation and observing practices provided a great deal of invaluable information.[1]

WMO also collects information from unmanned, automated drifting surface buoys and other surface platforms that are essential for the calibration or "ground-truthing" of satellite observation.

All the operational ocean observing systems referred to above provide an integrated stream of oceanographic and related marine meteorological data, in both real-time and delayed mode, for use by national and international agencies and institutions. These observational data have immediate and critical application to global climate monitoring, research and prediction, including El-Niño/La Niña prediction, maritime safety and marine environmental protection and management.

II. PROTECTION OF MARINE METEOROLOGICAL AND OCEANOGRAPHIC OBSERVATIONS IN THE CONTEXT OF THE NEGOTIATION PROCESS LEADING TO THE UN CONVENTION ON THE LAW OF THE SEA

During the Third United Nations Conference on the Law of the Sea, WMO sought and received assurances that the pertinent provisions of the United Nations Convention on the Law of the Sea on marine scientific research would not have a detrimental impact on routine meteorological and oceanographic observations from ocean areas, including areas within the exclusive economic zone, carried out in the framework of existing international programmes.

These observations were judged to be of common interest to all countries and to have universal significance.[2]

Already in May 1979 the Eight World Meteorological Congress expressed its concern at the potential implications of draft articles 238 to 249 of the Part XIII on Marine Scientific Research of the Informal Composite Negotiating Text prepared by the Third UN Conference on the Law of the Sea, in the context of the World Weather Watch and the Integrated Global Ocean Services System from within the

1 Based on: The WMO Voluntary Observing System – An Enduring Partnership. Geneva, WMO 2000.

2 Official Records of the UN Conference of the Law of the Sea, vol. XIV (UN Publ. Sales No.E.82.V.2), Plenary, 134th meeting, para 43, and Third Committee, 46th meeting, paras. 4 and 5.

Exclusive Economic Zone and Territorial Sea. The concern was expressed formally when it was adopted by the WMO Congress Resolution 16.

By this Resolution the WMO Congress referred to the fact that activities of the Members of WMO over the oceans fall into two major categories:

(a) Operational activities, such as the collection of meteorological information from voluntary observing ships, buoys, other ocean platforms, aircrafts and meteorological satellites;

(b) Research activities, both meteorological and oceanographic, such as those carried out during the Global Weather Experiment.

The Congress also emphasised that an adequate marine meteorological data coverage from ocean areas including the Exclusive Economic Zone is indispensable for the issue of timely and accurate storm warnings for the safety of life at sea and the protection of life and property in coastal and off-shore areas, and that the International Convention for the Safety of Life at Sea (SOLAS, 1960) specifies that the Contracting Governments undertake, *inter alia*, to issue warnings of gales and storms, and to arrange for selected ships to take meteorological observations. According to internationally agreed procedures, the Members of WMO have undertaken the responsibility of issuing warnings for the high seas and coastal waters.

The Congress expressed the hope that the legal provisions contained in the Informal Composite Negotiating Text prepared by the Third UN Conference of the Sea would not result in restriction to operational meteorological and related oceanographic observations carried out in accordance with WMO international programmes, in particular in the context of the WWW and Global Ocean Services System (IGOSS).

The Resolution adopted at the WMO Congress was formally brought to the attention of the Third Conference of the Law of the Sea, namely to its Committee dealing, *inter alia*, with the issues of Marine Scientific Research (Third Committee).

At the 46th Meeting in August 1980 the Chairman of the Third Committee, Ambassaor A. Yankov, announced that in the Resolution adopted at the Eight World Meteorological Congress which had been distributed to the participants of the Law of the Sea Conference as doc. A/CONF.62/80, the WMO Congress referred to some of the activities carried out in accordance with international programmes such as WWW and IGOSS. "… Now that the Third Committee had completed the negotiations on the substantive questions before it, it was in a position to reply to the Secretary-General of the WMO."

According to the extract from the Third UN Conference on the Law of the Sea, Ambassador Yankov at the 46th meeting of the Third Committee stated that: "Since the formulation of draft articles on the legal régime for the conduct of marine scientific research came under his mandate as Chairman of the Third Committee, he was able to share the view of the Eighth Meteorological Congress that adequate marine meteorological data coverage, including that from areas within the exclusive economic zone, was indispensable for timely and accurate storm warnings for the safety of navigation and for the protection of lives and property in coastal and offshore areas. In his opinion, the provisions on marine scientific research would not create any difficulties and obstacles hindering adequate meteorological coverage from ocean areas, including areas within exclusive economic zone, carried out both within the framework of existing international programmes and by all vessels, since such activities had already been recognized as routine observations and data collecting which were not covered by Part XIII of the negotiating text. Furthermore, they were in the common interest of all countries and had undoubted universal significance."

Amb.Yankov further stated at the 134th Plenary Meeting of the Third Conference that in his reply to the Secretary-General of the WMO he would state that: "in his view the provisions of the second revision of the negotiating text on marine scientific research would not hinder adequate meteorological coverage from ocean areas, including areas within the exclusive economic zone, since such operational and research activities had already been recognized as routine activities within the Organisation's terms of reference and were of common interest to all countries".

Indeed in his letter to the Secretary-General of WMO dated 29 August 1980 Amb. Yankov referred to the above points.

Accordingly the Ninth World Meteorological Congress was informed of the letter and views expressed by Amb. Yankov.

The Congress expressed satisfaction with the interpretation of the provisions of the UNCLOS as they relate to routine meteorological and oceanographic observations. The Congress emphasised that the WMO-coordinated research programmes will require extensive marine meteorological and oceanographic data sets from the world ocean including the Exclusive Economic Zone, and urged its Members to continue to promote marine meteorological and related oceanographic observational programmes over the ocean, for both operational and research purposes.

The Congress requested the Executive Council of WMO and its Secretary-General to arrange for continuing review of the implications of the legal provisions of the Convention on the ocean-related activities of WMO with a view to informing the United Nations and Members of WMO as appropriate, and to take, as necessary, action to ensure that the ocean-related activities of WMO, both operational and scientific, are undertaken under the most favourable conditions.[3]

UNCLOS entered into force in November 1994. In the light of this, in August 1994 the Secretary-General of WMO circulated among WMO Members represented on the Commission for Marine Meteorology the letter in which he presented the background related to the routine meteorological and oceanographic observations in the context of UNCLOS, with a view to facilitating national discussions related to the marine observation networks. In his letter the Secretary-General also emphasised: (a) the indispensable nature of routine marine meteorological and oceanographic observations, including from the EEZ and Territorial Sea, to the provision of services in support of the safety of life and property at sea; (b) the fact that these observations are made in the context of agreed, long-standing operational systems of WWW and the Integrated Ocean Services System, and that they are freely exchanged among, and are of benefit to, all countries; (c) that these observations are generally made on a voluntary basis by officers on merchant vessels engaged in normal trading activities, who should be reassured where necessary of the continuing legality and importance of their work.

3 Ninth WMO Congress – Resolution 9 (Cg-IX) – United Nations Conference on the Law of the Sea.

Part XIII of the UNCLOS, entitled "Marine Scientific Research" (Articles 238–249), addresses and promotes international cooperation in marine scientific research for peaceful purposes. Article 243, entitled "Creation of favorable conditions", stipulates that States and competent international organizations shall cooperate, through the conclusion of… agreements, to create favourable conditions fort the conduct of marine scientific research in the marine environment and to integrate the efforts of scientists in studying the essence of phenomena and processes occurring in the marine environment and the interrelations between them. The Convention addresses the issue of Publications and dissemination of information and knowledge by encouraging States and international organizations to promote the flow of scientific data and information and the transfer of knowledge resulting from marine scientific research.

In Section 3, entitled "Conduct and Promotion of Marine Scientific Research" of Part XIII, it is clearly stated that the coastal States shall grant their consent for marine scientific research projects by other States or competent international organizations in their exclusive economic zone or on their continental shelf to be carried out in accordance with the Convention exclusively for peaceful purposes and in order to increase scientific knowledge of the marine environment for the benefit of all mankind (Art. 246).

Marine scientific research projects undertaken by or under the auspicies of international organizations are further addressed in Art. 247 of the UNCLOS.

It is worth mentioning that in 1988 the IOC Executive Council decided, particularly with regard to the deployment of floating buoys, to invite the Inter-secretariat Committee on Scientific Programmes Relating to Oceanography agencies to consider establishing a group of experts to lay the groundwork for a global convention on the legal status of Ocean Data Acquisition System (ODAS). ODAS refers to structures, platforms, installations, buoys or other devices, together with the associated equipment, which are deployed at sea essentially for the purpose of collecting, storing or transmitting samples or data on the marine environment or the atmosphere. ODAS can be manned or unmanned, anchored or drifting, at the surface, below or at the bottom. The term does not include ships. It was agreed that a special study be prepared on the issue of the legal aspects of ODAS with a view to the preparation of a draft convention.[4]

III. ROLE AND ACTIVITIES OF THE NEWLY ESTABLISHED JOINT WMO/IOC TECHNICAL COMMISSION FOR OCEANOGRAPHY AND MARINE METEOROLOGY

The main scientific operational ocean observing systems recently have been carried out by the newly created intergovernmental technical body, namely the Joint WMO/IOC Technical Commission for Oceanography and Marine meteorology (JCOMM). The Commission was established in 1999 by the World Meteorological Congress and the IOC Assembly through the merger of the existing WMO

4 Annual Review of Ocean Affairs: Law and Policy, Main Documents, 1988, vol. III; pp. 972, 1394–6.

Commission for Marine Meteorology and the Joint IOC/WMO Committee for the Integrated Global Ocean Services System. JCOMM is an intergovernmental body, with the status in WMO of a technical commission and in IOC of a Technical and/or Scientific Committee.

One of the main reasons for the creation of the Joint Commission was the pressing need for a fully coordinated joint mechanism for implementing the stated requirement for ocean and surface marine meteorological data. The Commission is responsible for the development, maintenance, coordination and guidance of the operation of the global marine meteorological and oceanographic observing system and supporting communications facilities. It monitors the use of observations and derived products and suggests changes to improve their quality. Coordination of the safety-related marine meteorological and associated oceanographic services is an integral part of the Global Maritime Distress and Safety System of the International Convention for the Safety of Life at Sea (SOLAS).

It is important to emphasise that the observational data carried out within the Joint Commission as well as in all other WMO Programmes are made freely available to all countries through the Global Telecommunication System of WMO. This also includes data from drifting surface buoys and subsurface floats. Some concern has been, expressed however, about the status of such platforms in the context of UNCLOS, in particular that member States should receive appropriate notification of any platform drift into, and report observation from, exclusive economic zones.

In response to these concerns, and at the initiative of Intergovernmental Oceanographic Commission (IOC) of UNESCO, various actions are being undertaken, most specifically through the new Array for Real-time Geostrophic Oceanography project for a global network of drifting surface buoys, as follows:

(a) through a joint IOC/WMO circular letter, member States are being informed of the project, its formal acceptance by IOC and WMO as an integral part of existing international programmes of the two organisations, how to access float data and positions, and how to participate in and benefit from the project;

(b) an international Array for Real-time Geostrophic Oceanography information centre is being established through IOC, to work in conjunction with a similar technical unit for surface drifting buoys (the centre will, in particular, maintain a web site accessible to all member States, to provide real-time information on individual float status); and

(c) operational coordination of float and buoy programmes will take place within the overall international coordination of ocean observing systems to be undertaken by the newly created Joint WMO/IOC Technical Commission for Oceanography and Marine Meteorology (JCOMM) floats.

Inter-Agency Collaboration or Inter-Agency Competition – A Challenge for the UN System

*Moira L. McConnell**

1. INTRODUCTION

In December 2001 the Secretary General of the United Nations identified the need for a "Formulation of Common Responses Within the United Nations System" noting that:

> Successful coordination and cooperation among United Nations organizations, agencies and programmes in important sectoral areas such as energy, water, forests and oceans have contributed to the strengthening of programmes in these areas and provided deeper insights into the inter-linkages between the social, economic and environmental dimension of human activities…*Still an important challenge remains to ensure better linkages between inter-agency work at the global level and regional and national implementation… The adoption of national sustainable development strategies has facilitated the coordination of programmes among international agencies*…Further efforts are still needed to realize the full potential of the CSD to improve intergovernmental decision-making and to fully integrate the multi sectoral dimension of sustainable development. *There is also a need to strengthen and, where necessary, reform the governing structures and decision-making processes of international institutions* dealing with economic, social and environmental aspects of sustainable development. An important challenge for the Summit is to provide direction for a stronger and more coherent system of global governance for sustainable development.[1] (emphasis added)

This paper considers the question of the relationship amongst UN organisations[2] concerned with marine environmental protection. It was originally prepared as a

---

* Dr. *Moira McConnell* is Professor of Law at the Marine and Environmental Law Programme, Dalhousie University, Nova Scotia (Canada). Contact: moira.mcconnell@dal.ca.

This paper was prepared during my secondment as Professor of Maritime Affairs (2000–2002), World Maritime University, Sweden. The support of the University is gratefully acknowledged as is the support of the sponsors of ICMEL, Bremen, April 2002.

1 *Implementing Agenda 21*, Report of the Secretary General, Economic and Social Council, ECOSOC, Doc. Number.E/CN.17/2002/PC.2/7. Available at: http://www.johannesburgsummit.org/html/documents/prepcom2.html.

2 It is understood that the United Nations Environment Programme and the United Nations Development Programme are not specialised UN organisations *per se* but may instead be viewed as cross cutting activities. For purposes of this discussion the terms agency and institution are used more generally to include all of these organisations. Although the distinction is often considered important, for purposes of this paper the functional jurisdiction and activities are more relevant.

A. Kirchner (ed.), International Maritime Environmental Law, 69–91.

contribution to the International Conference on Marine Environmental Law (Bremen, April 2002) discussion on the implementation of international marine environmental law.[3] The latter is usually understood as being concerned with an examination of domestic or national efforts to give effect to a developing body of law and norms generally classified as international marine environmental law. The former, by contrast, is more concerned with an examination of the activities and roles of international institutional actors, or governance as it is sometimes called. At first sight the connection between these two concerns may not be obvious. The argument presented in this paper is that they are, in fact, intimately connected and that good international institutional relationships are central to implementation and, more importantly, effectiveness[4] – the ultimate measure of implementation – of environmental protection efforts.

The rapid expansion and influence of scientific information, models and methodology, particularly that known as ecology,[5] over the last 30 years, has led to a more holistic and dynamic system- (ecosystem-) based understanding of the nature of the relationships among various levels of human interaction. The emergence of a holistic approach both to understanding the relationship between human activity and the environment and to governing that relationship provides a number of challenges to the existing institutions at the domestic and international level. The phenomenon of globalisation, particularly as manifest in patterns of economic activity and electronic communication, has exacerbated this situation. An expanding awareness of the causal connections amongst myriad activities now presents opportunities to revisit the classification of issues that has structured all levels and fields of institutional interaction and organisational culture. The ecosystemic worldview has spawned a new generation of environmental concerns such as biodiversity/biosecurity, climate change and the goal of sustainable development, which defy these traditional legal and political classifications and the related governmental structures. These developments are combined with concern about the rising number of environment-related disasters, many of which have undermined the socio-economic and political stability in affected countries and revealed alarming gaps in their capacity to respond.

Not surprisingly, this has given rise to a change in contemporary perceptions of the environmental problematique, its causes, effects and also possible solutions. The most notable solution is the development and global endorsement of Integrated Management (IM) as the primary strategic process for achieving sustainable

---

3 It is focused on UN or formal agencies largely because of the legal relationships between the international and domestic systems. The influence of other groups, such as the Commission on Global Governance, various councils and environmental advocacy and industry organisations on the process of policy and lawmaking, is acknowledged.

4 That is, evaluating whether the lawmaking activity correlates with any positive change in the regulated field of activity. Too often it is assumed that adoption of a law will achieve the expected result with little or no attention devoted to follow-up activities to assess the impact of the lawmaking activity.

5 Peter Haas, *Saving the Mediterranean: the politics of international environmental cooperation* (New York: Columbia University Press, 1990), presents an interesting case study examining, in part, the rise of ecology and an ecological point of view within UNEP and its influence on the Regional Seas Programme in the Mediterranean.

development, particularly in relation to the management of ocean and coastal activities and interactions.[6] It was endorsed in 1992 by the international community of nations participating in the United Nations Conference on Environment and Development (UNCED). IM and the associated principles and practices have influenced the implementation processes and substantive content of environmental law and policy, including much of the body of law that relates to protection of the marine environment. At the international level, implementation of integrated management activity is often situated in the call for improved governance, a concept involving a more interactive and "open" process,[7] than the more specific institution and practice of "government".

This paper considers the challenges and opportunities these developments pose in the context of effective implementation of marine environmental protection law and policy. It focuses, in particular, on the issue of integrating governance and laws relating to ocean-based activities, such as shipping, with the regulation of land-based activities affecting the marine environment, as a means of helping to achieve sustainable development. In this context it is interesting to note the comment of the Secretary-General of the International Maritime Organization (IMO) in late 2001: "A strong transport and communication infrastructure is essential to achieving sustainable development."[8] The Secretary-General also highlighted the importance of marine environmental protection in view of the dependency of many nations on the sea as a source of food. These comments reflect an increasingly holistic view of the role of shipping as a positive force to promote sustainability, alleviate poverty and help to minimize and eliminate ecosystem security risks.

At the same time the hegemony of flag State supremacy (and even State sovereignty), the core of IMO's international regulatory mechanisms, and the divide between ocean- and shore-based activities is increasingly in question as States move to integrated domestic polices and institutional structures.[9] The same forces tending to global integration can also be observed in related areas such as international trade. There are also countervailing forces that focus on protecting local or domestic concerns. The term "fragmegration" – fragmentation and integration – is sometimes

6 Integrated management in the context of Integrated Coastal and Ocean Management (ICOM) has gone through a number of metamorphoses – moving from the narrow coastal land zone (CZ, ICZ, ICM, etc.) to include ocean use management and more recently ICARM (Integrated Coastal Area and River Management). To avoid debates on terminology the term Integrated Management (IM) is adopted in this paper and refers generally to the management model as opposed to a particular spatial context.

7 Evangelos Raftopoulos argues, in the context of multilateral environmental negotiations, that one can view multilateral negotiations as an ongoing process of uncovering or defining the nature of the relationship between the various actors: "International Environmental Negotiation as a Process of Governance Technique: Deconstructing the Negotiating Process in the Mediterranean Environmental Regime" (working title) Lecture Paper for the MEPIELAN Seminar, Athens, Greece, February 18–21, 2002 (copy on file with author). Publication forthcoming in the Proceedings and on the MEPIELAN website at: http://www.mepielan.gr.

8 William O'Neil, "IMO – Globalization and the Role of the Seafarer". A message from the Secretary-General of the International Maritime Organization. World Maritime Day 2001. Circular Letter No. 2335. Ref: A4/A/1.17 (London: IMO, 2001) p. 2.

9 See: Awni Behnam and Peter Faust, "The Twilight of Flag State Control", publication forthcoming in the Ocean Yearbook, Vol. 17 (Chicago: U of Chicago Press, 2002).

used to describe the fact that both of these forces operate concurrently and intersect.[10] This dynamic is important to understanding contemporary issues regarding effective implementation of marine environmental protection policy and law. For example, although the "flag State" is aligned with the traditional notions of State sovereignty and nationality, the interests described as "flag State" can be cast as globalising or internationalising forces that accord prominence to the international character of regulatory activity and concerns. By contrast, the interest captured by the idea of the "coastal State" is more aligned with local, domestic or regional concerns. Many States have both interests, with a third concept – that of the port State interest – straddling the two. The tension between these forces is played out internationally and domestically since most States have multiple faces. The differing, sometimes contrary, faces of national interest and identity are, in turn, presented, often by different people, in international *fora* such as UNEP, UNCTAD and IMO. At times, in relation to differing concerns, these forces will tend to override or "trump" each other. Increasingly this is related, particularly on the domestic level, to the classification of an issue relative to these forces. For example, despite commitment to sustainable development, most States will tend to give primacy to immediate economic matters rather than longer-term environmental concerns. However, matters perceived as threats to human health or safety or security of the State are more likely to override economic concerns in the short term. Reactive policy development with sudden shifts in approach and classification can result in conflicts and poor decision-making at all levels. The IM approach discussed later in this paper favours explicitly reflective and precautionary governance/regulatory design that seeks to develop common information and identify common interests and long-term goals among all concerned, to facilitate cooperative and collaborative activities of governance.

2. TERMINOLOGY

Before examining the development of an ecosystem worldview and Integrated Management as the corresponding institutional response, it is important to emphasise the significance of the terminology used in this paper.

---

10 A term adopted by James Rosenau, an international relations theorist, to describe the interaction of the globalizing (integration) and localizing (fragmentation) forces affecting domestic and international relationships. He argues that it is the boundary or frontier where these forces intersect that provides the challenge for governance: See: James Rosenau, *Along the Domestic – Foreign Frontier. Exploring Governance in a Turbulent World* (Cambridge, UK: Cambridge University Press, 1997). For an exploration of similiar themes in the environmental governance see: Moira McConnell, "Centralization–Decentralization of Environmental Governance: Constitutive Tensions in a Transnational Interdependent Era", paper presented at the World Jurist Conference, Montreal, August 1995 (published in the Proceedings). The idea of fragmegration is also discussed in the context of the intersection of security and environmental interests by Peter H. Liotta, "Military and Environmental Security: Revisiting the Concepts in the Euro-Mediterranean", paper presented at the Canterbury Workshop "Security and the Environment in the Mediterranean in the 20th Century", Canterbury, AFES-PRESS, 8–10 September 2001. Publication forthcoming as Chapter 14 in H. Bauch, A. Marquina, M. Selim, P. Liotta, P. Rogers (eds). *Security and the Environment in the Mediterranean in the 20th Century – Conceptualising Security and Environmental Conflicts* (Berlin: Springer, anticipated 2003).

"Collaboration", "competition", "challenge" and "system", all words found in the title, were chosen to reflect the themes that are explored in this paper. Collaboration is a word often used in negotiation theory, particularly by advocates of principled negotiation theory[11] and management theory, to describe a result that maximizes gains for all parties. A collaborative approach is one that leaves as little "value on the table" as possible. The word "competition" by contrast tends to describe a win-lose situation, perhaps with less regard for the ultimate impact of the process on the all players. "Challenge" is a word often understood to acknowledge difficulties that offer opportunities and growth. A system can be defined, *inter alia*, as "a group of things or parts working together or connected in some way as to form a whole".[12] That is, a system involves a relationship of some sort between discrete parts. In order to understand better the implications of the idea of a system in the context of the United Nations, the following description from the field of inquiry called systems science or system dynamics is helpful.

> The central concept to system dynamics understands how all the objects in a system interact with one another. A system can be anything from a steam engine, to a bank account, to a basketball team. The objects and people in a system interact through "feedback" loops, where a change in one variable affects other variables over time, which in turn affects the original variable, and so on.[13]

Thus the UN can be understood as a system comprising actors, ideas and institutions constantly interacting, through their reaction to issues and to each other's actions and reactions relating to the same or other issues. The point of interest here is the everchanging and conditional nature of these interactional relationships.

The word "ecosystem" presents a further elaboration on the idea of a system. An ecosystem is legally defined in the 1992 *Convention on Biological Diversity*[14] as:

> Article 2 ... "Ecosystem" means a dynamic complex of plant, animal and microorganism communities and their non-living environment interacting as a functional unit.

Researchers involved in the study of complex systems[15] have described this biological/ecological concept and its relationship to the process of human governance as follows:[16]

> In biology/ecology an ecosystem is the collection of organisms in one area that interact and therefore depend on each other. It is to be contrasted with the notion that organisms

11 The ideas were popularised by Roger Fisher and William Ury of the Harvard Negotiation Project in *Getting to Yes. Negotiating Agreement Without Giving* (Bruce Patton is also a co-author for the 2nd edition) (New York: Penguin: 1981, 1991). There are many variations on this approach to analyzing negotiations found in the work of other negotiation theorists: See, for example, Roy Lewicki, David Saunders & John Minton, *Essentials of Negotiation* (Chicago: Irwin, 1997).

12 David B. Guralnik (Gen. Editor), *Webster's New World Dictionary*, 2nd concise edition (New York: Simon & Shuster, 1979) p. 760.

13 Sloane School of Management, MIT. Undated Document. Available at: http://web.mit.edu/sdg/www/sysdyna.html.

14 Available at: http://www.biodiv.org.

15 For example, the New England Complex Systems Institute, see http://www.necsi.org/.

16 Yaneer Bar-Yam, 2000, "Ecosystem. Concepts in Complex Systems" in *Guide to Complex Systems* online publication by New England Complex Systems Institute. Available at: e/guide/concepts/ecosystem.html.

> are in deadly competition with each other for evolutionary survival. *The notion of ecosystem recognises the many ways an organism interacts with and is dependent for its own survival on various parts of its environment.*
>
> ...
>
> In ecology, the term also refers to the system (collective) behaviors of an ecological system (e.g. forest, wetland, coral reef, etc.) consisting of interdependent biological organisms and their physical context. The large scale collective behaviors include, for example, the forest lifecycle that might in some places include destruction by fire and stages of regrowth. We see that, *in principle, the idea of an ecosystem corresponds to viewing an organism or company (etc.) as part of a larger scale system whose parts are interacting and interdependent.* (emphasis added)

This explanatory model proffered by the sciences has profound implications when transplanted to the sphere of human activity. There are least two levels of analyses relevant to this paper. First, this model can be applied to the nature of the relationship amongst human/institutional actors. Second, and the primary focus of this paper, there are implications of this model or view for human activities that seek to manage this more fluid interactive situation. This issue has been explained as follows:[17]

> *The contrast between the idea of survival through competition and the idea of an ecosystem has also been transferred to social and economic systems.* The term ecosystem is used when people talk about the environment that a company is part of, when they think about how it interacts with various suppliers (of equipment, of parts, of services, of knowledge, of financial liquidity, etc.), partners in its primary activity, consumers or users of the products or services it provides, and the underlying structure and behavior of the technology, markets and social context. *The idea of establishing alliances with companies that might otherwise have been thought of as competitors reflects the notion that cooperation in an ecosystem is part of how the organisms that comprise it survive.*
>
> In the general usage one can contrast "ecosystem" to the term "system" which focuses on the collective behaviors. *The term ecosystem is typically used to describe the internal dependencies of the larger system especially as they pertain to a particular part. For example, one might say "he/it is part of my ecosystem" to refer to recognizing one's dependence on the other in the larger context.* Thus, ecosystem is almost a substitute for the term environment, but it emphasizes the existence of various parts of the environment, rather than the environment as a single entity. (emphasis added)

This squarely raises the crux of the contemporary governance concerns. How can we best manage these myriad relationships in a system where the underlying dynamic suggests that cooperation will, in the long run, result in survival, but the tendency to competition is ingrained in world history and the international legal system that gives primacy to the sovereignty and autonomy of each State? We must deal with the fruit of the past and the seeds of the future because both comprise and, perhaps, compromise the present.[18]

---

17 *Ibid.*

18 This thought draws on a comment made by Elisabeth Mann Borgese in somewhat different terms in her address "The Years of My Life", The Nexus Lecture, The Netherlands, May 1999. Her comment was cited in R. St John Macdonald, "Elisabeth Mann Borgese, *The Oceanic Circle: Governing the Seas as a Global Resource*", Book Review, *Canadian Yearbook of International Law*, Vol. 37 (Vancouver: UBC Press, 1999) p. 472.

3. FROM ENVIRONMENT TO ECOSYSTEM: 1972–2002

A consideration of the key international environmental agreements and events over the last 30 years illustrates the emergence of the, now pervasive, influence of the ecosystemic worldview. The 1972 Stockholm Conference on the Human Environment is often seen as a milestone for the global articulation of the "environment" as an issue area and as a matter for specific concern. Although some of the language (e.g., the move to preferring gender neutral language to describe humans) and framing of concerns has altered in the last 3 decades, most contemporary environmental and economic development concerns and even proposed solutions were expressed in 1972 in the Stockholm Declaration on the Human Environment.[19] It is instructive to review some the principles propounded in 1972. For example (emphasis added),

> Principle 2
> The natural resources of the earth, including the air, water, land, flora and fauna and *especially representative samples of natural ecosystems, must be safeguarded for the benefit of present and future generations* through careful planning or management, as appropriate.
>
> Principle 4
> Man has a special responsibility to safeguard and *wisely manage the heritage of wildlife and its habitat,...*
>
> Principle 13
> In order to achieve a more *rational management* of resources and thus to improve the environment, *States should adopt an integrated and coordinated approach to their development planning* so as to ensure that development is compatible with the need to protect and improve environment for the benefit of their population.
>
> Principle 14
> *Rational planning constitutes an essential tool for reconciling any conflict* between the needs of development and the need to protect and improve the environment.
>
> Principle 17
> *Appropriate national institutions must be entrusted with the task of planning, managing* or controlling the 9 environmental resources of States with a view to enhancing environmental quality.
>
> Principle 18
> *Science and technology, as part of their contribution to economic and social development, must be applied to the identification, avoidance and control of environmental risks* and the solution of environmental problems...
>
> Principle 19
> *Education in environmental matters*... is essential in order to broaden the basis for an enlightened opinion and responsible *conduct by individuals, enterprises and communities* in protecting and improving the environment in its full human dimension. It is also

---

19 Declaration Of The United Nations Conference On The Human Environment. Available at: http://www.unep.org/documents.

> essential that mass media of communications avoid contributing to the deterioration of the environment....
>
> Principle 20
> Scientific research and development in the context of environmental problems, both national and multinational, must be promoted...

The fact that the Stockholm Conference is noted as marking the beginning of these concerns does not mean there were no environmental concerns previously. For example, even in the 1950s the problem of discharges of oil and oily water resulting from shipping activities led to the 1954 *International Convention for the Prevention of Pollution of the Sea by Oil* (OILPOL).[20] The importance of the Stockholm Conference, Declaration and the resulting Framework is that it emphasised, at a global level, a comprehensive array of linked issues.

The Stockholm Conference also set in motion a number of institutional responses at the international and other levels, not the least of which was the creation of the United Nations Environment Programme (UNEP). UNEP in turn initiated regionalism based on marine ecological considerations with the creation of its Regional Seas Programme, with the first regional sea regime being that of the Mediterranean.

The 1970s were also a period that began to focus on the interests of the developing economies – many of which were in the process of decolonisation. The Group of 77 articulated these interests throughout this decade and particularly during the Prep Com sessions leading up to the third United Nations Conference on the Law of the Sea. The problems of poverty and environmental degradation, and concerns about equity and transfer of technology more fully entered the international political agenda and, ultimately, the text of many international agreements, in particular, the 1982 *United Nation Convention on the Law of the Sea* (UNCLOS).[21]

UNCLOS is frequently described as the constitution for the ocean. It is clearly a creature of the issues that surfaced in the 1970s. In addition to codifying existing international law on some ocean-related matters such as navigational rights and boundary determination, it also includes ideas of equity, trade, and economic rights and, importantly, advocates a holistic approach to ocean management. Part XII of UNLCOS provides a comprehensive management regime, albeit ocean-impact oriented, covering land, air and ocean. This regime, if fully implemented, could potentially govern all human activity. It provides the legal foundation for later instruments such as the 1995 *Global Programme of Action for the Protection of the Marine Environment from Land-based Activities (GPA)*[22] and encourages the development of regionalism and cooperation. The inclusion of economic considerations such as technology transfer and the institutional framework to implement the concept of the "Common Heritage" also reflects the more integrated approach to managing the interaction between human activities and the environment that emerged in the 1970s and 1980s, and culminated in the 1990s generation of conventions and other instruments.

---

20 1954. 327 UNTS 3.
21 Available at: http://www.un.org/Depts/los/.
22 See website at: http://www.gpa.unep.org/.

UNCLOS and the Stockholm Declaration, with their concern for economic development and environmental protection, also prepared the ground for the mid-1980s Report of the World Commission on Environment and Development, which popularised the term "sustainable development".[23] This term, essentially a political concept, sought to reconcile issues that had been perceived as being fundamentally in conflict: economic development and environmental protection. Incorporating the time- and morality-based concepts of intra- and inter-generational equity, both of which are related to environmental protection, into the notion of economic development, broadened the constituency to be considered in economic decision-making.

The lack of progress, despite an abundance of research and discussion, over the intervening 20 years and the worsening environmental situation in most countries, combined with an increasing gap between the wealth of the industrialized countries and the deepening poverty of most less developed economies, led to the UNCED in Rio de Janeiro in 1992. This Conference entrenched the concept of sustainable development and the associated principles and strategic action seen as necessary to its achievement.

A number of key documents emerged from UNCED. The Rio Declaration on Environment and Development [24] set out 27 Principles to guide achievement of sustainable development, "Recognizing the integral and interdependent nature of the Earth, our home".[25] *Agenda 21*,[26] a comprehensive 300-page management plan for achieving sustainable development, was also promulgated, as was a new generation of environmental instruments reflecting an ecosystem approach.

Agenda 21 has, as one of its core organising principles, IM at all levels of decision-making. This is set out in Chapter 8. As noted in the 1995 report of the Expert Group on Identification of International Law for Sustainable Development:

> The Expert Group considered that the principle of interrelationship and integration forms the backbone of sustainable development. Integration is the underlying theme of the Rio Declaration and Agenda 21 ... Interrelationship and integration reflect the interdependence of social, economic, environmental and human rights aspects of life that define sustainable development ...[27]

At the same time *Agenda 21* is a creation of the UN system. This means that all existing institutional arrangements are retained and their role in IM in each of *Agenda 21*'s topic areas is specifically mentioned. The situation it portrays is that of a complex,

---

23 World Commission on Environment and Development, *Our Common Future* (Oxford: Oxford University Press, 1987).

24 Available at: http://www.unep.org.

25 Although not the specific focus of this paper, it is interesting to observe the use of the metaphor of "home" in light of the recent national-security-based-action framed as "homeland defence", the exact parameters of which are not yet is defined. A linkage to Rosenau's idea of the "frontier" (see note 10 above) between what we imagine as domestic and foreign is also suggested by "homeland defence". It may be that we are indeed entering the "wild west" as portrayed in the history of the USA. Certainly there is increasing debate about the continued relevance of the rule of law, at least as it has been imagined to date.

26 Available at: http://www.unep.org.

27 Geneva, Switzerland, 26–28 September 1995. Background Paper #3, para. 15 (prepared by the Division for Sustainable Development for the United Nations' Commission on Sustainable Development).

multifaceted, highly coordinated, *managed* approach to addressing all of these issues at all levels. It is, perhaps, an idealistic picture of what "ought" to be, rather than what is. Certainly its materialisation is more difficult than the document suggests.

Relevant to the context of this paper, *Agenda 21* also includes Chapter 17 – "Protection Of The Oceans, All Kinds Of Seas, Including Enclosed And Semi-enclosed Seas And Coastal Areas And The Protection Rational Use And Development Of Their Living Resources" which reflects the ecosystemic world view. It provides, *inter alia*, that

> 17.1. The marine environment – *including the oceans and all seas and adjacent coastal areas – forms an integrated whole that is an essential component of the global life-support system* and a positive asset that presents opportunities for sustainable development. International law, as reflected in the provisions of the United Nations Convention on the Law of the Sea, referred to in this chapter of Agenda 21, sets forth rights and obligations of States and provides the international basis upon which to pursue the protection and sustainable development of the marine and coastal environment and its resources. *This requires new approaches to marine and coastal area management and development, at the national, subregional, regional and global levels, approaches that are integrated in content and are precautionary and anticipatory in ambit*, as reflected in the following programme areas:
>
> (a) Integrated management and sustainable development of coastal areas, including exclusive economic zones;
> (b) *Marine environmental protection*;
> (c) Sustainable use and conservation of marine living resources of the high seas;
> (d) Sustainable use and conservation of marine living resources under national jurisdiction;
> (e) Addressing critical uncertainties for the management of the marine environment and climate change;
> (f) Strengthening international, including regional, cooperation and coordination;
>
> 17.10. The *role of international cooperation and coordination* on a bilateral basis and, where applicable, within a subregional, interregional, regional or global framework, is to support and supplement national efforts of coastal States to promote integrated management and sustainable development of coastal and marine areas.
>
> 17.22 (c) Integrate protection of the marine environment into relevant general environmental, social and economic development policies;[28] ... (emphasis added).

---

28 The last of these is particularly relevant in that, at a domestic level, protection of the marine environment from sea-based activities is largely dealt with by specialized shipping or other sector specific agencies and legislation and is not located within the general domestic environmental law or practices. The reasons for this, in the case of shipping, are generally presented in terms of the uniquely international nature of shipping and ship nationality that requires a different regime. This division is now under a legal challenge in one jurisdiction and is likely to be the subject of future challenges in matters such as marine biodiversity protection. For example, it has been argued that provisions of the USA 1972 *Clean Water Act*, which requires a permit to discharge a pollutant into any navigable water in the USA, should apply to ships' ballast water, in that the *Act* includes biological materials as pollutants. The US Environmental Protection Agency has adopted regulations to exempt ships' operational discharges (such as ballast water) from the discharge permit requirements of the *Clean Water Act*. This is now being challenged in the courts. In September 2001, the Office of Water, Office of Wetlands, Oceans and Watersheds, Office of Waste Water Management of the US Environmental protection Agency issued a comprehensive "Draft Report for Public Comment" entitled *Aquatic Nuisance Species in Ballast Water Discharges: Issues and Options*. The Report is in response to the legal application to eliminate the exemption for ballast water under the *Clean Water Act*. Report available at: http://www.epa-ov/owow/invastive_species/ballast/report/reg.html.

This extract highlights the need for institutional change in order to develop a more holistic approach to management of activities affecting the marine environment. At the same time Chapter 17 is circumspect in acknowledging and confirming preexisting international agency demarcations of fields of interest and responsibility.

The Conference also adopted two conventions,[29] the *Convention on Biological Diversity and the Convention on Climate Change*. Much like UNCLOS, they have the potential to radically affect all areas of human enterprise. Both reflect an ecosystem perspective and present concepts of harm and responsibility which challenge pre-existing environmental and other law. To varying degrees both potentially govern and provide a source of State legal obligations to address many of the problems already subject to governance by UNCLOS and its institutional and legal regime. In both cases the issues are framed more broadly and systemically – preserving biodiversity, for example – and, arguably, enlarge the preexisting obligations. In this sense there is no inconsistency with UNCLOS. However the conceptual underpinning, regulatory approach and norms differ significantly between them, as do the responsible international (UNEP-based secretariats) and corresponding domestic agencies. Accordingly the situation demands a higher level of coordination in order to avoid conflicts at all levels.

As was the case in Stockholm in 1972, UNCED also generated new institutional structures, most notably the Commission on Sustainable Development,

> …to ensure effective follow-up of UNCED; to monitor and report on implementation of the Earth Summit agreements at the local, national, regional and international levels. The CSD is a functional commission of the UN Economic and Social Council (ECOSOC), with 53 members. [it is also responsible for UN agency relations with]…Inter-agency Coordination in the area of sustainable development is undertaken through the Inter-Agency Committee on Sustainable Development (IACSD).[30]

In 1995 the GPA was adopted under the auspices of UNEP. Given the fact that majority of marine environmental degradation is the result of land-based activities, this was an important step in protecting the marine environment. The GPA Secretariat notes that:

> Some 80% of the pollution load in the oceans originates from land-based activities. This includes municipal, industrial and agricultural wastes and run-off, as well as atmospheric deposition. These contaminants affect the most productive areas of the marine environment, including estuaries and near-shore coastal waters. The marine environment is also threatened by physical alterations of the coastal zone, including destruction of habitats of vital importance to maintain ecosystem health.[31]

As will be discussed below at least two of these issues, sewage and agricultural runoff (resulting in eutrophication), relate directly what is now seen as ship-source marine pollution. The GPA is also involved in supporting UNEP's Regional Seas Programme.

---

29 A soft law instrument was also adopted, the Forest Principles.

30 Website links at "About CSD" and "Inter-Agency Coordination". Available at: http://www.un.org/esa/sustdev.

31 http://www.gpa.unep.org/about/.

In 1997 more explicit efforts were also made to integrate the international economic/trade regime with the environmental regime. A lengthy round of trade negotiations resulted in the creation of the World Trade Organization (WTO) and the formal adoption of sustainable development as an aspect of the international trade regime. A Committee was set up under the WTO to consider the relationship between trade and environment. This too reflects an ecosystemic worldview in that interaction and dynamics between a range of sectors and activities are implicated. The potential use of the trade regime's regulatory tools and norms as a means of improving domestic environmental practices is still a relatively unexplored and controversial topic.

Similarly, developments in the international health community to focus more on preventing the root causes of lack of health (broadly defined) are closely aligned with concerns specially tied to poverty and environmental degradation.

A redefined notion of security proposed by UNDP and, more recently, triggered by concerns for biological pollution, scarcity of water and the conflicts arising from movements of environmental refugees, suggests that ecological concerns can now also be seen though the prism of human security.

UNDP's *Human Development Report, 1994*[32] argues:

> The threats to human security are no longer just personal or local or national. They are becoming global: with drugs, AIDS, terrorism, pollution, and nuclear proliferation. Global poverty and environmental problems respect no national border. Their grim consequences travel the world.... For too long, the concept of security has been shaped by the potential for conflict between states ... [and] security has been equated with the threats to a country's borders ... [and] nations have sought arms to protect their security ... Job security, income security, health security, security from crime – these are the emerging concerns of human security all over the world.

These issues and many others were discussed at the World Summit on Sustainable Development in late August and early September 2002.[33] The outcome was a decision to recommit to the Commission on Sustainable Development and its role as a facilitator of integration in this area as well as stressing the roles of the "United Nations Chief Executives Board for Coordination, the United Nations Development Group, the Environment Agency Group and other inter-agency coordination bodies".[34] In addition a new "effective transparent and regular inter-agency coordination mechanism on ocean and coastal issues within the United Nations system" is to be established.[35] Among the objectives to be achieved is that of:

> 121(f) Increasing effectiveness and efficiency through limiting overlap and duplication of activities of international organizations, within and outside the United Nations, based on their mandates and comparative advantages;

---

32 Available at: http://www.undp.org.

33 Interestingly, ocean issues were not among the core themes originally scheduled for discussion at the World Summit, although there was a strong advocacy effort to move them on to the agenda and to put ICOM ideas forward as a model for environmental governance.

34 See: "Key Commitments, Targets and Timetables from the Johannesburg Plan of Implementation" and the "World Summit on Sustainable Development Plan of Implementation" Advance unedited Text, 5 September 2002. Available at: htttp//www.johannesburgsummit.org/index.html.

35 *Ibid.* Para 29(c).

In summary, the last 30 years have witnessed a rapid expansion in both the availability and extent of scientific information on the environment and the cause and effects of environmental degradation.[36] The emergence and importance of an ecosystemic worldview, a view strongly influenced by ideas of continual change, interaction and notions of holism has been briefly outlined in this Section. Specifically, there is an enhanced awareness of the connections between human health and pollution of environment and between the long-term effects of environmental degradation and the socio-economic security of a country, its neighbouring States and, ultimately, global peace and security.[37] It must of course be remembered that the physical world has not changed. It is a living system that is not fragmented, however human understanding and institutional responses to the natural world do not perceive nor reflect this fact.[38]

The next Section examines the management/institutional response – integrated management (IM) – to this shift in understanding regarding the nature of the environment and human activity. This heightened awareness has generated numerous regulatory and administrative responses, thereby creating a potential for conflict or, at best, wasted resources and ineffective and problematic implementation efforts. Attention must therefore be paid to managing these aspects of human enterprise.

4. INTEGRATION AND INTERNATIONAL ENVIRONMENTAL GOVERNANCE (IEG)

The issues explored in this paper can be seen as falling within the more general rubric of "international governance". This topic is the subject of extensive contemporary discussion and study by scholars,[39] non-governmental organizations[40] (NGOs)

---

36 The simple fact of increased dissemination and public access, often to "undigested" or conflicting information, in the form of media coverage and the Internet, is a critical feature of this change.

37 Irrespective of moral or philosophical debates about the anthropocentrism and utilitarianism inherent in these linkages, they have been important in bringing the "environmental agenda" to the forefront of political concerns. At the same time, the traditionally polarized approach to matters of environment and economy still dominates decision-making, particularly in the short term in domestic politics. This is despite efforts to integrate the two under the umbrella of sustainable development and to adopt the tools of economic analysis (e.g., valuing natural resources in monetary terms to allow for a cost-benefit analysis of decisions regarding activities affecting the environment).

38 This refers to the general understanding in post-industrial western society as reflected in governmental organizations. Most indigenous peoples and eastern societies have a more organic world view.

39 See for example, Lee A. Kimball, *International Ocean Governance Using International Law and Organizations to Manage Marine Resources Sustainably* (Gland, Switzerland: IUCN, 2001); United Nations University, Tokyo, Peace and Governance Research areas and projects therein such as "The Legitimacy of International Organizations" http://www.unu.edu/p&g/legitimacy.html; "Global Environmental Governance Dialogue" Yale University, http://www.yale.edu/gegdialogue/ to name only a very few.

40 For example, The Commission on Global Governance: http://www.cgg.ch/millenium.htm; Third World Network: http://www.twnside.org.sg/title/ieg.htm.

and within the UN system itself.[41] Many of these discussions are prescriptive and involve matters such as co-management and engagement of civil society (usually divided between the "private sector" (meaning industry) and NGOs advocating for interests seen as unrepresented by State leaders). Irrespective of the solution advocated, the underlying premise is that the *status quo* is not working well and may even have failed. In the environmental sector the national and international failure to prevent further degradation of environment (or deal with other pressing related social issues such as poverty, disease, conflict etc.) is attributed to a poor, or at best outdated, management/regulatory system at all levels of governance system. Despite a massive increase in global, regional and national regulatory instruments and management activities and a proliferation of scientific and other data collection activities, indicators suggest that the environmental situation (and many other concerns) is getting worse, not better.[42] The goal of sustainable development, which is believed to rest on coordinated activities among its three pillars,[43] environmental, economic and social, has not been achieved. The diagnosis, and therefore the prescription, is that the specific management problem is the lack of integration of activities carried out by institutional actors within the three pillars. This is a problem found at both the domestic and international levels of governance. The problem is further exacerbated by the lack of coordination among levels of government. The problem is therefore cast as a management issue that has both a horizontal and vertical component.

As noted in the Introduction and in Section 3, given this definition of the problem, the proposed cure, or at least part of the cure, is integration, and specifically IM, including integrated management of activities affecting the marine environment. Integrated management (of coastal and ocean activities) has now emerged as a field of knowledge, if not a discipline.[44] In fact one its main claims is that it does not accept the assumptions of traditional disciplinary approaches to understanding phenomena and activities. It is a radical approach which aims at a long-term culture shift in human thinking and behaviour by consciously changing patterns of human behaviour. This approach is related to and reflects the thinking also found in the parallel development of the field of dispute resolution (DR). DR is also a cross-disciplinary field which focuses on moving away from a narrow framework of rights and claims to one based on interests, relationships and process as a means of reducing immediate conflict and changing the way that people deal with conflict.

41 For example, United Nations Environment Programme, *International Environmental Governance, Report of the Executive Director to the Open Ended Intergovernmental Group of Ministers or their Representatives on International Governance*, first meeting, 18 April 2001. UNEP Doc. No: UNEP/IGM/1/2, 4 April 2001. p. 4. Available at: http://www.unep.org/: or see the United Nations Informal Consultative Process on the Law of the Sea (UNICPOLOS).

42 Compare, for example, the UNEP State of the Environment Reports in 1997 and 2000. Available at: http://www.unep.org.

43 Chee Yoke Ling & Martin Khor, Third World Network, *International Environmental Governance: Some Issues from a Developing Country Perspective*, Working Paper, September 2001. Paper prepared at the request of the Chair of the Group of 77. Available at: http://www.twnside.or.sg/title/ieg.htm.

44 Aldo Chircop, "Teaching integrated coastal management: lessons from the learning arena", (2000) 43 *Ocean & Coastal Management* 343 at p. 345.

It is also radical in its aspiration to a more peaceful sustainable society.[45] The values and practices embodied in both fields of theory, knowledge and skill overlap and inform each other.[46]

One of the objectives of IM is to approach issues in a more holistic way and avoid fragmented or compartmentalised institutional decision-making and programmes that can often result in a waste of precious natural, human and economic resources. An Integrated Management approach does not necessarily mandate new administrative agencies but, rather, builds upon existing sectoral expertise to ensure that decisions are based on open discussion, review and analysis of the implications for the environment and other sectors and interests. This may in turn generate new organisational structures, partnerships and alliances to respond more effectively to questions relating to implementation. However, this often manifests as an evolutionary, rather than revolutionary, process. From a more pragmatic perspective an IM approach can also serve to ensure better compliance with regulatory requirements by coordinating and rationalising regulatory activity.

At the domestic level when implementing an IM approach, a key question is determining the nature of the institutional arrangements to be adopted. In this matter at a domestic level IM also presents an example, and even a model, for improving the effectiveness of marine environmental protection through integrated international institutional activities. The problem of institutional change and design is a difficult question for any government seeking to implement an IM approach. Consolidating, rationalising, eliminating or even changing existing governmental agencies inevitably generates political and other resistance at any level of governance. Such decisions affect individuals' jobs, perceived power, identities and relationships with regulated sectors and other interests. The problem is magnified at the international level where even the location of an institution or a secretariat can be a sensitive political matter. In many cases such an approach is not feasible at the domestic level because of vested interests and constituencies and is, forseeably, politically impossible at the international level. The tendency at all levels is to leave existing structures in place and instead create new ones to coordinate the existing issues or even become another specialized agency to address the issue.[47] This is understandable as a response to conflict, although it is clearly known that a major problem in the environmental and marine environmental field arises from overlapping and, at times, potentially conflicting institutional activities. The problem has been observed with regard the plethora of environmental convention secretariats and the costs of duplicating core administrative systems and committees with escalating numbers of meetings and cost of participation. For example, the Executive Director's Report (April 2001) to the first meeting of the Intergovernmental Group

45 Moira L. McConnell, (ed.) *Attitudes Skills Knowledge. Recommendations for Changes to Legal Education to Assist in Implementing Multi-Option Civil Justice Systems in the 21st Century*, Report prepared by the Joint Multi-disciplinary Committee on Legal Education. *Final Report* August 2000. (Ottawa, Canada: Canadian Bar Association, 2000). See also: Moira McConnell, "Capacity building for a sustainable shipping industry: a key ingredient in improving coastal and ocean management" (2002) 45 *Ocean and Coastal Management* 617 at 628.

46 C. A. Davos, "Sustaining co-operation for coastal sustainability" (1998) 52 *Journal of Environmental Management* 379.

47 For example, as noted above, the World Summit agreed that a new mechanism to coordinate ocean activities is to be developed.

on International Environmental Governance (under the auspices of UNEP) comments that:

> 7. This conclusion [of the Malmö meeting] was based, in part, on the present *proliferation of structures, agreements and conferences, which has resulted in a heavy burden on developing countries in particular, many of which simply do not have the necessary resources either to participate in an adequate and meaningful manner, or to comply with the complex and myriad reporting requirements associated therewith. It is also becoming apparent that weak policy coordination is resulting in missed opportunities to enhance coherence and synergy among the various instruments.* The number of legal agreements dealing with environment and sustainable development is increasing while the average time taken to negotiate each treaty is decreasing. At the same time, the scale of problems to be addressed has widened – from the regional through the hemispheric to the global – while the number of sovereign States that have to participate in the negotiation of such legal arrangements has gradually burgeoned. Whereas the creation of the various legally binding conventions and protocols on the environment constitutes an outstanding achievement on the part of the international community, it also raises the need for continuing policy coherence among the various instrumentalities that exist in this area, at both the inter-agency and intergovernmental levels.[48] (emphasis added).

The role of the Commission for Sustainable Development (CSD) as a facilitator, an agency devoted to coordinating, encouraging and monitoring activities of other agencies and countries to achieve sustainable development, can be seen as an example of such a coordinating institution.

Development of a more integrated approach to managing human activities is still at a relatively early stage at the international level. The United Nations General Assembly Informal Consultative Process on the Law of the Sea (UNICPOLOS), which has as one of its main concerns better integration of international ocean management activities, was only formed in last few years.[49] The CSD, which monitors and supports the process of integration of management and sustainable development in all sectors of activity, was only created in 1992. Discussion and activities at varying stages of development are occurring in most countries, particularly in connection with management of activities in increasingly urbanised and threatened coastal zones.

The issue of global governance and the UN system is by no means a new concern for the UN system. As the Secretary General of the UN pointed out in December 2001, "[t]he United Nations system has grappled with the problem of system-wide cooperation since its founding without reaching any ideal solutions".[50]

---

48 United Nations Environment Programme, International Environmental Governance, Report of the Executive Director to the Open Ended Intergovernmental Group of Ministers or their Representatives on International Governance, First meeting, 18 April 2001. UNEP Doc. No.: UNEP/IGM/1/2, 4 April 2001. p. 4. Available at: http://www.unep.org/.

49 It should be noted that "... protection of coastal areas from the introduction of non-native species has been prepared for inclusion on the agenda of further meetings of the Consultative Process": see A. de Marffy, "The Marine Environment and the Implementation of the United Nations Convention on the Law of the Sea and Related Agreements", paper presented Dec 3, 2001, UNESCO conference on Oceans and Coasts at Rio + 10.

50 Economic and Social Council, ECOSOC, Doc. No.E/CN.17/2002/PC.2/7 at p. 39, para. 174. Available at: http://www.johannesburgsummit.org/html/documents/prepcom2.html.

In 2000 the first meeting of the Global Ministerial Environment Forum agreed that the World Summit on Sustainable Development (2002) would:

> ... review the requirements of a greatly strengthened institutional structure for international environmental governance based on an assessment of future needs for an institutional architecture that has the capacity to effectively address wide ranging environmental threats in a globalizing world ...[51]

In February 2002 a meeting of the UNEP Governing Council responding to the work of the IEG Group concluded, *inter alia*, that:[52] (emphasis added)

(a) *The international environmental governance process encompasses all international environmental efforts and arrangements within the United Nations system, including at the regional level, and is not restricted to UNEP;*
(f) The design and implementation of environmental policy at all levels requires a clear link to the sustainable development context as well as greater involvement and engagement of non-governmental organizations, and civil society and the private sector, allowing them a meaningful role in intergovernmental policy-making, and also requires strengthened national frameworks of governance;
(h) An essential complement to international cooperative arrangements is the requirement to strengthen the capacity of developing countries to participate actively in policy formulation and implementation. In this regard there is a need to emphasize and support capacity-building and technology transfer, and the role of UNEP in this regard was emphasized;
(k) The Global Ministerial Environment Forum should be placed as the cornerstone of the international institutional structure of international environmental governance;
(m) *The proliferation of institutional arrangements, meetings and agendas, while having the benefit of specialization, may weaken policy coherence and synergy and put further strain on limited resources;*
(n) The clustering approach to multilateral environmental agreements holds some promise, and issues relating to the location of secretariats, meeting agendas and also programmatic cooperation between such bodies and with UNEP should be addressed.

These conclusions, as mentioned earlier, were part of the discussion at the World Summit although they do not appear to have resulted in any significant institutional change. The proposals envisage more than the issues and regulatory regime operating under the auspices of UNEP. They clearly point to the problem of an overabundance of specialised arrangements and the resulting lack of coordination, and possibly even competition for financial resources, private sector partners and participatory time and costs. They also point to the very serious problem of a systemic barrier to genuine participatory decision-making. A plethora of secretariats, meetings,

---

51 United Nations Environment Programme, International Environmental Governance, Report of the Executive Director to the Open Ended Intergovernmental Group of Ministers or their Representatives on International Governance, First meeting, 18 April 2001. UNEP Doc. No.: UNEP/IGM/1/2, 4 April 2001. p. 4. Available at: http://www.unep.org/.

52 UNEP. Seventh Special Session of the Governing Council/Global Environment Forum Cartagena, Colombia, 13–15 February 2002, Decision adopted by the GCSS.VII. Doc. No. SS.VII/1. International Environmental Governance. Available at: http://www.unep.org/governing_bodies/gc/specialsessions/gcss_vii/.

advisory groups etc., whilst overtly "open" are, *de facto*, closed to many. Only countries and NGOs and private sector representatives with an excess of available trained personnel, and the resources to send them to meetings, can effectively participate. It is simply beyond the capacity of many countries, and only a relatively small number can attend or even comment on the avalanche of documents, reports, surveys etc. The international environmental governance system is itself a drain on the capacity of countries to address problems at a domestic level. In addition, the intensity of efforts in each secretariat or forum can breed a tendency to technocracy. That is, the discussions can become so inordinately technical and arcane that they discourage participation: decisions are *de facto*, if not *de jure*, left to the experts and the secretariat to debate. This may lead to better informed "expert" decision-making, but it can also simply lead to decisions that are not well understood or that lack genuine commitment and participation, despite "on paper" endorsement.

The IEG conclusions set out above point to some benefits that can perhaps be be gained from strategies such as clustering issue areas and meetings. This may generate new crossover ideas and solutions, and enable greater domestic cohesion and integration, with representative teams attending and formulating an integrated response to a number of related issues. However, such an approach requires a high level of cooperation and commitment to collaboration on the part of international organisations, as each will struggle with questions of budgets, constituencies and other matters when trying to make such changes.

It should be noted that there are similarities between the international discussions and discussions regarding the governance in the European Community. In 2001 the European Commission released a *White Paper*, "European Governance".[53] Superficially, some concerns such as developing a European identity, appear dissimilar. However much of the effort internationally is also oriented to developing a cohesive global entity, a world community.[54] The *White Paper* sets out five principles of "good governance":

- openness;
- participation;
- accountability;
- effectiveness;
- coherence.

The application of these five principles is said to reinforce the important principles of proportionality and subsidiarity,[55] both of which require reflection and a careful exercise of choice as to the most appropriate regulatory level/forum and instrument. As is the case in the IEG discussion, the changing configuration of actors, issues and ideas has generated a need to coordinate and integrate policies and law making within the European Community and, as the *White Paper* notes, contribute to global good governance practice. These are essential practices in IM and should inform

53 Commission of the European Communities, Doc. No. COM (2001) 428 Final, July 2001. Available at: http://europa.eu.int/comm/governance/index_en/html.

54 Although one can say that there is already a preliminary adjustment in norms to meet group identity matters in order to be given admission to the EC/EU. The same does not apply internationally.

55 *Ibid.* p.10

and characterise efforts to improve institutional arrangements to better protect the marine environment.

5. OPPORTUNITIES AND IMPLICATIONS

Section 4 outlined the development of an ecosystemic worldview and the corresponding adjustment in the institutional and regulatory paradigm at all levels of governance. The need for an integrated approach in order to achieve the common goal of sustainable development is well accepted and, indeed, obvious. The question of how to implement an integrated approach is less obvious for the reasons already discussed above in connection with IM. The dilemma is a very human problem experienced at every level from the individual to international organizational collectives. It remains the core problem in connection with environmental protection in that there is agreement on the need to change, but only without experiencing any change that is perceived to be negative. Often change only occurs when a problem reaches a crisis. The message of the environmental movement is that many problems are already close to or past redemption and that there is very little elasticity in the system. The call for IM is clearly oriented to the need to prevent crises through careful planning and developing regulatory systems that explicitly take into account uncertainty and monitor and revisit decisions and actions to examine their impact. At its heart IM is simply a common-sense solution to an old problem. It seeks to forestall and avoid conflicts between people, policies, laws and institutions and in so doing it can help improve the effectiveness of laws and actions taken to protect the environment and, in the context of this paper, the marine environment.

Despite the development of an ecosystem worldview and the centrality of the ocean to the global ecosystem, the governance system relating to the ocean remains perversely fragmented. The need for integration in the context of ocean activity was recognised in the preambular declaration of UNCLOS in 1982 "that the problems of ocean space are interrelated and need to be considered as whole".[56] UNCLOS sought to resolve the tension between what was described earlier as the globalising/internationalising (flag State) forces and the decentralising/localising (coastal State) interests through a careful delineation of agreed rights and responsibilities. This was combined with the adoption of zoning as a mechanism to resolve conflicts in specific situations. But the tension between the two still remains at the international level and within the internal dynamics of the national regulatory structures. The current tussle for supremacy between port State control and enforcement and the much maligned flag State jurisdiction is illustrative. The increased resort to and expansion of the variety of maritime zones developed in a number of *fora* (and associated as well as increased

56 This is by no means an orginal point. In 1983, J. Alan Beesley, Canada's Ambassador for Disarmament, spoke to the 17th Annual Conference of the Law of the Sea Institute in Oslo (paper on file with the author). His speech, entitled "An Action Plan for Competent International Organizations on Marine Pollution", noted (at p. 16ff) several studies of this issue, including one by the UN Economic and Social Council, "Cross Organizational Programme Analysis of the Activities of the United Nations System in Marine Affairs" (March 15, 1983, No.E/AC.51/1983/2) that identified 456 distinct marine activities over 1982–83 involving 17 major organisational units of the UN and 11 specialised agencies.

cases of what is described as "unilateralism" by IMO Member States), also testifies to the unsettled and difficult relationship between these forces at both the domestic and international level.

One of the difficulties is that this dynamic is, essentially, reproduced at the international institutional or agency level, a fact that serves to reinforce these divisions at the domestic level. There are numerous agencies involved in ocean governance, in one way or another. Each is, in a sense, specialised or has a particular focus that appears, at least on paper, to make sense and constitutes a reasonable division of effort and expertise. But this is a structure that has been built over time and reflects an ongoing process of accommodation and *ad hoc* renovation rather than design. International marine environmental protection is both institutionally and substantively fragmented and should be better integrated. There is a sea-shore divide and even within that divide there are further divisions relating to sea-based activities (shipping) and living-resources-based activities (fishing), as well as overall biodiversity preservation. This has led some to advocate in favour of ocean governance and describe a body of law called "international oceans law".[57]

However, the process of integration is gradually affecting the institutions in this sector. The post-UNCED emergence of what James Cameron has called the "ecological state"[58] has been accompanied by a more sophisticated generation of environmental concerns, particularly related to oceans. These more abstract issues such as biodiversity, biosecurity and climate change, refer to relationships, processes and interactions rather than observable, point-in-time evaluations of substance-based pollution and cause and effect. This means that these issues cross and sometimes fall between sectors, institutions, disciplinary lines, activities, countries and responsibilities. They demand new regulatory and management approaches and with them enhanced human resource capacity to develop and work with these ideas. This intellectual shift has resulted in a number of new less permanent institutional arrangements, projects and programmes particularly at a global and regional level.[59] Such agencies seek to establish flexible cooperative arrangements to deal specifically with these problems outside the pre-existing jurisdictional and sectoral constraints. They operate as forces of institutional integration, triggered, as they often are on a domestic level, by shared ecological and socio-economic concerns.

The parallel between the international and domestic systems and the process of institutional and regulatory integration are important in terms of observing models or mechanisms to help create change and implement IM. In many cases, at a domestic level, the first step to a more integrated approach to management of these issues is generated by a problem (or a new opportunity or entrant into one sector) that affects many sectors. The example of the international legal obligation to protect biodiversity and

57 Lee A. Kimball, note 3. The approach argued for by Kimball has the advantage of according recognition the unique nature of the ocean as largely outside national jurisdiction and, therefore, *sui generis*, in terms of governance. It also seeks to recognise the extra pressures placed on the ocean because of human demographic patterns. The view argued for in this paper is that, rather, because of the centrality of the ocean for sustainable development and its interaction with most environmental concerns, it should be integrated and woven into the fabric – a whole cloth – of environmental law.

58 James Cameron, "Globalization and the Ecological State" 1999 8(3) *RECIEL* 243.

59 The Global Environmental Facility projects are a good example.

the related obligation to prevent the spread of alien species among marine ecosystems is one such issue. Responding to the specific problem of the transfer of potentially harmful aquatic organisms and pathogens in ships' ballast water can itself become a step, or even a catalyst in some cases, in the direction of a more integrated management approach at the international, regional, national and even sub-national level.

The problem of harmful aquatic species and pathogen transfer in ships' ballast water and through other ship vectors and their impact on food, health and economic security and on biodiversity is a topic of concern to the environmental community and is governed by a strongly supported multilateral environmental agreement, the 1992 *Convention on Biological Diversity* (Article 8(h)) that is affiliated with UNEP. It is also governed by UNCLOS (Article 196) and will be the subject of discussion at an upcoming UNICPOLOS meeting. Voluntary Guidelines responding to what was seen as a ship's operational problem were developed by IMO in the early 1990s.[60] In addition, an international convention focused primarily on flag State responsibilities to regulate the problem, now characterised as a ship-source marine pollution problem, is currently under negotiation by IMO Member States. The fact that carriage of marine organisms and pathogens in ships' ballast water can spread human, fish and animal diseases and may affect human health and economic security relating to the human food chain has also engaged the concern of the Food and Agricultural Organisation (FAO) and the World Health Organisation (WHO). It is also matter of importance to ports and port management because the problem is directly related to the condition of port waters. This can have consequences for the competitiveness of ports and economically efficient carriage of goods.[61] It should be noted that one of the more important marine pollution prevention initiatives that will have implications for the problem of harmful aquatic organisms and pathogens in ships' ballast water is the November 2001 recommitment of States to implementation of the *GPA*. One of the main issues that States have agreed to take action on is preventing untreated sewage from entering coastal waters. If this occurs it will have the effect of reducing the likelihood of pathogens and some harmful organisms entering or growing in port or near port waters. This in turn reduces the "riskiness" of the port waters that ships must take on board as ballast.[62] The relevance of this, aside from reducing risk, is that in the long

60 The latest version is 1997 IMO Resolution A.868 (20) *Guidelines for the control and management of ships' ballast water to minimise the transfer of harmful aquatic organisms and pathogens. Available at http://globallast.imo.org*

61 I have argued elsewhere for the future economic significance of biosecure ports. See: Moira McConnell, "Ballast and Biosecurity: The Legal, Economic and Safety Implications of the Developing International regime to Prevent the Spread of Harmful Aquatic Organisms and Pathogens in Ships' Ballast Water" forthcoming, Vol. 17 *Ocean Yearbook* (Chicago: University of Chicago Press, 2002). An earlier version of this paper was presented June 2001 at the University of the Aegean – 2nd International Conference 2001 "Safety of Maritime Transport", Chios, Greece.

62 See also the emphasis placed on the problem of sewage and eutrophication in a recent report, GESAMP (IMO/FAO/UNESCO/-IOC/WMO/IAEA/UN/UNEP Joint Group of Experts on the Scientific Aspects of Marine Environmental Protection) and Advisory Committee on Protection of the Sea, *Protecting the Oceans from land-based activities – land-based sources and activities affecting the quality and uses of the marine, coastal and associated freshwater environment*, Rep. Stud. No. 71 (GESAMP, 2001). Available at http://gesamp.imo.org/no71/. However, it does not address the problem of transferring species between marine ecosystems thereby disrupting the biodiversity of the receiving system.

term if the problem of land-based marine pollution, the source of most marine environmental pollution, is not fully addressed, then eventually there will be no "clean" coastal, or possibly even any, waters. It is a problem that affects fisheries, ports, human health, international trade and ships' operations. It can also be seen as a threat to national biosecurity, thereby also falling within maritime security concerns. In short, it is a problem that does not fit neatly into specialised international and domestic shipping regulations or administrative structures.[63]

The point to take from this example is that domestic regulatory efforts to address this marine environmental/biodiversity/border control problem need to do so in an integrated manner that addresses the full range of issues in order to ensure that the response is effective. It requires extensive interaction amongst agencies and sectors and people that may have widely differing expertise, values and practices. In other words, it requires integrated management in order to develop an effective response to the threat this problem presents.

In this context the GEF/UNDP/IMO Global Ballast Water Management Programme responding to this problem provides an example of an international-level institutional mechanism that can "seed" the integration of the sea-based and land-based concerns.[64] This Programme includes maritime administrators, environmental agencies, environmental non-governmental organisations (ENGOs), IMO, the shipping industry, marine scientists, engineers and naval architects, as well as collaborative work with WHO, FAO, UNEP and UNDP to name but a few concerned international agencies. Although it is based in IMO, its proactive stance and many of the activities it undertakes and supports, such as biological surveys of ports and other aspects of coastal/port State responsibilities, are outside the more usual role of IMO, which is primarily that of a specialised UN technical agency focusing on promoting economic development and international trade, and ensuring ship safety and protection of the marine environment through uniform regulatory standards for ships and seafarers. The Programme, with its limited life span, can be understood as a mechanism for enabling activities that operate across institutional boundaries at the domestic level and international level. This type of interstitial organisation that is flexible and relatively unthreatening to the existing organisational structures may then act as a catalyst for increased connection and collaborative activities among organisations at all levels of governance.

The Regional Seas and other emerging regional arrangements (regionalism) may also prove to be mechanisms and also the site of integration of the land-sea-based regulatory regimes and interests. Certainly the renewal and development of the Barcelona Convention system in the Mediterranean suggests that this may be possible.

These are but two examples of gradual change based more on responding to the task or problem effectively with less emphasis on formal classifications or institutional jurisdiction. This can perhaps be seen as starting to reflect a more collaborative

63 The developing national laws deal with it in many different ways. For example, in some countries, such as Australia and Chile, it is a quarantine matter. In the USA it is a mix of fisheries and coastguard activity. In Canada it is dealt with under Federal Transport regulations and port notices. In New Zealand it is part of a new biosecurity regime.

64 Another example is the IMO affiliated programme, Partnerships in Environmental Management for the Seas of East Asia (PEMSEA), that focuses on a range of activities and initiatives at the regional and domestic levels.

response that achieves more value than if the issues were divided up (a more competitive approach) amongst agencies. Unfortunately the potential offered by these models can be undermined by legal agreements/conventions that have not been explicitly developed with a view to promoting collaborative efforts specifically intended to encourage flexibility and effectiveness. It requires leadership and vision within UN agencies to promote such an approach and it also requires personnel with the sufficient skill and a commitment to the value of an IM approach.

The emergence of more holistic concerns such as biodiversity and sustainable development that are articulated in almost universally adopted international legal instruments means that there is an increasing overlap in the mandates of a number of agencies. This can lead to competition and conflict, and ultimately to less effective implementation and indeed undercutting of otherwise compatible and complementary programmes. Alternatively, there are opportunities presented for collaboration and fruitful, innovative, synergistic relationships among agencies and perhaps, ultimately, development of new organisational configurations combining the strength of the predecessor agencies but oriented to dealing with new concerns. This appears to be happening in some cases at the domestic level.[65]

Given the centrality of the ocean in the ecosystem it is not surprising that most of these concerns overlap in fact and at the level of institutional activities. The harmful aquatic organism and pathogen transfer issue as well as other issues such as ship-source air emissions, port expansion and marine biodiversity protection are demanding integration through the process of dissolving the boundaries between sea and land.[66] Whatever the eventual meaning of these trends, it is clear that they are placing new and different demands on all participants. The new system based on ecological system concerns means that it is imperative that the agencies working to protect the marine environment both domestically and internationally, particularly those in the shipping sector, need to develop a broader awareness and capacity[67] to work easily in a cross-disciplinary way within the contemporary IM governance framework.

---

65 For example, in the last decade New Zealand developed a regime dealing with biosecurity including reconfigured agencies and combinations of responsibilities.

66 This is evidenced at a domestic level by the greater involvement of, for example, the US Environmental Protection Agency in the development of ship-source air emission controls, or the Indian government's decision to transfer port development approvals from the Shipping Ministry to the Environment Ministry. In the former case these shifts have been construed by the shipping industry as acts of unilateralism and a challenge to the hegemony of the IMO regime. They can also be viewed as simply part of the more general process of mainstreaming the impacts of shipping-related activities into the domestic environmental regime. This may result in the feared patchwork of standards. However, the globalisation of environmental standard setting through the MEA process and the World Trade Organisation processes may also mean that these standards are equally international, albeit negotiated in different *fora* with differing actors influencing the balances and values set out in the standards.

67 I have discussed the question of capacity building in the maritime industrial sector elsewhere: See, Moira McConnell, note 45. Although not the topic of this paper, there is also a need for greater integration of the regime and trade issues generally in ICOM and oceans issues. It was interesting to observe that the topics of trade and, except for a few marginal references and the above noted paper, also shipping, were absent from a week of intensive discussions on protection of the marine environment and ocean governance.

Capacity-Building in International Marine Environmental Law: Perspectives of Developing Countries

*Aref Fakhry**

INTRODUCTION

There is a pressing need to look at the views of developing countries in the study of the international rules pertaining to the marine environment.

The IMO International Maritime Law Institute (otherwise known as "IMLI") was set up in 1988 under the auspices of the International Maritime Organization for the provision of specialized training in international maritime law, including marine environmental law, particularly for lawyers and legal advisers from developing countries lacking educational facilities and resources. So far, close to 274 men and women representing about 95 countries have graduated with a Master's degree in international maritime law. Graduates typically return home to fill high-ranking positions in the Government or the private sector. A number of graduates have been promoted to the office of chief justice, attorney general, director of maritime transport and so forth.

IMLI was one of the first international training facilities to implement an equal gender access policy. In fact, the Institute continues to reserve 50% of seats for women. The Institute's web of overseas graduates ensures that a nucleus of knowledge in international maritime law is constituted in every country of the world.

At the outset, it may be useful to define some of the recurring terms in this paper, including capacity-building and international marine environmental law.

Capacity-building is the training of human resources and the acquisition and maintenance of equipment and facilities necessary to attain defined objectives.

On the other hand, international marine environmental law relates to the rules adopted internationally for the protection of the marine environment from all sources of pollution and damage, including rules on prevention, response, liability and compensation.

The expression "capacity-building" connotes an element of dependency, inasmuch as reaching a higher level of education or technological capability means that Party A must acknowledge that it has needs which can only be fulfilled provided Party B offers the required assistance. This sense of dependency pervades a large

* Mr. *Aref Fakhry*, LL.M. (Montreal), M.M.M. (Dalhousie), is a Lecturer at the IMO International Maritime Law Institute (IMLI), Malta. Contact: aref.fakhry@imli.org.

A. Kirchner (ed.), International Maritime Environmental Law, 93–99.

part of marine environmental law and has placed developing countries in the dependency state. It is this sort of dependency which will be the focus of the current paper.

It should be said, however, that another sort of dependency operating in the opposite direction also exists, insofar as developed countries depend on their less developed partners with regard to the attainment of certain levels of knowledge and technical know-how, for example ancestral or local knowledge, in order to meet their own environmental objectives.

Capacity-building is a key component of marine environmental law, because of the profuse interrelationships existing in the marine environment between the various states, bolstered by the fact that there is only one environment for all. In a world of increasingly complex science and technology and with the gap between rich and poor widening further, there is an ever stronger demand for the sharing of know-how and resources.

I will start by looking at the main achievements owed to international marine environmental law in developing countries and then proceed to assess some of its salient shortcomings in those same countries.

ACHIEVEMENTS OF INTERNATIONAL MARINE ENVIRONMENTAL LAW IN DEVELOPING COUNTRIES

I have identified three areas of success which are owed to international marine environmental law in the developing world. These are:

(1) Raising of environmental awareness,
(2) Technical cooperation and
(3) Raising of environmental standards.

1. Raising of Environmental Awareness

The environmental paradigm of the second half of the 20th century has travelled the world over. It has unquestionably raised awareness about the fragility of the Earth in the face of the relentless industrial and technological advances of humankind. The realization that the sea could not continue to serve as the dumping site of man's unearthly levels of waste is due to the alarming signals of environmentalists and scientists, carried forward into international political and legal statements, including the Stockholm Conference Declaration on the Human Environment and the Declaration of the Rio Conference on Environment and Development.

Developing and developed countries alike have, at different stages, laid the founding blocks for the new international environmental law. The case of Malta, a small developing country in the sixties, is illustrative. It was the representative of Malta who called for the adoption of the concept of the common heritage of mankind relating to the seabed beyond areas of national jurisdiction. The idea was later codified in the United Nations Convention on the Law of the Sea.

Both developed and developing countries are also the ones that ultimately embrace and apply the rules thus laid down. Through the processes of international debate and standard-setting, as well as the role of media and emulation, the "good word" has spread across the economic and political divide. Environmental awareness may now be present, to varying degrees, in every country of the world and in the relevant international organizations.

Recent campaigns on flag state implementation in the shipping sector have, for instance, led to increased awareness among developing countries regarding the need to enforce internationally agreed ship safety and environmental standards. Open registries such as Belize and Honduras have, as a result, sought to downsize their merchant fleet in order to rid their flags of substandard shipping.

It is arguable whether awareness exists as a result of the consideration of the environment as a value *per se* or of other considerations, including economic welfare. Very often, environmentally friendly behaviour emanates from the realization that it makes sense economically. But in many countries, unfortunately, short-term gains, which are often at odds with sound environmental policies, may be systematically preferred over more environmentally sustainable long-term profits. It is clear, however, that civil society movements in developing countries help promote the idea of protecting the environment as an intrinsic value.

A case in point is perhaps Lebanon, which, coming out of a long and devastating war, initially sought to rebuild itself with little or no consideration for the environment. Today the country realizes that the sustainability of its recovery and the preservation of public health require prioritization of environmental measures. Large coastal dump sites directly bordering the Mediterranean Sea have, as a result, been closed. There is still a long way to go for that country, but mentalities have already started to change.

2. Technical Cooperation

Various international agencies have responded to the need to promote environmental awareness in developing countries. The IMO, for instance, was the first UN specialized agency to include a technical cooperation branch within its administrative structure. Developing countries have been the prime recipients of technical cooperation programmes.

As a means to help enforce international standards, technical cooperation is essential in a world marked by wide gaps in economic, technological and skill-based development. Programmes are still called for to transfer know-how and build self-sustainable capacity in the less-developed countries. The excellent universities in Nigeria, for instance, have been battered lately by civil strife and national economic downturn. Throughout West Africa, lack or insufficiency of training facilities is a serious problem stifling economic progress and environmental protection.

Despite their key role in promoting international environmental standards, various technical cooperation institutions are faced with serious budgetary constraints. The last Assembly of the International Maritime Organization called on States Parties to consolidate their support to the training institutions of the IMO family, of which IMLI is a member.

It should be stressed that technical cooperation is a tool, not an aim in itself. It is not suggested that technical cooperation has succeeded in fully enabling states to look after their environmental policies. It will be seen further below that there are still shortcomings in the knowledge and equipment base of developing countries. Perhaps it is not incorrect to say that technical cooperation becomes meaningful when recipient countries genuinely embrace the underlying programmes and objectives.

Technical cooperation should not become a tool for developed states to pursue selfish policies which are unrelated to environmental protection. The international community must be increasingly vigilant in safeguarding the real nature of technical cooperation and not letting it become an instrument of political trade or other forms of hegemony by one or a few powers at the expense of others. After all, the real objective should be the protection of our waters and through this objective the whole world stands to gain.

3. Raising of Environmental Standards: A Measured Assessment

Undoubtedly, the rules already devised have helped secure a more livable world than would have otherwise been the case with no rules at all. Many will question, however, whether environmental protection has been effective or whether – and the answer is obvious – more could and should have been achieved.

Unquestionably, a measure of environmental success has been achieved in developing countries thanks to the adoption of globally binding norms and standards in the marine field. Perhaps land-based marine pollution continues to be a black spot, but strides in ship-source pollution prevention, liability and response are incontestable. For instance, the International Convention for the Prevention of Pollution from Ships 1973/1978 (Marpol) has helped reduce oil pollution significantly. The Civil Liability and Fund Conventions appear, on the other hand, to have met the objective of quick and adequate compensation for oil pollution victims.

The adoption of global rules for the protection of the marine environment has filled a gap in those countries whose national legislation lags behind. It is essential in this area to have international rules that transcend the inconsistencies which often arise from varying national and regional practices.

Yet the very nature of international law – its predominantly voluntary character – would entail that the mere adoption of international rules is not sufficient. Conventions still have to be ratified and implemented. One of the major challenges facing, for instance, the International Maritime Organization is the implementation of its already adopted rules.

Capacity-building in this respect is essential. IMLI's core maritime legislation drafting course seeks to instil in candidates the techniques commonly used to give a treaty legal effectiveness in the internal order of a state. It is not enough to lay down rules without also giving the means for the less advanced to implement them.

FAILURES OF INTERNATIONAL MARINE ENVIRONMENTAL LAW IN DEVELOPING COUNTRIES

In terms of failures of the current law, I will consider:

(1) The environmental tragedy,
(2) Lack of faith in international standards,

(3) Globalization and
(4) Sustainable development.

1. The Environmental Tragedy

Despite measured success, there is arguably an environmental tragedy unfolding before our eyes. The world's oceans have borne the brunt of continuous and accumulative pollution from air, land and sea activities. The coastal zone, home to one billion of the world's population and harbouring the Earth's most productive areas, is under constant threat from wide-ranging human activities.

It is clear that the marine environment is witnessing alarming degradation in various parts of the world, the Mediterranean Sea, cradle of civilisations, being the perfect example. Land-based sources of marine pollution bear perhaps a significant part of the blame. But one must add other serious factors, including sprawling urban development, arms stockpiling and warfare.

The picture may not be so bleak in other parts of the world, and improvements have in fact been reported. But the overall picture remains of an ocean pressured to its limits under the weight of overpopulation, development and an "I am free to do what I please in my own backyard" approach.

Perhaps this tragedy represents the major failure of the existing rules. It may, however, be true that the problem could have been much more serious had there been no effort to tackle it. In a sense, some optimism may be called for.

2. Lack of Faith in International Standards

As in other areas of international law, developing countries may often perceive in environmental law the tarnishing effects of the democratic shortage of institutions of global governance as well as the colonial legacy of some of its rules. As a result, a diminution or lack of faith in those organizations and rules may develop, leading to lax enforcement.

This is not simply a question of perspective. Developing countries often perceive a great discrepancy in terms of scientific, technological and financial capabilities *vis-à-vis* their more developed partners. In other words, the starting point for developing countries is often simply not comparable.

Another problem may be of the developing countries' own doing, that is their lack of commitment to the international law-making processes. Lack of commitment erodes faith in the rules ultimately adopted.

Developing countries may furthermore view international marine environmental law as offering too inadequate an answer to their needs. For instance, the United Nations Convention on the Law of the Sea requires enforcement of shipping standards by the flag State; in other words, the burden is placed on the nominal player, not the real economic stakeholder (the State of beneficial ownership of the ship).

With a few exceptions, international marine environmental law is often seen to be driven by and large by the needs and imperatives of developed countries. The *Exxon Valdez*, *Erika* and *Prestige* disasters brought to bear the unilateralist tendencies of major players in pressing forward their own agendas, while developing countries have remained largely passive. So many oil spills have gone unnoticed in the waters of developing countries. On the other hand, opposition by some coastal states to shipments of toxic waste transiting off their coastlines may herald a reversal of the traditional dynamic processes and the respective roles of developing and developed countries.

The current international political scene may further undermine the coercive value of international marine environmental law, with a large portion of the Earth's population having lost trust in international law as a guardian of world peace and basic human rights. This comes at a time when more cooperation is needed in tackling environmental destruction.

3. Globalization's Uncharted Prophecy

Globalization has intrinsic effects on the environment which are still largely unknown. An additional area of uncertainty emanates from the disturbances of world affairs and the upheavals of developing countries' policies and practices resulting from globalization. It will be some time before members of the international community come to terms with the fast-changing patterns of the current world. For developing countries, this may be profoundly perturbing, with the result that environmental considerations are sidelined.

Ever larger markets and fledgling technological advancement pose an increasing threat to the environment. In ancient times, humans seemed to be at the mercy of nature and this ensured environmental stability. Since this simple equation was reversed, our relationship with nature has deteriorated gradually.

In today's age of globalization, man seems to have tamed the whole planet for his own benefit. But it is often forgotten that globalization may mean different things to different people. Repercussions of globalization in one country may not be the same as those affecting another.

The question is therefore as follows: In a world of increasing market competition, where will environmental considerations come into play?

4. Environment and Development: The Ongoing Dilemma

Ten years after the Rio Conference, developing countries are still grappling with the need to balance development and environmental protection.

In the pursuit of development, we often see in developing countries today the same mistakes being made as those which developed countries made in recent history.

Because it leaves much manoeuvrability to States, sustainable development may be an important but yet insufficient tool in protecting the environment. This may be the reason why another key principle has emerged, namely the precautionary principle, which complements the concept of sustainable development.

It is questionable, however, whether controls on unsustainable development could be devised on an international level. Currently, an array of safeguards are being practised by certain States and international organizations, particularly in the area of development aid.

CONCLUSION

Having taken stock of the achievements and failures of international marine environmental law in developing countries, it is indispensable to sketch suggested avenues for addressing current and future challenges.

A great many of the problems highlighted above can be traced to the perceived lack of symbiosis of the developing world with the forces taking shape elsewhere. Another reason is undoubtedly the democratic shortage in a large part of the developing world itself.

There should be a closer integration of developing countries in every step of the environmental process.

Developing countries need to do their share also by committing themselves to the task of protecting our common environment.

Effectiveness of International Environmental Protection Treaties on the Sea Transport of Mineral Oil and Proposals for Policy Revision

Thomas Höfer and Lutz Mez***

SUMMARY

This study examines the effectiveness of international treaties and regulations concerning environmental protection during sea transport of mineral oil. Attendant circumstances and basic international legal structures for environmental policy in this field are explained, and direct as well as indirect effects of policy instruments are discussed. Although the declared aims – the elimination of intended, and the minimization of accidental discharge of mineral oil into the sea – have not been accomplished, a marine environmental policy success must be acknowledged. Today, the problems surrounding flags of convenience and the limitations in authority and competence of the United Nations International Maritime Organization (IMO) impede more effective policy instruments for marine environmental protection.

The analysis concludes with proposals for policy revision. These include a fortification of environmentally conscious coastal states within the political regime by reducing the influence of flags of convenience, and a conversion of the IMO to a specialized UN organization for marine environmental protection and maritime affairs.

1. INTRODUCTION

1.1. Effectiveness of International Treaties

Since the 1960s, evaluation and implementation research has examined policy in terms of its success or failure. This branch of research investigates the content, patterns of development, and effects of political programs and compares the original policy aims with measurable policy results. In this tradition, environmental policy, too, has focused on the evaluation of results and the assessment of success of

* Dr. *Thomas Höfer*, Federal Institute for Risk Assessment, Berlin (Germany). Contact: thomas.hoefer@bfr.bund.de.

** Dr. *Lutz Mez*, Environmental Policy Research Unit, Free University Berlin (FFU), Otto-Suhr-Institute for Political Science, Berlin (Germany). Contact: umwelt1@zedat.fu-berlin.de.

A. Kirchner (ed.), International Maritime Environmental Law, 101–121.

environmental regulations, especially in the international context (Jänicke and Weidner 1995; Kern and Bratzel 1996). Policy research takes effectiveness as its standard criterion and the aims established by the policymakers as its starting point. Contrary to a common argument of, in particular, experts from the natural sciences, the effectiveness of environmental policy measures cannot be determined in terms of reduction in pollution or improvement in the ecological situation alone. Other effects, such as change in the general awareness of environmental problems, slowing of pollution increase under conditions of economic growth, or initiatives to establish new environmentally friendly technologies on the market, are also important.

The demand of political scientists for a comprehensible standard is legitimate, so as to prevent judgments at the level of the armchair politician. Nonetheless, clearly formulated, and thus checkable, goals are missing from many environmental programs and treaties. In the past, the mere existence of measures was often regarded as a success. In assessing the effectiveness of an environmental program, however, the question must be posed as to whether its implementation has in fact led to the intended results. The degree to which program goals have been met and the time frame in which this has taken place are of significance in this regard. In our view, an assessment of the success of an environmental policy requires a considerable period of time, generally ten years or more.

From 1998 to 2000, in international workshops within the framework of the Concerted Action "Effectiveness of International Environmental Agreements", previous experience was discussed and standards for political-scientific methods, criteria, and evaluation procedures were developed (Underdal 1999; Wilkinson 1999). This study, with its analysis of a treaty that has been in place for decades, was intended as a contribution to the broader evaluation of international environmental agreements. In our view, special importance must here be placed not only on the formulation of policy, but also on policy revision or termination, and thus the completion of the policy cycle. The study represents a contribution to the means of evaluating the effectiveness of environmental policy instruments.

1.2. Legal Framework for Shipping and Marine Pollution (Law of the Sea)

Maritime traffic has always operated under the general understanding that the oceans are free for the ships of all nations. Freedom of the oceans is the underlying maritime legal principle. This principle was also valid for fishing and, aside from acts of war or piracy, ran up against its limits only when the interests or rights of coastal states were involved. It was not until the 1950s and 1960s that the traditional principles (free use of the sea and free innocent passage) that had been reconfirmed during the Law of the Sea Conferences of 1958 and 1960 were called into question. The technical means of exploiting the seabed and the global erosion of fishing grounds in coastal waters made clear that a new maritime law covering fishing and economic zones was necessary. The third Law of the Sea Conference (1973–1982) was one of the longest international conferences in the history of the United Nations. The "Constitution of the Ocean", accepted in December 1982, came into force in November 1994 as the "UN Convention on the Law of the Sea"

(UNCLOS) and is now the legal basis for maritime business and marine environmental protection. This treaty distinguishes between territorial waters, economic zones and the high seas. Technical regulations for ships under the umbrella of the International Maritime Organization, IMO (IMO 1998a, IMO 2001a), are accepted as the standard allowing free passage. In general, the enforcement of rules aboard ships was left in the hands of the flag states. The freedom of shipping reaches its limit and interventions become legal when the interests of coastal states, in particular within the 200-mile economic zone, are violated by significant pollution. If clear indications for violations within this zone exist, information on the identity and routes of ships concerned can be demanded. National sovereignty is reduced for straits within national waters that are used as international shipping routes. Only after entering a port "voluntarily" can ships be checked by harbour states for internationally required equipment. In such cases, coastal states may impose requirements supplementary to international standards (Lagoni 1993, p. 140). Violations within a 200-mile zone can be punished in such situations at the request of the coastal state concerned (see Biermann 1994a, p. 105).

To adjudicate disputes, an International Tribunal for the Law of the Sea was established in Hamburg, and this could become one of the most important bodies in regulating marine environmental conflicts (see Biermann 1994a, p. 89).

According to international law, the water column, the seabed and the air space above the sea belong to the "marine environment". This term includes vegetable and animal life in the water. Preservation and use of the so-called "living resources", however, primarily serves not ecological but economic interests. The Law of Sea therefore regulates this aspect in Part VII, separate from "Protection and Preservation of the Marine Environment" in Part XII. The Law of the Sea does not list detailed prohibitive or protective regulations for the marine environment, but presents a general package of principles for possible regulations and treaties on marine environmental protection (see Lagoni 1993). It uses a definition of "marine pollution" based on the wording introduced by GESAMP 1969 and the Conference on Human Environment in Stockholm 1972: "Pollution (of the marine environment) means the introduction... of substances..., resulting in such deleterious effects as harm to living resources, hazards to human health, hindrance to marine activities... and reduction of amenities." The inclusion of the preservation of the oceans as a "heritage of mankind" under this damage-orientated definition is generally viewed as a misinterpretation (see Lagoni 1993, p. 121 or Caldwell 1996, p. 202).

1.3. Genesis and Structure of the Convention (MARPOL Annex I)

The most important regions for oil extraction have always been located far away from the chief consumers. The simplest transport from a technical standpoint has been the use of vessels. In the 1870s, petroleum and kerosene were carried in drums from the Caspian Sea and southern United States to Western Europe and the East Coast of the US. The first tankship was introduced in the Caspian Sea in 1878. The first regulations for the handling of mineral oil during sea transport were intended to protect harbours and canals from fire and explosion hazards. The ecological dimension had not yet been recognized at that time. In 1888, harbour regulations in

New York defined limits for the discharge of oil from tankships. In 1892, equipment standards were introduced for tankships in the Suez Canal. It was not until the 1920s that environmental pollution due to oil was discussed from scientific (see overview by Höfer 1998), political and legal (see overview by Lagoni 1993) perspectives. Because of rising numbers of cargoes from the oil fields of Iran/Iraq (1920s) and Bahrain/Saudi Arabia (1930s), as well as tankship damage by German submarines in the 1940s, oil pollution on the eastern coast of North America became evident. The coastal zones of the USA and the United Kingdom were particularly polluted. The Second World War put a stop to international activities. The first important initiative following the war came from Great Britain in 1952/53. Non-governmental organizations held a scientific conference. One year later an international conference took place in London (see Mitchell 1994). The first treaty, the "International Convention for the Prevention of Pollution of the Sea by Oil" (OILPOL), was accepted in 1954. This was one of the reasons for the involvement of the London-based "Intergovernmental Maritime Consultative Organization" (IMCO), which had been established in 1948 as a UN body specializing in maritime safety. The delays in signing the convention, the lack of control instruments, and the slow processing of technical regulations prevented progress and success. In 1962, new scientific findings on the persistence of mineral oil were presented during talks with ship owners and oil companies at the IMCO. OILPOL, however, remained unsuccessful. From 1967 to 1969 this changed, with resolutions allowing amendments to the regulations without diplomatic conferences being held and solely based on decisions by an IMCO "Sub-Committee on Oil Pollution" established in 1965. Within a short time, 95% of the world tanker tonnage came under OILPOL regulation. The most important stakeholders wanted to secure their right to share in decisions on and amendments to environmental protection regulations. In 1969, the IMCO committee was renamed the "Sub-Committee on Marine Pollution" and its terms of reference were amended (history, see IMO 1998b). While all of this took place against the backdrop of the heavy oil pollution of extensive coastal areas after the wreck of the Torrey Canyon in 1967, preparations for the 1972 United Nations Conference on Human Environment in Stockholm also influenced this sudden progress. The national delegations at IMCO were competing to secure a leading role in this organization for global marine environmental protection.

In November 1973, during the "International Conference on Marine Pollution", the MARPOL Convention (International Convention for the Prevention of Pollution from Ships) was passed (text in IMO 1992).

Several activities are named as having occasioned the international conference in 1973 in London, and for the amendment and reissue of the OILPOL regulations to develop a treaty with stronger rules for the transport of mineral oil (Moore 1976):

1. the resolutions passed at the United Nations Conference on Human Environment 1972 in Stockholm, which received high-profile news coverage;
2. the passage of the "Ports and Waterways Safety Act 1972" by the US Congress, which required the United States Coast Guard unilaterally to establish construction and operation standards for oil tankers in the event that no international standards were created;
3. political action by Canada to motivate coastal states, particularly developing nations, to protect their territorial coastal (fishing) interests by sending delegations to the international conference.

Despite a promising start, the treaty was not brought into effect. Very few nations ratified it. Several years later, additional negotiations were necessary. Protocols hereto were adopted which weakened certain of the original requirements, and regulations on chemical tankers were transferred to a second annex to MARPOL. The next oil tanker spill on the European coast (Amoco Cadiz) in 1978 induced more extensive requirements that became part of the treaty text: *inter alia* expensive equipment regulations, transfer of responsibility from the captain to the owner, and separate regulations for the transport of other bulk liquid cargoes. This so-called "MARPOL 73/78" treaty became the basic environmental protection convention for the sea transport of mineral oil. The main part of this MARPOL Convention contains the principles and the rules and procedures for amendments. The annexes target special problems. Annex I focuses on the reduction of discharge of mineral oil into the sea. In contrast to the 1973 treaty text and the 1978 protocols hereto, the annexes are open to amendment without new diplomatic conferences being held. Amendments can be decided on by committees of the "International Maritime Organization" (IMO), the former IMCO, which was renamed in 1982. The environmental protection treaties for the sea transport of mineral oil (OILPOL/MARPOL) are generally recognized as the oldest globally enforced regulations. The even older whale protection regime is often named as an environmental protection treaty in publications in the field of environmental research (e.g. Underdal 1999), though this is dubious from a legal standpoint (Lagoni 1993), as the treaty regulates stocks and catch quotas for living resources.

2. POSITIVE ASPECTS

2.1. Primary Objectives

The objectives of the MARPOL Convention are covered by very general paragraphs, which is common for international treaties of this kind. They do not contain any fixed goal in terms of quantitative exposure limits or reduction aims. The preamble states that the parties of the convention desire "to achieve the complete elimination of intentional pollution of the marine environment and… the minimization of accidental discharge of such substances". The genesis of the treaty negotiations, however, makes obvious that the nations involved only intended to minimize the intentional discharge of mineral oil to a level within the technological and financial capacities of all parties. The treaty includes discharge and ship safety aspects. The scientific and technological state of the art alone was not viewed as a sufficient basis for the definition of new standards under this treaty. Concerning these objectives, important questions concern progress (measurable in principle) and whether success could have been achieved more efficiently and quickly (speculative in general).

2.2. Successful Policy Instruments

The integration of all stakeholders in negotiations with regulatory consequence under the auspices of the United Nations was surely the first and most important success. The tacit acceptance procedure for amendments, introduced by IMCO in 1969, means that decisions can only be blocked by a written veto by a third of all nations submitted to the Secretary General of the organization. This procedure, together with the regularly convening Marine Environment Protection Committee, MEPC, led to a rapid expansion of the technical standards in the agreement. For technical and legal reasons, most such new rules only came into effect after an interim period, during which new additional regulations were often passed. This procedure is regarded as one of the reasons for the increasing gap between the adoption of and compliance with rules.

Four developmental steps can be identified in the shift in power of influence between environmental and shipping interests during the negotiations within IMO's committees:

1. During the 1970s some important stakeholders (national delegations, e.g. of the United Kingdom and the United States) developed rules and standards together with owners of large fleets (a small number of extremely large oil companies and some independent ship owners), who were represented by a non-governmental organization but had no voting rights under IMO's rules of procedure.
2. The influence exercised by these "important" governmental delegations became limited in the 1980s as delegates representing flag-of-convenience states, acting and voting in the interests of ship owners, surfaced. It is a central aspect of the definition of "flag of convenience" by the International Labor Organization (ILO 1990) that the vessel not be beneficially owned and controlled within the flag state. This means that there is no genuine link between the flag state and the persons or corporate entities that effectively control the vessel.
3. The proponents of better environmental protection benefited increasingly during this period from a sympathetic media and, especially, news coverage of media-effective actions by environmental organizations (in particular Greenpeace). The media and environmental organizations, however, exerted only indirect influence on a limited number of governmental delegations (primarily in Europe) and on the image of the ship owners.
4. Since the 1990s, ship management has been dominated by globally active financial interests, which often own ships for the purpose of offsetting depreciation against taxes and whose activities reflect none of the "natural" behavior of traditional ship owners. In general, these investment companies operate their ships under flags of convenience and low-cost conditions ("low-price flags"). Additionally, such companies are not represented either by Western European or US ship owner associations or by governmental delegations in the classical sense. The interests of these ship-owning companies are now represented predominantly by developing nations, while the true owners reside in Western Europe or the US.

Because of this shift in influence and representation, the concept for creating better environmental protection standards for oil tankers as developed under MARPOL Annex I began to lose effectiveness during the late 1980s. Today, with voting taking place in IMO committees, environmentally concerned stakeholders (in particular coastal state delegations with small fleets) are confronted with a large number of representatives from flag-of-convenience states. Non-governmental organizations (NGOs) have no voting power within IMO bodies. Even if they had a vote, they would predominantly represent industry interests. Only 10% of all NGOs registered with the IMO represent associations for the environment or the personnel employed on ships (IMO 2000a).

One reason for the lack of success in enforcing IMO standards is the lack of implementation of IMO guidelines and circulars by many states (flag state principle). This has been noted by IMO committees. Flags of convenience are not genuinely interested in activities furthering enforcement of IMO rules. However, to compensate for the lack of interest by many flag states, port state control rights have been enlarged. These allow the enforcement of many standards by administrations working in keeping with the public's desire for better marine environmental protection (in particular in northwestern Europe). Originally, port state control was restricted to the checking of technical equipment (and thus the monitoring of the activities of classification societies) and the ship's documents (and thus the tasks of the captain). Their effectiveness has increased in Europe due to the Memorandum of Understanding on Port State Control of 1980. In 1992, the signatories decided to include all conventions and standards connected with IMO instruments, later also including social standards as defined by the International Labor Organization (ILO). Results of controls are circulated through a central office. In the 1990s, such organizational structures were also created for the American region and the Pacific. However, there are no effective means for coastal states, port states or the IMO administration to punish violations against MARPOL rules on the high seas.

The protocols and amendments to Annex I of MARPOL also deal with technical means to eliminate the oil input into the sea by oily ballast. The most important achievement was the introduction of separate ballast tanks for large tankers to separate sea water and cargo as far as technically possible. In times of over-capacity of cargo space, ship owners accepted this solution because it reduced the unused capacity of the oil tanker fleet by regulatory means. Ballast tanks make up about 30% of the cargo tank volume of a vessel.

In the aftermath of the Exxon Valdez spillage in 1989, the US demanded the introduction of double-hulled oil tankships to prevent discharge of oil in the event of "soft" groundings. The competent IMO committee passed an amendment to Annex I of MARPOL (Regulation 13 F/G) requiring a double hull for new ships. Vessels without such a double hull were to be taken out of business within 30 years. The world fleet would not have had to meet this requirement until 2020. However, under public pressure in Europe following the Erika disaster off the French coast in 2000, IMO's Marine Environment Protection Committee decided to impose an earlier date (IMO 2000b, IMO 2001b). Enhanced surveys of old ships ("Condition Assessment Scheme") and step-by-step dates for the introduction of new requirements are intended to lead to faster introduction of new double-hulled ships. By 2016 no tankship without a double hull is to be in service. Certain ships can obtain an exemption, but port states may deny their entry (summaries of decisions in: IMO 2001c).

Ship owners cannot ignore technical requirements. Installed technology can be checked at any point – during classification as well as by port state control. These are measures that contributed to the success of MARPOL, but which needed long introductory periods. The classification societies play one part in this strategy by replacing administrative execution by flag states. These privately organized companies (like the Germanische Lloyd in Germany) conduct business internationally and are empowered to enforce standards and conduct technical inspections worldwide. In the shadow of the flags of convenience, however, new classification societies have started performing their business to a low standard. From this point forward there is some legitimacy in talking of "low-price flags", "low-level registers" and "sub-standard ships". Lax controls are criticized especially by ship owner associations and insurance companies that relied on technical surveillance (ICS 2001, p. 14/15). The classification societies' function of enforcing MARPOL's standards has lost its authority during the last decade and needs to be newly defined.

2.3. Secondary Achievements (Side Effects)

Based on the open rules of procedure of IMO's Marine Environment Protection Committee and the flexibility of the MARPOL Convention in taking in new aspects of regulation, it has been possible to bring all aspects of maritime environmental protection under the administration of the IMO, which is organizationally optimized to coordinate negotiations and draft regulations. An outstanding instrument of environmental policy has thus been created to place new problems on the international maritime agenda. Using this instrument, issues such as anti-fouling, engine exhaust (NOx, SOx) and the scrapping of ships have been put on the agenda, leading to new annexes to MARPOL or new conventions alongside MARPOL. All practicable drafted regulations have had to be discussed.

Under international law, the freedom of the seas and the sovereignty of flag states determine the conditions surrounding maritime shipping. Global marine environmental protection and the interests of coastal states are often contrary to the interests of flag states. One significant success of MARPOL is the gradual undermining of flag state rights. Port state control and the administrations of flag states complement each other. An ever-rising number of protocols and technical equipment are checked on board ships during port stays. When severe defects or a lack of standard performance is detected, corrections – even those requiring shipyard work on the spot – can be enforced. Without proof of repair, entry to other ports may be restricted. Within this control regime, the main impetus lies in producing economic damage to ship owners through keeping ships in harbour, not in ordering penalties which might be difficult to collect under international law. Port state nations have been able to act together within the framework of MARPOL without having to compete with each other economically. The authority of the concerned states has been enlarged. Increasingly, these controls include aspects such as social regulations by the International Labor Organization (ILO) concerning supplies for and the accommodation of the crew.

Some treaties which were primarily demanded and developed for the tanker business as a supplement to Annex I of MARPOL have assumed particular importance for all maritime affairs. These include regulations on liability and damages, on performance and training of crews, and the safety management of ships. Taken together, these standards contribute significantly to the safe operation of ships.

The genesis of the treaty makes clear how neglect on the part of ship owners and relevant flag states was able to hinder the successful creation of international agreements. The policy instruments of MARPOL, in combination with other IMO instruments and the IMO's secretariat work, has nonetheless brought about progress. A productive collaboration of all involved parties can now be observed. Ship owner and industry associations are introducing technical solutions. Coming under pressure during negotiations in committees and working groups within the

"IMO community", delegates from such flag-of-convenience states as Panama and Liberia have signalled their willingness to cooperate to achieve practicable solutions. But most delegates from flag-of-convenience states (even Cyprus) continue their attempts to delay further accomplishments in the area of environmental protection. These states provide cover for the profit-oriented position of many European and North American ship owners who would otherwise face criticism in countries with a high standard of environmental protection for their opposition to marine environmental protection measures.

2.4. External Factors (Free Effects)

The completion of the convention in 1973 took place during the most severe crisis in the world oil market and the tanker industry. After the US market was opened to Arabian oil in early 1973, a ship-building boom started. The closure of the Suez Canal in connection with the war between Israel and Egypt (as well as Syria) had almost no effect, as there was sufficient fleet capacity to be used for the route around Africa. However, in late 1973 a boycott against the USA and the Netherlands, home of the most important transit oil port for Europe, Rotterdam's Europort, had a catastrophic effect on the oil tanker business. Cargo volumes declined despite an existing over-capacity. In 1975 the tanker fleet increased by 24%, whereas trade in oil decreased by 8%. These circumstances made possible the belated adoption of the Protocols of MARPOL in 1978, as these reduced the loading capacity of each vessel and, accordingly, the over-capacity of the fleet.

In the first months of 1974, hundreds of tankships, including many recently completed Very Large Crude Carriers ("Supertankers"), had to be taken out of operation. Ship owners as well as crews began to change their minds: mineral oil that had become expensive should not be discharged "free of charge" into the sea. The over-capacity in cargo tank volume created interest among ship owners in reducing the global tank capacity. For them the introduction of separate ballast tanks (SBTs) was of interest, because this would reduce transport tonnage. New ship-building regulations could be accepted as long as so many newly built ships were waiting for cargo. Many ships were scrapped; the construction of new ones was out of the question (see Figure 1). The reduction in size and modernization of the fleet lowered the number of accidents. These external factors helped in achieving the success of the treaty.

The reduced transport volume had an additional influence in the 1980s. Nautical experts point out that changed shipping routes may also have had an influence on the reduced number of tanker accidents in the 1980s and 1990s. A large part of the increasing oil transported was loaded in the Persian Gulf and transferred to Asian countries, crossing the Indian Ocean and passing through the Strait of Malacca. This route holds fewer dangers for tankships than the route around the Cape of Good Hope into the North Atlantic and the English Channel. For some regions, pipelines replaced the tank shipping route from the Gulf to Western Europe. There is a lack of high-quality data by which to calculate the sea miles, loadings and transport volumes that were saved. We were therefore not able to extrapolate the effect of pipelines on the success of MARPOL.

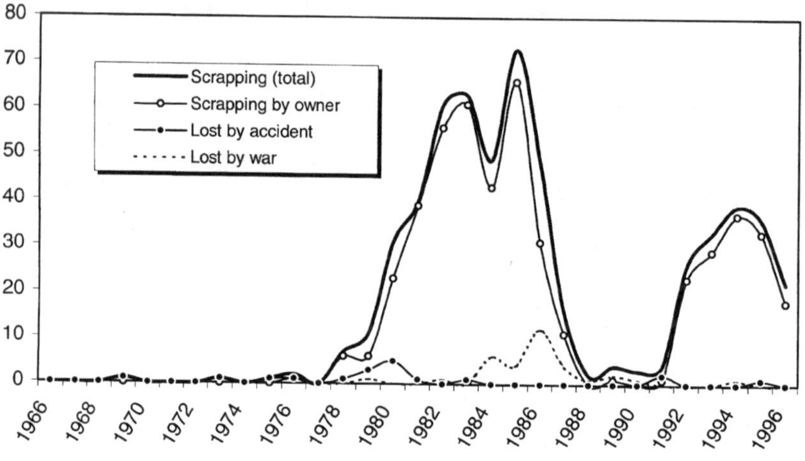

Figure 1. Number of oil tankers over 200,000 tons capacity scrapped or lost 1966–1996
Source: Analysis of data published by Pein (1996).

3. NEGATIVE ASPECTS

3.1. External Factors (Complicating Factors)

The change in ownership and management of the tanker fleet created a negative impact. During the period of decommissioning of many new ships, some important "independent" ship owners went bankrupt (Pein 1996, p. 47 ff.). For some time, oil companies and oil-producing countries dominated the ownership of the fleet. In the 1980s more and more ships were transferred to cheaper registries. European owners started to change flags in large numbers, transferring ships to the Isle of Man or the Bahamas. As early as the 1950s many US-owned tankships had been registered under the flags of Liberia and Panama. A further reason for establishing anonymous management companies in such countries was the negative press coverage received by mineral oil companies in connection with every tanker accident. These multinationals transferred ships to "independent" owners. Most of these ship owners reinvented themselves as investment companies, transferring the ship management and crewing to ship agents. This was a means of reducing costs. Because of international safety and pollution protection standards, cost-reduction strategies target social costs and occupational protection standards. Whereas in the past permanent crews had taken responsibility for the ship (and the ship owner), crews from low-wage countries that signed on for one period dominated. Because of poor social and hygiene conditions, as well as a lack of good occupational standards aboard ships, such crews generally showed a lack of motivation and responsibility for environmentally friendly procedures (Höfer 1999). In addition, under most of the flags of convenience and the low-level flags, proceedings against ship owners or crew members are extremely rare in instances of violations of MARPOL regulations. This is important, keeping in mind that, in principle, flag states must enforce standards on the high seas. In the 1990s, within the system of checking technical safety standards, some new companies started low-price classification of ships. In light of these developments, talks within the IMO committees were slow-moving, if not inconsequential. In some areas it was possible to develop treaties that regained lost ground (e.g. for training: International Convention on Standards of Training, Certification and Watchkeeping for Seafarers, STCW). Additionally, coordinated port state controls could compensate for lack of interest on the part of flag-of-convenience administrations. In total, however, these factors limited the effectiveness of the policy instrument.

3.2. Failed Approaches (Policy Instruments)

Calls for the establishment of land-based reception facilities for oily residues from cargo tanks must be judged as not fully successful. Ship owners today still criticize a lack of such installations in countries with low interest in environmental policy. Such installations should have been established in the 1970s and 1980s, in particular in the oil-exporting countries of the Arab world. The majority of these nations, however, had neither taken part in the development of MARPOL nor ever signed the treaty at that time. Calls for action within the convention thus were aimed at non-signature states who responded with predictable indifference.

OILPOL included discharge limit values that could not be measured at the place of discharge and were solely dependent on the standard of procedures on board. To prevent crusts and coating, the cleaning of tanks, pumps and pipes had to take place after unloading. Oily waste water was created on the way to the oil fields because ballast water loading was necessary to give the ship sufficient stability and draft (for the propeller). At the end of the journey, ballast water had to be discharged. Before 1980, when using empty oil tanks without special measures, this water was heavily oiled. Tar balls on beaches became common during the 1960s. During the negotiations on the MARPOL Annex I regulations between 1973 and 1978, proposed measures to reduce the input of oil into the oceans were one of the most important matters of dispute. Under OILPOL, special deposition tanks had been demanded for remaining water, while most of the mineral oil that remained on top of the ballast or wash water could be mixed with newly loaded oil. MARPOL introduced a new technique: washing of the walls of the tanks and the pumps with light oil under pressure. Both measures together led to a reduction in the input of oil into the sea of about 80%. Both procedures were carried out based on instructions on board and could be measured. The allowable oil content in discharged ballast water is limited legally, but there is no means of control during discharge into the sea. According to MARPOL, there is a requirement for a report in an Oil Record Book, and a check on the documentation can be done in port. There is little that can be done against intentional violations.

In addition to the discharge regulations for tank ships within Annex I of MARPOL, there are regulations on the discharge of oils from engines of all types of ships. The contamination of coasts with mineral oil and the extrapolation of oil input into the oceans (see Figure 2) show that the discharge of oily bilge water and oil from engines has become the most important source of marine oil pollution. However, different polluters (in terms of personnel and equipment) call for different

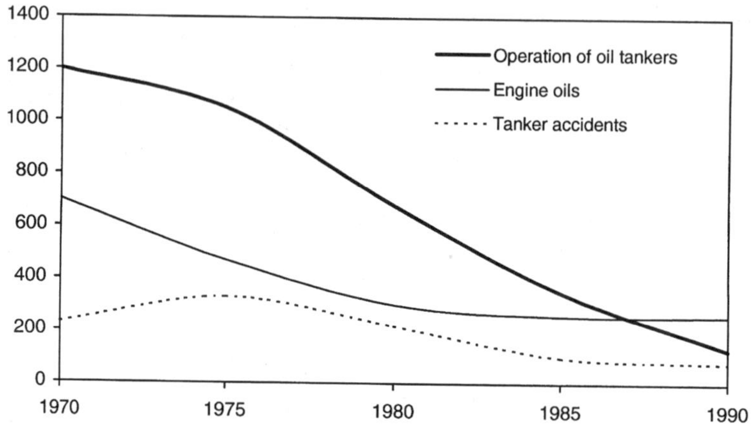

Figure 2. Input of mineral oil into the sea by different polluters, shown in kilotons
Source: Figure showing smooth tendency line of extrapolations by different authors for 1970, 1975, 1980, 1985 and 1990; Data according to Höfer 1998.

political instruments. In the area of machinery effluent, fundamentally misguided approaches within the principles of the Law of the Sea were taken: MARPOL calls for legal action by non-motivated parties (the flag states) and uses a method-oriented approach that cannot be easily implemented on the high seas. This failure casts unfavorable light on even the successful parts of MARPOL. Specific ideas for new international regulations and a change in responsibility are lacking.

3.3. Side Effects

As has already been discussed, the requirement for double-hulled tankers introduced unilaterally by the Oil Pollution Act (OPA) in the US began to shift single-hulled tankers to the routes to Asia and Europe. It can be assumed that the new MARPOL Annex I regulations taking such old ships out of the mineral oil business will motivate ship owners to use such vessels in the chemical tanker business as long as the rules within MARPOL's Annex II are not changed accordingly. The unwillingness of IMO committees to introduce the demands of environmental pioneers into further regulations produces such irregularities and failures in environmental protection. Owners of ships with obsolete technology continue to avoid new requirements for better environmental protection.

IMO committee decisions have continually produced new technical requirements for tankships. Such new regulations have generally been restricted to newly built vessels for technical, economic and diplomatic reasons. Existing ships are subject to fewer requirements, so-called grandfather clauses, and benefit from such exceptions. This requirement gap creates an economic advantage for old ships under old regulations because of the higher costs for new ships that have to be financed. Through this system, ship owners with low-standard vessels are rewarded. Incentives for building new ships are missing from the environmental policy of the IMO. This situation hinders innovation-friendly, pioneering ship owners.

The slow enforcement of measures for better environmental protection is due to two problems. First, in general, delegations from environmentally interested nations are dominated by shipping interests. Second, within IMO's bodies an international policy network has developed which opens prospects for broadly accepted solutions, but on the other hand is self-contained and reluctant to accept stakeholders representing environmental interests. In the public mind, there is a growing tendency to define the IMO as an international lobbyist for maritime shipping, much like the International Atomic Energy Agency, which in public perception stands for nuclear energy interests. The IMO framework offers no sufficient antidote to the anti-environmental strategies of flag-of-convenience states. Delegates from low-price flags do not actively participate and often are only present in the plenary for important votes. The delegations from flags of convenience like the Bahamas and Panama employ experts from Europe with long-time experience in IMO bodies, who are known for their weak interest in environmental protection, and who are able to represent the interests of their delegations successfully.

4. EXTRAPOLATION OF SUCCESS

4.1. Effects on the Marine Environment

The convention provides no instruments for measuring success. The participation of all stakeholders, including the non-governmental organizations, enables the presentation of reports which must then be discussed. In this way, specific aspects can be presented and weak points named. There are no independent experts or research budgets available within IMO to evaluate the outcome of the work. IMO entrusts this responsibility to a group of experts named by several United Nations organizations (e.g. IMO, FAO, UNESCO, WHO, UNEP) which were involved in the scientific work for the MARPOL Convention in 1972. GESAMP (Joint Group of Experts on the Scientific Aspects of Marine Environmental Protection) published its last study on mineral oil pollution for IMO in 1993 (GESAMP 1993). A new study is in preparation and will soon be finished (GESAMP 2002). Past studies have also been financed by the US government (NRC 1985, IMO 1990). An organization established by ship-owner interests presented the best data on accidental oil pollution by tankships (ITOPF 1997). However, the correctness and independence of these studies as far as operational discharge is concerned is open to question (v. Bernem 1997, p. 13). Certain experts involved in preparing the GESAMP study were also delegates who dominated policy decisions in IMO's competent body. Emission rates that were used as fundamental data for all further extrapolations were derived from an extrapolation using legally defined discharge limits together with an extrapolation on the violation rate. No scientific and independent monitoring has been realized since the MAPMOPP project in the 1970s (see Höfer 1998). Despite these criticisms, an analysis of all existing studies (Höfer 1998) suggests a reduction in operational discharge from tankships (Figure 2).

Even taking into account the reduced transport volumes, the reduction in discharges is significant. The input of oil into the ocean dropped from 1 (in 1971) to 0.2 parts per thousand (in 1989) of all traded mineral oil. Measurements of oily residues on beaches also suggest a significant reduction (Höfer 1998). Current studies of oil discharges from tankships confirm this trend up to the year 2000 (GESAMP 2003).

Despite rising transport volumes in recent years (Figure 3), a significant reduction in rate and volume of accidental discharge has been observed (Figure 4). This development is confirmed by GESAMP's new study (GESAMP 2003).

The real reasons for this development are still unclear. Ship owners argue that higher safety standards for ships are one reason. However, as already discussed, changed routes and tank sizes could also play a role. The scrapping rates for Very Large Crude Oil Carriers (above 200,000 tons loading capacity) are shown in

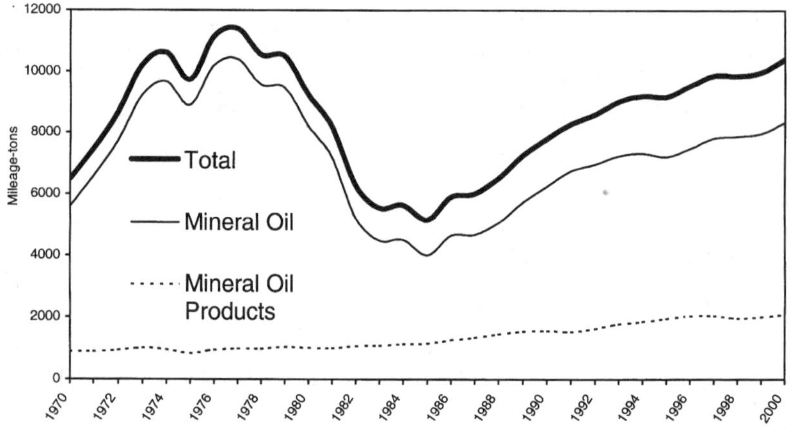

Figure 3. Development of sea transport volumes of mineral oil and mineral oil products 1970–2000
Source: Fearnresearch, Norway (private communication).

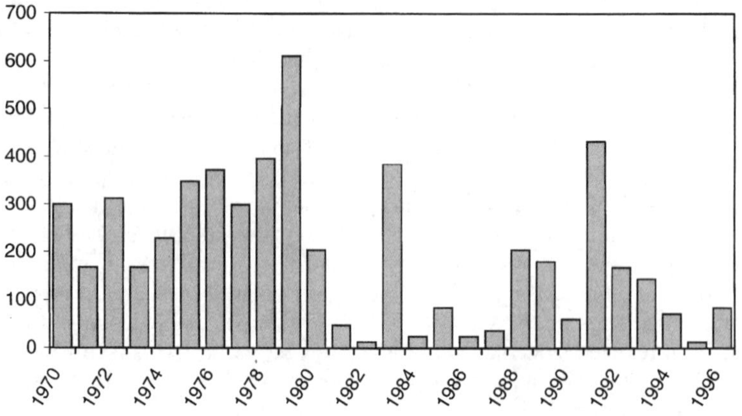

Figure 4. Input of mineral oil into the sea due to tankship accidents in kilotons
Source: ITOPF 1997.

Figure 1 as an example of a part of the fleet. A comparison of both statistics without a differentiated analysis of data suggests that ship quality and crew training have an influence on the rate of accidents. Replacement of old ships in the fleet by new ones for either regulatory or economic reasons seems to enhance the level of marine environmental protection. A reduction in accidental discharge during the MARPOL period has to be accepted as fact, independent of any determination of specific reasons.

4.2. Turning Away from Damaging Tradition

Environmentally harmful ways of scrapping tankships on the beaches of Asia that have been reported recently (Greenpeace 1999), as well as harmful occupational health standards (Johnsson 1996), show that there is no tendency within this branch of the shipping industry to behave responsibly of its own accord as long as profit is involved and legal standards are lacking. It has to be assumed that, without the convention, no turning away from damaging tradition would have occurred. Participants in IMO meetings even state that from the 1980s to date there has been a change in mood in the administrations and delegations of the most important flag-of-convenience states, such as Liberia, Panama and the Bahamas. But new flags of convenience have appeared and, according to shipping experts, produced different qualities of flags of convenience. Some of these offer second registers under flags of high-standard shipping nations (e.g. Norway, Germany and the Netherlands). Others have reasonably good administrations (like Liberia, the Marshall Islands and Panama with offices in New York) and are known for productive work within IMO bodies. Others, for example Malta and Cyprus, have come under pressure because of their interest in joining the European Union. Delegates from some other flag states are known for a destructive role or lack of activity in IMO bodies and have no actively working maritime administrations. Fleets with extremely low standards have surfaced. The “Flag State Conformance Index” names Honduras, Cambodia, St. Vincent and Belize among the low-standard flags (SIRC 2001).

4.3. Environmental Policy: Proposals for Further Projects

The portrayal of the history of the MARPOL treaty shows the evolutionary character of this convention. Over four decades, ideas for environmental policy and for the reduction of oil discharge from tankships have been developed. Attention has been given to operational effluents from tank washings as well as discharges of ballast and accidental spillage. Tankship accidents in particular have led to stricter shipping standards, although many standards introduced in the aftermath of such events did not have any direct connection to the cause of the accident. For example, following the stranding of an oil tanker, lower limits for routine operational discharge were set. After the sinking of a tanker on the open sea, the future use of single-hulled ships was limited. Ideas are continually being developed and future regulations drafted within the IMO committees and working groups. These regulations are then put into effect when accidents occur in Europe or near the US coast and the public and press complain about lax regulations. In this climate, training standards, liability rules and high-quality safety management have been developed (see Höfer 1999). This is one of the greatest values of the convention.

5. INTEGRATED EVALUATION

The success of Annex I of MARPOL is based in particular on its integration into, and the involvement of, a United Nations organization. This is the reason that the environmental protection initiative has developed a dynamic of its own and a momentum of expansion. While negotiations and decisions involving ship owners and ship management appear to be slow-moving, they promote diffusion of innovation.

The main aims of the convention, "reduction of input of mineral oil from tankships" and "fewer shipping accidents", have been achieved. Serious accidents due to substandard ship management and ongoing oil pollution of the sea by other maritime polluters have not convinced the public that the convention has done well. Stricter means of enforcement against violations are necessary, but cannot be introduced for conceptual grounds. On balance, however, the results are positive, chiefly because of positive side effects. It is our view that without the convention, the environmental performance of this industry would be far worse than it is at present.

Other authors have arrived at similarly positive conclusions. Biermann (1994a) *inter alia* studied the question of whether the treaties on marine environmental protection have taken on the character of an environmental protection regime. He named MARPOL's tankship regulations in particular as building blocks for such a regime. In his study on marine oil pollution, despite some reservations concerning the enforcement of regulations on operational discharges of oil from the world fleet, Mitchell (1994) also arrived at a positive assessment. Hartje (1995) presented the regulations on oil discharge from tankships as a partial environmental success story.

Within our assessment, there are some significant negative moments, particularly concerning the environmental policy-making framework and the enforcement of existing rules. It is our impression that developments during the last twenty years have shown increasingly negative results and point up a lack of potential for future developments within MARPOL's regulatory framework. The restrained willingness regarding environmental protection measures has been characterized by Caldwell (1996, p. 136): "Pollution prevention measures have proceeded very slowly against resistance from shipping nations."

6. POLICY REVISION

6.1. Institutional Policy Organization

The importance of the International Maritime Organization should not be underestimated (Biermann 1994b). However, because of IMO's orientation to the reduction of emissions from shipping and ship technology, this organization is not able effectively to administrate coordinated measures for marine environmental protection and their enforcement. Neither the administrative inclusion of the secretariats of the London Dumping Convention and GESAMP, nor its local and political connection to the liability funds change the situation. From an environmental policy viewpoint, stimulation of the internal dynamic within IMO has been neglected. Positive impulses could be brought in by the expansion of rights of the IMO secretariats to introduce their own proposals, as well as the change to a programmatically oriented organization within the United Nations framework, with budgets for specific projects, thus ending the strict limitation on the management of international negotiations. Biermann (1994a) stated that the Regional Seas Programmes of the United Nations Environmental Programme UNEP were a success in terms of conflict theory. However, looking at their effectiveness in terms of environmental policy, their success must be judged as meager. They must additionally be viewed as underfinanced and weak in enforcement. According to Liersch (1994), the North Sea Conferences of the nations bordering the North Sea can be termed a success.

From an environmental protection standpoint, the hazard for coastal zones created by city sewage and ship traffic, the total input of pollutants from land which dominates the input into the oceans, and the international fishery management which has become essential, need a coordinated and enforcable regulatory organization for the use of the seas (Mann Borgese 1998). A "World Organization for Environment and Development", as postulated by Biermann and Simonis (1998), however, would be overburdened if it took on these tasks, including the enforcement of maritime rules.

The discharge of mineral oil on international shipping routes or on the high seas by individual acts of ships' crews that generally go unprosecuted calls for an international enforcement agency to ensure the sovereignty of coastal states as far as environmental protection, fisheries and use of amenities are concerned. A transfer of flag state rights to a United Nations body would make this possible.

The fragmentation of competencies between a number of specialized United Nations organizations with regard to the operation of cargo fleets and fishing vessel fleets, the dumping of wastes and the discharge of other pollutants into the sea, as well as the evaluation of and research on marine pollutants, hinder the effective protection of the marine environment. In this area, the following UN organizations and programs are involved: the International Maritime Organization (IMO), the Food and Agriculture Organization of the United Nations (FAO), the United Nations Education, Scientific and Cultural Organization (UNESCO), the Intergovernmental Oceanographic Commission (IOC), the United Nations Environmental Programme (UNEP), and the International Seabed Authority (ISBA). Additionally, nearly all of these UN organizations run the Joint Group of Experts on the Scientific Aspects of Marine Environmental Protection (GESAMP). While an evaluation of GESAMP praised the quality of its scientific projects, it also drew attention to its insufficient organization and integration, as well as its general under-funding (GESAMP 2001).

Elisabeth Mann Borgese (1998) introduced the International Seabed Authority (ISBA) into the debate, although this would require a tremendous enlargement of this institution of the United Nations. She explained that only the General Assembly, with its all-inclusive membership (not all nations are members of the UN organizations listed above), would be able to deal with all problems of the sea, to coordinate conventions, treaties and programs, and to develop an integrated marine policy. The establishment of the "United Nations Informal Consultative Process on the Oceans and the Law of the Sea (UNICPOLOS)" under the General Assembly must be seen as a breakthrough. The discussion of illegal, unregulated and undocumented fishing during its first session in 2000 (see Mann Borgese 2001) also focused on the problems associated with the flags of convenience and the roles of IMO and FAO in this context, albeit restricted to the special viewpoint defined by the agenda (as we did with regard to oil transport).

6.2. Proposals for Policy Formulation

The positive balance of the MARPOL Convention is increasingly overshadowed, as we have explained in detail, by a development that is calling the future of the regulatory network and the policy organization into question. Seven areas of concern dominate the critical side of the balance:

1. The insufficient prosecution and punishment by flag-of-convenience administrations of violations, in particular on the high seas, hinders policing-oriented parts of the regulations.
2. IMO instruments lack the economic incentives necessary to promote innovation-oriented projects by environmentally pioneering ship owners and thus offset the consequences of grandfather clauses. Instruments for a new environmental policy by port states are already being discussed (Green Shipping 2000).
3. The social situation on board many ships under flags of convenience has reduced the crews' identification with ship owner and vessel. Environmental awareness is low among crews from poor developing nations, who work for low pay and are given no motivation for environmentally friendly behaviour by flag states or ship owners.
4. Classification societies, in particular the newly introduced low-priced ones, conduct business without any real control or quality checks. Because these companies are in paricular supposed to assure the quality standards on ships internationally (including flags of convenience), a softening of IMO standards is observed.
5. The limitation of IMO's competence to standards for ships, in connection with very small competence for marine environmental protection, has allowed the rise of a political network of stakeholders in maritime shipping interests. Coastal and environmental protection interests are not present in committees at the ministry level (with e.g. the exception of the Netherlands). There are no continuous expert groups within IMO that discuss matters of environmental protection.
6. The orientation and also limitation of IMO's work as a UN agency specializing in the management of international negotiations constricts initiatives by the international expert personnel working in the organization.
7. The fragmentation of competencies between a number of specialized United Nations organizations concerning the use of the sea, the exploitation of the sea, and marine pollution hinders the effective protection of the marine environment.

Based on our observation and analysis of developments, we suggest activities in regulatory policy in two areas: the national supervision of ship owners; and new international control to counterbalance the perspectives for ship owners in globalization and strengthen the effectiveness of MARPOL regulations.

National Supervision: The Role of the Flags of Convenience

A study by the British Parliament acknowledged the problems explained here and called for political initiatives, such as (a still lacking) quality check for classification societies, or even the withdrawal of flag state licence under MARPOL in the case of a continuous high rate of deficiencies during port state controls on ships flying such flags (Donaldson 1994). The inclusion of social and health standards developed by the International Labor Organization (ILO) or the World Health Organization (WHO) in IMO treaties concerning environmental protection and ship safety could enhance the enforcement of such standards. The registration of tankships under their "true" flag should be encouraged. To ensure legal prosecution of violations and prevent oil pollution, flags of convenience should be withdrawn from tankships. Economic stimulus by the large oil-importing nations could induce a change of flags by large oil companies. A proposal by the US House of Representatives was a move in this direction, amending the Maritime Safety Act and enabling the State Department to prohibit loading and unloading by tankships flying the flags of states that do not enforce IMO standards adequately (House of Representatives 2000).

International Regulatory Policy: The United Nations Organizations

Biermann proposed the establishment in London of a joint administration for the use of the sea and marine environmental protection, with power to organize research and campaigns (Biermann 1994a). It is our opinion that such an "International Organization for Marine Environment Protection and Maritime Affairs" could enhance the discussed effectiveness of MARPOL, as well as integrate regional treaties, take over national prosecution of violations committed in international waters, and become a maritime Interpol. A reduction in national activities (administrations) with respective transfer of personnel and competence to the UN administration would enable the establishment of such an organization under low budget rise. This would offer a special opportunity for the International Tribunal for the Law of the Sea in Hamburg, as the introduction of UN regulatory policing in the area of sea traffic would inevitably call for personnel enlargement and a general enhancement of this institution.

ACKNOWLEDGEMENTS

We wish to thank Frank Biermann for his suggestions for improving the first draft of the report, Manfred Binder for critical review and Michael Dills for his assistance in editing the English version of the manuscript.

LITERATURE

Bernem, C.v.; Lübbe, T. (1997): Öl im Meer, Katastrophen und langfristige Belastungen. Wissenschaftliche Buchgesellschaft. Darmstadt

Biermann, F. (1994a): Internationale Meeresumweltpolitik. Verlag P. Lang, Frankfurt/M.

Biermann, F. (1994b): Schutz der Meere. Internationale Umweltpolitik nach Inkrafttreten der Seerechtskonvention der Vereinten Nationen. Wissenschaftszentrum Berlin WZB FS II 94-405

Biermann, F.; Simonis U.E. (1998): Plädoyer für eine Weltorganisation für Umwelt und Entwicklung. FS II 98-406. Wissenschaftszentrum Berlin für Sozialforschung WZB, Berlin

Biermann, F. (2000): Regionalismus oder Globalismus in der Meeresumweltpolitik? Zeitschrift für Umweltpolitik und Umweltrecht, H. 1. S. 99–117

Caldwell, L.K. (1996): International environmental policy. 3rd Ed. Duke University Press. Durham NC

Donaldson (1994): Safer ships, cleaner seas, report of Lord Donaldson's inquiry into the prevention of pollution from merchant shipping. Her Majesty's Stationary Office HMSO, London

GESAMP. IMO/FAO/UNESCO/WMO/WHO/IAEA/UN/UNEP Joint Group of Experts on the Scientific Aspects of Marine Pollution (1993): Impact of oil and related chemicals and wastes on the marine environment. GESAMP Reports and Studies No. 50. IMO, London

GESAMP. IMO/FAO/UNESCO/WMO/WHO/IAEA/UN/UNEP Joint Group of Experts on the Scientific Aspects of Marine Environmental Protection (2001): Independent and indepth evaluation of GESAMP. Report of the Evaluation Team, July 2001. IMO Publication 482/01. IMO London

GESAMP. IMO/FAO/UNESCO/WMO/WHO/IAEA/UN/UNEP Joint Group of Experts on the Scientific Aspects of Marine Environmental Protection (2003): Estimates of oil entering the sea from ships and other sea-based activities. GESAMP Reports and Studies (to be published). IMO, London

Greenpeace (1999): Ships for Scrap: Steel and toxic wastes for Asia. Greenpeace, Hamburg

Green Shipping (2000): Proc. of the International Conference on Incentives for Environmentally Sound Maritime Transport. Umweltbehörde, Hamburg

Hartje, V.J. (1995): Ocean pollution by tankers: regulating operational discharges as a partial policy success. In: Jänicke, M., Weidner, H. (eds.): Successful environmental policy. S. 379–393. Edition Sigma, Berlin

Höfer, T. (1998): Tankships in the marine environment, marine transport of bulk liquids and cargoes spilt. Environmental Science and Pollution Research, H. 5, S. 97–104

Höfer, T. (1999): Tankships in the marine environment, regulations to prevent marine pollution. Environmental Science and Pollution Research, H. 6, S. 107–114

House of Representatives (2000): Draft Maritime Safety Act introduced by Congressman DeFrazio. Reference HR 5025. Washington

ICS. International Chamber of Shipping (2001): Annual Review 2000/2001. ICS, 12 Carthusian Street, London.

ILO. International Labour Office (1990): Labour Standards on Merchant Ships. ILO International Labour Conference, 77th session, Geneva

IMO. International Maritime Organization (1990): Petroleum in the marine environment. Submitted by the United States. MEPC 30/Inf.13. IMO, London

IMO. International Maritime Organization (1992): MARPOL 73/78. Articles, protocols, annexes, unified interpretations of the International Convention for the Prevention of Pollution from Ships, 1973, as modified by the protocol of 1978 relating thereto. IMO, London

IMO. International Maritime Organization (1998a): IMO Conventions Status. Focus on IMO. IMO, London

IMO. International Maritime Organization (1998b): IMO – the first 50 years. IMO News, Nr. 1, S. 3–14. IMO, London

IMO. International Maritime Organization (2000a): Basic facts about IMO. Focus on IMO. IMO, London

IMO. International Maritime Organization (2000b): Report of the Marine Environment Protection Committee on its forty-fifth Session. MEPC 45/20 Annex 9. IMO, London

IMO. International Maritime Organization (2001a): Status of conventions, note by the secretariat. MEPC 46/18. IMO, London

IMO. International Maritime Organization (2001b): Report of the Marine Environment Protection Committee on its forty-sixth Session. MEPC 46/23. IMO, London

IMO. International Maritime Organization (2001c): Accelerated phase-out for single hull tankers. IMO News 2/2001, Seite 5. IMO, London

ITOPF. The International Tanker Owners Pollution Federation (1997): Oil spill statistics. Ocean Orbit Newsletter of ITOPF. August 8. London

Jänicke, M.; Weidner, H. (eds.) (1995): Successful Environmental Policy. A Critical Evaluation of 24 Cases. Edition Sigma, Berlin

Johnsson, L. (1996): Funny Flags. Utbildingsförlaget Brevskolau (German edition: Oertel u. Spörer, Reutlingen)

Kern, K.; Bratzel, S. (1996): Umweltpolitischer Erfolg im internationalen Vergleich. Zum Stand der Forschung. In: Jänicke, M. (Hg.): Umweltpolitik der Industrieländer. Edition Sigma, Berlin. S. 29–58.

Lagoni, R. (1993): Die Abwehr von Gefahren für die marine Umwelt. In: Umweltschutz im Völkerrecht und Kollisionsrecht. Berichte der deutschen Gesellschaft für Völkerrecht, H. 32, S. 87–152

Liersch, K.-M. (1994): Der Schutz der Meeresumwelt – Instrumente und Maßnahmen. Wasser u. Boden, H. 8, S. 15–20

Mann Borgese, E. (1998): The Oceanic Circle. Governing the seas as a global resource. United Nations University Press N.Y.

Mann Borgese, E. (2001): UNICPOLOS. The First Session. Environmental Policy and Law 30(5): 224–232

Mitchell, R.B. (1994): Intentional oil pollution at sea – environmental policy and treaty compliance. The MIT Press, Cambridge MA

Moore, G. (1976): Legal aspects of marine pollution control. In: Johnston, R.: Marine pollution. S. 589–697. Academic Press, New York

Newcombe, J.; Wilkinson, D.; Coffey, C. (2000): Report from the Workshop on the Effectiveness of EU-Environmental Legislation, Copenhagen November 11–13, 1999, London

NRC National Research Council (1985): Oil in the sea, inputs, fates, and effects. National Academy Press, Washington D.C.

Pein, J.W. (1996): Giganten der Weltmeere. Koehlers Verlagsgesellschaft, Hamburg

SIRC Seafarers International Research Centre (2001): Distribution of Flasci Scores. Cited from: Lloyds: Flags of Convenience. LSM 2001 (6): 42–43 (Details on SIRC via Prof. Tony Lane, Cardiff University, GB)

Underdal, A.; Andresen, St.; Ringius, L.; Wettestad, J. (1999): Evaluating regime effectiveness: developing valid and usable tools. Agenda-setting paper for the Workshop on Global and Regional Agreements, 10–12 September, Oslo

Wilkinson, D.; Coffey, C.; Newcombe, J. (1999): The effectiveness of EU environmental policy: How do we assess effectiveness? Agenda-setting paper for the Workshop on effectiveness of EU environmental policy, 11–13 November, Copenhagen.

Ending Flag State Control?

*Awni Behnam**

This paper is dedicated to the memory of Professor Elisabeth Mann Borgese.[1]

I. SETTING THE SCENE

While the inexorable processes of liberalization and privatization continue to spread as a response to the forces of globalization, uneasiness persists in many quarters that the promotion of equity and balanced economic growth based on just social values, respect for nature and protection of the environment, including the sustainability of the oceans, is being placed on the back-burner in the pursuit of the elusive promises held out by globalization.

The international community so far appears generally satisfied with the existing governance framework of market forces in conjunction with traditional tools of governance – namely, treaties and instruments (such as the United Nations Convention on the Law of the Sea (UNCLOS), Agenda 21, IMO conventions and legal instruments of numerous multilateral institutions).

However, the institutions that were endeavouring to provide the necessary framework for global governance have proved to be less than effective and often incapable of ensuring implementation of their policies, rules and conventions, as they have lacked powers of enforcement.[2]

---

* Dr. *Awni Behnam* is Senior Adviser to the Secretary-General of the United Nations Conference on Trade and Development (UNCTAD), Geneva (Switzerland). Contact: awni.behnam@unctad.org.

The views expressed in this paper are those of the author and do not necessarily reflect those of the UNCTAD secretariat.

An extended version of this paper, entitled "Twilight of flag State control", was written jointly by Dr. Awni Behnam and Dr. Peter Faust at the request of Professor Elisabeth Mann Borgese to be included in Volume 17 of the Ocean Yearbook, published by the University of Chicago Press in cooperation with the International Ocean Institute and Dalhousie University Law School.

1 The topic addressed in this paper is one that Elisabeth always found fascinating. She felt very concerned with Flags of Convenience from two perspectives. One was the exploitation of ship labour from developing countries, and the second that Flags of Convenience were a tool that inhibited developing countries' integration into the world maritime economy.

Many call her the "Mother of the Oceans" and very rightly so. She strove for fairness and prosperity based on just social values, respect for nature and protection of the Oceans.

2 The UN agencies of the ILO, the IMO and UNCTAD have undoubtedly worked assiduously over the years in facilitating and steering these conventions through committees and diplomatic meetings in order to protect the welfare and safety of seafarers. They could not prevent dilution and they have

A. Kirchner (ed.), International Maritime Environmental Law, 123–135.

Shipping is one sector in the use of the oceans where the global implications of this reality has been clearly demonstrated. It is one sector where the direct impact of globalization is clearly discernible. Unfettered liberalization, mergers and acquisitions, massive accumulation and concentration of capital in a few hands, unadulterated use of economic power, and mastery of technology, compounded by an amazing loophole in international law – "the legal fiction of flag territory at sea" – have contributed to the current global deficit in governance of the oceans.

The first to experience the downside of globalization were the fledging fleets of developing countries, particularly the least developed among them, who, during the 1990s, were first driven out of mainstream operations and forced into secondary roles, and then driven out completely from the secondary roles as well. The gains of the 1970s and 1980s, when institutions such as UNCTAD placed economic justice and participatory international economic systems at the forefront of their shipping work programmes in order to help developing countries make headway in the development of shipping capabilities, were lost in the 1990s.

The marginalization of developing countries in shipping during the last decade was evident as they were increasingly forced out of the mainstream of the global economy into the secondary subsectors of the shipping industry and subsequently into what may be termed "the informal sector of international shipping".[3]

The experience resembles that of the poor and underprivileged in national societies who have been forced to eke out a living in the informal sector. One consequence is that this so-called "informal sector" in shipping attracts substandard vessels for its marginal operations – a recipe for environmental disasters both physical and social (seafarers' welfare and safety) – and constitutes an open invitation to carry out illegal, unregulated and unreported (IUU) fishing.

Equally disturbing is the fact that many developing countries have begun to resort to flags of convenience that traditional owners have exploited for decades. This itself fuels a vicious circle of more substandard ships and a proliferation of small flags of convenience from States with no, or totally ineffective, maritime administrations. The inability of a large majority of developing countries, particularly the least developed countries, to participate more effectively in world shipping characterized by equal opportunities and shared benefits deprives them of the capacity to develop competent maritime authorities that can and should exercise effective control. However, the issue is not confined to the impact on developing countries but embraces all members of the international community.

II. THE EMERGING GOVERNANCE DEFICIT

Shipping continues to represent the most valuable use of the oceans. More than 90 per cent of world trade moves by sea. In 2001, seaborne trade approached 6 billion

---

Cont.

no powers of enforcement, which rest with flag States which, as sovereign nations, have always been considered the primary regulators of vessels flying their flags. A.D. Couper, Voyage of Abuse, Sea-Farers, Human Rights and International Shipping. London. Pluto Press, 1999, p. 168.

3 Emerging Institutional Framework for Ocean Governance. Awni Behnam. Hamburg, Pacem Maribus, 2000.

tons and the world fleet reached 808 million deadweight tons (DWT).[4] However, hidden beneath this apparently healthy global growth and progress lies a very disturbing reality – that at the start of the new millennium, half of the world fleet is under flags of convenience (FOC). This phenomenon is spreading out of control. Efficient world shipping, with generally low freight rates and sophisticated use of advanced technology, is only one aspect of the equation. The other, darker aspect is the unchecked market forces, alongside a great myth called flag State control.

The post-Second World War expansion of trade changed the qualitative and quantitative distribution of shipping and flags, apart from the economic implications of the engagement of nations in shipping. The technological revolution ushered in a vast increase in ship size and the ability to carry unconventional cargoes, such as bulk, oil, gas, toxic chemicals and radioactive materials. These cargoes brought into the limelight both environmental and safety issues that had to be addressed in terms of flag State control.

Churchill and Lowe explain that "the ascription of nationality to ships is one of the most important means by which public order is maintained at sea. As well as indicating what rights a ship enjoys and to what obligations it is subject, the nationality of a vessel indicates which State is to exercise flag State jurisdiction over the vessel".[5] Nationality is granted when a ship is entered on the national register of the country authorizing it to fly its flag. The exercise of control, however, is not automatic; it is generally dependent on the ability and willingness "vigour". The first, relating to the existence of the flags of convenience, is dependent on the existence or absence of a genuine link between the vessel and the flag State. The latter is applicable to all flag registries. The Convention on the Law of the Sea, in its articles 91–94, recognized the obligations of flag States in the exercise of jurisdiction and control, but did not impart any solution to the basic problem in so far as obligating a genuine link. Consequently, the Convention on the Law of the Sea did not in essence strengthen the genuine link between a ship and its flag State.

This became evident when major international conventions relating to safety standards, pollution and social conditions were being drafted in the 1970s and 1980s in the IMCO (precursor to the IMO), ILO, UNCTAD and other international organizations. Enforcement lay squarely and largely with the flag States, but in the late 1980s and early 1990s, it became apparent that the root cause of the problem had not been addressed. Consequently, the role of port State control in maritime governance increased.

Edgar Gold captured this in his article on "Learning from disaster",[6] in which he explained that, as international organizations had no enforcement power (which had traditionally been left to flag States), acceptance or adherence to international codes and conventions did not entail that the accepting State was willing or able to enforce such codes. Moreover, in the case of the flag of convenience, flag States had little or no actual jurisdiction controls, which resulted in some open registry States not being

4 UNCTAD Review of Maritime Transport, 2001 – UNCTAD/RMT/2001.

5 R.R. Churchill and A.V. Lowe, The Law of the Sea, third edition. Manchester University Press, 1999, p. 205.

6 Edgar Gold, Review of European Community & International Environmental Law, Learning from Disaster: Lessons in Regulatory Enforcement in the Maritime Sector. Vol. 8, No. 1, 1999.

involved in any enforcement at all. Gold agrees that the governance deficit, which he terms "enforcement leakage", was at the root of the major disasters, and that the sub-standard shipping of the 1980s was a major impetus for seeking alternative methods of control. Consequently, there are two avenues to explore, the first relating to the erosion of sovereignty and the second to the existence or absence of a genuine link.

III. THE EXISTENCE OR ABSENCE OF A GENUINE LINK

Flag-of-convenience fleets (or "open registry fleets") expanded at a faster rate than any other flags of the world merchant fleet. In fact, these vessels now account for one-half of the world's deadweight tonnage, consisting mainly of tankers and bulk carriers. This in itself is a cause for serious concern, as the system permitted owners of vessels to be replaced by "faceless men" who concealed their identities behind a veil of nominal holding companies. Trading nations dependent upon shipping cannot fail to be alarmed at the prospect of the shipping industry falling increasingly into the hands of shipowners who cannot be identified.

A significant controversy is the occurrence in recent decades of a number of alarming incidents involving shipwrecks, scuttling of vessels, maritime fraud, abuse of seafarers, breach of United Nations embargoes and environmental disasters. These incidents clearly illustrate the problems of enforcing the law when flag States have no more than a nominal connection with the shipowners who fly their flags. This means that half of the world fleet is technically an international anomaly and not subject to the jurisdiction of the State of the flag they fly.

In general terms, it can be said that a vessel flies a flag of convenience when it has no real economic connection (or no "genuine economic link") with the country whose flag it flies. From the viewpoint of the countries of registration, an "open registry" country is one which accepts vessels on its shipping register with which it has no genuine economic link.

Although the Convention on the High Seas of 1958[7] and later UNCLOS states that there must be a "genuine link" between a vessel and its country of registration, it does not define what is meant by "genuine link". UNCTAD states that the following elements are normally relevant in determining whether a genuine link exists:

(a) The merchant fleet contributes to the national economy of the country;
(b) Revenues and expenditures of shipping, as well as purchases and sales of vessels, are treated in the national balance-of-payments accounts;
(c) The employment of nationals on vessels; and
(d) The beneficial ownership of the vessel.

---

7 Convention on the High Seas, United Nations, Treaty Series Vol. 450, p.11. In addition, article 91 of the Convention on the Law of the Sea states:

1. Each State shall fix the conditions for the grant of its nationality to ships, for the registration of ships in its territory, and for the right to fly its flag. Ships have the nationality of the State whose flag they are entitled to fly. There must exist a genuine link between the State and the ship.
2. Each State shall issue to ships to which it has granted the right to fly its flag documents to that effect.

However, the Law of the Sea Conference did not define what constitutes a genuine link.

There are numerous reasons why shipowners register vessels under flags of convenience – including evasion of taxes, avoidance of various governmental regulations and freedom from restrictions on the use of cash flows. Some of the less reputable shipowners undoubtedly use these flags with the specific aim of concealing their identities and escaping the responsibilities and law enforcement procedures relating to maritime safety, pollution prevention, obligation towards seafarers, etc., which apply under normal flags. However, there are also numerous transnational corporations of good standing involved in open registry operations. The reasons why these companies choose flags of convenience relate principally to crew costs.

IV. CONSEQUENCES OF OPEN REGISTRY OPERATIONS: THE ISSUE OF JURISDICTION AND CONTROL

One of the main consequences of open registration is that it enables the traditional maritime operators[8] (countries) to maintain their domination over world shipping – despite their increasing inability to operate under their own country flags – on account of their high labour costs and the scarcity of seafarers. However, another consequence that has aroused the most public discussion over the years has been the amount of misconduct and irresponsible conduct associated with the operation of open registry vessels. There are, of course, a large number of companies that operate FOC vessels in a responsible manner, not because of the open registry system, but because they believe that safety and respect of international standards is good business.

Nonetheless, the same system that permits these companies to operate with more freedom than they could achieve under their home flags also permits the operation of vessels by irresponsible owners. The problem arises from the fact that, whereas a country with a normal registry can exercise authority over the owners, crew and vessel, an open registry country can exercise authority only over the nominal owners listed on its register book. Since these countries, unlike the normal registry countries, do not impose taxes, they do not have an incentive to identify the real owners; the key crew members of these vessels are non-nationals, and consequently the only real remedy which an open registry country can apply in the event of misconduct is to "de-register" a vessel. However, de-registering is not an effective measure, since nominal owners can circumvent deregistration by changing their company and ship name, and subsequently re-register.

Some of the ILO and IMO conventions are enforceable by port States – but what action can be taken by a port State? A port State can take action against the crew of a vessel, but the owners are effectively outside its jurisdiction. Some of the traditional maritime countries were urging action to correct the "abuses" of the open registry system without altering the system itself. But the abuses are an inherent part of

8 The existence of globalized shipping with its substandard sector clearly represents unfair competition to decent shipping companies. But it is more socially pervasive than that. Because of competitive pressures, some FOC ships (in the absence of an ITF Blue Certificate) can induce a downward levelling in the conditions of seafarers under all flags by undermining the economic viability of socially responsible owners. A.D. Couper, *op. cit.*, p. 173.

the system, stemming from the fact that the real owners live outside the jurisdiction of the flag State. Consequently, it is simply not possible to take effective action in respect of the abuses without taking action to ensure that there is a genuine economic link between owners and countries of registration.

As ships are considered parcels of the national territory and come under the jurisdiction of the flag State, in the high seas, only international rules and regulations are applicable, provided they bind the flag State either directly (ratification) or indirectly (common use).

For decades, the international community has faced a challenge: the proper exercise of jurisdiction and control over vessels by a flag State was not only of national concern but above all of international concern. It would be futile to expect a flag State to exercise such control unless minimum requirements were laid down in an international convention on the registration of vessels.

The principle that a State must effectively exercise its jurisdiction and control in administrative, technical and social matters over ships flying its flag was embodied in the United Nations Convention on the Law of the Sea, in particular with respect to the provisions relating to the nationality of vessels and the duties of flag States (articles 91 to 97). Under article 91, each State shall fix the conditions for the granting of its nationality to ships, for the registration of ships in its territory and for the right to fly its flag. However, there must exist a "genuine link" between the State and the ship. Article 94 sets forth various duties of the flag State concerning the exercise of its jurisdiction and control in administrative, technical, safety and social matters.

To reflect on some arguments that have been made with regard to the Law of the Sea: one is reminded by statements highlighted in the media that there was no need for an international agreement on conditions for registration of ships, as that had been adequately covered by the Law of the Sea Convention.

It is clear from an analysis of the relevant provisions of the Law of the Sea Convention that although individual States have certain flexibilities to establish conditions concerning the granting of their nationality, registration and right to fly their flags, there must exist as a very minimum a "genuine link" between the State and the ship. The Convention provides no definition of this genuine link nor in any other way gives guidance as to the conditions required for the registration of ships to meet the genuine link requirement. Article 94 deals with the separate question of the duties of a State *vis-à-vis* vessels flying its flag. In this respect the Convention sets forth international norms for the exercise of jurisdiction and control by flag States.

Since the absence of a genuine link between open registry vessels and the flag State makes it impossible for the flag State to fulfil its international obligations to exercise jurisdiction and control over vessels flying its flag. The Convention left unresolved the issue of what exactly the elements were that constitute the genuine link between State and vessel and that are necessary to enable a State effectively to exercise its jurisdiction and control under article 94. In this context it is important to note that the statement in article 91 that "Each State shall fix the conditions for the registration of ships" is a statement of *obligation* and not one of freedom. It does not say, "Each State shall *remain free* to fix the conditions for the registration of ships". Thus, having neither defined nor obligated the components of a genuine link, the Law of the Sea text does not preclude, and is not inconsistent with, establishing by another international agreement minimum conditions for the registration of ships.[9] In fact, such an international agreement would be complementary to the Law of the Sea Convention by, in effect, establishing the minimum conditions for registering ships without affecting the right of individual States actually to fix conditions for the granting of nationality, registration and right to fly its flag which are more stringent than the stated minimum. Such a definition, in the form of establishing minimum conditions upon which vessels may be registered in a State, would result in fulfilment of the duties of flag States, as set forth in article 94.

V. AN INTERNATIONAL INSTRUMENT TO REGULATE FLAGS-OF-CONVENIENCE

The United Nations Convention on Conditions for Registration of Ships,[10] adopted in 1986, introduced new standards of responsibility and accountability for the world shipping industry. For the first time there was an international instrument that defined the elements of the "genuine link" that should exist between a ship and the State whose flag it flies. The Convention filled a major gap in international maritime jurisprudence, as the components of the "genuine link" had never previously been identified.

Articles 8, 9 and 10 – the heart of the Convention – provided for participation by nationals of the flag State in the ownership, manning and management of ships, thus establishing key economic links between a ship and the flag State that are often missing in present practice. A distinctive feature was that States had a choice of two mandatory articles on ownership and manning. This element of flexibility was introduced to take account of the different conditions prevailing in flag States. Some flag States might lack sufficient manpower among their nationals or "persons domiciled or lawfully in permanent residence" within their territory to provide for significant participation by nationals in the crews of ships flying their flag, while other flag States might not have sufficient capital to participate effectively in ship ownership. Among the important provisions of the article on manning is the statement that the State of registration shall ensure that the manning of its ships "is of such a level and competence as to ensure compliance with applicable international rules and standards, in particular those regarding safety at sea". Another provision of that article stipulates that the State of registration shall ensure that the terms and conditions of employment "are in conformity with applicable international rules

---

9 *"In spite of the fact that the 'genuine link' requirement appears to have had little influence on State practice since the High Seas Convention came into force, the requirement is repeated in the Law of the Sea Convention (art.91), although the requirement is not linked to the effective exercise of jurisdiction by the flag State, as it is in article 5 of the High Seas Convention. (The effective exercise of flag State jurisdiction is dealt with by article 94, discussed below.) There seems little reason for supposing that article 91 will have any more influence on State practice than article 5 of the High Seas Convention. The direct attack mounted on flags of convenience in the past few years by UNCTAD may prove more effective."* R.R. Churchill and A.V. Lowe, The Law of the Sea, *op. cit.*

10 United Nations Convention on Conditions for Registration of Ships, TD/RS/CONF/25, 1990.

and standards" and that "adequate procedures exist for the settlement of civil disputes between seafarers employed on ships flying its flag and their employers".

A balanced approach is evident in the article on management. On the one hand, the principle was set out that before entering a ship on its register of ships, a registration State would ensure that the shipowning company or its subsidiary was established and/or had "its principal place of business within its territory". On the other hand, where this was not the case, the flag State was expected to ensure that there was "a representative or management person who shall be a national of the flag State or be domiciled therein". The article on management is also significant in that it makes the State of registration responsible for ensuring that persons accountable for the management and operation of ships are in a position to meet the financial obligations that may arise from the operation of such ships and to cover risks which are normally insured in international maritime transportation in respect of damage to third parties.

Another important article (article 5) in the instrument provides for the establishment by a flag State of a "competent and adequate national maritime administration which shall be subject to its jurisdiction and control" and which is charged with a number of specific mandatory tasks, such as ensuring that a ship flying its flag complies with a State's "laws and regulations concerning registration of ships and with applicable international rules and standards concerning, in particular, the safety of ships and persons on board and the prevention of pollution of the marine environment" and ensuring that it carries on board documents, "in particular, those evidencing the right to fly its flag and other valid relevant documents". At present, a number of States have no such national maritime administrations.

In addition, the article on identification and accountability (article 6) provides that a State shall take the necessary measures to ensure that owners and operators of a ship on its register are "adequately identifiable for the purposes of ensuring their full accountability". This provision was of particular importance in identifying and punishing perpetrators of maritime fraud.

The Convention did not please all concerned. It was a product of compromise necessitated by the divergent positions held by States on flags of convenience. Some criticized the Convention, claiming that it did not change the *status quo*. Others accepted realities and saw the Convention as a step forward in the struggle to limit flags of convenience and their undesirable side effects. Some claimed that open registry countries were the real beneficiaries, as they would not need to make any changes. The truth was thought to be somewhere inbetween. The Convention would provide a possibility as an international legal instrument for States to take sanctions at national level against the more undesirable aspects of the phenomenon of flags of convenience. It also provided a policy platform for developing countries for their future planning. Perhaps most importantly, it provided those countries that supplied labour and wished to attract vessels to their national register to adapt their standard of registration without compromising the integrity of their registers and thus have their national labour manning vessels under their own flags. Thus, it opened the door to competition which the traditional open registry countries perhaps could not afford to ignore, as they would have to tighten their control over vessels under their register in accordance with the minimum conditions set out in the Convention.

The Convention induces greater transparency in the operations of open registry vessels through articles 6 and 11. It also provides the legal basis for registration of bareboat chartered vessels in article 12.

Referring to article 5 of the Convention on national maritime administration, S.G. Sturmey[11] admits that this is one of the strongest provisions of the Convention. Moreover, he makes a sound proposal for the improvement of this article – namely, for an appropriate United Nations agency to be set up to review the structure and performance of the maritime administration of States, upon their request, and to recommend what measures might be taken to enable them to meet the standards set out in the Convention.

One could agree with him that if the Convention was to enter into force, it would not only be the present open registry countries that would need to act, since plenty of "normal" registers are defective with respect to some of the provisions of the Convention. The Convention would also render an international service if it was responsible for an improvement in maritime administrations throughout the world, including parastatal and private bodies, e.g. the classification societies and surveyors that work in conjunction with administrations in so many ways.

Unfortunately, the Convention on ship registration still awaits ratification and is unlikely to enter into force. Its die-hard supporters believed that it nevertheless provides sufficient guidance to national maritime administrations and standard-setting for new registries.

Since the adoption of the Convention in 1986, the use of flags of convenience (open registries) has increased even further. There appear, however, to have been some qualitative changes. First of all, the Convention may have been the catalyst for Norwegian and Danish international ship registries to be opened and modelled along the provisions of a genuine link, thus allowing those countries' vessels to be registered under their national flags but along the lines of an offshore tax haven concept. At the same time, some developing countries decided to follow the concept "if you can't beat 'em, join' em". Operators from such countries as China (with Hong Kong, China, and Taiwan Province of China), Saudi Arabia, Republic of Korea and Singapore became fully involved in open registry operations by registering some of their vessels under open registry flags.

Clearly, the attempt to bring flags of convenience under a new international regime of jurisdiction and control has totally failed.

Professor Alastair Couper[12] has poignantly documented the continuing and tragic predicament and suffering of seafarers in his recent book, *Voyages of Abuse*, which shows how the human rights of seafarers are flagrantly violated on a daily basis. The book shows the failure of the international legal framework to provide seafarers with even the minimum protection. It describes cases of their mistreatment outside of territorial seas, their servitude on substandard vessels, their mounting loss of life and their disenfranchisement, as FOC States abandon them in a flagrant dereliction of duty, which contravenes international law and minimum norms of decent behaviour. Clearly, there exists today a major lacuna between the intention of the drafters of UNCLOS and the applicability of the law as it concerns the duties and responsibilities of the flag States. This lacuna, as demonstrated by the

---

11 See also S.G. Sturmey, "United Nations Convention on Conditions for Registration of Ships", *Lloyds Maritime and Commercial Law Quarterly*, February 1987".

12 A.D. Couper, Voyages of Abuse, *op. cit.*

extensive details in the elaboration of the International Convention on Registration of Ships, remains one of the greatest challenges to the international community.

VI. ALTERNATIVE MEASURES

Port State control, coastal State control and other measures, such as the International Safety Management (ISM) code and quality management, have evolved as alternative tools to reverse the governance deficit of the oceans.

As mentioned earlier, the hard reality of today's shipping is that flag States are not universally doing their duty to regulate and effectively police tonnage included in their registers. There is often little identifiability and even less accountability, particularly in relation to the owners and operators of substandard ships. The shipping scene under some flags continues to be characterized by unidentifiable and consequently unaccountable one-ship companies.

While the international community has not been able to reach agreement on an instrument defining the genuine link and setting minimum obligations for flag States, it has recognized that the situation of substandard shipping has become untenable. Consequently, those directly and adversely affected by these operations have either unilaterally or plurilaterally taken some necessary measures to protect their environmental and maritime safety.

Port State control is not meant to be a substitute for flag State obligations, but rather a complementary instrument. It is clear that port State control, on the scale observed today, would not be necessary if flag States were to discharge their duties in a more responsible manner.

The concept of port State control is not new but was already contained in the SOLAS Convention and later on in UNCLOS. Similarly, it is commonly recognized that the coastal State has full authority to determine the conditions of, and prescribe the policy for access to and use of, its port. In fact, a number of modern international instruments recognize not only the power but also the duties of port States to undertake inspections of vessels to ensure compliance with international rules and regulations.[13]

Up to now, it has been fair to assert that port State control has been a relatively efficient instrument for eliminating or at least reducing substandard shipping. Nevertheless, the general level of maritime safety and pollution prevention could be raised to standards acceptable to the global community only if all flag States lived up to their obligations and implemented mechanisms to ensure identifiability and accountability of owners and improve general standards of maritime operations.

In contrast to port State control, coastal State control is not clearly defined or integrated into a coherent concept of protecting marine safety and the environment by combating substandard shipping. While the Coastal States Authority with regard to the prevention of pollution is established in UNCLOS, it is not clear to what

---

13 For a discussion of the roles of flag States, coastal States and port States, see J. Hare, "Flag, coastal and port State control – Closing the net on unseaworthy ships and their unscrupulous owners", in SEA CHANGES, No. 16, 1994, p. 57.

extent measures to prevent, reduce and control pollution may interfere with the concept of innocent passage of foreign vessels.[14]

The issue of coastal State control has, however, become more topical in the context of increasing problems related to illegal, unreported and unregulated (IUU) fisheries. Fishing in areas under national jurisdiction without the authorization of the coastal State has become a major offence of IUU fishing, requiring active cooperation between flag States, coastal States and port States in combating these malpractices.[15]

Another instrument to combat substandard shipping that is closely linked to flag State control is the ISM Code. Its introduction primarily involved a cultural change that had gradually affected the way shipping companies were being managed. This change involved an integration of ship- and shore-based management in pursuit of the common goals of improving maritime safety, protection of the environment and consequent improving of the profitability of shipping operations. In so doing, it was necessary to redirect behavioural patterns away from activity-based to results-based patterns. Thus, for instance, companies should change from the "inspection culture" that was widely accepted in the context of flag State and port State control mechanisms to a "safety culture" in which the systematic improvement of operational safety becomes the underlying principle of the companies' activities. This changeover is to be achieved gradually through a disciplined approach to ship operations.

VII. CONCLUSION

A cursory review of the sections of the reports of the United Nations Secretary-General to the fifty-fourth and the fifty-fifth sessions of the General Assembly dealing with the shipping industry, navigation and fisheries reveals the problems relating to safety of navigation, safety of ships, welfare of crews, IUU certification fishing and related re-flagging issues. The reports consistently placed responsibility on the flag State for the exercise of the State's jurisdiction and duties. They stressed that the primary responsibility for the enforcement of IMO and other regulations lies with the flag State. However, the truth was, and remains, that flags of convenience were created with the very intention that the flag State, even if it had the will, would not and could not exercise such duties *ipso facto*.[16] To go any further and pretend that flag-of-convenience States can abide by voluntary guidelines from intergovernmental international organizations or by self-imposed rules is tantamount to placing arsonists in charge of the fire brigade.

---

14 See J. Hare, *op. cit.*

15 The problem of IUU fishing and potential solutions were debated at length at the first meeting of the United Nations Open-ended Informal Consultative Process on Oceans and the Law of the Sea, the proceedings of which are contained in its report (A/55/274, New York, 2000).

16 "The State has sovereign rights over the ships and seafarers as part of its territory. This is now a form of political sophistry in the global industry. The flag State is in control *de jure*, but only theoretically; in practice, the *de facto* authority lies with the foreign-based beneficial owner (via the master), who can dictate procedures and conditions on board regardless of the flag of the ship" (A.D. Couper, *op. cit.*).

Port State control has been a natural response by coastal/port States that are most directly and adversely affected by safety and environmental consequences of irresponsible operations. Nevertheless, it can bring only a partial solution to the problem, as it relies too heavily on *ad hoc* measures and regionalizes the issue of substandard shipping. Similarly, it must be seen that the concept of ISM and the related code, both of which attempt to set operational standards and disciplines, stop short of addressing the real flag State issues. It does little, if anything, to create the genuine link called for in UNCLOS, with the legal, economic and operational consequences thereof. The link, which could be created through certification mechanisms, is too weak to be effective. The code undoubtedly presents a step towards improving ship management, but its implementation is still flawed, and existing problems might well have been amplified since July 2001, when the bulk of the world fleet became subject to the provisions of the ISM Code.

It is also clear that while a flag-of-convenience State does not have the leverage of the genuine link to exercise control, other flag States which do have a genuine link to the vessel do not exercise that control with the required vigour, for well-known reasons that include the unfair competition that flag-of-convenience operators enjoy. Consequently, it is not only a regulatory issue but an issue that permeates the whole structure of the industry, technological change, concentration of capital, economic performance, etc.

The issue, therefore, is one of governance, as part of the global governance of the oceans. As Gold indicates, there is a multitude of actions that could be taken by Governments, civil society, international organizations, port States, coastal States, the business community and the media, among others, to provide the global community with "safer ships and cleaner seas".

The thesis of this presentation is that flag State control is no longer a viable proposition. However, it is not our intention to propose alternatives or to resolve the lacuna, but rather to point out certain needs to be addressed by the international community, including the need to:

- Elaborate an international instrument designed to deal with the problems of a variety of illegal maritime acts and fraud, and specifically the problem of jurisdiction and extradition. Such a convention could expand the jurisdiction of States and list the illegal maritime acts to be covered. This expansion of jurisdictional capabilities of States should be linked to extradition requirements, so that a State could either prosecute offenders in its custody or extradite them to a requesting State. So far, Governments have not found any existing international legal instruments to govern illegal maritime acts or offences appropriately. Crimes which lead to the destruction of living resources, endanger safety of life and result in pollution are not "extraditable crimes", governed by international treaty. It seems that the time has come for the international community to address these issues seriously, in the same way as it rose to the challenge of air piracy, drug trafficking and terrorism

  (The Hamburg Declaration on the Ocean: The European Challenge emerging from the PACEM in Maribus XXVIII states: "Particular attention should be paid to the issues of the effective exercise of jurisdiction and control, including the need for elaboration of an international instrument relating to extradition in maritime crimes, fraud, piracy and for the protection of seafarers against abuse and violence");
- Ensure and promote coherence among all involved institutions relative to their work on the oceans and the Law of the Sea and Agenda 21;

- Promote increased political accountability as regards the various uses of the oceans through a vigorous approach to regional cooperation and coordination
  (In this regard, it is to be noted that the Group of 77, at the latest meeting of its Intergovernmental Follow-up and Coordination Committee, IFCC-X, Tehran, 21 August 2001, adopted a recommendation addressed to the UN General Assembly to "establish regional centres for technology, development and transfer, with the objective of creating synergies between public and private investment, equipped with contemporary high-tech management tools and serving the technological needs of all conventions, agreements, codes and programmes of the UNCLOS/UNCED process in a regional context");
- Involve all stakeholders of the oceans, particularly civil society and non-governmental organizations, in the evolving framework of governance;
- Pay greater attention to the recent proposal on levying of charges for the use of "global commons in high seas"
  (*The German Advisory Council on Global Change presented a paper at the International Conference on Financing for Development (Monterrey, March 2002) in which it described the use of the high seas for transportation as an example of global open access where the high seas are not subject to the legal sovereignty of any State. It argued in this context for levying user charges to create incentives to reduce shipping-induced marine pollution and to close the prevailing regulatory gap*);[17]
- Set higher goals and prepare the ground for further progress in promoting a system of global governance of the oceans that is comprehensive and interdisciplinary; that is democratic, inclusive and transparent; and that can contribute to addressing universal concerns. It may be necessary to establish an OCEANS SENATE. This could be a quasi-legislative or deliberative body composed of elected members from member States, heads of multilateral institutions, eminent persons who have made significant contributions to the oceans, and representatives of civil society and industry. The deliberations or recommendations of the OCEANS SENATE could be transmitted to the General Assembly for endorsement and legitimacy.

Professor Elisabeth Mann Borgese at the Algiers meeting on Reshaping the International Economic Order in 1976, expressed a vision of world shipping sailing under a single international flag. Perhaps the time has come to consider a single international registry for ships.

---

17 See WBGU Special Report, charging the use of the global commons, Berlin 2002.

Port State Control as an Instrument to Ensure Compliance with International Marine Environmental Obligations

*Lorenzo Schiano di Pepe**

1. INTRODUCTORY NOTE

The present paper is aimed at discussing the port State *régime*, and in particular the concept of "port State control" (or, in brief, "PSC"), *i.e.* the range of control powers that may be exercised by the competent authorities of a given port on ships flying a flag that is foreign in respect of the State of the visited port.[1] As is widely recognised, this is a very complex and fast-developing topic in the international arena: its complexity derives from the fact that PSC is a truly interdisciplinary issue, raising questions that are at the same time of a legal, economic and administrative nature;[2] as to its rapid evolution, this is very well demonstrated by the steadily increasing number of instruments (of international, regional and national scope of application) making reference to it.[3] Thus, due to the material limits of the present paper, the decision has been made that, rather than giving a general – and necessarily superficial – overview of PSC and its current *status* in international law,[4] a somewhat expanded answer will be provided to the following question: "What is, and what is going to be in the future, the role of PSC in ensuring compliance by States with international law provisions relating to the protection of the marine environment?"

* Dott. Lorenzo Schiano di Pepe, LL.M. (London), LL.M. (Georgetown) is currently a doctoral candidate in international law at the University of Milano (Italy). Contact: lorenzoschianodipepe@slac.it

1 For a comprehensive, in-depth analysis of port State control and jurisdiction issues, see George K. Kasoulides, *Port State Control and Jurisdiction. Evolution of the Port State Regime*, Martinus Nijhoff Publishers (Dordrecht/Boston/London), 1993 and, more recently, Z. Oya Özçayır, *Port State Control*, LLP (London/Hong Kong), 2001.

2 Ted L. McDorman, "Regional Port State Control Agreements: Some Issues of International Law", 5 *Ocean and Coastal Law Journal* 207 (2000), for example, emphasises the competition aspects that characterise relationships among ports.

3 This is exemplified by the ample documentary appendices in the recent work of Özçayır, *supra* fn. 1, 403 *et seq*.

4 For an account of the origins of port State jurisdiction and control and their evolution, in addition to the monographs cited *supra* at fn. 1, see also Tatjana Keselj, "Port State Jurisdiction in Respect of Pollution from Ships: The 1982 United Nations Convention on the Law of the Sea and the Memoranda of Understanding", 30 *Ocean Development and International Law* 127 (1999) and John Hare, "Port State Control: Strong Medicine to Cure a Sick Industry", 26 *Georgia Journal of International and Comparative Law* 571 (1997).

A. Kirchner (ed.), International Maritime Environmental Law, 137–156.

It is therefore evident that the primary focus will be on the existing interconnections between port State powers and international law provisions relating to the protection of the marine environment, particularly those on vessel-source pollution prevention, and on the role of the former in ensuring that the latter are effectively complied with by States. The relevance of port State powers in connection with other kinds of international regulations, such as, for example, safety- or working standard-related instruments, will not be considered *per se* in the present paper.

In this respect, it is important to note that, by mentioning international law obligations relating to the protection of the marine environment, we are in fact talking about two different, yet equally important and mutually influent, fields of international law, namely, international law of the sea and international environmental law. Although the areas covered by the two subjects clearly overlap to some extent (manifestly with regard to rules relating to prevention of marine environmental damage or degradation, response in case of voluntary or accidental contamination, and management of marine natural resources), the fact remains that these were born as separate branches of international law and are rightly still considered as such.

Law of the sea is notably one of the oldest fields of international law, for some of its governing principles were developed as early as the fifteenth or sixteenth century;[5] moreover, it is nowadays virtually entirely codified in a single international law instrument, the United Nations Convention on the Law of the Sea,[6] opened for signature in Montego Bay on 10 December 1982 (hereinafter, in brief, "Montego Bay Convention"), which largely corresponds to customary law and counts, as of April 2003, 142 contracting parties.[7] International environmental law, in contrast, is relatively young and there exists no single and comprehensive international treaty dealing with environmental issues and concerns, but, rather, a myriad of both binding and non-binding instruments. As is widely known, moreover, this field of international law is characterised by the existence of an intricate web of regional and bilateral agreements and, finally, by the development of a very limited number of customary principles of general application.[8]

---

5 Treatises on international law of the sea include, for example, Robert R. Churchill & Alan V. Lowe, *The law of the sea*, Manchester University Press (Manchester), 3rd ed., 1999; Laurent Lucchini and Michel Voelckel, *Droit de la mer*, Pedone (Paris), 1990; Edward D. Brown, *The International Law of the Sea*, vol. I, Dartmouth (Aldershot/Brookfield USA/Singapore/Sydney), 1994.

6 The text of the Convention is published in 21 *International Legal Materials* 1261 (1982). For an article-by-article analysis of the Montego Bay Convention see Myron H. Nordquist (ed.-in-chief), *United Nations Convention on the Law of the Sea 1982. A Commentary*, Martinus Nijhoff Publishers (Dordrecht/Boston/London), 1985–1995. On the law of the sea codification process, see also Tullio Treves, "Codification du Droit International et Pratique des États dans le Droit de la Mer", in 223 *Recueil des Cours* 9 (1990).

7 As at 11 April 2003 (source: Treaty Section of the Office of Legal Affairs of the United Nations, Status of Multilateral Treaties Deposited with the Secretary-General).

8 Treatises on international environmental law include, for example, Patricia W. Birnie and Alan E. Boyle, *International Law and the Environment*, Clarendon Press (Oxford), 2nd ed., 2002; PHILIPPE SANDS, *Principles of international law*, vol. I, Manchester University Press (Manchester/New York), 1995; Edith Brown Weiss et aa., *International Environmental Law and Policy*, Aspen Law & Business (Gaithesburg/New York), 1998; Alexandre Kiss & Jean-Pierre Beurier, *Droit international de l'environnement*, 2e éd., Pedone (Paris), 2000; JOSÉ JUSTE RUIZ, *Derecho internacional del medio ambiente*, Mc Graw-Hill (Madrid), 1999.

The fact that a number of agreements have been adopted in recent years dealing with prevention of, and response to, marine environmental degradation, especially within the institutional framework provided by the International Maritime Organization (IMO),[9] demonstrates the ever-increasing need for interaction between, on the one hand, principles and rules of international law of the sea and, on the other hand, instruments and concepts that are typical of international environmental law.[10] The view is taken here that PSC, in itself, is one of the clearest examples of the fact that the interaction between such different normative systems is becoming more and more inevitable, and will constitute the necessary theoretical legal background for any future development of marine environmental regulation at the international level.

Given such a complex scenario, the decision has been taken to focus on compliance issues, since it is believed that, at the present stage of development of international environmental law, and – in particular – of marine environmental law, compliance represents "the" crucial question to be addressed. As authoritatively noted in a recent thorough study on compliance with international environmental agreements, "we know very little about actual implementation and compliance with treaties and other international instruments that have been negotiated, despite their importance and growing number".[11] This is an especially topical issue with regard

---

9 IMO's work in the marine environmental field covers *inter alia* civil liability as well as pollution prevention issues. Examples of the former include the International Convention on Civil Liability for Oil Pollution of 29 November 1969 (published in 8 *International Legal Materials* 453 (1969), entered into force on 19 June 1975 and subsequently amended in 1976, 1984, 1992 and 2000); the Convention on the Establishment of an International Fund for Compensation of Oil Pollution Damage of 18 December 1971 (published in 11 *International Legal Materials* 284 (1972), entered into force on 16 October 1978 and subsequently amended in 1976, 1984, 1992 and 2000); the International Convention on Liability and Compensation for Damage in Connection with the Carriage of Hazardous and Noxious Substances by Sea of 3 May 1996 (published in 35 *International Legal Materials* 1406 (1996), not yet in force). An example of the latter is provided by the 1973/1978 Marpol Convention, on which see *infra*, text at fn. 32. For an analysis of IMO's role with specific regard to PSC, see Heike Hoppe, "Port State Control – an update on IMO's work", *IMO News*, 2000, vol. 1, 9.

10 For similar perspectives, see Patricia W. Birnie, "Implementation of IMO Regulations and Oceans Policy Post-UNCLOS and Post-UNCED", in Myron H. Nordquist and John Norton Moore (eds.), *Current Maritime Issues and the International Maritime Organization*, Martinus Nijhoff Publishers (The Hague/Boston/London), 1999, 361; Louise De La Fayette, "The Marine Environment Protection Committee: The Conjunction of the Law of the Sea and International Environmental Law", 16 *The International Journal of Marine and Coastal Law* 155 (2001); Sergio M. Carbone, "Diritto internazionale e protezione dell'ambiente marino dall'inquinamento: sviluppi e prospettive", 103 *Il diritto marittimo* 956 (2001); Tullio Treves, "Il nuovo diritto del mare e le convenzioni internazionali sulla protezione dell'ambiente marino", 101 *Il diritto marittimo* 201 (1999).

11 Edith Brown Weiss and Harold K. Jacobson, "A Framework for Analysis", in Edith Brown Weiss & Harold K. Jacobson (eds.), *Engaging Countries. Strengthening Compliance with International Environmental Accords*, MIT Press (Cambridge, Mass./London), 1998, 1. Works on compliance with international environmental agreements are increasing in number; in addition to the one that has just been cited see e.g. Rüdiger Wolfrum, "Means of ensuring compliance with and enforcement of international environmental law", in 272 *Recueil des Cours*, 9 (1998) (for a comprehensive discussion on existing mechanisms for ensuring compliance with international environmental obligations) and Malgosia A. Fitzmaurice and Catherine Redgwell, "Environmental Non-Compliance Procedures and International Law", in 31 *Netherlands Yearbook of*

to marine environmental law, considering the fact that a constant tension exists between, on the one hand, the continuing search for new, more sophisticated and more effective regulatory instruments, and, on the other hand, the need to ensure that existing agreements are implemented and complied with by the greatest possible number of States. As it will be seen later on in more detail, PSC represents a unique standpoint in this respect, for it may give rise to a number of compliance-related considerations.

After this brief introduction, a basic overview of the existing legal framework relating to port State control and jurisdiction will be set out (§ 2), with a view to providing the fundamental background to the ensuing discussion. The paper will then analyse the role of PSC as an instrument for ensuring compliance with relevant international obligations (§ 3) and some of the peculiar features of PSC as a compliance tool (§ 4). An examination of the recently approved EC Directive on PSC (§ 5) and a series of final remarks (§ 6) will follow.

2. THE EXISTING LEGAL FRAMEWORK ON PORT STATE JURISDICTION AND CONTROL: AN OVERVIEW

As already noted, specific powers of port States are provided for by various kinds of international instruments: codification conventions (such as the aforementioned Montego Bay Convention), multilateral "technical" treaties, agreements among maritime authorities belonging to a particular region, domestic legislations (including EC legislation) and administrative acts. It is therefore virtually impossible to provide a full account of all legal implications of port State jurisdiction[12] and control[13] within the limits of the present paper. An attempt will be made in this section to outline some of the most prominent features of this increasingly important subject of international law.

The first instrument that must be taken into account with regard to port State jurisdiction is undoubtedly the Montego Bay Convention of 1982, which, along

Cont.

International Law, 35 (2000) (with a particular focus on non-compliance procedures and their role as an alternative to State responsibility). On the broad topic of compliance with international agreements generally, reference should also be made to Abram Chayes and Antonia Handler Chayes, *The New Sovereignty: Compliance with International Regulatory Agreements*, Harvard University Press (Cambridge, Mass.), 1995, as well as to the review essay by Harold Hongju Koh, "Why Do Nations Obey International Law?", 106 *Yale Law Journal* 2599 (1996/1997).

12 In the present context, and for the purpose of the following discussion, "port State *jurisdiction*", encompassing both *prescriptive* and *enforcement* jurisdiction, relates to a particular State's right to enact, and react to possible violations of, regulations for the protection of the marine environment. For an in-depth discussion on the concept of jurisdiction, reference can be usefully made to Özçayır, *supra* fn. 1, at 61 *et seq*.

13 "Port State *control*" is the expression used by a number of regional Memoranda of Understanding (on which see *infra* under §§ 3 and 4); it relates to the possibility for the competent authority within a given port to inspect a foreign vessel's documentation and, under particular circumstances, the vessel itself and to take appropriate measures if any deficiency is found (see *infra* under § 4). See Özçayır, *supra* fn. 1, at 93 *et seq*.

with provisions relating to flag States and coastal States, deals with port State powers in its Part XII – "*Protection and preservation of the marine environment*", and particularly at articles 211 and 218, setting out "prescriptive powers" and "enforcement powers" of port States, respectively.[14]

Article 211, at its paragraph 3, recognises the right of States to establish

> particular requirements for the prevention, reduction and control of pollution of the marine environment as a condition for the entry of foreign vessels into their ports or internal waters or for a call at their off-shore terminals

and requires them to give

> due publicity to such requirements and… communicate them to the competent international organization.[15]

Whilst article 211 sets out the limits within which port States may enact domestic rules and standards, article 218,[16] under the heading "*Enforcement by port States*", establishes, at its paragraph 1, that

> [w]hen a vessel is voluntarily within a port or at an off-shore terminal of a State, that State may undertake investigations and, where the evidence so warrants, institute proceedings in respect of any discharge from that vessel outside the internal waters, territorial sea or exclusive economic zone of that State in violation of applicable international rules and standards established through the competent international organization or general diplomatic conference.[17]

Furthermore, according to paragraph 3,

> [w]hen a vessel is voluntarily within a port or at an off-shore terminal of a State, that State shall, as far as practicable, comply with requests from any State for investigation of a discharge violation referred to in paragraph 1, believed to have occurred in, caused, or

---

14 On articles 211 and 218, and for exhaustive documentary references, see Nordquist (ed.-in-chief), *supra* fn. 6, vol. IV, at 176 and 258, respectively.

15 Article 211, paragraph 3, also provides that, "[w]henever such requirements are established in identical form by two or more coastal States in an endeavour to harmonize policy", parties are bound to indicate "which States are participating in such cooperative arrangements". In addition, "[e]very State shall require the master of a vessel flying its flag or of its registry, when navigating within the territorial sea of a State participating in such cooperative arrangements, to furnish, upon the request of that State, information as to whether it is proceeding to a State of the same region participating in such cooperative arrangements and, if so, to indicate whether it complies with the port entry requirements of that State". As made clear by article 218, this is without prejudice to the continued exercise by a vessel of its right of innocent passage or to the application of article 25, paragraph 2, of the Convention (recognising the coastal State's right to take the necessary steps to prevent any breach of the conditions to which admission of ships to internal waters, or a call at a port facility outside internal waters, is subject).

16 For a comprehensive analysis of article 218 of the Montego Bay Convention see Ted L. McDorman, "Port State Enforcement: A Comment on Article 218 of the 1982 Law of the Sea Convention", 28 *Journal of Maritime Law and Commerce* 305 (1997).

17 It is however stipulated, in paragraph 2, that "[n]o proceedings pursuant to paragraph 1 shall be instituted in respect of a discharge violation in the internal waters, territorial sea or exclusive economic zone of another State unless requested by that State, the flag State, or a State damaged or threatened by the discharge violation, or unless the violation has caused or is likely to cause pollution in the internal waters, territorial sea or exclusive economic zone of the State instituting the proceedings".

threatened damage to the internal waters, territorial sea or exclusive economic zone of the requesting State.[18]

Some clarifications in relation to the above provisions may be appropriate. First of all, it has to be remembered that, as unanimously recognised, it is a cardinal principle of international law that "the jurisdiction of the flag State follows the ship wherever it goes and is not limited to the territory of the flag State",[19] although such a rule is not free from exceptions, as both coastal States and port States (as mentioned above) are recognised limited powers over a foreign vessel under particular circumstances. In this respect, it has also been observed that "[t]he [Montego Bay] Convention makes radical changes in the exclusive character of flag state jurisdiction, but still leaves intact the central principle of earlier conventions that the flag state has primary responsibility for the regulation and control of pollution from its ships".[20] Hence, it may confidently be said that port States appear to be emerging – or have indeed emerged – along with coastal States, as "complementary" or "secondary" jurisdictions, in respect of flag States.[21]

Four aspects of the normative framework provided for by the Montego Bay Convention are generally regarded as of particular importance. First of all, the use of the term "voluntarily" in article 218 excludes from the application of the Convention any vessel that has been compelled howsoever to enter the port at issue.[22] Secondly, both article 211 and article 218 recognise the primacy of international legal standards:[23] States, in fact, on the one hand "shall establish *international rules and standards* to prevent, reduce and control pollution of the marine environment"[24] whilst on the other hand "may undertake investigations and... institute proceedings in respect of

18 The port State shall likewise, as far as practicable, "comply with requests from the flag State for investigation of such a violation, irrespective of where the violation occurred". Finally, according to paragraph 4, "[t]he records of the investigation carried out by a port State pursuant to this article shall be transmitted upon request to the flag State or to the coastal State. Any proceedings instituted by the port State on the basis of such an investigation may, subject to section 7, be suspended at the request of the coastal State when the violation has occurred within its internal waters, territorial sea or exclusive economic zone. The evidence and records of the case, together with any bond or other financial security posted with the authorities of the port State, shall in that event be transmitted to the coastal State. Such transmittal shall preclude the continuation of proceedings in the port State".

19 Özçayır, *supra* fn. 1, at 81.

20 Mario Valenzuela, "Enforcing Rules against Vessel-Source Pollution Degradation of the Marine Environment: Coastal, Flag and Port State Jurisdiction" in Davor Vidas and Willy Østreng (eds.), *Order for the Oceans at the Turn of the Century*, Kluwer Law International (The Hague/Boston/London), 1999, 485, at 492. On the respective roles of flag States and port States, cf. Philippe Boisson, "Le Pouvoir de Police en Matière de Navigabilité; État du Port et État du Pavillon", in 12 *Espaces et Ressources Maritimes* 79 (1998).

21 For a complete analysis of coastal States' jurisdictional powers see Erik Jaap Molenaar, *Coastal State Jurisdiction over Vessel-Source Pollution*, Kluwer Law International (The Hague/Boston/London), 1998. See also the "Final Report" of the International Law Association's Committee on Coastal State Jurisdiction Relating to Marine Pollution, 2000, available at the ILA's website at the address http://www.ila-hq.org (visited on June 24, 2003).

22 See Özçayır, *supra* fn. 1, at 81–82; Kasoulides, *supra* fn. 1, at 125 and Nordquist (ed.-in-chief), *supra* fn. 6, vol. IV, at 272.

23 See Özçayır, *supra* fn. 1, at 84–85. This has to be appreciated in connection with the fact that a need exists for a non-discriminatory use of PSC – a need which is also recognised in the preambular language of the Paris Memorandum of Understanding (on which see *infra*).

24 Emphasis added.

any discharge in violation of applicable *international rules and standards* established through the competent international organization".[25] Thirdly, as far as enforcement is concerned, the *régime* of the Montego Bay Convention can certainly be qualified as a permissive one, since port States have the right to establish particular requirements and "may" institute proceedings, rather than being under a duty to do so.[26] Fourthly, and finally, the proceedings referred to in article 218 may be instituted only in cases where a discharge has actually occurred beyond the territorial waters of the port State concerned: the triggering of the port State's enforcement jurisdiction is thus conditional upon the occurrence of a discharge event.[27]

Before moving to the analysis of other relevant international instruments, it is important to note the content of yet another provision of the Montego Bay Convention, namely article 219, according to which,

> [s]ubject to section 7, States which, upon request or on their own initiative, have ascertained that a vessel within one of their ports or at one of their off-shore terminals is in violation of applicable international rules or standards relating to seaworthiness of vessels and thereby threatens damage to the marine environment, shall, as far as practicable, take administrative measures to prevent the vessel from sailing. Such States may permit the vessel to proceed only to the nearest appropriate repair yard and, upon removal of the causes of the violations, shall permit the vessel to continue immediately.[28]

With regard to article 219, which – as it is quite clear – allows port States to adopt administrative measures in respect of foreign ships, it is interesting to point out the use of the verb "shall" (though somehow limited by the words "as far as practicable") instead of "may", the fact that it appears to be irrelevant whether or not a discharge has previously occurred (as the wording refers to a mere "threat" thereof), and the circumstance that the article does not differentiate between vessels that are voluntarily and vessels that are not voluntarily in a port.[29]

The inclusion of port State-related provisions within the Montego Bay Convention is undoubtedly of paramount importance, due to the almost universal acceptance of the Convention and the general understanding that large portions thereof correspond to international customary law and, as such, may be considered binding on all States, including non-parties, irrespective of ratification. It is, however, doubtful whether this is true as far as port State jurisdiction provisions are concerned. In particular, the view has been taken some time ago that "it cannot be confidently concluded that the provisions [of article 218] have entered into the corpus of customary international law".[30]

---

25 Emphasis added.

26 Both Özçayır, *supra* fn. 1, and McDorman, *supra* fn. 15, at 319, stress the permissive nature of the enforcement regulation provided by the Montego Bay Convention. See also Kasoulides, *supra* fn. 1, at 126: "The port state has only a discretionary power to enforce and may decline to do so" and Nordquist (ed.-in-chief), *supra* fn. 6, vol. IV, at 271: "The article does not impair the primacy of the flag State in enforcement jurisdiction, and is essentially permissive".

27 On the concept of "discharge" reference can be made to Nordquist (ed.-in-chief), *supra* fn. 6, vol. IV, at 271.

28 Section 7 – "Safeguards" establishes the conditions under which proceedings may be instituted under Part II of the Montego Bay Convention.

29 See Nordquist (ed.-in-chief), *supra* fn. 6, vol. IV, at 273.

30 McDorman, *supra* fn. 16, at 320.

Besides the Montego Bay Convention, a number of other international treaties exist containing provisions that recognise and regulate the powers of port States, including a number of conventions adopted under the auspices of IMO.[31] Generally speaking, such agreements, besides providing the right of port States to exercise their jurisdiction over accidents in which the ship may have allegedly been involved, also recognise the possibility for port State authorities to verify whether vessels calling at their ports are carrying the appropriate certificate and, under certain circumstances, ascertain whether the content of the certificate corresponds to the actual condition of the ship.

In particular, if we focus on marine environment-related instruments, mention must be made of the so-called Marpol Convention 1973/78,[32] and in particular of its articles 5 and 6.

Article 6 of the Marpol Convention, "*Detection of violations and enforcement of the Convention*", dealing with port State jurisdiction, introduces, at its paragraph 2, the possibility for port officials in contracting States to inspect a foreign vessel

> for the purpose of verifying whether the ship has discharged any harmful substances in violation of the provisions of the Regulations

annexed to the Convention itself. Moreover, paragraph 5 clarifies that a right of inspection exists in cases where port officials have received a request for an investigation together with "sufficient evidence" that the discharge has taken place.

As for port State control, article 5 "*Certificates and special rules on inspection of ships*", at paragraph 2 provides that

> [a] ship required to hold a certificate in accordance with the provisions of the Regulations is subject, while in the ports or off-shore terminals under the jurisdiction of a Party, to inspection by officers duly authorized by that Party.

Inspections must be limited to verifying that there is on board a valid certificate, unless there are "clear grounds" indicating that the condition of the ship or its equipment does not correspond substantially with the particulars set out by the relevant certificate:

> [i]n that case, or if the ship does not carry a valid certificate, the Party carrying out the inspection shall take such steps as will ensure that the ship shall not sail until it can proceed to sea without presenting an unreasonable threat of harm to the marine environment.

Finally, but most importantly (especially for application purposes), PSC provisions are contained in a number of agreements concluded at a regional level by competent maritime administrations for the purpose of strengthening the enforcement of provisions contained in relevant international treaties such as, for example,

---

31 Özçayır, *supra* fn. 1, at 113 *et seq*. lists five IMO and one ILO (International Labour Organization) conventions providing for PSC, including the Marpol 1973/1978 Convention.

32 Convention for the Prevention of Pollution from Ships of 2 November 1973, as modified by the Protocol of 17 February 1978; the texts of the 1973 Convention and the 1978 Protocol are published in 12 *International Legal Materials* 1319 (1973) and 17 *International Legal Materials* 546 (1978), respectively. For information on the Marpol Convention and its subsequent amendments, reference can be made to the website of the IMO, at the address www.imo.org (visited on June 24, 2003).

Marpol 1973/1978 (and specifically article 5 thereof). The first example of such an endeavour is the Memorandum of Understanding (hereinafter, in brief, MOU) agreed in Paris in 1982 by the representatives of the maritime administrations of 14 European States, and whose membership has subsequently been increased so as to embrace, as of today, 19 parties, including countries such as Canada and the Russian Federation.[33]

The key feature to the Paris MOU is that no new standard or substantive rule is provided for, in addition to the ones contained in the applicable international conventions. Rather, what is required by its members is the fulfilment of a specific target in inspecting vessels that happen to visit any particular port in a participating State in relation to the requirements imposed by "relevant international instruments".[34] The same also holds true in relation to the other regional Memoranda that have followed the European example; in fact, subsequent to the Paris MOU, regional arrangements have so far been concluded in relation to as many as seven maritime regions, namely Latin America, the Asia-Pacific Region, the Caribbean Sea, the Mediterranean Sea, the Indian Ocean, West and Central Africa, and the Black Sea.[35]

As it is quite evident, although no additional obligations are imposed, with respect to such relevant international instruments, and although there is no duty to inspect any given ship, the Paris MOU represents a substantial step forward in the establishment of a port State *régime*, for it discards (in part) the permissive approach taken by the Marpol 1973/1978 Convention, by establishing a system whereby participating maritime administrations are indeed *required to* inspect at least a certain number of ships visiting their ports.[36]

In particular, while recognising that the flag State remains primarily responsible for ensuring compliance with relevant obligations,[37] the Paris MOU calls for maritime authorities of member countries to inspect 25% of the foreign merchant

---

33 The maritime authorities of Belgium, Canada, Croatia, Denmark, Finland, France, Germany, Greece, Iceland, Ireland, Italy, The Netherlands, Norway, Poland, Portugal, the Russian Federation, Spain, Sweden, the United Kingdom are members of the Paris MOU. Slovenia's authority adhered on 15 May 2003, with effect from 22 July 2003.

34 Such "relevant instruments" are listed in section 2.1 of the Paris MOU and consist of ten international conventions including Marpol 1973/1978, the others being: the International Convention on Load Lines, 1966; the Protocol of 1988 relating to the International Convention on Load Lines, 1966; the International Convention for the Safety of Life at Sea, 1974; the Protocol of 1978 relating to the International Convention for the Safety of Life at Sea, 1974; the Protocol of 1988 relating to the International Convention for the Safety of Life at Sea, 1974; the International Convention on Standards of Training, Certification and Watchkeeping for Seafarers, 1978; the Convention on the International Regulations for Preventing Collisions at Sea, 1972; the International Convention on Tonnage Measurement of Ships, 1969; and the Merchant Shipping (Minimum Standards) Convention, 1976. The discussion in the present paper is based on the version of the Paris MOU which is in force at the time of writing. A new, amended version will enter into force on 22 July 2003; this will include reference to two further instruments, namely the Protocol of 1996 to the Merchant Shipping (Minimum Standards) Convention, 1976 and the International Convention on Civil Liability for Oil Pollution Damage, 1992.

35 For an examination of such regional instruments, see McDorman, *supra* fn. 2 and Özçayır, *supra* fn. 1, at 113.

36 See Kasoulides, *supra* fn. 1, at 159 and Özçayır, *supra* fn. 1, at 119. On selected aspects of the Paris MOU, see also "Le contrôle des navires par l'État du port: régime et conséquences commerciales (droit français et droit anglais)", 17 *Annuaire de droit maritime et océanique*, 237 (1999).

37 Paris MOU, Preamble.

ships that entered in their ports in a twelve-month representative period.[38] In connection with the Paris MOU, it is important to note the fact that in 1995 a European Directive was adopted for the purpose of facilitating the application of the Paris MOU across the EC.[39]

3. PORT STATE CONTROL AS AN INSTRUMENT TO ENSURE COMPLIANCE WITH INTERNATIONAL OBLIGATIONS RELATING TO THE PROTECTION OF THE MARINE ENVIRONMENT

Two aspects, at this stage of the discussion, need further explanation. First of all, as we are dealing with compliance issues, it is essential to clarify the meaning of "compliance". Secondly, it is equally important to specify what are the international obligations relating to the protection of the natural environment that come under consideration when analysing the role of PSC.

As regards the first question, *i.e.* the definition of the term "compliance", this – it has to be recognised – is by no means an easy task, especially within the limits of the present paper. Reference will therefore be made, in this respect, to a recent authoritative study, according to which compliance "refers to whether countries in fact adhere to the provisions of the accord and to the implementing measures that they have instituted".[40]

Thus, compliance may be distinguished from implementation (which relates to the adoption by States of domestic laws and regulations pursuant to relevant international obligations), effectiveness (which indicates whether or not the final aim of a given international regulation has actually been achieved, either partially or in its entirety),[41] and enforcement (as this, as mentioned above when discussing jurisdiction, refers to the actual application of a given set of laws or regulations to a particular case).

Moving now to the second question, that is to the range of relevant international obligations that are at issue here, one should recall the introductory remarks regarding the need for a greater interaction between international law of the sea and international environmental law. In fact, on the one hand, it is quite evident that when exercising their PSC powers, States are taking an important action so as to ensure that flag States comply with international obligations imposed on them by instruments such as, for example, the Marpol 1973/1978 Convention. On the other hand, as it is perhaps less evident but equally important, by performing the very same action, port States are actually complying with an international obligation of their own that, although "general", appears to be fundamental, *i.e.* the one

38 Paris MOU, section 1.3.

39 Directive 95/21/EC of the Council of 19 June 1995, in OJEC L 157, p. 1; the Directive and its subsequent developments are dealt with in § 5, below.

40 Brown Weiss and Jacobson, *supra* fn. 11, at 4; according to Wolfrum, *supra* fn. 11, at 29, "compliance means that commitments entered into by a State are fully effectuated in practice".

41 Brown Weiss and Jacobson, *supra* fn. 11, at 4. On "implementation", "compliance" and "enforcement" see also Molenaar, *supra* fn. 21, at 25 *et seq.*

enshrined in article 192 of the Montego Bay Convention, according to which, crucially

> States have the obligation to protect and preserve the marine environment.[42]

Such a general obligation is somehow specified in a subsequent provision of the Convention, paragraph 1 of article 194, where it is stated that

> States shall take, individually or jointly as appropriate, all measures consistent with this Convention that are necessary to prevent, reduce and control pollution of the marine environment from any source, using for this purpose the best practicable means at their disposal and in accordance with their capabilities, and they shall endeavour to harmonize their policies in this connection.

Although, as noted earlier, the Paris MOU does not envisage the kind of port State powers referred to by article 218 of the Montego Bay Convention,[43] measures such as the ones included in article 5 of the Marpol 1973/1978 Convention or in the Paris MOU may certainly be said to be "consistent with" the 1982 Convention. Moreover, one should stress the use of the term "any" to indicate the kind of source that is relevant for the application of article 194, paragraph 1, in contrast, for example, with the wording contained in the following paragraph 2, where it is established that

> States shall take all measures necessary to ensure that activities under their jurisdiction and control are so conducted as not to cause damage by pollution to other States and their environment, and that pollution arising from incidents or activities under their jurisdiction or control does not spread beyond the areas where they exercise sovereign rights in accordance with this Convention.[44]

Clearly, in the context of PSC, international rules relating to the various possible uses of the sea and its resources and international rules on the protection of the environment, intersect and influence each other to an extent that has to be taken into due account.

If we move on, and examine the importance of PSC as a compliance tool in some more detail, it is possible to say that, generally speaking, the range of port State powers (including both jurisdiction and control powers) that have been briefly outlined above has been defined in legal literature as an instrument which is *new*

---

42 See Nordquist (ed.-in-chief), *supra* fn. 6, vol. IV, at 35. Accordingly, it has been clearly stated that "[The Montego Bay Convention] contains comprehensive rules for the protection and preservation of the marine environment and imposes a duty on states to protect the oceans from all sources of pollution": cf. Satya Nandan, "An Introduction to the 1982 United Nations Convention on the Law of the Sea", in Davor Vidas and Willy Østreng (eds.), *supra* fn. 20, 8, at 9.

43 According to McDorman, *supra* fn. 16, at 320, "[t]he MOU is *not* an example of port State enforcement against foreign vessel discharges on the high seas or in the waters of other States" (emphasis in the original).

44 See Nordquist (ed.-in-chief), *supra* fn. 6, vol. IV, at 53. As for the meaning of the phrase "in accordance with this Convention", this should be intended as recalling "that States may only enforce protection measures which are compatible with the Convention as a whole" (*ibid.*, at 64).

and, as already said, *subsidiary in character*, if compared to flag State jurisdiction and control.[45]

Such statements are in principle undoubtedly correct, especially if one takes into account that the principle of a State's jurisdiction over vessels flying its own flag is probably nearly as old as international law itself, whilst port State enforcement in relation to accidents occurring beyond territorial waters belongs, to an area of international law that is still developing and that has probably not yet found its way into customary international law. In addition, Marpol 1973/1978, although establishing a "right of inspection", falls short of making it an international duty imposed on States.

It is submitted, however, that by taking such an approach, and in particular by stressing the subsidiary (or even exceptional) nature of port State powers, rather than its complementary character, one runs the risk of disregarding, or minimising, two fundamental aspects: first of all, the circumstance that a complex regulatory web is already in place, governing the powers of port States in connection with marine environmental protection; secondly, the fact that – especially from a compliance standpoint – PSC is becoming a critical element and a tool that cannot be renounced in the fight against marine environmental degradation.

As was made clear above,[46] the position now is such that international rules and standards (both safety- and environment-related) not only *may be*, but indeed *are*, daily enforced by port State authorities. This is done, as already said, on the basis of relevant regional arrangements among competent maritime authorities and applicable international regulations embodied in instruments such as the Marpol 1973/1978 Convention. Furthermore, additional evidence of this current trend derives from the analysis of the recently approved EC Directive that will be dealt with later on by the present paper.

Of course, it is not possible to deny the primacy of flag State control, nor to forget that vessel-source pollution may be successfully fought on the basis of a wide range of measures, including, but of course not limited to, PSC. However, it is crucial that statements stressing the primacy of flag States in combating marine pollution are not used as arguments so as to reduce the importance of port States in policing the quality of oceans and seas and ensuring that substandard vessels and the pollution problems caused by them are denied citizenship by the world shipping community in the twenty-first century. It must be clearly spelled out that any

45 Port State *jurisdiction* has been characterised as "an innovative expansion of international law" (Kasoulides, *supra* fn. 1, at 126); "a novel development" (Valenzuela, *supra* fn. 20, at 496); "new in the general international law of the sea" and with an "element of innovation" (Nordquist (ed.-in-chief), *supra* fn. 6, vol. IV, at 260); moreover, it has been observed that the adoption of a port State jurisdiction provision does not "not impair the primacy of the flag State in the enforcement jurisdiction" (Nordquist (ed.-in-chief), *supra* fn. 6, vol. IV, at 260), and that "[f]lag state jurisdiction has not been altered" (McDorman, *supra* fn. 2, at 212). As to port State *control*, the view has been taken that although "[i]nternationally the control of foreign merchant ships by port States has been a feature of the Conventions since the 1929 SOLAS Convention…the coordinated application of port State control is a relatively recent development" (Özçayır, *supra* fn. 1, at 93); port State control, moreover, is still generally considered as "the last safety net" within the existing normative system (*ibid.*).

46 See *supra* under § 2.

diminutio of the recognised role of PSC and, more generally, of port States can no longer be accepted at the present stage of development of international environmental regulation.

In connection with what has just been said, the circumstance has to be recognised that the evolution of the PSC *régime*, far from being the "cause" of the erosion of flag State powers, is a mere consequence thereof. In fact, as it has been recently argued, the principle of freedom of the seas (to which the concept of flag State jurisdiction and control is strictly linked) is undergoing a process of profound modification, as an increasing number of limitations and exceptions apply to the traditional rule according to which on the high sea a vessel is only subject to the jurisdiction and control powers of the flag State.[47] The emergence of new interests (such as, for example, a sound management of marine resources) and concepts (such as, for example, the concept of common heritage of mankind) indicates that the traditional principle of freedom of the seas is being progressively replaced by an evolving body of international regulation.[48]

4. THE FEATURES OF PSC AS A COMPLIANCE TOOL

It is well established that compliance with international obligations, and in particular international environmental obligations, is at least as crucial as the drafting and adoption of appropriate treaties and conventions. Fundamental as compliance may be, however, it is probably not yet focussed upon enough by competent institutions and organisations.

Obviously, in order to achieve compliance, it is necessary to have in place appropriate compliance tools, *i.e.* instruments or mechanisms that are able to induce States and other relevant actors to abide by the regulations that have been stipulated at the international level. PSC, clearly, is one such tool. In fact, as seen above in § 3, PSC is primarily designed to compel States to live up to the commitments they have subscribed to. As a matter of fact, as has already been explained in § 3, through PSC both flag States and port States fulfil their obligations relating to the protection of the marine environment.

The view is taken here that, in addition to the arguments that have been presented above, the centrality of PSC is further demonstrated by some of the peculiar

47 Tullio Scovazzi, "The Evolution of International Law of the Sea: New Issues, New Challenges", in *Recueil des cours*, vol. 286 (2000), 41, at 228 *et seq*. According to this author, "the [Montego Bay Convention] should be interpreted in an evolutionary way, especially where the most undesirable consequences of the principle of freedom of the sea and its corollary of exclusive flag State jurisdiction over ships on the high seas become evident and new concepts are not given due consideration" (at 232).

48 "After the adoption of the [Montego Bay Convention], the principle of fishing on the high seas has been practically contradicted by the 1995 UN Fish Stocks Agreement, which introduce the revolutionary idea that States which persistently undermine the measures agreed upon by the others can be excluded from an activity taking place on the high seas. New instances confirm the assumption that régimes based on "first come, first served" criteria are highly undesirable to regulate various matters, be they the protection of underwater cultural heritage or the use of genetic resources of the deep seabed" (*ibid.*).

aspects that – it is submitted – render it a fundamental instrument in the fight against substandard shipping and, in turn, marine environmental degradation. The discussion in the present section is based on the Paris MOU, as that is the first example of a regional arrangement on PSC. It goes without saying, however, that some of the other regional Memoranda that have subsequently been adopted may diverge in one or more respects from the provisions of the Paris MOU, thus lacking some of the features referred to hereunder. The focus has nevertheless been maintained, for the purposes of the present analysis, on the Paris MOU, since this, being the first of this kind of regulatory arrangements, has set the path that has been followed (and, most probably, will continue to be followed) by the other Memoranda, the oldest of which, in any event, was adopted in 1992, *i.e.* ten years after the Paris MOU.

It is generally agreed among international law scholars that compliance may be better pursued when a number of different instruments exist for the purpose of "encouraging" States that are parties to a particular convention to implement the necessary measures at the domestic level and, most importantly, abide by them once they have been put in place. In particular, it is now widely accepted that successful international *régimes* are rarely based solely on the provision of punitive or coercive measures for those States that fail to fulfil their obligations, and that a mixture of performance-based mechanisms has to be established for the purpose of ensuring compliance with international treaties. Whilst writers have proposed different approaches and answers to the question "why" in fact States comply with their international law obligations,[49] with particular regard to international *environmental* treaties, three broad categories of legal and institutional strategies have been identified that are particularly useful for the purposes of the present paper: (i) transparency-based methods; (ii) "positive incentives", or awards *lato sensu*; and finally (iii) "coercive measures", or penalties.[50] These, it has been recommended, should be used in combination with one each other in order to "engage" countries and strengthen compliance with international environmental agreements.[51]

Experience with international environmental treaties that have been in force for some time has demonstrated that all such strategies promote compliance, although the respective relevance of each of them will vary depending, *inter alia*, on the

49 Harold Hongju Koh, *supra* fn. 11.

50 For such a categorisation see Edith Brown Weiss and Harold K. Jacobson, "Assessing the Record and Designing Strategies to Engage Countries", in Brown Weiss and Jacobson (eds.), *supra* fn. 11, 511, at 542. With a somewhat different approach Wolfrum, *supra* fn. 11, at 151, states that it is "appropriate to distinguish between compliance instruments of command and control and incentive-based instruments, the latter being, by their very nature, self implementing" and that "[a]dditionally, it is appropriate to distinguish between confrontational and non-confrontational means of enforcement". From a different (though closely linked) perspective, this appears to hold partly true also as regard the use of economic instruments: cf. Peter H. Sand, "International Economic Instruments for Sustainable Development: Sticks, Carrots and Games", in Peter H. Sand, *Transnational Environmental Law. Lessons in Global Change*, Kluwer Law International (The Hague/Boston/London), 313.

51 Edith Brown Weiss and Harold K. Jacobson, *supra* fn. 50, 511, at 542. As indicated by the following discussion, "sanctions" on, and "incentives" for, ships flying a particular State's flag, because of the consequences they entail and their interplay with the "transparency" element, may be considered as if they were addressed at the State itself and are treated as such.

characteristics of the agreement at issue as well as on the contracting party by which compliance is sought.

If we consider the example of the Paris MOU and the PSC *régime* embodied by it, it is possible to conclude that these represent a very good "mixture" of the three strategies referred to above (or, to put it differently, of "confrontational" and "non-confrontational" compliance methods[52]) and, for this reason, constitute a finely balanced mechanism to ensure compliance with marine environment-related international obligations.

If we focus on sanctions first, it is important to note that the Paris MOU provides for serious penalties in cases where ships are found to be in violation of applicable regulations.

In particular, both detention and banning are provided for as sanctions. As a matter of fact,

> [i]n the case of deficiencies which are clearly hazardous to safety, health or the environment, the [Maritime] Authority will... ensure that the hazard is removed before the ship is allowed to proceed at sea. For this purpose, appropriate action will be taken, which may include detention or a formal prohibition of a ship to continue an operation due to established deficiencies which, individually or together, would render the continued operation hazardous.[53]

Moreover, it is also established that: (i) ships found to be in violation that proceed to sea without complying with the conditions by the relevant maritime authority in the port of inspection and (ii) ships which refuse to comply with the applicable requirements of the relevant instruments by not calling at the indicated repair yard will be refused access to any port within the States the authorities of which are parties to the MOU.[54]

However, "awards" *lato sensu* or, rather, positive incentives, are also recognised as an important element within the Paris MOU system: in fact, the Memorandum provides that the Authorities "will seek to avoid inspecting ships which have been inspected by any of the other Authorities within the previous six months, unless they have clear grounds for inspection"[55] and unless the vessel at issue falls within the ambit of application of section 3.3 of the MOU and section 1 of Annex I to the MOU (so-called "priority inspection").[56] In this respect, mention must also be made by the fundamental "targeting factor", a complex mechanism that enables participating Authorities' resources "to be used more effectively while rewarding well-managed vessels with less frequent inspections"[57] by establishing, also on the basis of previous inspections to which any given ships have been subject in the past, which vessels have priority for inspection purposes.

Finally, as to the transparency element, this is satisfied by the classification system developed within the Paris MOU, whereby flag States are grouped according to

---

52 See Wolfrum, *supra* fn. 11, at 56 *et seq.*, 110 *et seq.*, 151.

53 Paris MOU, section 3.7.1.

54 Paris MOU, section 3.9.1. Banning rules have been further strengthened in the new, amended version of the MOU, in force from 22 July 2003.

55 Paris MOU, section 3.4.

56 On priority inspections see Özçayır, *supra* fn. 1, at 122.

57 Özçayır, *supra* fn. 1, at 123.

their performance under white, grey, and black lists corresponding to very good, average, and poor behaviour, respectively. Moreover, within the black list, flag States are separately listed as posing a "very high risk", a "high risk" or a "medium risk".

The results of such a survey on flag States' performance is published annually as part of the Paris MOU Annual Report,[58] which also details, on a country-by-country basis, the number of inspections that have been carried out by participating maritime authorities and the number of vessels that have been detained: this allows the maritime community to identify "good" and "bad" actors and, according to the "reputation factor",[59] this – at least in theory – should constitute an incentive for bad performers to improve their conduct. The reliability of such data is ensured by the independent nature of the emanating institution and by its frequent updates. Authorities that belong to the Paris MOU, in fact, are required to publish, on a quarterly basis,

> information concerning ships detained during the previous 3-month period and which have been detained more than once during the past 24 months.[60]

In addition, the activities of the Paris MOU are explained and documented in a well-organised Internet website, which among other things lists up-to-date information on ships that have been detained or banned, as well as a database of all inspections that have been carried out.[61] This, arguably, constitutes a further element of transparency: flag States and port States will do their best in order to avoid being regarded as "bad players" within the international community of maritime countries.

5. RECENT DEVELOPMENTS: ADOPTION OF DIRECTIVE 2001/106/EC OF THE EUROPEAN PARLIAMENT AND THE COUNCIL

The concept of PSC has undergone substantial developments not only at the international level, but also within the European legal system. In fact, in order to discourage substandard vessels from calling at European ports, Council Directive 95/21/EC was adopted on 19 June 1995

> concerning the enforcement, in respect of shipping using Community ports and sailing the waters under jurisdiction of Member States, of international standards for ship safety, pollution prevention and shipboard living and working conditions (port State control).[62]

As to the relationship between the Directive and the Paris MOU, it has to be considered that the former was introduced at a time in which the effectiveness of the

58 See e.g. Paris MOU on port State control, *Annual Report*, 2001, at 16 *et seq*, available at the address www.parismou.org (visited on June 24, 2003).
59 Brown Weiss and Jacobson, *supra* fn. 50, at 543; Chayes and Chayes, *supra* fn. 11, at 119.
60 Paris MOU, section 3.14.
61 At the address www.parismou.org (visited on June 24, 2003).
62 OJEC L 157 of 7 July 1995, 1.

latter was under serious criticism, as the available data were showing substantial discrepancies and various degrees of non-compliance among States participating in the Paris MOU. Hence, the decision was made to adopt a legally binding instrument that would require EC member States to enact the necessary domestic measures so as to ensure the effective application of the Paris MOU.[63]

According to its article 1, the Directive aims at reducing

> substandard shipping in the waters under the jurisdiction of Member States by: increasing compliance with international and relevant Community legislation on maritime safety, protection of the marine environment and living and working conditions on board ships of all flags, establishing common criteria for control of ships by the port State and harmonizing procedures on inspection and detention, taking proper account of the commitments made by the maritime authorities of the Member States under the Paris Memorandum of Understanding on Port State Control (MOU).

Under article 5 of the Directive, every member State is required to

> carry out an annual total number of inspections corresponding to at least 25% of the number of individual ships which entered its ports during a representative calendar year.

In addition, vessels that have undergone inspections within the previous six months are not subject to further controls, provided that the ship is not listed in Annex I ("Ships to be considered for priority inspections") to the Directive, no deficiencies were reported following a previous inspection and no clear grounds exist for carrying out an additional inspection. In general, provisions and procedures within the Directive follow the ones of the Paris MOU.

Amendments to Directive 95/21 were adopted in 1998[64] and 1999[65] for the purpose of keeping European legislation up-to-date with international applicable standards and regulations that had been modified since 1995. However, it was after the infamous disaster of the oil tanker *Erika* that the European Commission initiated a comprehensive revision process with the aim of reconsidering some of the substantial aspects of the Directive.

As a matter of fact, the EU has been playing a major role in the aftermath of the *Erika*, by proposing, on the one hand, a thorough revision of international law

---

63 For an in-depth account of the 1995 Directive and its application see Erik Jaap Molenaar, "The EC Directive on port State control in context", 11 *The International Journal of Marine and Coastal Law* 241 (1996) and Özçayır, *supra* fn. 1, at 209 *et seq.*

64 Directive 98/25/EC of the Council, of 27 April 1998, concerning the enforcement, in respect of shipping using Community ports and sailing in the waters under the jurisdiction of the Member States, of international standards for ship safety, pollution prevention and shipboard living and working conditions (port State control) (OJEC L 133 of 7 May 1998, 19) and Directive 98/42/EC of the Commission, of 19 June 1998, amending Council Directive 95/21/EC concerning the enforcement, in respect of shipping using Community ports and sailing in the waters under the jurisdiction of the Member States, of international standards for ship safety, pollution prevention and shipboard living and working conditions (port State control) (OJEC L 184 of 27 June 1998, 40).

65 Directive 99/97/EC of 13 December 1999 amending Council Directive 95/21/EC concerning the enforcement, in respect of shipping using Community ports and sailing in the waters under the jurisdiction of the Member States, of international standards for ship safety, pollution prevention and shipboard living and working conditions (port State control) (OJEC L 331 of 23 December 1999, 67).

instruments relating to both prevention of (and compensation for) oil pollution damage, as well as, on the other hand, the introduction of a novel body of EC legislation (the so-called *Erika I* and *Erika II* packages).[66] It is within such a framework that Directive 2001/106/EC "amending Council Directive 95/21/EC" was adopted by the European Parliament and the Council on 19 December 2001.[67]

An in-depth analysis of Directive 2001/106, let alone of the *Erika* packages and reforms as a whole, clearly goes beyond the scope of the present paper: such an exercise will therefore not even be attempted. What may be of interest, however, is a brief examination of some of the amendments that have been introduced in 2001, for the purpose of locating them within the discussion that has been conducted so far.

---

66 "Communication from the Commission to the European Parliament and the Convention to the European Parliament and the Council on the Seaborne Oil Trade", including a proposal for a "Directive of the European Parliament and of the Council amending Council Directive 95/21/EC concerning the enforcement, in respect of shipping using Community ports and sailing in the waters under the jurisdiction of the Member States, of international standards for ship safety, pollution prevention and shipboard living and working conditions (port State control)", a proposal for a "Directive of the European and of the Council amending directive 94/57/EC on common rules and standards for ship inspection and survey organizations and for the relevant activities of maritime administrations", and a proposal for a "Regulation of the European Parliament and of the Council on the accelerated phasing-in of double hulls or equivalent design requirements of single hull oil tankers" (document COM(2000)142 final of 21 March 2000); "Communication from the Commission to the European Parliament and the Council on a Second Set of Community Measures on Maritime Safety Following the Sinking of the Oil Tanker *Erika*", including a proposal for a "Directive of the European Parliament and of the Council establishing a Community monitoring, control and information system for maritime traffic", a "Regulation of the European Parliament and of the Council on the establishment of a fund for the compensation of oil pollution damage in European waters and related measures" and a "Regulation of the European Parliament and of the Council establishing a European Maritime Safety Agency" (document COM(2000)802 final of 6 December 2000). For a discussion of the consequences of *Erika* and the two European "packages", see Z. Oya Özçayır, *supra* "The 'Erika' and its Aftermath", 7 *International Maritime Law Journal* 230 (2000) and, by the same author, "Erika I' and 'Erika II' packages", 8 *International Maritime Law Journal* 129 (2001). Subsequent to the above Communication, the following acts have been adopted *inter alia* at the EC level: Directive 2001/105 of the European Parliament and of the Council, of 19 December 2001, amending Council Directive 94/57 on common rules and standards for ship inspection and survey organisations and for the relevant activities of maritime administrations (OJEC L 19 of 22 January 2002, 9); Directive 2002/59 of the European Parliament and of the Council, of 27 June 2002, establishing a Community vessel traffic monitoring and information system and repealing Council Directive 93/75/EEC (OJEC L 208 of 5 August 2002, p. 10); Regulation 417/2002 of the European Parliament and of the Council, of 18 February 2002, on the accelerated phasing-in of double hull or equivalent design requirements for single hull oil tankers and repealing Council Regulation (EC) no. 2978/94 (OJEC L 64 of 7 March 2002, 1); Regulation 1406/2002 of the European Parliament and of the Council, of 27 June 2002, establishing a European Maritime Safety Agency (OJEC L 208 of 5 August 2002, 1). For an overview of European initiatives following the disaster of the tanker "Prestige", see also the "Communication from the Commission – Report to the European Council on action to deal with the effects of the Prestige disaster", doc. COM (2003) 105 final, of 5 March 2003.

67 OJEC L 19 of 22 January 2002, 17. Further amendments to Directive 95/21/EC have subsequently been introduced by Directive 2002/84/EC of the European Parliament and of the Council, of 5 November 2002 (OJEC L 324 of 29 November 2002, 53).

As has been observed by a commentator, the *Erika* "focused attention on several weaknesses in the current system of port State control and made it clear that inspections made by the port State control authorities and the classification societies' as well as the oil companies' private inspection systems were insufficient to detect failures in the safety net system".[68]

Among the important innovations brought about by the new Directive, the most crucial is probably represented by the introduction of a requirement for mandatory port State control. According to the amended version of article 5(2)(a), in fact,

> [t]he competent authority shall... ensure that an inspection... is carried out on any ship not subject to an expanded inspection with a target factor greater than 50 in the Sirenac information system, provided that a period of at least one month has elapsed since the last inspection carried out in a port in the MOU region.

A high target factor, however, is not the only ground on which a mandatory inspection may be required, since, according to article 7.1,

> [a] ship in one of the categories in Annex V, section A, is liable to an expanded inspection after a period of 12 months since the last expanded inspection carried out in a port of a State signatory of the MOU,

where Annex V, section A, according to the 2001 text, includes gas and chemical tankers older than 10 years of age, bulk carriers older than 12 years of age, oil tankers with a gross tonnage of more than 3000 gross tonnes and older than 5 years of age and, finally, passenger ships older than 15 years of age other than those falling within the scope of application of Directive 1999/35/EC on a system of mandatory surveys for the safe operation of regular ro-ro ferry and high-speed passenger craft services.

Another novel element provided for by Directive 2001/106/EC is the concept of "access refusal measures" embodied in the amended version of article 7(b) of the 1995 Directive, whereby gas and chemical tankers, bulk carriers, oil tankers, and passenger ships will be refused access to European ports if they *either* fly a black-listed flag according to the Annual Report of the Paris MOU and have been detained more than twice in the preceding 24 months in a port of Paris MOU member State *or* fly the flag of a "very high risk" or "high risk" State according to the Annual Report of the MOU and have been detained more than once in the course of the preceding 36 months in a port of a Paris MOU member State.

An overview of the recent European measures appears to confirm the ever-increasing relevance of PSC in ensuring that members of the maritime community comply with *all* applicable rules and regulations. It has to be recalled that within the last 20 years port State powers have evolved from the initial "permissive" approach to the establishment of precise inspection targets to the creation of a duty to inspect the most dangerous ships, although only at the European level. Undoubtedly, Europe has so far played a major role in this respect, by indicating the path towards effective compliance with international marine environmental regulations. It is very likely that this will continue to be the case in the years to come.

---

68 Özçayır, *supra* fn. 1, at 225.

6. CONCLUDING REMARKS

An attempt has been made in the previous pages to discuss the role of port States and their organs in ensuring that international obligations relating to the protection of the marine environment are effectively complied with.

First of all, the argument has been presented that the future of compliance with international law obligations relating to the protection of the marine environment will increasingly depend on the interaction between international law of the sea and international environmental law. PSC, in particular, clearly constitutes an exemplary mechanism that requires States to fulfil their legal obligations under both *régimes*.

It has also been maintained that, whilst the primacy of the flag State's control powers has surely to be confirmed, PSC must be recognised as an essential function for the purpose of ensuring effective compliance with relevant environmental regulations: by exercising their powers to inspect foreign vessels, in fact, port States not only promote implementation and enforcement by flag States of existing and applicable international standards and rules, but also directly fulfil their own basic obligation, enshrined in article 192 of the Montego Bay Convention, to "protect and preserve the marine environment".

The above view is further strengthened by some of the peculiar features of PSC, as these support the argument that controls carried out by port States, because of their approach based on a "mixture" of performance-based ingredients, represent a uniquely effective method for guaranteeing compliance by both flag and port States with their marine environment-related international obligations.

The most recent development of the field at issue is constituted by the adoption of European Directive 2001/106/EC, which, *inter alia*, establishes for the first time ever a duty to inspect certain vessels whose conditions appear to be particularly threatening. Such a move, part of the post-*Erika* reform packages, has to be welcomed with approval: although the risk exists that European harbours will be regarded hereinafter as "less convenient" because of the increased level of involvement by port organs, this should not necessarily be considered with alarm. On the contrary, the stepping up of port State powers within EU member States may well set an important precedent, as has happened with the adoption of the Paris MOU, for other regional pacts or, perhaps, for the setting up of a global arrangement.

Marine Protected Areas in the Exclusive Economic Zone

*Rainer Lagoni**

INTRODUCTION

The exclusive economic zone (EEZ) is one of the most important developments in the modern law of the sea. With the exception of the Mediterranean Sea, almost all coastal States have established such a zone,[1] and already in 1985 the International Court of Justice[2] considered it as incontestable that the "institution of the exclusive economic zone" had been "shown by practice of States to have become a part of customary international law".

The EEZ forms a "specific legal régime",[3] which is laid down in part V of the UN Convention on Law of the Sea of 1982 (UNCLOS). According to this part, the coastal State has sovereign rights for the purpose of exploring and exploiting, conserving and managing the living or non-living natural resources, and with regard to other economic activities in its EEZ.[4] In addition, the coastal State has, *inter alia*, the exclusive right and jurisdiction with regard to artificial islands, installations and structures.[5]

But the specific legal régime of the EEZ is not limited to the coastal State's rights and jurisdiction. It also provides for the rights and duties of other States in the zone, in particular the freedoms of navigation and overflight and the laying of submarine cables and pipelines.[6] Therefore, with regard to the uses of the sea and the natural resources in the zone, it is an interest-balancing régime: the régime of the EEZ provides a delicate balance between the rights and jurisdiction of the coastal State on the one hand and the rights and freedoms of other States on the other hand.

In recent years, however, the exclusive economic zone has also continued to gain importance from an environmental point of view. Coastal States increasingly tend to consider their EEZ as a zone in which they can designate marine areas for the protection of particular sensitive ecosystems and habitats of threatened and

---

* Professor Dr. *Rainer Lagoni*, LL.M. is the Director of the Law of the Sea and Maritime Law Institute at the University of Hamburg (Germany). Contact: r-lagoni@jura.uni-hamburg.de.

1 There are presently 150 coastal States.

2 Case Concerning the Continental Shelf (Libyan Arab Jamahiriya/Malta), I.C.J. Rep. 1985, p. 33, para. 34; ironically this *obiter dictum* refers to the Mediterranean Sea.

3 Art. 55 UNCLOS.

4 Art. 56(1)(a) UNCLOS.

5 Art. 56(1)(b)(i), Art. 60(1) UNCLOS.

6 Art. 58(1) UNCLOS.

A. Kirchner (ed.), International Maritime Environmental Law, 157–167.

endangered species. Thereby certain obligations to designate such protected areas under the Directive 92/43/EEC on the conservation of natural habitats and of wild fauna and flora of the European Council and the 1992 Convention on Biological Diversity often play a role.

The Law of the Sea Convention mentions marine protected areas in the exclusive economic zone only in Art. 211(6). In State practice, however, there are examples of other kinds of protected areas in the sea. Therefore, in order to avoid confusion, whenever one speaks about marine protected areas one has to say which kind of area is meant. Taking this into account, this paper will deal with the question of whether or not such other kinds of protected areas are compatible with the Law of the Sea Convention. If not, they are incidents of creeping jurisdiction that are incompatible with the specific legal régime of the EEZ.

THE ENVIRONMENTAL RÉGIME OF THE EEZ

When considering the different marine protected areas in the exclusive economic zone, one has to start with the legal régimes of that zone. The Convention contains not only the specific legal régime of Part V relating to the uses of the EEZ and its resources. It also provides a separate régime on the protection and preservation of the marine environment in that zone. This environmental régime of the EEZ is contained in Part XII of the Convention.[7] Nevertheless, the régimes are closely linked to each other. Part V refers to the environmental protection régime in Art. 56(1) lit. (b). According to this provision the coastal State also has in its EEZ "jurisdiction as provided for in the relevant provisions of this Convention with regard to: (iii) the protection and preservation of the marine environment". The plain text of this article leaves no doubt that this is merely a rule of reference, which does not provide any right or jurisdiction for the coastal State.

The environmental régime for the EEZ laid down in Part XII of the Convention is much more complex than the specific legal régime of Part V. It serves different purposes and its provisions have different functions, three of which shall briefly be mentioned here in order to explain the legal foundation and structure of the different marine protected areas.

First, Part XII of the Convention contains certain general obligations of all States to protect and preserve the marine environment.[8] Accordingly, Art. 193 UNCLOS stipulates that States have the sovereign right to exploit their natural resources "in accordance with their duty to protect and preserve the marine environment". The respective obligations of coastal States also apply, of course, in their exclusive economic zone. But these general obligations don't provide any particular right or jurisdiction of the coastal State with regard to its zone.

Second, the environmental régime contains certain duties for coastal States to regulate pollution from sea-bed activities in their exclusive economic zone[9] and to

7 The situation is similar with regard to marine scientific research, which is regulated in Part XIII of UNCLOS.

8 Art. 192 to 196 UNCLOS.

9 Art. 208 UNCLOS.

enforce their respective laws and regulations in the EEZ.[10] Similar duties exist for the regulation and enforcement of dumping in the zone.[11] These duties to regulate and to enforce do necessarily include the respective jurisdiction of the coastal State in its EEZ. Accordingly, the coastal State may designate in its domestic law certain areas in its exclusive economic zone where off-shore activities or dumping are not permitted. Or it may indicate an artificial island as an environmentally protected area. Similarly the coastal State may, on the basis of its sovereign rights over the living resources in the EEZ,[12] determine certain areas of this zone, for example, for the protection of marine mammals. And, taking the aforementioned general obligations to protect the marine environment into account, the coastal State may indeed be obliged to take such measures if, for example, the particular circumstances of a rare and fragile ecosystem so require. Notwithstanding this, such areas which are unilaterally designated by way of the coastal State's domestic law on the basis of its sovereign rights and jurisdiction provided in Part V of the Convention, or on its duty to regulate off-shore activities and dumping in the EEZ, don't affect the freedoms of navigation, overflight and the laying of submarine cables[13] of other States and other lawful uses of the sea related to these freedoms.

Third, under the specific conditions of Art. 211(6) UNCLOS the coastal State may adopt laws and regulations for a particular clearly defined area in its exclusive economic zone, which may become applicable to foreign vessels after a certain period of time. These laws and regulations may be enforced against foreign vessels pursuant to Art. 220(1) and (3) UNCLOS. In this respect the environmental régime of the EEZ is not merely a protective but an interest-balancing régime which is taking the rights and freedoms of other States into account.

In conclusion, beyond its rights and jurisdictions mentioned in Part V and apart from the special provision of Art. 211(6), the Law of the Sea Convention does not provide any general jurisdiction of the coastal State to unilaterally determine marine protected areas in its EEZ. Without the necessary jurisdiction under the Convention, the coastal State may not designate such an area in its EEZ, even if it considers such a measure necessary for the protection of the environment in the zone. However, whether it is possible to set up such marine protected areas on the basis of other international agreements is another question. I will come to this question in a moment.

Nevertheless, before turning to the specific conditions under which the different areas may be designated in the EEZ, I will make a few remarks about pollution and the protection of ecosystems and habitats, because some protected areas shall prevent pollution of the marine environment from vessels, whereas others shall protect the ecosystem and certain habitats against other deleterious effects.

---

10 Art. 214 UNCLOS.

11 Arts 210 and 216 UNCLOS. Criteria to identify sensitive areas, where dumping shall not be permitted, are contained in Annex III B of the 1972 London Dumping Convention.

12 According to Art. 193 UNCLOS, States have the sovereign right to exploit their natural resources "in accordance with their duty to protect and preserve the marine environment."

13 In the case of the laying of a submarine pipeline, however, pursuant to Art. 79(2) UNCLOS the delineation of the course is subject to the consent of the coastal State.

POLLUTION, ECOSYSTEMS AND HABITATS

Part XII of the Convention starts with the straightforward obligation of States "to protect and preserve the marine environment".[14] Although the concept of the protection and preservation of the sea includes more than merely pollution of the marine environment, most provisions of this Part relate expressly to pollution. For the purpose of the Convention "pollution" is defined in Art. 1(1) no. (4) as

> the introduction by man, directly or indirectly, of substances or energy into the marine environment, including estuaries, which results or is likely to result in such deleterious effects as harm to living resources and marine life, hazards to human health, hindrance to marine activities, including fishing and other legitimate uses of the sea, impairing of quality for the use of sea water and the reduction of amenities.

Whilst the definition also mentions harm to "marine life", it is nevertheless limited to the introduction of substances or energy into the marine environment.

Despite the fact that Principle 2 of the 1972 Stockholm Declaration on the Human Environment had already stated the common conviction that "the natural resources of the earth, including the air, water, land, *flora and fauna* and especially representative samples of *natural ecosystems* must be safeguarded for the benefit of present and future generations",[15] the Third United Nations Conference (1973 to 1982) focused on pollution. Pollution was obviously the principal concern of the States at that time with regard to the environmental protection of the sea, and it was an issue on which the Conference could most easily reach consensus.

Nevertheless, the Conference adopted with Art. 194(5) at least one provision which deals with rare and fragile ecosystems and certain habitats of species. It reads:

> The measures taken in accordance with this Part shall include those necessary to protect and preserve rare or fragile ecosystems as well as the habitat of depleted, threatened or endangered species and other forms of marine life.

The protection of ecosystems and habitats is a goal which has to be distinguished from the prevention of pollution. Accordingly, section 5 of Art. 194 UNCLOS provides a separate and independent legal obligation, whilst it is systematically included in an article that deals in its sections 1 to 4 with measures to prevent pollution. This obligation to protect ecosystems and habitats relates to all measures taken in accordance with Part XII. But again, stipulating a general obligation of all States, Art. 194(5) of the Convention is not a jurisdictional rule. It does not create any jurisdiction of the coastal State with regard to its EEZ.

MARINE PROTECTED AREAS WITH REGARD TO POLLUTION FROM VESSELS: MPAs, PSSAs, MARPOL SPECIAL AREAS

Turning now to the marine protected areas, I begin with such areas that shall protect against pollution and other deleterious effects from vessels. These are, first, the

---

14 Art. 192 UNCLOS. This makes clear that pollution is no longer just another freedom of the sea.

15 Stockholm Declaration of the United Nations Conference on the Human Environment, 16 June 1972, ILM Vol. 11 (1972), p. 1416 (emphasis added).

marine protected areas (MPAs) pursuant to Art. 211(6) UNCLOS; second, Particularly Sensitive Sea Areas (PSSAs) identified and designated on the basis of Guidelines of the International Maritime Organization (IMO); and third, Special Areas adopted under MARPOL 73/78. They shall all balance conflicting interests between navigation and the protection of the marine environment. Therefore they have in common that IMO is involved in their designation. The Organization does not miss an opportunity to express its view that "IMO is the only recognised body for introducing measures affecting international shipping in international waters".[16] Nevertheless, the areas differ greatly in the scope of their application, the criteria for their designation, their legal structure, and, last but not least, with regard to the jurisdiction of the respective coastal State or States.

1. Marine Protected Areas Provided for in Art. 211(6) UNCLOS

A marine protected area, in which the coastal State has additional jurisdiction to regulate in its exclusive economic zone, is provided in Art. 211(6) UNCLOS. Pursuant to Art. 211(6) lit.(a) the coastal State may, under specific conditions, designate marine protected areas in its EEZ. The first condition is that the established international rules and standards to prevent, reduce and control pollution from vessels and the adopted ships' routeing systems designed to minimise the threat of accidents must be inadequate to meet the special circumstances of a clearly defined area in the EEZ. And secondly, there must be "recognised technical reasons" that the adoption of "special mandatory measures for the prevention of pollution from vessels is required". The recognised technical reasons shall relate to the "oceanographical and ecological conditions of the area […] and the particular character of its traffic".[17] The same criteria serve for the designation of a Special Area under MARPOL. But as Art. 211(6) lit.(a) additionally mentions the "utilisation or protection of resources" as criteria, the marine protected areas under this provision cover a broader range of purposes than a Special Area under MARPOL 73/78.[18]

Despite these strict requirements, which together must be satisfied in order for an area to be designated,[19] the coastal State cannot proceed on its own. It has to direct a communication to IMO submitting "scientific and technical evidence in support and information on necessary reception facilities".[20] And it is the Organization which shall determine within 12 months "whether the conditions in that area correspond to the requirements set above".[21] Only if IMO so determines, the coastal State may adopt laws and regulations for that area, and it may apply them to foreign vessels 15 months after their submission. But the coastal State's jurisdiction

16 See e.g., IMO Resolution A.720(17), Guidelines for the Designation of Special Areas and the Identification of Particularly Sensitive Sea Areas. Adopted on 6 November 1991, Annex 3.8.2; similarly in: SOLAS 1974, Annex Chapter V Rule 8 b).

17 Art. 211(6) lit.(a) 1st sentence.

18 Identification and Protection of Special Areas and Particularly Sensitive Sea Areas, IMO Doc. MEPC 43/6/2 of 31 March 1999, para. 26.

19 IMO Doc. MEPC 43/6/2 (note 18), paras. 26, 30.

20 Art. 211(6) lit.(a) 2nd sentence.

21 Art. 211(6) lit.(a) 3rd sentence.

to regulate is limited, because it is not free to adopt any laws and regulations it considers appropriate. Only such laws and regulations for the prevention, reduction and control of pollution from vessels, which implement international rules and standards or navigational practices as made applicable through IMO for Special Areas under MARPOL 73/78,[22] may be adopted.

Accordingly, Art. 211(6) lit.(a) UNCLOS provides for the designation of protected areas in the EEZ, which permit the coastal State the same measures that would apply in a Special Area under MARPOL 73/78. As these international rules and standards relate only to discharges from vessels and to navigational practices accepted for Special Areas under MARPOL, this means in practice that the navigation of foreign vessels as well as other internationally lawful uses of the sea cannot be excluded from the said marine protected areas. On the other hand, when a sea is already a Special Area under MARPOL, as for example the Baltic Sea is, there is in practice no reason to designate a marine protected area pursuant to Art. 211(6) lit.(a) UNCLOS.

Yet, the Convention contains in lit.(c) of Art. 211(6) UNCLOS an important alternative to lit.(a). This provision adds to its jurisdiction to regulate, because the coastal State may, again with the approval of IMO, adopt additional laws and regulations relating to discharges or navigational practices to those provided under MARPOL 73/78. However, these additional laws and regulations shall not provide for standards of design, construction, manning or equipment other than generally accepted by international rules and standards.

Of considerable practical effect on navigation could be the regulation of navigational practices. Such practices include normally recommendatory measures of ships' routeing, vessel traffic services (VTS) and pilotage.[23] But if IMO would specify that a marine protected area should not only be avoided, but navigation should be prohibited for all or certain classes of ships, the coastal State could even close the respective area in its EEZ. This shows that measures taken under Art. 211(6) lit.(c) of the Convention may go considerably beyond those in Special Areas under MARPOL.

Nevertheless, under both alternatives of Art. 211(6) UNCLOS, the enforcement jurisdiction of the coastal State pursuant to Art. 220 UNCLOS is not affected. The strict requirement for their designation and the limited effects of its first alternative might explain why no protected areas have been designated under Art. 211(6) UNCLOS up to now.

2. Particularly Sensitive Sea Areas (PSSAs)

Of quite a different legal nature are the Particularly Sensitive Sea Areas (PSSAs). In November 2001 the IMO adopted Guidelines for the Identification and

22 Art. 211(6) lit.(a) 4th sentence. Even within IMO there are different interpretations as to whether it is the onus of the coastal State to submit measures to the Organization for approval, or whether IMO itself shall determine the measures, see IMO Doc. MEPC 43/6/2 (note 18), para. 22. The text of lit.(a), the existence of lit.(b) as well as the unilateral nature of the marine protected area give more weight to the first interpretation. Therefore, contrary to the view of the MEPC, the reference to the "special areas" appears to mean MARPOL Special Areas, *id.* para. 30.

23 Only traffic separation schemes, where behaviour of ships is regulated pursuant to Rule 10 of the 1972 Collision Regulations, are mandatory.

Designation of Particularly Sensitive Sea Areas,[24] which replace earlier Guidelines of 1991[25] and 1999.[26] According to the present Guidelines, a "PSSA is an area that needs special protection through action by IMO because of its significance for recognized ecological, socio-economic, or scientific reasons and which may be vulnerable to damage by international shipping activities".[27] Besides vessel traffic, international shipping activities also includes other vessel-based operations that are subject to international regulation in the purview of IMO.

There are considerable differences between the conditions and procedures for the identification of PSSAs, on the one hand, and marine protected areas under Art. 211(6) UNCLOS on the other. The PSSA is identified and the associated protective measures are adopted by IMO upon a proposal of one or more coastal States, whereas a marine protected area under Art. 211(6) UNCLOS is designated by the coastal State or States with the permission of IMO. The procedure to identify a PSSA, for example, does not contain the time-frame stipulated in Art. 211(6) UNCLOS. The two also differ in the scope of their implementation. Unlike a marine protected area under Art. 211(6) UNCLOS, a PSSA is not confined to the EEZ but can be designated in internal waters (where IMO has no competence), archipelagic waters, or in the territorial sea as well, and it may also include a buffer zone.[28] The existing PSSAs, – the Great Barrier Reef,[29] the Cuban Archipelago of Sabana-Camaguey,[30] the Colombian Malpelo Island, the sea areas around the Florida Keys and the Wadden Sea[31] – extend from internal waters[32] into the territorial sea. The Wadden Sea PSSA is almost completely situated in the internal waters of Denmark, Germany and the Netherlands.[33] On the other hand, a PSSA could also include a marine protected area designated under Art. 211(6) UNCLOS.

A PSSA may be identified for ecological socio-economic or scientific reasons. Unlike under Art. 211(6) UNCLOS, these reasons are not cumulative, so that each one can be sufficient to identify a PSSA. The criteria for the identification of a PSSA mentioned in the Guidelines[33] go beyond those of the Convention, because they include social, cultural, scientific, educational and historical reasons as well. These criteria obviously have a greater relevance in the internal waters or territorial sea than in an exclusive economic zone.

Another important difference is the adoption of protective measures associated with the respective area. Whilst under Art. 211(6) UNCLOS either strict MARPOL

---

24 Guidelines for the Designation of Special Areas under MARPOL 73/78 and Guidelines for the Identification and Designation of Particularly Sensitive Sea Areas, IMO Resolution A.927(22). Adopted on 29 November 2001. Published in: IMO Doc. A.22/Res. 927, 15 January 2002.

25 IMO Resolution A.720(17). Adopted on 6 November 1991.

26 IMO Resolution A. 885(21). Adopted on 25 November 1999.

27 Guidelines (note 24), Annex 2, 1.2.

28 Guidelines (note 24), Annex 2, 6.3.

29 Designated through IMO Doc. MEPC 44(30) of November 1990.

30 Designated through IMO Doc. MEPC 74(40) of September 1997.

31 The last three PSSAs are designated in 2002, see IMO Docs. MEPC 46/6/3 and 46/6/2.

32 With the exception of Art. 8(2) UNCLOS, the coastal State has unlimited jurisdiction in its internal waters so that there is hardly a reason to designate a PSSA in these waters. Only a few parts extend into the territorial sea of Germany and the Netherlands.

33 Guidelines (note 24), Annex 2, 4 and 5.

discharge standards (lit.(a)) or additional mandatory discharge measures or navigational practices (lit.(c)) may be adopted, there is a greater variety of protective measures in a PSSA. The Guidelines mention ships' routeing measures, discharge restrictions, operational criteria, and prohibited activities,[34] which shall be specifically tailored to meet the need of the area at risk.[35] The PSSA of the Great Barrier Reef, for example, includes compulsory pilotage and mandatory reporting for certain ships as associated protective measures, and the Cuban PSSA contains, *inter alia*, an area to be avoided. On the other hand, the Wadden Sea PSSA in the North Sea does not envisage any additional protective measures. The purpose of its identification is that consideration shall be given to the particular sensitive environment of the Wadden Sea, which is located in the internal waters. Whether this constitutes more than a sheer act of symbolic environmental policy could certainly be disputed.

Finally, there are two important restrictions with regard to the associated protective measures. First, these measures shall fall within the competence of IMO.[36] The Organization can, upon the application of the coastal State or States, determine only such protective measures for application in the PSSA for which it has competence and a legal basis in existing international agreements such as MARPOL, SOLAS or the Collision Regulations. Therefore the designation of a PSSA provides only for jurisdiction of the coastal State to implement the associated protective measures indicated by IMO for the respective area.

Second, measures proposed for adoption in the territorial sea cannot derogate from the rights and duties of the coastal State in the territorial sea as provided in the Law of the Sea Convention.[37] Accordingly, the designation of a PSSA can affect navigation only by measures that are compatible with the Convention. And, in the same strand, the coastal State cannot take any action against a foreign ship which is not complying with the requirements of the protective measures by means other than those consistent with the Law of the Sea Convention.[38]

3. MARPOL Special Areas

The oldest institutions of this kind intended to prevent pollution of the sea from discharges of ships are the Special Areas designated under MARPOL 73/78 and its Annexes I, II, V.[39] A Special Area is defined as "a sea area where for recognised technical reasons in relation to the oceanographical and ecological conditions and the particular character of its traffic, the adoption of special mandatory methods for the prevention of pollution by oil, noxious liquid substances, or garbage, as applicable, is required".[40] This has been amended by SOx emission control areas under Annex VI[41] against pollution of the sea by ships.

34 Guidelines (note 24), Annex 2, 7.4.2.1(b).
35 Guidelines (note 24), Annex 2, 7.4.2.
36 Guidelines (note 24), Annex 2, 7.4.2.1(a)(ii); otherwise IMO would act *ultra vires*, the measure would be void.
37 Guidelines (note 24), Annex 2, 7.4.2.1(a)(iii) and related footnote.
38 Guidelines (note 24), Annex 2, 7.7.
39 MARPOL Annex I regulation 10(1)(b); Annex II regulation 1(7); Annex V regulation 5.
40 Guidelines (note 24), Annex 1, 2.1.
41 MARPOL Annex VI regulation 14(3)–(7) applying to the Baltic Sea.

Special Areas under MARPOL 73/78 encompass entire seas such as the Baltic and the Mediterranean Sea and other enclosed or semi-enclosed seas[42] including maritime zones of several States. In these areas stricter regulations apply with regard to discharges from ships than in other parts of the sea. Within a MARPOL Special Area, PSSAs as well as marine protected areas under Art. 211(6) UNCLOS may be designated, because the criteria for the designation of these areas are not mutually exclusive.[43]

The criteria for the designation of Special Areas as well as guidance to States in the formulation and submission of applications for the designation are also provided in the Guidelines of IMO.[44] However, unlike PSSAs and marine protected areas under Art. 211(6) UNCLOS, Special Areas under MARPOL are designated by way of an amendment to the relevant MARPOL Annex. Accordingly, they have a conventional basis, which means they are not merely designated by a decision of IMO but agreed by the Contracting Parties to MARPOL 73/78.

OTHER AREAS FOR THE PROTECTION OF THE ENVIRONMENT IN THE SEA

Apart from protected areas unilaterally designated by the coastal State on the basis of its jurisdiction in the different maritime zones, and the three kinds of marine protected areas affecting navigation, international law knows various other protected areas in the sea, which are designated on the basis of global or regional agreements. In order to indicate their compatibility with the Law of the Sea Convention, I can only mention a few examples here, without dwelling on their details.

Art. 237 UNCLOS provides that Part XII is without prejudice to existing conventions and agreements for the protection and preservation of the marine environment and to future agreements which may be concluded of the general principles set forth in the Convention. Furthermore, it states that specific obligations assumed under special conventions shall be carried out in a manner consistent with UNCLOS. The general rule of Art. 311(2) adds to this, providing that rights and obligations under other agreements compatible with UNCLOS shall not affect the enjoyment by other States Parties of their rights or the performance of their obligations under the Convention.

Perhaps the most important example of a global convention in point is the 1992 Convention on Biological Diversity (CBD).[45] With regard to "marine and other aquatic ecosystems",[46] it applies, subject to the rights of other States, to processes and activities under the jurisdiction or control of each Contracting Party "within the area of its national jurisdiction or beyond the limits of national jurisdiction".[47] Under the CBD each Contracting Party shall, as far as possible and as appropriate,

42 See MARPOL 73/78 Annex I regulation 10.
43 The Guidelines (note 24), Annex 2, 4.5, confirm this with respect to PSSAs.
44 Guidelines (note 24), Annex 1.
45 Of 5 June 1992, BGBl. 1993 II 1742.
46 Art. 2(1) CBD.
47 Art. 4(b) CBD.

establish “a system of protected areas or areas where special measures need to be taken to conserve biological diversity”.[48] The collision rule of Art. 22(2) CBD stipulates that the Contracting Parties “shall implement this Convention with respect to the marine environment consistently with the rights and obligations of States under the law of the sea”. The “law of the sea” in the sense of this provision, no doubt, means the Law of the Sea Convention and the relevant customary law. Hence, the CBD does not change the régime of coastal States' jurisdiction provided in Parts V and XII of the Convention. It does not add to the jurisdiction of the coastal State with regard to the designation of a protected area, but presupposes it and dwells upon it. Accordingly, the CBD also does not affect other lawful uses of the sea, such as fishing or the laying of submarine cables or pipelines. Therefore, a protected area established pursuant to the CBD could only be designated as a PSSA if it would affect navigation.

The situation is in principle the same under regional conventions for the protection of enclosed or semi-enclosed seas in Europe. In 1994 the Helsinki-Commission recommended the establishment of a system of Baltic Sea Protected Areas (BSPAs) and in 1995 adopted Guidelines for the designation of such BSPAs.[49] Similarly the OSPAR Commission in 1998 adopted a new Annex V[50] to the OSPAR Convention for the Protection of the Marine Environment of the North-East Atlantic of 1992[51] in order to implement the respective obligations of the CBD. For the Mediterranean Sea, where no exclusive economic zones have been established as yet, a Protocol of 1995 on Specially Protected Areas of Mediterranean Importance (SPAMIs)[52] to the 1976 Barcelona Convention exists. In addition, a sub-regional sanctuary for the protection of marine mammals was designated in 1999.[53] Measures taken in these protected areas within the realm of coastal States' jurisdiction, as recognised in the Law of the Sea Convention, are mandatory *erga omnes*, that means for all ships. If, however, such measures exceed the jurisdiction of the coastal State, they are binding only *inter partes* for the States Parties to the respective regional agreement forming their legal basis. This is the case, for example, if the Contracting Parties to the Helsinki-Convention would include military activities in their management plans for the BSPAs,[54] or for measures taken in the Mediterranean Sea based on coastal States' jurisdiction with regard to the EEZ before such a zone has been established.

---

48 Art. 8(a) CBD.

49 Guidelines for Designating Marine and Coastal Baltic Sea Protected Areas (BSPA) and Proposed Protection Categories, Helsinki-Commission, 16th Meeting, Helsinki 14–17 March 1995, Helcom 16/17.

50 Ministerial Meeting of the OSPAR Commission, Sintra: 22–23 July 1998, Annex V On the Protection and Conservation of the Ecosystems and Biological Diversity of the Maritime Area.

51 BGBl. 1994 II 1360.

52 Protocol Concerning Specially Protected Areas and Biological Diversity in the Mediterranean, Madrid 14 October 1994, Art. 8.

53 France, Italy and Monaco: Agreement on the Creation of a Mediterranean Sanctuary for Marine Mammals, Rome 25 November 1999; non-official translation in: International Journal of Marine and Coastal Law (IJMCL), 16 (2001), 142–145.

54 HELCOM Recommendation 15/5 of 10 March 1994, lit.(d).

CONCLUSION

Marine protected areas may only be designated in conformity with the régime of coastal States' jurisdiction as it has been recognised in the 1982 Law of the Sea Convention. Particularly with regard to the exclusive economic zone, the coastal State has no freewheeling jurisdiction to designate such areas unilaterally and to adopt binding measures *vis-à-vis* other States. States can, however, by way of a global or regional agreement, establish such areas, as, e.g., Special Areas under MARPOL 73/78 prove.

Marine protected areas do not affect other internationally lawful uses of the sea, unless the coastal State designating the area has the relevant jurisdiction to adopt mandatory measures. Measures affecting navigation outside the internal waters can only be introduced with the agreement of IMO, the most appropriate way for this being the designation of a PSSA.

Nevertheless, the practice of designating marine protected areas specially tailored for the particular environmental problems of the region – be it the prevention of pollution or the protection and preservation of a rare and fragile ecosystem or the habitat of depleted, threatened or endangered species – as it has internationally increased in particular since the 1992 Rio Summit, is in every respect an important step towards implementing Part XII of the Law of the Sea Convention and the related conventions.

Approaches to the Establishment of Protected Areas on the High Seas

Hjalmar Thiel[1]

1. BACKGROUND

In contrast to the coastal environment, where historical overfishing has been viewed as the first in a sequence of man-induced changes to marine ecosystems (Jackson *et al.* 2001), human interest in the living and non-living resources of the high seas, including the deep sea, only dates from about 40 years ago. Interest initially was in mining mineral resources, then in using this remote space as a repository for waste, also to harvest its living resources and, finally, to prospect for commercially valuable genetic resources at the seafloor. One might assume that there exists little life in this vast habitat which needs protection, but the occurrence of exploitable living resources contradicts this assumption. Fishing for tuna and hunting whales in the surface waters of the high seas is of long standing and well known. Impacts on exploited species have been described, and protective measures discussed (e.g. Fonteneau 2001), and partially realised through regional fisheries organisations and the International Whaling Commission. Their limited success is well known and will not be considered further in this paper. Protective regulations were also issued for bycatch such as seabirds caught in tuna fisheries (e.g. Cousins *et al.* 2001, Gilman 2001, Thiel and Gilman 2001). Hereon I concentrate on resources of the deep sea, and on the impacts on this remote world caused by their exploitation.

Activities by scientists, national or international committees, governmental and non-governmental organisations and industry are reported. But this paper would certainly not be complete if the protection of deep-water species, communities, habitats and biodiversity were considered broadly. It focuses on the high seas, i.e. those regions beyond national jurisdiction. However, many of the ecological facts and the results from discussions related to Exclusive Economic Zone conditions would apply also to the high seas.

2. DEEP-SEA RESOURCES, THEIR USE AND ENVIRONMENTAL IMPACTS

Various resources have been identified in the deep sea, and these are briefly summarised, together with their exploitation methods and impacts on the environment, in Table 1.

---

1 Professor Dr. *Hjalmar Thiel* is an emeritus professor at the University of Hamburg (Germany). Contact: hthiel@uni-hamburg.de.

A. Kirchner (ed.), International Maritime Environmental Law, 169–192.

Table 1. Deep-sea resources, their exploitation methods and environmental impacts

Resource	*Exploitation*	*Impacts*
Fish	Fishing	Over-exploitation, community and habitat disturbance
Ores	Mining	Habitat disturbance and community changes
Space	Waste Storage	Contamination, habitat and community changes
Genetic material	Sampling	Species and habitat disturbance

2.1. Deep-water Fish Stocks and Benthos

Because of over-exploitation of commercial fish populations on the continental shelf, the increasing efficiency in fishing methods, and use of ever more powerful boats and heavier fishing gear, fishing activity has moved slowly from the shelf down the continental slope. It now reaches to a depth of about 2000 m and has expanded to seamounts in Exclusive Economic Zones (EEZs) and high sea areas. Fish stocks of various species do live in high sea habitats and some of them have been exploited at that depth in certain places (e.g. Rogers 1994, Clark 1995, Koslow 1997, Merrett and Haedrich 1997, Clark 1999, Koslow *et al.* 2000, Gordon 2001a, b, International Council for the Exploration of the Sea 2001, Koslow 2001). However, initial profits soon dropped, and in all cases the fisheries did not develop sustainability. Furthermore, over-fishing became noticeable within just a few years (Clark 1995, International Council for the Exploration of the Sea 2001).

The reasons for this are based on the ecology of deep-sea fish species in general, and some plankton species exhibit the same characteristics (Koppelmann pers. comm.). Populations are structured with high percentage of adult specimens of high age and only few young individuals. Reproductive and growth rates are low, and maturity is reached only after many years, in some species only after two or three decades. Such populations are over-fished in periods of a few years and it takes many more years for the stocks to recover, if this does occur at all. The very slow recovery rate of deep-sea populations may result in altered community composition due to competitive energy foraging of opportunistic species and modified numerical dominance. The term "fishing down the food web" (Pauly *et al.* 1998, Williams 1998) well describes the process of top predator reduction and changes in species composition applying also to deep-water communities. Calculations for deep-living species have resulted in sustainable fishing rates of stocks at no more than about 1–2% per year, and for the sake of protection of fish stocks one can only hope that such low rates would preclude commercial fishing, because catch per unit effort would be too low. In unregulated situations, fisheries may move to other places, leaving behind devastated habitats, with the same fate predicted for other habitats and communities subsequently exploited. Clearly, some directives are necessary for the protection of deep-living demersal fish stocks and the benthic communities of which fish and bycatch species are integral parts.

Fishing also has severe impacts on the seafloor and the benthos. Communities in the deep sea exhibit high diversity, *i.e.* they are composed of many species in relation to total biomass. Therefore, fisheries bycatch, of no value for the fishermen and thrown back into the sea, is high, and destructive for all life at the seafloor. This is particularly well described by Richer de Forges *et al.* (2000) and Koslow *et al.* (2001) for seamount communities off southern Australia. In general, deep-sea communities are very sensitive to the extraction of living resources and to severe human disturbances. Both fishery stakeholders and political decision makers have yet to reconcile short-term interests with the long-term need for sustainable fishing and conservation measures for seafloor communities. Until they agree on the introduction of much reduced fishing efforts and catch rates, areas for the protection of deep-living fish and benthic species are an absolute requirement (see below, 3.4).

2.2. Deep-water Coral Reefs and Associated Communities

It is still not widely appreciated that colony-building corals not only exist in the tropical shallow seas, but also flourish in northern cold deep water. The species *Lophelia pertusa* (L.) occurs along the European coast of the Atlantic and in the Norwegian Sea (Long *et al.* 1999, Fossa *et al.* 2000), while species having similar reef-building potential live in other regions (Wilson 1979). The reefs are particularly endangered by bottom trawling (Rogers 1999), and reef structures even have been intentionally destroyed by dragging heavy chains over the seafloor in order to minimise subsequent damage to fishing nets. Cold-water coral reefs may also be stressed or potentially decimated by other activities, such as discharges from oil and gas drilling wastes.

Deep-water corals are important species not only *per se*, but also because of their formation of a carbonate skeleton that may eventually form a structure tens of metres high and kilometres in length. This constitutes a hard substrate for the establishment of specific communities. These are different from the communities living in and on the muddy seafloor around the reef. This coral-determined system requires particular protection (Jensen and Fredriksen 1992, Mortensen *et al.* 1995, Freiwald *et al.* 1997, Rogers 1999, Grehan 2001). Conservation of the deep cold-water reefs is necessary to protect many species within these highly biodiverse communities and their genetic resources (Mortensen *et al.* 1995, Rogers 1999, Baker *et al.* 2001, Grehan *et al.* 2001).

2.3. Chemosynthesis-based Communities

Communities associated with hydrothermal vents, and subsequently cold seeps and gas (methane) hydrates, were first discovered in 1977 (Lonsdale 1977) and, although these specific areas are not commercially exploited, some of them have already been found to be under stress and deserving protection. At these specific places live large numbers of endemic (restricted to these habitats) and unusual species, probably close relatives of ancient life. Many of these organisms are able to thrive in an extreme range of conditions, similar to those found at various times during millions of years in the development of Earth (Gebruk *et al.* 1997, Van Dover 2000, Juniper 2001).

The existence of such life forms has raised considerable interest in various scientific disciplines, including biotechnology (Jannasch 1995). The fascinating hydrothermal vent communities and their geological formations with black and white smokers (seafloor chimneys) have also become targets for eco-tourism. Observations of animals, their collection, and the installation of permanent stations for the observation and recording of various parameters at the vents and seeps is achieved from manned submersibles. Already scientists have noticed their own impacts on the relatively small areas occupied by these faunas. In particular, repeated observations within long-term studies may disturb some of these communities, and scientists are now concerned about the impact of their own intrusion (Mullineaux *et al.* 1998).

Eco-tourism, using the Russian Mir submersibles, down to some vent sites with spectacular black smoker chimneys shooting a muddy hot water fountain into the cold deep-sea water at 2500 m depth, began in 1999, and further dives for tourists are planned. Those dives are conducted in international waters and require no clearance by any governing body. Ballast weights are left behind during each dive, and tourists may want to collect souvenirs. The community of the vent site selected will be disturbed by repeated tourist dives. For example, strong light beams used with the submersibles may have negative effects on the eyes of shrimps concentrating at some of the vents in the Atlantic Ocean (Herring *et al.* 1999).

Hydrothermal vent sites are also locations of polymetallic sulphide precipitation and ore development so that mining – technically feasible today – could impact on these sites and their communities in the future, unless only inactive vent sites sufficiently distant from active ones become the target of miners. The Australian company Nautilus Minerals Corporation Ltd holds two exploration licences, covering massive sulphide deposits (see 3.5) in the Papua New Guinea EEZ, but no such activities are known beyond national jurisdiction (Nautilus Minerals Corporation 2001).

3. APPROACHES FOR THE ESTABLISHMENT OF BIODIVERSITY, SPECIES AND COMMUNITY PROTECTION IN THE DEEP SEA

In the past, various approaches have been initiated for the protection of deep-sea species and communities. These were all launched by scientists realising the threats to species or communities and effects on biodiversity. The creation of reserves for scientific investigations is an approach proposed only recently (Thiel 2001, 2002a, b, see also below, 4).

3.1. Stable Reference Areas

The concept of Stable Reference Areas (SRAs) was first suggested during a conference by the International Union for the Protection of Nature (IUCN, now the World Conservation Union) at Ashkhabad in 1978, and it was further discussed by the Ocean Policy Board of the National Research Council of the United States of America's National Academy of Sciences (National Research Council 1984). These discussions were stimulated by the development of polymetallic nodule mining from the deep sea during the 1970s, and it was concluded that two categories of SARs should be established:

- the Preservational Reference Area (PRA) to serve as a reference area for the natural community development in undisturbed regions, and, for comparison,
- the Impact Reference Area (IRA) to monitor community development after severe disturbance by polymetallic nodule mining.

Both areas must be of sufficient size for a monitoring programme lasting for about two decades. Ecologically they must be similar to mining areas in the wider vicinity, in terms of physical, sedimentological and topographical characteristics, and also the seafloor dwelling community. The PRA must remain undisturbed by all mining activities, and this is the same for the IRA following the primary disturbance by mining.

For the last two decades discussion on SRAs has become rather dormant, as a result of industrial nations stepping back from further developments in deep-sea mining. But they are not forgotten; and now and again they re-appear in discussions. The concept and the need to establish them are known to the International Seabed Authority. However, the development of the mining code is restricted in its first phase to exploration activities of polymetallic nodule mining, and the code for the exploitation phase will be considered in the future. This must include discussions on PRAs and IRAs, where they should be established and to what extent the scientific and monitoring activities are to be conducted by the mining contractors. The number of SRAs is still in ongoing debate. One PRA and one IRA should be established in, or close to, the Indian and the German mining claims in the central Indian Ocean and the Peru Basin in the Southeast Pacific Ocean, respectively. In the North Pacific Ocean, where most of the claims are lined up along the Clarion Clipperton Fracture Zone, probably four PRAs and four IRAs will be sufficient throughout this region.

SRAs – so far restricted to their application with polymetallic nodule mining – can and will be established through regulations by the International Seabed Authority (Lodge in press), having the responsibilities for environmental protection of the Area in relation to seabed mining. The establishment of conserved areas outside the mining claims needs special regulations to result in internationally accepted protection measures.

3.2. The UN Convention on the Law of the Sea

Within the 1982 United Nations Convention on the Law of the Sea (UNCLOS), the protection of the marine environment is well presented in various parts and articles on Fisheries and the Environment Regimes, and these are also relevant for the high seas, although there is no reference explicitly given to regions beyond national jurisdiction. The conservation of resources, based on best scientific evidence, constitutes the aim of these regimes and

> nothing in the Law of the Sea Convention precludes the adoption of some form of marine protected areas on the high-seas

(de Fontaubert 2001, p. 79, also for more details). Protective measures laid down in UNCLOS are subject to various papers in this conference volume (see e.g. the papers from Anderson, Blanco-Bazán, Lodge and McConnell) and will not be considered further in this contribution.

3.3. Self-binding Code for Researchers at Hydrothermal Vents

Scientists have observed impacts on hydrothermal vent sites and their communities, and they are concerned about their own and those of other activities in the vicinity of these concentrations of rare animal species (Tunnicliffe and Juniper 1990, Sarrazin *et al.* 1997, Shank *et al.* 1998). A code of conduct for scientific work at vent sites was developed (Dando and Juniper 2000, Juniper 2001), but this remains a self-regulatory, voluntarily binding restriction within science. It is open for other vent-directed activities like eco-tourism, but it cannot become a binding agreement.

Protective issues should be developed for vent and seep areas and their communities, but certainly, on a global basis, there is no threat to these sites and faunas. Concentration of activities at some sites may result in local or even regional effects and some species may become endangered. It would be an unrealistic target to ask for general protection and management of hydrothermal vent and seep sites, but certain regulations for the protection of species and communities in international waters should be issued. These should include protection measures for sites inhabited by rare species, and also those sites of particular interest to science (see 3.4). Also, for the exploration and exploitation of polymetallic sulphides, binding environmental impact studies should be introduced, and these should be conducted by independent scientific specialists in ecological hydrothermal vent or cold seep research, respectively.

A first step in this direction has been taken by the International Seabed Authority in developing a code for the mining of polymetallic sulphides (International Seabed Authority 2001), which follows the mining code for polymetallic nodules. It seems necessary to take into account the fact that polymetallic sulphide mining will be more localised, penetrating deep into the seafloor, and will involve keeping the mining platform in position for longer periods, in contrast to polymetallic nodule mining, in which the collection of the ore concretions from the sediment surface takes place over large areas, and under slow but permanent steaming. Consequently, the environmental impacts will be different. Also, it remains difficult to evaluate the environmental impacts of polymetallic sulphide mining before sufficient knowledge on the mining techniques and related processes become known.

However, independent of any exploitation of polymetallic sulphide resources and independent from a mining code, protection of some vent and seep sites is necessary and legal provisions should be established.

3.4. Discussions by International Organisations

As an example for the management of deep-living fish species, reference may be made to the activities of the International Council for the Exploration of the Sea (ICES). In 2000 this scientific council received a request from the European Community (Directorate General for Fisheries) to provide potential management measures for deep-water fisheries, and an *ad hoc* working group was established under the Advisory Committee on Fisheries Management.

The working group expressed their concern and proposed very low exploitation rates because of the general ecology of deep-living species (see above, 2.1 and 2.2), but also as a precautionary measure. For many species such advice comes too late because European deep-water fisheries developed substantially throughout the 1980s and 1990s. However, numerous recommendations by the ICES for the immediate reduction of exploitation have not been implemented by political decision makers. Fishery management must learn and accept that deep-sea species and habitats exhibit much higher sensitivities to disturbances than those in shelf regions. Measures to be taken will certainly introduce changes to the structure of the fishing fleets, and this will also have an impact on individual fishermen. The group also stressed the need for intensive fundamental research to learn more about the ecology of the deep-living target species and to allow for extended science-based advice (International Council for the Exploration of the Sea 2001, Hammer 2001).

The discussions within the ICES may become effective for deep-water fish and other species only in European EEZ regions. But ICES recommendations would be the same and could also be applied in high sea regions beyond national or European legislation. ICES is also involved in other discussions, such as the protection of deep-water coral reefs, marine protected areas and the Directive on the Conservation of Natural Habitats and on Wild Plants and Animals issued by the European Community.

The obligations and activities of the International Seabed Authority (ISA), which in accordance with UNCLOS Article 157 (United Nations Convention on the Law of the Sea 1982) and the Agreement (1994) is the organisation through which States Parties to the Convention shall organise and control activities in the Area, are described by Lodge (in press). The important role the Authority has to play for the protection of the marine environment is expressed e.g. in Article 145 requiring this organisation

> to adopt rules, regulations and procedures for, *inter alia*,
>
> (a) the prevention, reduction and control of pollution and other hazards to the marine environment, including the coastline, and of interference with the ecological balance of the marine environment, particular attention being paid to the need for protection from harmful effects of such activities as drilling, dredging, excavation, disposal of wastes, construction and operation or maintenance of installations, pipelines and other devices related to such activities.
>
> (b) the protection and conservation of the natural resources of the Area and the prevention of damage to the flora and fauna of the marine environment.

(Lodge in press based on United Nations Convention on the Law of the Sea 1982). There are many more articles in UNCLOS demanding protective measures for the Area, and the SRAs (see above 3.1) will be included into the mining code phase 2 for the exploitation of deep-sea mineral resources (Lodge in press and pers. comm.). The ISA has also organised workshops for discussion of environmental problems, the development of environmental guidelines, and the stimulation of environmental reaseach and international cooperation (International Seabed Authority 1999, 2002).

Many other committees and organisations are occupied with the problems of marine protected areas, but for deep-water habitats activities are generally restricted to those within EEZs (see below, 3.6). There is one exception, the Convention on the Protection of the Marine Environment of the North-East Atlantic, the OSPAR Convention. The region considered has oceanic borders in 36°N to the South and in 42°W to the West, i.e. reaching from the European continent out to the Mid-Atlantic Ridge, penetrating far into the Area (Figure 1). An OSPAR working group has been established to propose protective measures. This group considers the entire OSPAR region, including the Area of the Northeast Atlantic Ocean (Convention on the Protection of the Marine Environment of the North-east Atlantic 2001). European decisions might become effective in this region (Czybulka 2001) (see below, 4).

Also, the concept of the Particular Sensitive Sea Areas (PSSAs), elaborated by the International Maritime Organization (IMO), are applicable to the high seas (Gjerde 2001a). This regulation, however, aims at protection of areas from shipping and dumping in respect of their renewable resources. It seems hardly possible to propose that a high sea region – particularly deep-sea habitats – should become a PSSA and justify it in terms of potential damage to renewable resources.

The Convention on Biological Diversity together with its Jakarta Mandate encourages states to establish marine and coastal protected areas. The scope of the Convention clearly extends beyond the limits of national jurisdiction, i.e. into the high seas (Vierros *et al.* 2001). Also, in Agenda 21, adopted by the UN Conference on Environment and Development (UNCED), protected areas are described as an important tool for the conservation of biodiversity and habitats in general, and the high seas are not precluded.

In analyzing the various regulations of the conventions and regimes, de Fontaubert (2001, for more details see her paper) arrives at the conclusion that

> the current legal regime should not be viewed as an obstacle to the designation of high-sea MPAs.

However, provisions and responsibilities for the high seas were not determined by UNCLOS and this vacuum should be filled, probably as amendments to this regulatory work already ratified by 136 States Parties, including European Community countries and the European Community as such. Various steps have been undertaken to discuss conservation measures for high sea habitats, such as the Vilm workshop in 2001 (see below, 3.8). Its results were incorporated into the Annual Report for 2001 of the US Secretary General (United Nations 2001a, p. 74; United Nations 2001b, p. 16).

Progress was also achieved during the Informal Consultative Process (ICP, the former UNICPOLOS, United Nations Open-ended Informal Process on Oceans and the Law of the Sea) held in the years 2000–2003. The ICP report (United Nations Open-ended Informal Consultative Process 2002) stresses the need for protective measures on the high seas. This attitude is expressed in many paragraphs, and it is proposed that the UN General Assembly should invite the various United Nations agencies and regional organisations

> to consider urgently how to integrate and improve on a scientific basis the management of risks to such (seamount) fauna … within the framework of the United Nations Convention on the Law of the Sea.

(p. 7, paragraph 20). In paragraph 40 (p. 9)

> It is proposed that the General Assembly should also invite each of the relevant fisheries bodies which have responsibilities for the management of fisheries on the high seas under article 11 of UNCLOS … to consider how to improve the regulation of all aspects of fisheries mangement … taking into account the ecosystem approach.

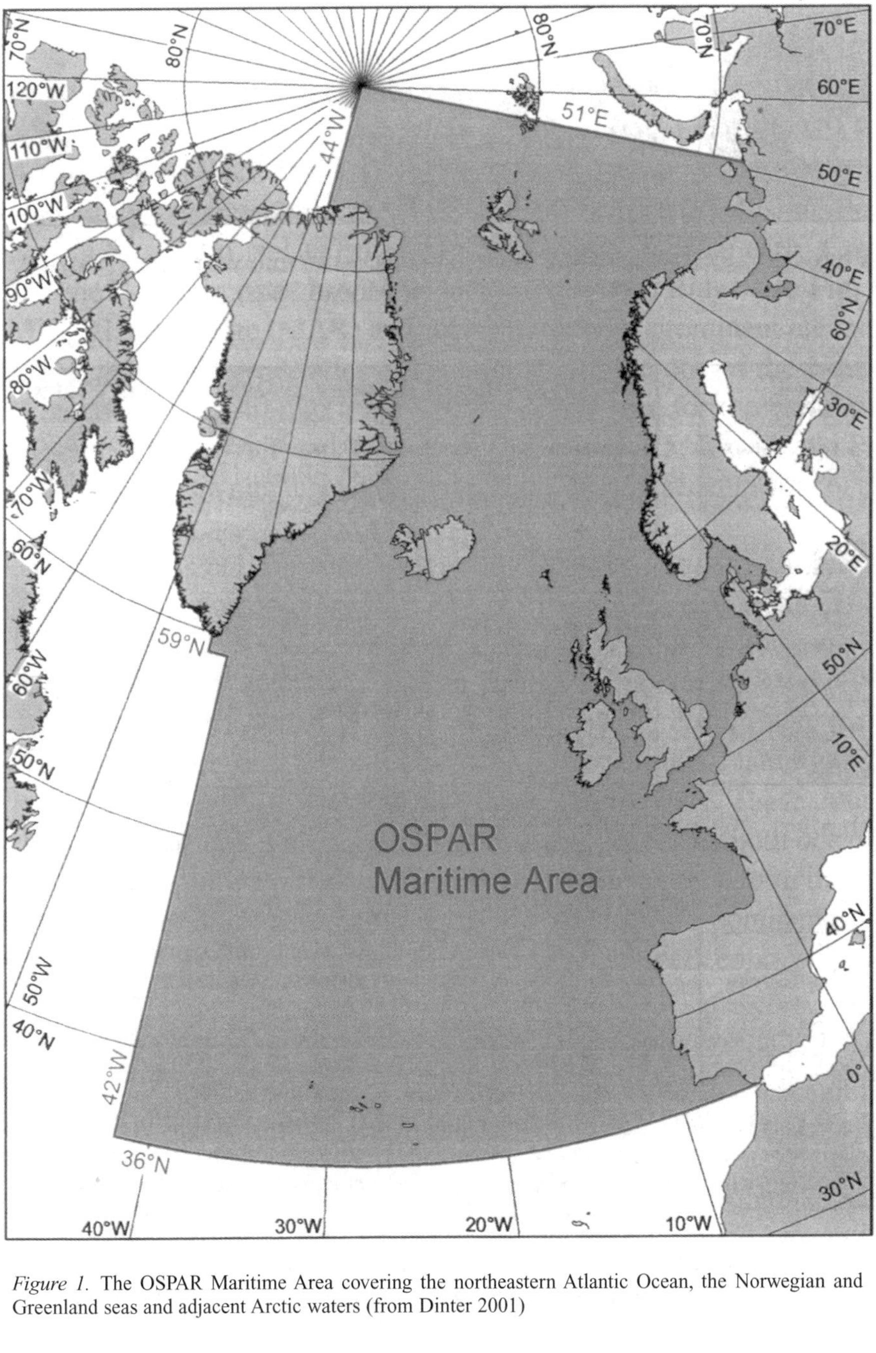

Figure 1. The OSPAR Maritime Area covering the northeastern Atlantic Ocean, the Norwegian and Greenland seas and adjacent Arctic waters (from Dinter 2001)

A subchapter in the ICP report is devoted to

> Protection of marine biodiversity on the high seas

(pp. 30–31, paragraphs 137–143).

> The various activities underline the importance given to the development of mechanisms for the establishment and the awareness for the need of high sea biodiversity protection. The adminstrative processes for arriving at effective protection measures seem to be well underway, and it is hoped that regulations will be available before further severe destruction of habitats, reduction in biodiversity and loss of sustainability in fish stocks occur.

3.5. Provisions for the Protection of Deep-sea Areas in EEZs by States

Protection of deep-water areas has occured in only a few instances. Since this falls into the responsibility of governmental agencies, protected areas were not established in offshore regions before the declaration of exclusive economic zones, followed by time-consuming administrative processes. Up to the present time it seems that only four deep-water regions have been placed under protection.

The United States of America have large regions off the Hawaiian Islands separated for the management of precious coral fishery. The area covers about 1000 km^2 at a depth range from 200 to 500 m.

Australia has been developing a policy for the protection of deep-water areas in national and international waters since 1998, and between various other activities distributed a non-paper during the first UNICPOLOS meeting in 2000 (Osborn 2001, p. 105)

> which expressed Australia's hope:
> that the international community will give serious consideration to the use of MPAs as a tool for integrated oceans management. More specifically, international commitment is needed to advance the global representative system of marine protected areas.

Australia established the Tasmanian Seamounts Marine Reserve, covering an area of 370 km^2 with about 15 seamounts, arising from 1000 to 2000 m depth on the continental slope, and the regions between them. The seamounts, elevating 200 to 500 m above the seafloor, support a benthic community with many rare and endemic species (see above, 2.1). The protected zone encloses the depth from 500 m below the ocean surface to 100 m into the seafloor. Fishing for demersal species, drilling for oil and gas, and exploitation of minerals is not permitted in order to preserve the fish species living above the seabed and the fauna of the seafloor. Such a vertical zonation is comparable to horizontal zoning structures of coastal and terrestrial protected areas to allow for multiple use. Above the Tasmanian Seamounts Marine Reserve access remains open to the long-line tuna fishery (Osborn 2001).

In 2000 Norway declared two neighbouring regions of the Sula Ridge lying to the northwest of Trondheim at depths between 240 to 270 m, altogether about 1300 km^2, to be excluded from all fishing activities. This marine protected area is characterized by reefs of the cold-water coral *Lophelia pertusa* and their communities (see above, 2.2; Freiwald and Wilson 1998, Fossa *et al.* 2000).

In 2002 Portugal established two protected areas in the southwest of the Azores. They cover the hydrothermal vent areas known as "Lucky Strike" (about 200 km^2, around 1700 m water depth) and "Menez Gwen" (about 100 km^2, 850 to about 1500 m water depth), to protect the specific vent communities and the specific geological settings (World-wide Fund for Nature 2001, pers. comm. S. Lutter and S. Christiansen 2002, see also Gebruk *et al.* 1997)

Great Britain is considering the protection of the Darwin Mounds (2002), discovered in 1998 within their 200 nautical miles offshore waters. This region, in depths of about 1000 m, is situated in the northeast corner of the Rockall Trough, immediately south of the Wyville Thomson Ridge and southwest of the Faroe Islands. The area measures about 100 km^2 and includes some hundreds of mounds, each one about 5 m high with a diameter of 100 m. There are living colonies of *Lophelia pertusa* and many other species adapted to this particular habitat. Drilling for oil and gas occurs on the continental margin in the close vicinity of the Darwin Mounds.

3.6. Code of Conduct Developed by Industry

The International Marine Minerals Society (IMMS) adopted in November 2001 a Code for Environmental Management of Marine Mining, demonstrating the awareness of environmental problems arising from mining at all ocean depths. Intensive activities of marine scientists during the 1980s, and for the deep sea particularly during the 1990s, has led to a wide distribution of basic ecological knowledge and the comprehension for the need of protective measures (e.g. Ellis 1989, Thiel and Schriever 1990, Thiel and Foell 1993, Schriever 1995, Foell *et al.* 1997, Thiel *et al.* 1998). The introduction to this IMMS document states (International Marine Mining Society 2002):

> The Code consists of a concise statement of Environmental Principles for the marine mining industry, followed by a set of Operating Guidelines for application as appropriate at specific mining sites. These Guidelines can function for industry as benchmarks for development of environmental management plans, and also for regulatory agencies and other stakeholders at sites targeted for exploration and extraction.

The Code is based on six principles to which marine mining companies commit themselves by their adoption. The principles are based on key phrases (International Marine Minerals Society 2002) such as

the application of
    best practical procedures for environmental and resource protection,
the consideration of
    environmental implications,
the facilitation of
    community partnership on environmental matters,
and reporting
    publicly on environmental performances and implementation of the Code.

Although this Code does not consider the establishment of protected areas, and may convey no relationship to conservational issues, it demonstrates the awareness of, and the attitude to, the oceanic environment on which negotiations with protection targets may be based. This is certainly different from the climate two decades ago and should lead to comfortable discussions and guide positive results for the declaration of protected areas.

3.7. Activities by Non-governmental Organisations

In relation to the exploitation of the deep-sea resources, IUCN already voiced their concern more than 20 years ago, when the SRA concept for the monitoring of polymetallic nodule mining impacts was laid down (see above, 3.1). For many years deep-sea issues remained rather unimportant to non-governmental organizations (NGOs), but were revived by the controversy over the disposal of the oil storage platform Brent Spar (Rice and Owen 1999) and the general trend to establish protected areas in marine environments. In 2000 IUCN held its Second World Conservation Congress in Amman, Jordan, and adopted a resolution on the conservation of marine biodiversity which calls for "implementing effective protection, restoration and sustainable use of biodiversity and ecosystem processes on the high seas" (de Fontaubert 2001, p. 76, Gjerde 2001b). The World Wide Fund for Nature (WWF) and the IUCN together with the World Commission on Protected Areas have commissioned an independent study of high sea habitats, resources and threats, and the legal status for conservative measures for the high seas (Baker *et al.* 2001, de Fontaubert 2001, see also Cripps and Christiansen 2001). These organisations also participated in the Vilm workshop (see 3.8) (Cripps and Christiansen 2001, Gjerde 2001b) and they, as well as Greenpeace (2002), played an active role in the annual ICP conferences in New York.

IUCN and WWF have recently initiated a project to evaluate the potential for high seas marine protected areas from ecological and legal perspectives, and have established a small working group to elaborate a plan for further action (World Conservation Union, IUCN 2002, see also Gerde 2003).

3.8. Workshop on "Managing Risks to Biodiversity and the Environment on the High Sea"

A few years ago some marine ecologists realised the insufficient legal background for the protection of biodiversity and habitats in the areas beyond national jurisdiction. The need for protective measures became apparent with the threats commercial exploitation of the deep-sea resources would have on species and communities. Therefore, an international workshop was organised, funded largely by the German Ministry of the Environment. It was held at the International Academy for Nature Conservation, Isle of Vilm, Germany, 27 February–4 March 2001. Most of the participants were experts on international law, though some came from various organisations for nature protection, and a few were marine ecologists.

A positive interaction between experts with rather different experiences, not always achieved in interdisciplinary conferences, led to the workshop report and to the acceptance of the "Conclusions and Summary Record", published with the report (Thiel and Koslow 2001, see also Gjerde 2001b).

More general key statements from a total of 31 (consecutive numbering of the Conclusions in brackets):

1 (1). The United Nations Convention on the Law of the Sea (UNCLOS) provides the framework for all action to conserve biodiversity and other components of the marine environment of the high seas. It is the bedrock on which all actions must be based.

2 (2). There are areas of the high seas where more effective means of sustainable management and conservation within this framework are considered desirable, and in some cases urgent, to give effect to the obligation to protect and preserve the marine environment.

3 (6). The meeting acknowledged that it had been set up to discuss marine protected areas on the high seas. It was recognized that the phrase 'marine protected areas' is an umbrella term with several applications and which covers a suite of ideas.

4 (8, in part). The conclusions reached by the meeting therefore are not based on any specific concept of 'marine protected areas', but rather discuss management of risks to biodiversity and other components of the marine environment in the high seas.

5 (11, in part). The meeting started with the example of seamount ecosystems. In the first instance, regional fisheries management organisations … (or, in some cases, regionalseas organisations) would be likely to be the appropriate competent international organisation.

6 (13). To provide a safety net and to avoid problems from the absence in some areas of competent regional organisations, global organisations with responsibilities for certain resources (for example, the Convention on Biological Diversity with respect to biodiversity, the Food and Agriculture Organization for living marine resources, the International Seabed Authority for mineral resources in areas beyond national jurisdiction) should consider whether significant threats arise in such areas and what mechanisms could be used to develop appropriate risk management approaches.

7 (15). In addition, it could be appropriate to consider global action to establish risk management approaches. This might *inter alia* take the form of either

(a) a resolution of the U. N. General Assembly on the model of the Driftnet Resolution; or

(b) an initiative to amend or apply an existing international agreement or to establish a new international agreement to cover all problems of a particular nature (for example, seamount ecosystems).

8 (22). Risk management measures would need to be tailored to the specific case, but would also need to be consistent with the obligations, powers and duties established by UNCLOS.

9 (26). The annual report of the United Nations Secretary General on Oceans and the Law of the Sea can be expected to report progress on risk management measures of this kind. This will provide a basis for comparison and evaluation.

10 (31, in part). The meeting suggested that an important subject for early discussion within the UN Informal Consultative Process on Oceans and the Law of the Sea should be the management of risks to biodiversity and other components of the marine environment in the high seas.

Other paragraphs consider risk management, and encourage states and NGOs to review knowledge about biodiversity and other components of the environment in the high seas and to draw connections with the Convention on Biological Diversity.

The Summary Record reports shortly on the papers presented during the workshop and on the results of the general discussion (2.4.7). Some of the topics seem to be of particular interest for further action (pp. 28 and 29, see also Gjerde 2001b):

> Many management measures that would be useful components of an MPA already exist in international law. A combination of actions under existing legal instruments could provide the same degree of protection as some of the hypothetical types of high sea MPAs.
>
> The interpretation of international law on environmental protection is still under debate, but many (of the participants) considered that under certain circumstances high sea MPAs might be established under UNCLOS. The question was however raised whether it is lawful for a country or group of countries to declare a high sea MPA binding on other states, since the freedom of the high seas is one of the most important themes actually defining the term high seas – in areas beyond national jurisdiction. It was agreed that any one attempt could only be legally binding on those nations setting up the MPA.

In every case the rights of legitimate users of the high seas are to be respected, and balanced against the requirements for the protection of biodiversity and habitats.

The "Conclusions and Summary Record" and also the total report were widely distributed, and they were also sent to the United Nations for discussion during the annual CIP conferences (see Simcock 2001 for background information). The workshop and its results, together with other activities, have immediately stimulated the discussion process on the need for high seas protected areas (see above, 3.4). Although fast progress was made from the level of the marine ecologists to the level of the United Nations, one must realise that a long time may elapse until regulations are issued and become effective. Gjerde (2001b), reporting on the workshop, and de Fontaubert (2001) listed some organisations and agreements relevant to the high seas which may achieve faster, or intermediate, protection and conservation (see also IUCN and WWF in 3.7).

However, some of the statements sound promising in terms of achieving the establishment of protected areas before effective UNCLOS regulations are available. According to the above paragraph quoted from p. 29, countries may declare high seas protected areas. There are regions in the deep ocean that could be of interest only to a limited number of countries, e.g. the OSPAR region of the Northeast Atlantic Ocean. The European Community could establish a protected area, and this should result in effective protection (see below, 4), retaining the principles of the freedom of the high seas.

4. UNIQUE SCIENCE PRIORITY AREAS (USPAs)

Effective and potential uses of the deep sea, particularly in the Area, were developed during the second half of the twentieth century, and are shown in Table 2. Dumping of low-level radioactive wastes, sewage sludge and redundant munitions occurred, and further, final storage of waste products was discussed e.g. for carbon dioxide. No ethical argument can be brought forward for land storage versus deep disposal, and a weighted ecological evaluation may argue for using the "deep-sea space" one day, although regulations like the London (Dumping) Convention exist and prevent this – yet are binding only for signatory states – for the time being (comp. Thiel *et al.* 1998, Thiel 2003).

Table 2. Seafloor resources of the high seas – past, present and potential uses

Living resources
Demersal fish stocks
Genetic material
Non-Living resources
Polymetallic nodules
Polymetallic crusts
Polymetallic sulphides:
metalliferous muds
consolidated sulphides
Phosphorites
Oil and gas
Gas hydrates
Resource space for disposal of
Munitions
Radioactive wastes
Sewage sludge
Dredge spoil
Offshore installations
Carbon dioxide

A decision on which area any ocean disposal should be conducted would be based on ecological arguments, but dissolved waste products would be dispersed by currents. Economic considerations will be of importance in such decisions, to limit transport costs. Some regions of the Area are certainly not suitable for waste disposal, and these are the localities of hydrothermal vents, seamounts and e.g. fish spawning grounds.

However, I would like to introduce arguments for reserved regions, independent of the issues of safeguarding species, habitat, community, or biodiversity: the conservation of unique science prioritiy areas (USPAs) (Thiel 2001, 2002a, b). Deep-sea research has developed with increasing intensity during the last 50 years, and progress has been made from descriptive to process and modelling studies. Whereas earlier investigations concentrated on near-continent mostly continental slope and rise regions, central oceanic habitats have been included during the last 20 years, and more importantly, long-term studies have been conducted to understand the natural processes of production and its variability within and between years. Researchers from Great Britain have studied by means of repeat sampling of the occurrence of organisms and the sedimentation of food resources in the region of the Porcupine Seabight (e.g. Rice *et al.* 1991), a wide indentation of the continental shelf in the southwest of Ireland (Figure 2), while another long-term programme was conducted in the area of the Rockall Trough to the west of Ireland and Scotland (Mauchline 1986). Research by scientists from various European nations at a deep position in the Porcupine Abyssal Plain was funded by the European Community through several subsequent contracts (see Thiel and Rice 1995).

During the 1980s and 1990s German activities in deep-sea benthos investigations concentrated some 500 nautical miles to the southwest of Ireland around a central position of 47°N and 20°W. Physical and sedimentological investigations were related to the questions of radioactive waste disposal (Mittelstaedt 1986), and ecological

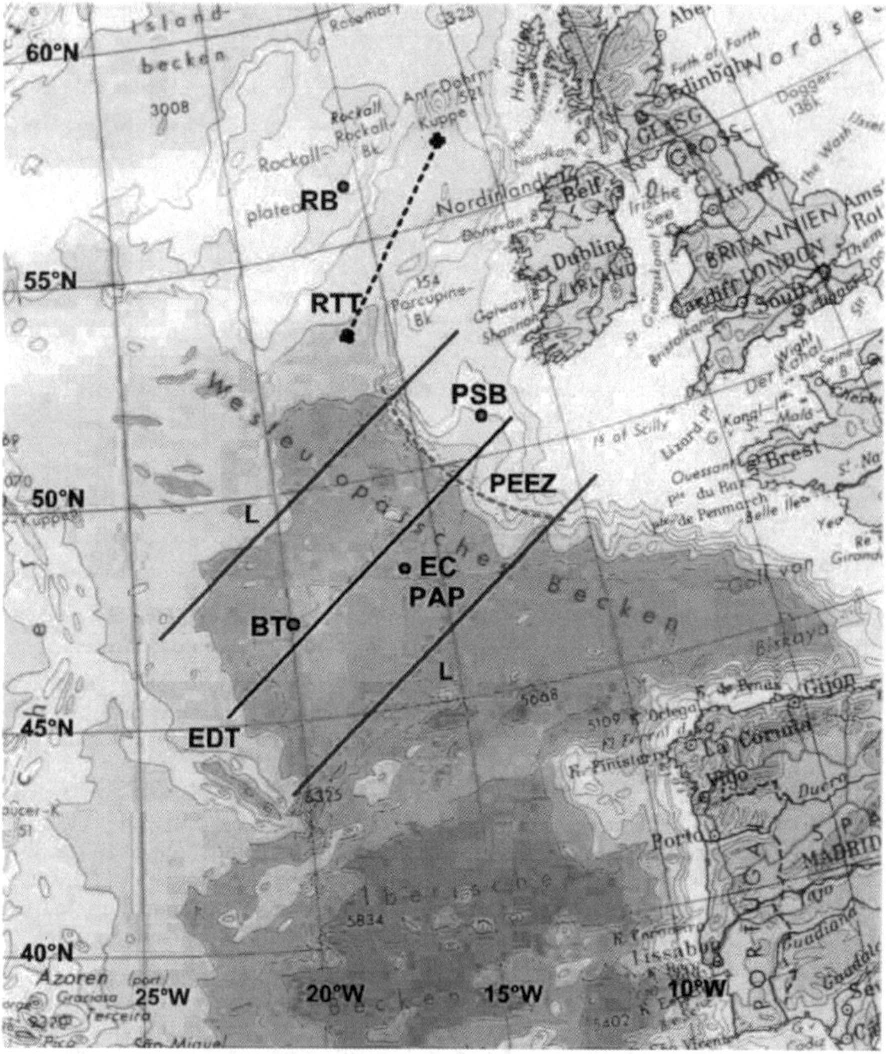

BT	-	BIOTRANS Station
EC	-	European Community Station=
PAP	-	Porcupine Abyssal Plain Station
EDT	-	European Deep-Sea Transect
L	-	Limit of proposed USPA
PEEZ	-	Potential Exclusive Economic Zone
PSB	-	Porcupine Seabight Station
RB	-	Rockall Bank Station
RTT	-	Rockall Trough Transect

Figure 2. "Hot spots" of long-term deep-sea investigations in the northeastern Atlantic Ocean and the Unique Science Priority Area (USPA) combining the stations BT (BIOTRANS/BIO-C-FLUX), EC/PAP (European Community/Porcupine Abyssal Plain) and PSB (Porcupine Seabight) to constitute the European Deep-Sea Transect (EDT) (from Thiel 2002)

studies concentrated on the abundance and distribution of organisms, on seasonally pulsed organic matter and energy income and dissipation, on turnover and production processes (Thiel *et al.* 1989, Pfannkuche *et al.* 1995). The German Ministry for Education and Research and the German Research Council together funded 25 cruises or cruise legs with various research ships to this research field. When the international Joint Global Ocean Flux Study (JGOFS) developed in the late 1980s, the 47°N, 20°W position became the central locality for many international studies, supplementing the existing broad knowledge of the benthic environment with ecological results from the water column (e.g. Lenz *et al.* 1993, Lochte *et al.* 1993).

These are some of the long-term deep-sea research activities of European scientists in the Area, and there exist others, however, in the 200 nautical mile zone, e.g. in the Golf de Gascogne (Laubier and Monniot 1985) and in the Pacific Ocean off the coast of California (Smith and Druffel 1998, Smith and Kaufmann 1999, Smith *et al.* 2001). A broad understanding of deep-sea ecological processes has been gathered at these sites. Those studies must be continued whenever new questions arise or global change monitoring becomes an important issue. The scientific results from these regions should be valued very highly by society. Not only have large investments been made in these and other research projects, but a valuable data base has been assembled which will be important for later, comparative studies. Assuming that waste products would be disposed of in one or more of these scientific "hot spot" areas, the loss of data for later comparisons would be tremendous. I dare to predict that such long-term reference stations would never be re-established. In the interest of society we have to make every effort to protect these long-term study areas for regular monitoring assessments and for research by future generations of scientists.

4.1. Proposal for a Unique Science Priority Area

The central positions of various long-term research programmes in the Northeast Atlantic are presented in Figure 2. Three of them constitute a rather straight line, termed the "European Deep-Sea Transect". These three areas should come under protection, and a buffer zone of 100 nautical miles around their central position should isolate them from other disturbing activities. Such an area is termed "Unique Science Priority Area" (USPA), focusing on its unique importance for past and future scientific work. However, for the demarcation of USPAs, rectangular fields better fulfil the bordering function. Therefore, I propose straight lines in parallel to the central transect at a distance of 100 nm to both sides. This is a proposal, and it needs to be discussed in respect of, various factors. I do not give any coordinates for the corners of this rectangular field, because these should be decided by negotiation, and because the two corners to the northeast fall into a potential Irish or European Exclusive Economic Zone (EEZ). A concerted effort would be necessary to establish such a science priority area. The total area would amount to 120 000 nm^2 or 400 000 km^2 corresponding to the area of Germany. This probably sounds rather unrealistic, but why not ban potentially adverse uses of the deep sea, except for scientific activities, from this region (Thiel 2001, 2002a, b)? European countries, having invested enormous sums of funds into these hot spots of deep-sea research, or even better the European Community, should establish a protected area in the Northeast Atlantic OSPAR region.

This European Deep-Sea Transect USPA is one example for those areas in which scientific investigations have been concentrated during the past two decades. Other such areas exist in the North Atlantic and the Pacific Oceans, and it is hoped that legal and organisational conditions will be developed in the near future to enable USPAs to be established in the deep sea beyond national jurisdiction, for reasons of science priority.

5. CONSEQUENCES

Society must realise that communities or the total organic energy content of deep-water ecosystems, manifested in the living biomass and non-living organic matter, and involved in the energy supply per unit time and organic matter turnover, are not structured for the exploitation of living resources in the context of catch per unit effort and ecological sustainability. This discrepancy cannot be modified or circumnavigated because of the underlying basic ecological rules of the deep-sea ecosystem.

I confess that marine scientists with almost no knowledge of marine environmental law believe it to be a simple process to arrive at legal regulations in respect of the aims of this paper, and to develop mechanisms for the establishment of regulations for the protection of areas on the high seas or in the deep sea. This view is also influenced by the positive evaluation of the total jurisdictional situation drawn by de Fontaubert (2001). Certainly, there are many more problems to be solved than a marine scientist can imagine. In particular, it seems to be the principle of the freedom of the high seas which may be brought forward against protected high sea areas. However, the conflict between the freedom of the high seas and our responsibility for the biosphere must be solved in a spirit of positive compromise. The deep sea as the common heritage of mankind, as formulated in 1967 by Pardo and ratified in 1970 by the United Nations (Pardo 1978), cannot only be used for resource exploitation, but also demands responsibility for the ocean commons as laid down by the United Nations Law of the Sea (1982).

We, the marine scientists, have made the first step. We have expressed our views; we have formulated the actual and potential threats to biodiversity, species and communities; and in precautionary terms we have also articulated the potential loss of biodiversity, and the need for reference areas and scientific decision potentials of interest for the society. We have realised the jurisdictional problems and finally voiced the need for protection measures. The second step falls into the obligation and responsibility of legal experts, politicians and international organisations, in order to establish effective protective regulations for species and communities, whose habitat is the high seas. I ask for help to find a solution for high sea protective measures without compromising the generally accepted principle of the freedom of the high seas.

ACKNOWLEDGEMENTS

I am most grateful to Prof. Dr. John Gage, Oban, for correcting the language of a former version of the manuscript and for providing valuable comments.

REFERENCES

Agreement, 1994. Agreement relating to the Implementation of the Part XI of the United Nations Convention on the Law of the Sea of 10 December 1982, A/RES/48/263, annex.

Anderson, D., 2003. The role of ITLOS as a means of dispute settlement under UNCLOS. pp. 19–30. in: A. Kirchner (ed.), *International Marine Environmental Law*. Kluwer Law International, The Hague.

Baker, C. M., B. J. Bett, D. S. M. Billett and A. D. Rogers, 2001. An environmental perspective. pp. 2–68 in: WWF/IUCN/WCPA (eds). *The Status of Natural Resources on the High-Seas*. WWF/IUCN, Gland, Switzerland.

Blanco-Bazán, A., 2003. The environmental UNCLOS and IMO rules and standards. pp. 31–48. in: A. Kirchner (ed.), *International Marine Environmental Law*. Kluwer Law International, The Hague.

Clark, M. R., 1995. Experience with the management of orange roughy (*Hoplostethus atlanticus*) in New Zealand, and the effect of commercial fishing on stocks over the period 1980–1993. pp. 251–266 in: A. G. Hopper (ed.), *Deep-water Fisheries of the North Atlantic Oceanic Slope*. Dordrecht: Kluwer Academic Publishers.

Clark, M. R., 1999. Fisheries for orange roughy (*Hoplostethus atlanticus*) on seamounts in New Zealand. *Oceanologica Acta* 22, 593–602.

Convention on the Protection of the Marine Environment of the North-east Atlantic (OSPAR Convention), 2001. Summary record. of the 3rd workshop on marine protected areas in the OSPAR region. Fiskbaeckskil, 11–14 June, 2001.

Cripps, S. and S. Christiansen, 2001. A strategic approach to protecting areas on the high-sess. pp. 113–121 in: H. Thiel and J. A. Koslow (eds). Managing Risk to Biodiversity and the Environment on the High Sea, Including Tools such as Marine Protected Areas – Scientific Requirements and Legal Aspects. Proceedings of the Expert Workshop held at the International Academy for Nature Conservation Isle of Vilm, Germany, 27 February–4 March, 2001.

Cousins, K., P. Dalzell and E. Gilman, 2001. International efforts to manage pelagic long-line albatross interactions in the North and Central Pacific Ocean. *Marine Ornithology* 28, 13–24.

Czybulka, D., 2001: The convention on the protection of the marine environment of the North-east Atlantic. pp. 175–184 in: H. Thiel and J. A. Koslow (eds). Managing Risk to Biodiversity and the Environment on the High Sea, Including Tools such as Marine Protected Areas – Scientific Requirements and Legal Aspects. Proceedings of the Expert Workshop held at the International Academy for Nature Conservation Isle of Vilm, Germany, 27 February–4 March, 2001.

Dando, P. and K. Juniper, 2001. Management of Hydrothermal Vent Sites. Report from the InterRidge workshop: Management and conservation of hydrothermal vent ecosystems. Institute of Ocean Sciences, Sidney (Victoria) , B. C., Canada, 28–30 September, 2000. 29 pp.

Darwin Mounds, 2002. See: www.soc.soton.ac.uk/GDD/DEEPSEAS/pages/projects/coral_page/fisheries/impact_fishing.html.

Dayton, P., 1998. Reversal of the burden of proof in fisheries management. *Science* 279, 821–822.

de Fontaubert, A. C., 2001. Legal and political considerations. pp. 69–93 in: WWF/IUCN/WCPA (eds). *The Status of Natural Resources on the High-Seas*. WWF/IUCN, Gland, Switzerland.

Dinter, W. P., 2001. Biogeography of the OSPAR Maritime Area. *A Synopsis and Synthesis of Biogeographical Distribution Patterns for the North-East Atlantic*. Federal Agency for Nature Conservation, Bonn. 167 pp.

Ellis, D., 1989. *Environments at Risk. Case Histories of Impact Assessment*. Springer Verlag, Berlin, Heidelberg. 329 pp.

Foell, E. J., H. Bluhm, C. Borowski, H. Thiel, A. Ahnert and G. Schriever, 1997. German environmental risk assessments in the Southeastern Pacific Peru Basin, DISCOL revisited. Proceedings of the Offshore Technology Conference, Houston, Texas 1997 (OTC Paper 8345), 549–566.

Fonteneau, A., 2001. Potential use of marine protected areas applied to tuna fisheries and offshore pelagic ecosystems. pp. 55–65 in: H. Thiel and J. A. Koslow (eds). Managing Risk to Biodiversity and the Environment on the High Sea, Including Tools such as Marine Protected Areas – Scientific Requirements and Legal Aspects. Proceedings of the Expert Workshop held at the International Academy for Nature Conservation Isle of Vilm, Germany, 27 February–4 March, 2001.

Fossa, J. H., P. B. Mortensen and D. M. Furevik, 2000. *Lophelia*-korallrev langs norskekysten forekomst og tilstand. *Fisken of Havet* 2, 94 pp.

Freiwald, A., R. Henrich, J. Pätzold, 1997. Anatomy of a deep-water coral reef mound from Stjernsund, West-Finnmark, northern Norway. *SEPM Special Publication* 56, 141–161.

Freiwald, A. and J.B. Wilson, 1998. Taphonomy of modern deep, cold-water temperate water coral reefs. *Historical Biology* 13, 37–52.

Gebruk, A. V., S. V. Galkin, A. L. Vareshchaka, L. I. Moskalev and A. J. Southward, 1997. Ecology and biogeography of the hydrothermal vent fauna of the mid-Atlantic ridge. *Advances in Marine Biology* 32, 94–144.

Gilman, E. L., 2001. Integrated management approach to address incidental mortality of seabirds in longline fisheries. *Aquatic Conservation: Marine and Freshwater Ecosystems* 11, 391–414.

Gjerde, K. M., 2001a. Protecting particularly sensitive sea areas from shipping: A review of IMO's new PSSA guidelines. pp. 123–131 in: H. Thiel and J. A. Koslow (eds). Managing Risk to Biodiversity and the Environment on the High Sea, Including Tools such as Marine Protected Areas – Scientific Requirements and Legal Aspects. Proceedings of the Expert Workshop held at the International Academy for Nature Conservation Isle of Vilm, Germany, 27 February–4 March, 2001.

Gjerde, K. M., 2001b. High seas marine protected areas. Participant report of the expert workshop on Managing Risks to Biodiversity and the Environment on the High Seas, Including Tools such as Marine Protected Areas: Scientific Requirements and Legal Aspects. *The International Journal of Marine and Coastal Law* 16, 515–528.

Gjerde, K. M., 2003. Towards a Strategy for High Seas Marine Protected Areas: Proceedings of the IUCN, WCPA and WWF Expert Workshop on High Seas Marine Protected Areas, 15–17 January 2003, Malaga, Spain. IUCN, Gland, Switzerland. 35 pp + 7 Annexes.

Gordon, J. D. M., 2001a. Deep-water fish and fisheries. pp. 31–37 in: H. Thiel and J. A. Koslow (eds). Managing Risk to Biodiversity and the Environment on the High Sea, Including Tools such as Marine Protected Areas – Scientific Requirements and Legal Aspects. Proceedings of the Expert Workshop held at the International Academy for Nature Conservation Isle of Vilm, Germany, 27 February–4 March, 2001.

Gordon, J. D. M., 2001b. Deep-water fisheries at the Atlantic frontier. *Continental Shelf Research* 21, 987–1003.

Greenpeace, 2002. Deep sea marine biodiversity: Fishing the final frontier to extinction? Prepared for the 3rd meeting of the United Nations Open-ended Informal Consultative Process on ocean affairs, New York, 8–15 April, 2002. 3 pp.

Grehan, A. J., 2001. Deep-water coral conservation. pp 67–74 in: H. Thiel and J. A. Koslow (eds). Managing Risk to Biodiversity and the Environment on the High Sea, Including Tools such as Marine Protected Areas – Scientific Requirements and Legal Aspects. Proceedings of the Expert Workshop held at the International Academy for Nature Conservation Isle of Vilm, Germany, 27 February–4 March, 2001.

Grehan, A. J., A. Freiwald and ACES Consortium, 2001. The Atlantic Coral Ecosystem Study (ACES): Forging a new partnership between scientists and principal stakeholders. Proceeding of the First International Symposium on Deep Sea Corals. S. Gass (ed.) EAC/NSIS, Halifax, Nova Scotia, in press.

Hammer, C., 2001. Response by the International Council for the Exploration of the Sea (ICES) to the request for advice on deep water fisheries management by the European Community (EC). pp. 39–40 in: H. Thiel and J. A. Koslow (eds). Managing Risk to Biodiversity and the Environment on the High Sea, Including Tools such as Marine Protected Areas – Scientific Requirements and Legal Aspects. Proceedings of the Expert Workshop held at the International Academy for Nature Conservation Isle of Vilm, Germany, 27 February–4 March, 2001.

Herring, P. J., E. Gaten and P. M. J. Shelton, 1999. Are vent shrimps blinded by science? *Nature* 398 (6723), 116.

International Council for the Exploration of the Sea, 2001. Answer to EC Request for Advice on Deep Sea Fisheries Management. pp. 401–411 in: Reports of the ICES Advisory Committee on Fishery Management, 2000. ICES Cooperative Research Reports, no. 242, 911 pp.

International Marine Minerals Society, 2002. Code for environmental management of marine mining. International Marine Minerals Society, Hawaii, 8 pp. http://www.ngdc.noaa.gov/mgg/imms/imms.html.

International Seabed Authority (ed.), 1999. Deep-sea polymetallic nodule exploration: development of environmental guidelines. Proceedings of the International Seabed Authority's workshop held in Sanja, Hainan Island, People's Republic of China, 1–5 June 1998. Kingston, Jamaica, 289 pp.

International Seabed Authority, 2001. Considerations relating to the regulations for prospecting and exploration for hydrothermal polymetallic sulphides and cobalt-rich crusts in the Area. International Seabed Authority ISBA/7/C/2 (Seventh Session of Council), 11 pp.

International Seabed Authority (ed.), 2002. Polymetallic massive sulphides and cobalt-rich ferromanganese crusts: status and prospects. ISA Technical Study: No. 2. Kingston, Jamaica, 116 pp.

Jackson, J. B. C., M. X. Kirby, W. H. Berger, K. A. Bjorndal, L. W. Botsford, B. J. Bourque, R. H. Bradbury, R. Cooke, J. Erlandsen, J. A. Estes, T. P. Hughes, S. Kidwell, C. B. Lange, H. S. Lenihan, J. M. Pandolfi, C. H. Peterson, R. S. Steneck, M. J. Tegner and R. R. Warner, 2001. Historical overfishing and the recent collapse of coastal ecosystems. *Science* 293, 629–638.

Jannasch, H. W., 1995. Deep-sea hot vents as sources of biotechnologically relevant microorganisms. *Journal of Marine Biotechnology* 3, 5–8.

Jensen, A. and R. Fredriksen, 1992. The fauna associated with the bank-forming deepwater coral *Lophelia pertusa* (Scleractinia) on the Faroe shelf. *Sarsia* 77, 53–69.

Juniper, S. K., 2001. Background paper on deep-sea hydrothermal vents. pp. 89–95 in: H. Thiel and J. A. Koslow (eds). Managing Risk to Biodiversity and the Environment on the High Sea, Including Tools such as Marine Protected Areas – Scientific Requirements and Legal Aspects. Proceedings of the Expert Workshop held at the International Academy for Nature Conservation Isle of Vilm, Germany, 27 February–4 March, 2001.

Juniper, S. K. 2002. Impact of the development of polymetallic massive sulphides on deep-sea hydrothermal vent ecosystems. pp. 101–116 in: International Seabed Authority (ed.), Polymetallic massive sulphides and cobalt-rich ferromanganese crusts: status and prospects. ISA Technical Report No. 2, Kingston, Jamaica.

Koslow, J. A., 1997. Seamounts and the ecology of deep-sea fisheries. *American Scientist* 85, 168–176.

Koslow, J. A., 2001. Fish stocks and benthos on seamounts. pp. 43–54 in: H. Thiel and J. A. Koslow (eds). Managing Risk to Biodiversity and the Environment on the High Sea, Including Tools such as Marine Protected Areas – Scientific Requirements and Legal Aspects. Proceedings of the Expert Workshop held at the International Academy for Nature Conservation Isle of Vilm, Germany, 27 February–4 March 2001.

Koslow, J. A., G. W. Boehlert, J. G. M. Gordon, R. L. Haedrich, P. Lorance and N. Parin, 2000. Continental slope and deep-sea fisheries: implications for a fragile ecosystem. *ICES Journal of Marine Science* 57, 548–557.

Koslow, J. A., K. Gowlett-Holmes, J. K. Lowry, T. O'Hara, G. C. B. Poore and A. Williams, 2001. Seamount benthic macrofauna off southern Tasmania: community structure and impacts of trawling. *Marine Ecology Progress Series* 213, 111–125.

Laubier, L. and C. Monniot (eds), 1985. Peuplements profond du Golfe de Gascogne. Campagnes BIOGAS. Institut Francais de Recherche pour l'Exploration de la Mer, 629 pp.

Lenz, J., A. Morales and J. Gunkel, 1993. Mesozooplankton standing stock during the North Atlantic spring bloom study in 1989 and its potential grazing pressure on phytoplankton: a comparison between low, medium and high latitudes. *Deep-Sea Res. II* 40, 559–572.

Lochte, K., H. W. Ducklow, M. J. R. Fasham and C. Stienen, 1993. Plankton succession and carbon cycling at 47°N 20°W during the JGOFS North Atlantic bloom experiment. *Deep-Sea Res. II* 40, 91–114.

Lodge, M. W., 2003. Environmental regulation of deep seabed mining. pp. 49–60. in: A. Kirchner (ed.), *International Marine Environmental Law*. Kluwer Law International, The Hague.

Long, D., J. M. Roberts and E. J. Gillespie, 1999. Occurrences of *Lophelia pertusa* on the Atlantic margin. British Geological Survey Technical Report WB/99/24.

Lonsdale, P., 1977. Clustering of suspension-feeding macrobenthos near abyssal hydrothermal vents at oceanic spreading centers. *Deep-Sea Research* 24, 857–863.

Mauchline, J. (ed.), 1986. The Oceanography of the Rockall Channel. Proceedings of the Royal Society of Edinburgh, 88B, 356 pp.

McConnell, M., 2003. Inter-agency collaboration or inter-agency competition – a challenge to the UN system. pp. 69–92 in: A. Kirchner (ed.), *International Marine Environmental Law*. Kluwer Law International, The Hague.

Merrett, N. R. and R. L. Haedrich, 1997. *Deep-sea demersal fish and fisheries*. Chapman and Hall, London, 282 pp.

Mittelstaedt, E. (ed.), 1986. Ausbreitungsbedingungen für Stoffe in großen Ozeantiefen. Report, Deutsches Hydrographisches Institut, 202 pp.

Mortensen, P. B., M. Hovland, T. Brattegard and R. Farestveit, 1995. Deep water bioherms of the scleractinian coral *Lophelia pertusa* (L.) at 64°N on the Norwegian shelf: structure and associated megafauna. *Sarsia* 80, 145–158.

Mullineaux, L. S., S. K. Juniper, D. Desbruyères and M. Cannat, 1988. Deep-sea reserves at hydrothermal vents. *EOS, Transactions of the American Geophysical Union* 79 (44), 533–538.

National Research Council, 1984. Deep seabed stable reference areas. Ocean Policy Committee, National Research Council/US National Academy of Sciences,Washington DC, 74 pp.

Osborn, D., 2001. Challenges to conserving marine biodiversity on the high seas through the use of marine protected areas. pp. 103–112 in: H. Thiel and J. A. Koslow (eds). Managing Risk to Biodiversity and the Environment on the High Sea, Including Tools such as Marine Protected Areas – Scientific Requirements and Legal Aspects. Proceedings of the Expert Workshop held at the International Academy for Nature Conservation Isle of Vilm, Germany, 27 February–4 March, 2001.

Nautilus Minerals Corporation, 2001. Nautilus marine exploration licences renewed by PNG government. Press release 18th April, 2001, 1 p.

Pardo, A., 1978. The evolving Law of the Sea: A critique of the informal composite negotiating text. pp. 9–37 in: E. Mann Borgese and N. Ginsburg (eds), *Ocean Yearbook 1*, University of Chicago Press, Chicago.

Pauly, D., V. Christensen, J. Dalsgaard, R. Froese and F. Torres Jr., 1998. Fishing down marine food webs. *Science* 279, 860–863.

Pfannkuche, O., H.-G. Hoppe, H. Thiel, and H. Weikert (eds), 1995. BIO-C-FLUX – Biologischer Kohlenstofffluss in der bodennahen Wasserschicht des küstenfernen Ozeans. Berichte aus dem Institut für Meereskunde an der Christian-Albrechts-Universität Kiel, 280, 114 pp.

Rice, A. L., D. S. M. Billett, M. H. Thurston and R. L. Lampitt, 1991. The Institute of Oceanographic Sciences biology programme in the Porcupine Seabight: background and general introduction. *Journal of the Marine Biological Association of the United Kingdom* 71, 281–310.

Rice, T. and P. Owen, 1999. *Decommissioning the Brent Spar*. E. & F. N. Spon, London and New York, 182 pp.

Richer de Forges, B., J. A. Koslow and G. C. B. Poore, 2000. Diversity and endemism of the benthic seamount fauna in the southwest Pacific. *Nature* 405, 944–947.

Rogers, A., 1994. The biology of seamounts. *Advances in Marine Biology* 30, 305–350.

Rogers, A. D., 1999. The biology of *Lophelia pertusa* (Linneus 1758) and other deep-water reef-forming corals and impacts from human activities. *International Review of Hydrobiology* 84, 315–406.

Sarrazin, J., V. Robigon, S. K. Juniper and J. Delaney, 1997. Biological and geological dynamics over four years on a high-temperature sulphide structure at the Juan de Fuca Ridge hydrothermal observatory. *Marine Ecology Progress Series* 153, 5–24.

Schriever, G., 1995. DISCOL – disturbance and recolonization experiment of a manganese nodule area of the southeastern Pacific. Proceedings of the 1st Ocean Mining Symposium, Tsukuba, Japan, 223–235.

Shank, T. M., D. J. Fornari, K. L. von Damm, M. D. Lilley, R. M. Haymon and R. A. Lutz, 1998. Temporal and spatial patterns of biological community development at nascent deep-sea hydrothermal vents (9°50′N, East Pacific Rise). *Deep-Sea Research II* 45, 465–515.

Simcock, A. J. C., 2001. The UN open-ended Informal Consultative Process on Oceans and the Law of the Sea (UNICPOLOS)–current status. pp. 133–136 in: H. Thiel and J. A. Koslow (eds). Managing Risk to Biodiversity and the Environment on the High Sea, Including Tools such as Marine Protected Areas – Scientific Requirements and Legal Aspects. Proceedings of the Expert Workshop held at the International Academy for Nature Conservation Isle of Vilm, Germany, 27 February–4 March, 2001.

Smith, K. L., Jr. and E. R. M. Druffel, 1998. Long time-series monitoring of an abyssal site in the NE Pacific. *Deep-Sea Research II* 45, 569–913.

Smith, K. L. Jr. and R. S. Kaufmann, 1999. Long-time discrepancy between food supply and demand in the deep eastern North Pacific. *Science* 284, 1174–1177.

Smith, K. L. Jr., R. S. Kaufmann, R. J. Baldwin and A. F. Carlucci, 2001. Pelagic-benthic coupling in the abyssal eastern North Pacific: an 8-year time-series study of food supply and demand. *Limnology and Oceanography* 45, 543–556.

Thiel, H., 2001. Unique science and reference areas on the high sea. pp. 97–102 in: H. Thiel and J. A. Koslow (eds). Managing Risk to Biodiversity and the Environment on the High Sea, Including Tools such as Marine Protected Areas – Scientific Requirements and Legal Aspects. Proceedings of the Expert Workshop held at the International Academy for Nature Conservation Isle of Vilm, Germany, 27 February–4 March, 2001.

Thiel, H., 2002a. Schutzgebiete in der Hohen See pp. 227–231 in Bundesamt für Seeschifffahrt und Hydrographie, Hamburg und Rostock (ed.), Meeresumweltsymposium 2001: Aktuelle Probleme der Meeresumwelt, Vorträge des 11. Symposiums.

Thiel, H., 2002b. Science as stakeholder – a proposal for Unique Science Priority Areas. *Ocean Challenge* 12, 44–47.

Thiel, H., 2003. Anthropogenic impacts on the deep sea. pp. 427–471 in: P. A. Tyler (ed.) *Ecosystems of the Deep Ocean. Ecosystems of the World series*. Elsevier Science, Oxford.

Thiel, H. and E. J. Foell, 1993. Environmental risk assessment for manganese nodule mining and application of the precautionary principle. pp. 226–233 in: A. Couper and E. Gold (eds). *The Marine Environment and Sustainable Development . Law, Policy and Science*. Law of the Sea Institute, Honolulu, Hawaii.

Thiel, H. and E. L. Gilman, 2001. Protection of birds on the high seas. pp. 83–87 in: H. Thiel and J. A. Koslow (eds). Managing Risk to Biodiversity and the Environment on the High Sea, Including Tools such as Marine Protected Areas – Scientific Requirements and Legal Aspects. Proceedings of the Expert Workshop held at the International Academy for Nature Conservation Isle of Vilm, Germany, 27 February–4 March, 2001.

Thiel, H. and J. A. Koslow (eds), 2001. Managing Risk to Biodiversity and the Environment on the High Sea, Including Tools such as Marine Protected Areas – Scientific Requirements and Legal Aspects. Proceedings of the Expert Workshop held at the International Academy for Nature Conservation Isle of Vilm, Germany, 27 February–4 March, 2001. 216 pp.

Thiel, H. and A. L. Rice, 1995. Structure and variability of the deep-sea benthos – Results from EU funded research. *Internationale Revue der Gesamten Hydrobiologie* 80, 149–151.

Thiel, H, and G. Schriever, 1990. Deep-sea mining, environmental impact and the DISCOL project. *Ambio* 15, 245–250.

Thiel, H., O. Pfannkuche, G. Schriever, K. Lochte, A. J. Gooday, Ch. Hemleben, R. F. G. Mantoura, C. M. Turley, J. W. Patching and F. Riemann, 1989. Phytodetritus on the deep-sea floor in a central oceanic region of the North-east Atlantic. *Biological Oceanography* 6, 203–239.

Thiel, H., M. V. Angel, E. J. Foell, A. L. Rice and G. Schriever, 1998. Environmental risks from large-scale ecological research in the deep sea. A desk study. Contract No. MAS2-CT94-0086, European Commission, Directorate General for Science Research and Development, Marine Science and Technology. 210 pp.

Tunnicliffe, V. and S. K. Juniper, 1990. Dynamic character of hydrothermal vent habitats and the nature of sulphide chimney forms. *Progress in Oceanography* 24, 1–14.

United Nations Convention on the Law of the Sea, 1982. United Nations Convention on the Law of the Sea. A/Conf.62/122 and Corr. 1–11, ILM 21 (1982) 1261. The Law of the Sea: Compendium of basic documents, International Seabed Authority/The Caribbean Law Publishing Company, 2001.

United Nations, 2001a. Oceans and the law of the sea. Report of the Secretary General. General Assembly, A/56/58, 73–75. VI. Marine resources, marine environment and sustainable development. E. Protection of specific marine areas.

United Nations, 2001b. Oceans and the law of the sea. Report of the Secretary General. General Assembly, A/56/58/Add.1, 16. VI. Marine resources, marine environment and sustainable development. D. Protection of specific marine areas.

United Nations Open-ended Informal Consultative Process, 2002. Report on the work of the United Nations Open-ended Informal Consultative Process established by the General Assembly in its resolution 54/33 in order to facilitate the annual review by the Assembly of developments in ocean affairs at its third meeting, held at the United Nations Headquarter from 8 to 15 April, 2002. See: www.un.org/depts/los/consultative_process/consultative_process.htm.

Van Dover, C. L., 2000. *The ecology of deep-sea hydrothermal vents*. Princeton University Press, Princeton, New Jersey. 424 pp.

Vierros, M., S. Johnston and D. Ogalla, 2001. The Convention on Biological Diversity (CBD) and marine protected areas on the high seas. pp. 169–173 in: H. Thiel and J. A. Koslow (eds). Managing Risk to Biodiversity and the Environment on the High Sea, Including Tools such as Marine Protected Areas – Scientific Requirements and Legal Aspects. Proceedings of the Expert Workshop held at the International Academy for Nature Conservation Isle of Vilm, Germany, 27 February–4 March 2001.

Williams, N., 1998. Overfishing disrupts entire ecosystem. *Science* 279, 809.

Wilson, J. B., 1979. The distribution of the coral *Lophelia pertusa* (L.) (*L. prolifera* (Pallas)) in the north-east Atlantic. *Journal of the Marine Biological Association of the United Kingdom* 59, 149–164.

World Conservation Union – IUCN, 2002. IUCN website: www.IUCN.ORG/themes/marine/ → What's New?

World Wide Fund for Nature, 2001. Lucky Strike and Menez Gwen. The first deep-sea marine protected areas in the Northeast Atlantic. pp 1–6. WWF North-East Atlantic Programme (ed.), see: www.wwfneap.org.

Management of Marine Nature Reserves in East Asia: The Case of the People's Republic of China

*Zou Keyuan**

INTRODUCTION

The establishment of marine nature reserves is an indispensable link in the chain of protection of the marine environment. The designation and management of marine nature reserves is one of the best ways to conserve marine biodiversity and to prevent overall deterioration of the marine ecological environment. Marine nature reserves help to maintain ecosystem productivity, and to safeguard essential ecological processes by controlling activities that disrupt them or that physically damage the environment. Furthermore, a major role of the coastal and marine nature reserves is to preserve genetic resources. Both ecological processes and genetic resources must be maintained for the sustainable utilization of species and ecosystems. Thus they are regarded as key components of integrated management of coastal and marine areas and as part of sustainable development in the utilization of marine resources.[1]

China's sea areas cover three climatic zones (warm-temperate, subtropical and tropical zones). There is a great diversity of ecosystems, such as coast, estuary, coastal wetland, island, mangrove, coral reef, upwelling and oceanic ecosystems. In China's seas, the species of marine organisms, ecological groups and community structures all show diversified characteristics. The history of China's practice in establishing marine nature reserves is brief and short, despite the fact that China is a country of long history. The oldest marine protected area in the People's Republic of China (PRC) is the Snake Island Protected Area, located in Bohai Sea and established in 1963. Since then, a number of other marine nature reserves have been established. However, the work was still sporadic and unsystematic, that is, until 1988 – ten years after China carried out its economic reform and open-door policy.

In July 1988, the management system for the nature reserves in China was clearly defined as a combined mechanism of comprehensive and decentralized

---

* Professor Dr. *Zou Keyuan* is a Senior Research Fellow, East Asian Institute, National University of Singapore. Contact: eaizouky@nus.edu.sg.

The author is very grateful to the GAUSS Institute for the kind invitation to the Conference on Marine Environmental Law.

1 Graeme Kelleher (ed.), *Guidelines for Marine Protected Areas* (Gland: IUCN, 1999), vii.

A. Kirchner (ed.), International Maritime Environmental Law, 193–209.

management. It clearly stipulated that the Ministry of Forestry, the Ministry of Agriculture, the Ministry of Geology and Mineral Resources, the Ministry of Water Resources, and the State Oceanic Administration (SOA) were responsible for the management of various types of reserves. In November, the State Council decided that the SOA was responsible for the designation and management of marine nature reserves. In early 1989 five marine nature reserves, including Changli Golden Beach, Shankou mangrove ecosystem, and Dazhou Island marine ecosystem nature reserves, were selected, investigated and shown to have met certain standards set by the local marine administrations and relevant departments under the unified organization, and approved by the State Council in September 1990. In November 1991, the SOA set up a review board on national marine nature reserves which assessed and recommended to the State Council a group of national marine nature reserves for approval. In October 1992, the second group of national marine nature reserves, including Tianjin palaeocoast and wetland and Jinjiang ancient forest, was approved by the SOA. During that time numerous other local marine nature reserves were designated by the SOA and the local marine management departments and approved by local governments.

As of the end of 2001, 1,551 nature reserves had been established in China, with an area of 130 million ha, accounting for 12.9% of the territory.[2] Of the reserves, 3,643,000 ha were marine areas. Among 18 nature reserves established in April 2000, two were marine nature reserves (Xiamen Rare Marine Species Nature Reserve in Fujian Province, and Beilun Estuary Nature Reserve in Guangxi Autonomous Region).[3] In comparison with the "eighth five-year" period,[4] the quantity and size of the reserves in the "ninth five-year" period (1995–2000) increased respectively 53% and 37%, including 155 national nature reserves covering 57.515 million ha.[5] Unfortunately, the exact number of marine nature reserves within the above figure is not known because of the constant development. The figure in 1998 recorded 59 marine nature reserves with a total area of 12,900 km^2, covering gulfs, islands, estuaries, coasts, coral reefs, mangrove swamps, coastal lagoons, marine natural history sites, seaweed beds and wetlands.[6] The pace of establishing marine nature reserves is steadily moving on. Very recently in 2002, Shangdong Province established three such reserves at the provincial level.[7]

It should be noted that protection of marine areas was not a priority in China's early practice regarding the management of nature reserves. The establishment of the first set of nature reserves in China was aimed at protecting forest resources.

---

2 See *People's Daily* (in Chinese), 22 May 2002, at 2.

3 See "Circular of the General Office of the State Council on Publishing the List of Newly Established State-Level Nature Reserves", *Gazette of the State Council of the People's Republic of China* (in Chinese), No. 16, 10 June 2000, 11–12.

4 China prepares its development plan for every five years. The "eighth five-year" period is between 1990 and 1995.

5 See "Developments of nature reserves during 'ninth five-year' period", available in http://www.zhb.gov.cn/nature/index.php3?category (access date: 27 June 2001).

6 See "The Development of China's Marine Programs" (White Paper), *Beijing Review*, 15–21 June 1998, at 18.

7 They are Dagong Island, Haiyang Thousand Li Rock, and Wuti Island and Wetland, in http//www.soa.gov.cn/work/2002/05/01.htm (access date: 29 April 2002).

However, with economic development, closer attention has been paid to preserving and protecting the marine environment as well as the establishment and management of marine nature reserves.

LAW AND REGULATIONS

Marine nature reserves, though within the category of nature reserves, are different from terrestrial nature reserves and need special regulations for their management and protection. The term "marine nature reserves" first appeared in the 1982 Law on Marine Environmental Protection. Article 4 of the law stipulates that government departments under the State Council and at the provincial level "may, as the need to protect the marine environment requires, establish special marine reserves, marine sanctuaries and seashore scenic and tourist areas, and take corresponding measures to protect them. The designation of special marine reserves and marine sanctuaries shall be subject to the approval of the State Council".[8] Based on this stipulation, a dozen marine nature reserves were established in the coastal areas. However, due to the lack of detailed regulations for implementing the law and the issue being quite new, early practice showed that the establishment of the reserves was simply a paper exercise, and the so-called marine nature reserves actually enjoyed no protection.[9] It was necessary, therefore, to make a special regulation for the management and protection of the marine nature reserves. The SOA started the drafting work of the Measures on the Management of Marine Nature Reserves in 1988 and it was finally adopted in 1995 after the adoption of the 1994 Regulations on Nature Reserves.

The 1995 Measures on the Management of Marine Nature Reserves is the most important specific law on the management of marine nature reserves. It is a sort of administrative regulation and in China's legislation hierarchy, it is at the third level, lower than the status of the Regulations on Nature Reserves, and much lower than the Law on Marine Environmental Protection. It sets forth the guiding principle of "conservation first, appropriate exploitation and sustainable development". Following the legal practice set forth in the 1994 Regulations, the marine nature reserves are also divided into two categories: national and local. The marine nature reserves at the national level should be those which have great national and international impact and are of great scientific and protective values. Their establishment is subject to the approval of the State Council. The local ones are those which have great local impact and certain scientific and protective values, and their establishment is the responsibility of governments at the provincial level. When a certain area fulfils one of the following conditions, it should be established as a marine nature reserve: (a) locality of typical marine ecosystem; (b) area with abundant

8 The Law was first adopted on 23 August 1982 and amended on 25 December 1999. The 1982 English version is available in Office of Policy, Law and Regulation, State Oceanic Administration (ed.), *Collection of the Sea Laws and Regulations of the People's Republic of China* (Beijing: Ocean Press, 1998), 195–208.

9 See Li Mingfeng, "Legislation on Marine Nature Reserves (2)", *Ocean Development and Management* (in Chinese), Vol. 12 (4), 1995, at 27.

marine biodiversity or with precious and endangered marine species; (c) locality of marine natural relics with significant scientific and cultural values; (d) sea area, coastal belt, islands, or wetlands of special protective values; and (e) other areas which need protection.

In October 1998 the Principles on Categorising Marine Nature Reserves and Dividing Their Levels were approved and issued by the State Bureau of Quality Technology Supervision. According to these state standards, marine nature reserves are divided into three main categories and 16 sub-categories: (a) ocean and coastal natural ecosystems, including 10 subcategories such as river mouth, mangroves, bays, islands; (b) marine biological species, including two subcategories of precious and endangered species and of economic species; and (c) marine natural relics and non-living resources, including four subcategories such as marine geological relics, ancient biological relics, natural landscapes and non-living resources.[10] These standards play some guiding role in establishing marine nature reserves.

The Measures set forth the procedure for establishing marine nature reserves. The SOA is the competent authority in China which is responsible for the overall management of marine nature reserves. It prepares plans on national marine nature reserves, reviews any schemes or reports on marine nature reserves at the national level, and examines and approves the comprehensive programmes of national marine nature reserves. The departments of ocean management at the provincial level are responsible for preparing plans on marine nature reserves in the sea areas within their jurisdiction, and for making suggestions on selection of national marine nature reserves, and are in charge of the selection and establishment of marine nature reserves within the sea areas in their administrative competence. Although the Measures do not mention whether the marine nature reserves under the responsibility of the provinces are those at the local level, it is usually understood that the marine nature reserves under their competence are the local ones. The local marine reserves may also be divided into the province-level ones and the county-level ones.[11] When the department of ocean management at the provincial level applies to establish any national marine nature reserves, they should submit to the SOA the application together with supporting materials which have already been approved by the provincial governments. The SOA organises a review committee comprising experts and representatives from relevant government departments. Once the application has been adopted by the review committee with a majority vote, it is submitted by the SOA to the State Council for approval. The SOA may make suggestions to the State Council on the establishment of marine nature reserves. The establishment of local marine nature reserves is subject to the examination and approval of the provincial governments, and forwarded to the SOA for record.

Once a marine nature reserve has been established, it should have a clear demarcation line which should be made public. Any cancellation, adjustment or change of a marine nature reserve should be examined and reviewed by the original organ which approved its establishment. Change of marine nature reserves is

---

10 See *China Ocean News* (in Chinese), 17 November 2001, at 1.

11 See Li Guoqing (ed.), *Study on Marine Comprehensive Management in China* (Beijing: Ocean Press, 1998) (in Chinese), at 151.

not common, but it does exist in practice. In 1997, the State Council approved the adjustment of the Fujian Neilingding Island Nature Reserve in Guangdong Province.

For the marine nature reserves, there should be corresponding management organs equipped with professional and technical personnel. They have the following responsibilities: (a) to implement laws, regulations and policies relating to marine nature reserves; (b) to adopt detailed management methods and regulations for the protected areas, and to manage all the activities within the areas; (c) to prepare overall plans to build up protected areas; (d) to place boundary markers and other protective facilities for the protected areas; (e) to organize basic investigations and regular monitoring in the protected areas and to establish the archives for the protection work; (f) to organize ecological and environmental restoration and scientific research in the protected areas; and (g) to launch marine natural protection publicity and education work. The management organ is authorised to make detailed management rules.

A marine nature reserve may be divided into core zone, buffer zone, experimental zone in accordance with the natural environment, natural resource conditions, and the need of protection, or be determined as absolute protection period[12] or relative protection period[13] in accordance with different protected objects. No activities can be conducted in the core zone except for scientific investigations and research approved by the department of ocean management at the provincial level; in the buffer zone, appropriate fishing production, tourism, scientific research, and educational excursions may be conducted within limited time and scope, and subject to the approval of the management organ of the protected area, on the condition that the protected objects are not damaged or polluted; appropriate development activities with a plan may be conducted in the experimental zone under the guidance of the management organ. The following activities are prohibited in the marine nature reserves: (a) moving or damaging the boundary markers and other protection facilities; (b) illegal fishing or collecting marine living species; (c) illegal stone collecting, sand digging or mining; and (d) other activities damaging the natural environment and resources. No work unit or individual may build any installations in the marine nature reserves without the approval of the SOA or department of ocean management at the provincial level.

Any agreement signed between the Chinese side and foreign counterpart regarding marine nature reserves or any visit of foreigners to the marine nature reserves should be approved by the SOA. For local marine nature reserves, these matters are subject to approval by the provincial department. Any activities such as scientific research, excursions or tourism are subject to approval by a relevant competent authority. Any breach is dealt with in accordance with Articles 34, 35 and 38 of the Regulations on Nature Reserves.

---

12 Absolute protection period refers to a certain period when no adverse activities against the protected objects are prohibited; and appropriate scientific research or teaching excursion may be conducted subject to approval.

13 Relative protection period refers to the time except the absolute protection period when other activities can be conducted except for catching or harming the protected objects.

The Measures on the Management of Marine Nature Reserves was prepared by the SOA, which is the competent authority in the management of marine nature reserves. The legal basis of the Measures is Article 42 of the Regulations on Nature Reserves, which provides that competent departments for nature reserves under the State Council may set forth management measures on relevant types of nature reserves in accordance with the Regulations. It is clear therefore that many clauses in the Measures are consistent with the relevant provisions of the Regulations. Some of the provisions in the Regulations are directly borrowed from, or applied through the Measures to marine nature reserves. However, there are some inconsistencies between the two. For instance, regarding the legal liability, the Regulations has a provision on criminal liability to be imposed on persons who have caused serious damage to nature reserves, while the Measures only expressly adopts two kinds of administrative punishment: monetary fines and compensation for any loss or damage to the reserve (provided in Articles 34, 35 and 38 of the Regulations). Under such circumstances, it is not clear whether the criminal liability can be imposed in respect of marine nature reserves.

Although the Measures above are the major regulations for the management of marine nature reserves, other specific regulations relating to the management of marine nature reserves also exist, but they are issued by different government departments. The most relevant one is the Measures on the Management of Nature Reserves of Aqua Fauna and Flora promulgated by the Ministry of Agriculture in October 1997.[14] These Measures provide that an area with one of the following conditions should be established as a nature reserve of aquatic animals and plants: (a) concentrated areas, main habitats and breeding areas of aquatic animals and plants under State or local protection; (b) areas representing different ecosystems of typical aquatic plants; (c) main production areas of aquatic economic animals and plants of special importance; (d) concentrated areas of diversity of aquatic animals and plants; (e) natural habitats of aquatic plants without disturbance by humans and in natural conditions; (f) aquatic ecological environment of special protection values.[15] Like marine nature reserves, the nature reserves for aquatic animals and plants are also divided into national and local ones, including core zones, buffer zones and experimental zones. In comparison, there are a lot of similarities between these Measures and the ones on marine nature reserves introduced by the SOA. It may be assumed that the preparation of the 1997 Measures had made reference to the 1995 Measures or that the SOA was consulted during the preparation. There are two points which should be noted. First, the 1997 Measures apply not only to marine fauna and flora but also to freshwater fauna and flora. Second, for the purpose of establishing nature reserves, marine nature reserves are identical to nature reserves of aquatic fauna and flora when they are established in the coastal areas. Thus a problem of overlapping authority between the SOA and the Ministry of Agriculture in the management of marine nature reserves arises.

Another legal document that is closely connected with marine nature reserves is the Provisions Governing the Management of Coastal Forest Belts under Special

---

14 Text in *Gazette of the State Council of the People's Republic of China* (in Chinese), 24 December 1997, No. 37, 1997, 1614–1619.

15 Article 6 of the Measures on the Management of Nature Reserves of Aqua Fauna and Flora.

State Protection, adopted by the Ministry of Forest in December 1996.[16] Protection forest belts can be, subject to the approval of the State Council, established 200 metres along the coast for sand areas and no less than 100 metres for mangroves or other trees. The Provisions is particularly meaningful for the protection of mangroves in the coastal areas since it is designed for the management of coastal forests. However, the Provisions do not mention its relationship with the Measures on the Management of Marine Nature Reserves, nor with the management of forests including mangroves within marine nature reserves.

In order to emphasise the importance of marine nature reserves in the comprehensive protection of the marine environment, a new chapter on marine ecological protection with 9 clauses was added to the 1999 amended Law on Marine Environmental Protection (MEPL). The necessity came from the requirements set forth in China's *Agenda 21* and China's *Ocean Agenda 21*. The peculiarity of the marine environment makes the protection of marine ecology inseparable from the protection of the whole marine environment. According to the MEPL, mangroves, coral reefs, offshore wetlands, islands, bays, estuaries, and important fishing areas having typical marine ecological systems, zones where endangered and precious species live, and marine natural historic sites and natural landscapes should be protected (Article 20). When necessary, marine nature reserves should be established (Article 21). The development of marine resources should not cause any damage to the marine ecological system (Article 24). Although this chapter is new in the MEPL, it should be noted that there exist already the Regulations on Nature Reserves and the Measures on the Management of Marine Nature Reserves which contain similar provisions pertaining to the protection of the marine and coastal ecosystems. In that sense, the chapter in the MEPL may overlap with the existing regulations and thus create difficulties in implementation. However, the existence of certain stipulations in both the Regulations and the Measures indicates that China has realised fully the significance of the marine ecosystem, particularly the marine nature reserves in the context of marine environmental protection, and promoted the legal status of these stipulations so as to make them more authoritative.[17]

It should be noted that the management of marine nature reserves is related to other fields of marine environmental protection. The laws and regulations on marine environmental protection, such as prevention of vessel-source pollution, dumping at sea, land-source pollution, pollution from oil exploration and exploitation, are also applicable to the management of marine nature reserves.[18] It should also be noted that although the SOA is the competent authority in charge of the management of marine nature reserves, in reality not all marine nature reserves are

---

16 Text in *Gazette of the State Council of the People's Republic of China* (in Chinese), No. 37, 1996, 1518–1520.

17 In China, only the NPC and its Standing Committee have the competence to make laws. Regulations are made by the State Council, and measures by ministries. That means "law" is the first level legislation, "regulations" second level, and "measures" third level.

18 There are quite a number of laws and regulations in this respect. For details, see Zou Keyuan, "Implementing Marine Environmental Protection Law in China: Progress, Problems and Prospects", *Marine Policy*, Vol. 23, 1999, 207–225, and "Curbing Marine Environmental Degradation: China's New Legislation", *International Journal of Marine and Coastal Law*, Vol. 16, 2001, 347–360.

under its management. According to a statistic, as of 1995, there were 37 marine nature reserves, of which 13 were national. Based on the division of responsibility decided by the State Council, the SOA was responsible for managing 15, of which 7 were national.[19] The number of marine nature reserves under the authority of the SOA was thus only one-third of the total, and the other 22 were managed by other departments, such as the NEPA, Ministry of Agriculture.

IMPLEMENTATION AND MONITORING

Once laws and regulations are enacted, they should be implemented in practice. Enforcement is critical to the authority and validity of the relevant laws. Monitoring is an important part of the managerial work in the marine nature reserves, and its purpose is to ensure protected areas and their living species are not harmed or damaged. In accordance with Article 14 of the revised MEPL, the SOA is responsible for managing investigation, monitoring, and surveillance of China's marine environment, and for making relevant implementation measures. After the entry into force of the new MEPL, the SOA further strengthened its monitoring work, as an important undertaking for implementing the amended Law. The Programme of Marine Environmental Monitoring for 2000 defined 12 items as key monitoring areas, including the monitoring of environmental quality, important sea areas, areas vulnerable to land-based pollution, dumping areas, petroleum exploitation areas, mariculture areas, important beach areas, typical marine ecological system, air, radiation, red tides, and pollution accidents.[20] In 2001, China launched a marine satellite to improve monitoring capability.

The China Marine Surveillance subordinated to the SOA is the main force for implementing and enforcing marine nature reserve regulations. Established in 1983, it has since been gradually expanded. At present, it consists of the headquarters located in Beijing, the North Sea Brigade, the East China Sea Brigade and the South China Sea Brigade, and other surveillance teams formed by relevant coastal provinces.[21] It has the functions of inspecting China's jurisdictional waters to find and deal with violations of Chinese laws and regulations in respect of China's marine rights and interests, use of sea areas, marine environment and resources, damage of installations at sea, and the disturbance of order at sea. Monitoring of marine nature reserves is part of its responsibility. For example, from 1992 to the end of 1994, the Division of Management for Sanya Coral Reef Nature Reserve regularly sent monitoring vessels to survey the sea area with 256 cruises, dealt with more than 120 breaches, and imposed fines of 2,000 RMB.[22] In November 2000, the SOA East China Sea Bureau carried out an inspection of the management of marine nature reserves in the East China Sea area including three reserves: Jinshan Reserves in

19 SOA, "Working Summary of Twelve Years Implementation of the Law on Marine Environmental Protection", Discussion Paper (in Chinese), December 1995, at 8. (on file with the author).

20 See *China Ocean News* (in Chinese), 25 February 2000.

21 Relevant information is available on China's Marine Surveillance website: www.cms.gov.cn (access date: 31 January 2001).

22 SOA, "Working Summary", *supra* note 19, at 9.

Shanghai; Xiamen Precious Species Protection Reserves in Fujian; and Longhai Mangrove Reserves in Fujian. The problems discovered during the inspection included: (a) no sound management mechanism; (b) lack of professional knowledge of the management personnel; and lack of management means. The inspection team therefore made suggestions on how to improve the work in these nature reserves.[23]

Monitoring marine nature reserves is different from monitoring marine pollution and needs various methods. There are three major components in monitoring nature reserves: (a) surveillance – use of vehicles and equipment to observe and investigate living conditions of the protected species and changes in their quantity, the state of the environmental quality, and human activities; (b) law enforcement – use of laws to prevent violations, evidence collection, and reporting to competent authorities to punish law-breakers, education and publicity on laws relating to marine nature reserves; and (c) contingent protection – designed to deal with urgent incidents occurring within the nature reserves and to provide protection for the protected objects in the shortest possible time.[24] The following should be subject to monitoring: (a) damage of mangroves; (b) damage of coral reefs; (c) damage of scenic forests and stones; (d) digging of sand without approval; and (e) illegal fishing.[25]

There are a few case studies on marine nature reserves in China where the laws and regulations concerning marine nature reserves are implemented. Two are detailed below.

(i) Changli Golden Seashore Nature Reserve

The Changli Golden Seashore Nature Reserve, a national marine nature reserve, is located in Changli county, Hebei Province (119^{0}11'–119^{0}37'E, 39^{0}27'–39^{0}41'N), and covers a total area of 300 km^2. It was established in September 1990 under the approval of the State Council and was among the first group of marine nature reserves managed by the SOA. It was established to protect the coastal ecosystem which consists of the shelter-forest belt, dunes, sand dyke in the shore, lagoon and marine organisms in the coastal water. There are about 168 species of bird and about 300 marine species living in this reserve. Management of the reserve was shared between the local government and the SOA, and the Measures on the Management of the Changli Golden Seashore Nature Reserve were drawn up. With this, the management entered into a track with laws and standards.[26] In addition, three years were spent on six field scientific observations, particularly on sand. However, despite the protection efforts it is admitted that it will take a long time for ecological restoration to be achieved.[27]

---

23 "Law enforcement supervision over marine nature reserves was carried out in the East China Sea area", in *Marine Information* (in Chinese), No. 21, 2000, available at http://www.soa.gov.cn/work/2000/gzxx00–21.htm (access date: 15 November 2001).

24 See Division of Personnel and Adult Education Centre, SOA (eds.), *Marine Surveillance and Management* (Beijing: Ocean Press, 1998) (in Chinese), 105–106.

25 See Division of Personnel and Adult Education Centre, *ibid.*, at 108.

26 See Lü Caixia, "Changli Golden Seashore National Nature Reserve", *Ocean Development and Management* (in Chinese), Vol. 13 (4), 1996, 78–79.

27 Lü, *ibid.*, at 79.

(ii) Marine Nature Reserves in Shanghai

There are two marine nature reserves located in Shanghai municipality: (a) the Chongming East Beach Wetland Birds Nature Reserve and (b) the Three Jinshan Islands Marine Nature Reserve.[28] Both were established in 1991. The Chongming Island is the third largest island in China. The establishment of the Chongming East Beach Wetland Birds Nature Reserve is designed to protect the coastal wetlands for some 2–3 million birds consisting of more than 116 species, including 11 precious and endangered species subject to special protection by the state. On the other hand, the 1981 Agreement on the Conservation of Migratory Birds and Its Habitat between China and Japan listed 227 species of birds. In Chongming there are 179 and in East Beach 87 of the listed birds. The 1986 Agreement on the Conservation of Migratory Birds and Its Habitat between China and Australia listed 81 species, of which 56 are found in Chongming and 39 in East Beach.[29] This indicates that this marine nature reserve is very important in implementing international agreements to protect migratory birds.

Designed to protect tropic vegetation of Middle Asia, the Three Jinshan Islands Marine Nature Reserve, a local nature reserve, is located in offshore Shanghai. It is abundant with wild plants including precious and endangered species. It consists of two parts: the core zone (the Greater Jinshan Island) and the buffer zone (the Lesser Jinshan Island, Fushan Island and their surrounding sea area of one nautical mile).

To manage the two marine nature reserves, the Shanghai Municipality established the Committee of Management of Nature Reserves, which comprises government leaders, ecological specialists, and leaders of relevant departments. It aims to guide and coordinate protection and utilisation of the nature reserves. In addition, each marine nature reserve has an office of management to carry out national policy and laws on nature reserves, and to conduct routine management work for the two reserves. Respective Measures for the two marine nature reserves were adopted. The major problem which exists in these two nature reserves is the contradiction between protection and economic development. For example, in the Jinshan Nature Reserve, there is a monkey pasture within the reserve which has produced negative impact on the protected plants in the area.

INTERNATIONAL LAW IMPLICATIONS

International law may influence China's legislation and enforcement concerning the management of marine nature reserves. Of the various branches of international law, it is clear that two branches are most important for the management of marine nature reserves: the law of the sea and the international environmental law. The former guides China to establish its jurisdictional waters in the seas and along the coast, from where China is able to establish its marine nature reserves, while the

---

28 See Song Yufang, "Preliminary Discussion on Management System of the Two Marine Nature Reserves in Shanghai", *Ocean and Coastal Zone Development* (in Chinese), Vol. 9 (2), 1992, 35–39.

29 Song, *ibid.*, at 36.

latter sets forth a number of legal principles which should be complied with in the management of marine nature reserves, such as the principle of sustainable development, the precautionary principle, and the polluter-pays principle.[30] The following international treaties to which China has acceded are of relevance to China's management of marine nature reserves.

(i) The United Nations Convention on the Law of the Sea (LOS Convention)

The most important treaty is the LOS Convention. Under this, a coastal State has the right to create its jurisdictional waters of 200 nautical miles including territorial sea, exclusive economic zone and continental shelf. While the coastal State is granted the right to explore and exploit the marine resources within its jurisdictional waters, it also bears the responsibility of conserving and protecting them from being damaged or unsustainably exploited. In order to strengthen the protection of the marine environment, the LOS Convention contains a whole chapter (Part XII) on marine environmental protection, obliging signatory States to take measures to prevent, reduce and control pollution of the marine environment. Besides this, there are clauses concerning the preservation and conservation of marine resources. Although the Convention does not expressly mention the management of marine nature reserves, the provisions concerning marine environmental protection as well as marine resources preservation and conservation are of great help in the sound management of marine nature reserves. It is admitted that the LOS Convention makes limited references to specific marine species or areas, but the relationships between the limited references, the other environmental and conservation provisions in the Convention, and other international agreements are fundamentally important.[31]

---

30 There is abundant literature on these principles and the reader may consult relevant scholarly works. For the principle of sustainable development, see Winfried Lang (ed.), *Sustainable Development and International Law* (London: Graham & Trotman/M. Nijhoff, 1995); A.E. Boyle and D.A.C. Freestone (eds.), *International Law and Sustainable Development: Past Achievements and Future Challenges* (New York: Oxford University Press, 1999); and Konrad Ginther, Erik Denters, and Paul J.I.M. de Waart (eds.), *Sustainable Development and Good Governance* (Dordrecht: M. Nijhoff, 1995). For the precautionary principle, see David Freestone and Ellen Hey (eds.), *The Precautionary Principle and International Law: The Challenge of Implementation* (Boston: Kluwer Law International, 1995); Harald Hohmann, *Precautionary Legal Duties and Principles of Modern International Environmental Law: The Precautionary Principle: International Environmental Law between Exploitation and Protection* (London: Graham & Trotman/Martinus Nijhoff, 1994); and Emmanuel Agius and Salvino Busuttil (eds.), *Future Generations and International Law* (London: Earthscan, 1998). For the polluter-pays principle, see J. McLoughlin and E.G. Bellinger, *Environmental Pollution Control: An Introduction to Principles and Practice of Administration* (London: Graham & Trotman/ M. Nijhoff, 1993); Organisation for Economic Co-operation and Development (OECD), *The Polluter Pays Principle: Definition, Analysis, Implementation* (Paris: OECD, 1975); and Edward Dommen (ed.), *Fair Principles for Sustainable Development: Essays on Environmental Policy and Developing Countries* (Aldershot, Hants, England: E. Elgar, 1993).

31 IUCN, *The Law of the Sea: Priorities and Responsibilities in Implementing the Convention* (IUCN, 1995), at 84.

China put its signature to the LOS Convention in December 1982 on the occasion that it was adopted, and ratified it in May 1996. Based on this multilateral treaty, China has established its territorial sea, exclusive economic zone, continental shelf, part of its baselines to measure the above sea zones. However, there are still maritime boundary delimitation issues existing between China and its neighbouring countries in the bordering seas. So far there has been no marine nature reserve ever established beyond the range of China's territorial sea. Thus it is unlikely that there would be maritime disputes between China and other countries resulting from China's establishment of marine nature reserves. Nevertheless, there is one case which is perceived to disturb the normal relationship between China and another country. That is the case of the Xisha Islands (Paracel Islands) in the South China Sea, currently under China's control, but also claimed by Vietnam. It was proposed in 1991 to establish the Xisha Marine Ecological Nature Reserve so as to enhance the management of the natural resources on the Xisha Islands as well as in their surrounding sea areas.[32] So far there is no news about any further developments. Once established, the marine nature reserve will definitely become a target of dispute, challenged by Vietnam.

(ii) The Convention on Biological Diversity (CBD)

Another important treaty relating to the management of marine nature reserves is the Convention on Biological Diversity. This treaty contains many provisions supporting the case for marine conservation, including the management of marine nature reserves. States parties are obliged to develop national diversity strategies, to identify and monitor important components of biodiversity, to establish a system of protected areas to conserve biodiversity, to promote environmentally sound and sustainable development in areas adjacent to protected areas and to rehabilitate and restore degraded ecosystems. Under the Jakarta Mandate on Marine and Coastal Biological Diversity, adopted by the Parties to the CBD in 1995, governments affirmed the importance of marine and coastal diversity and promised to take action to implement programmes under the Mandate (which embraces five thematic areas: integrated marine and coastal management, marine and coastal protected areas, marine and coastal living resources, mariculture, and alien species), such as researching and monitoring the values of marine and coastal protected areas, and developing criteria for their establishment and management.[33] It can thus be seen that the CBD is more important than the LOS Convention in the management of marine nature reserves.

China played an active role in promoting the final adoption of the CBD, signed the Convention on Biological Diversity during the UNCED on 11 June 1992, and ratified it on 5 January 1993. It was one of the earliest countries to ratify the CBD. In order to implement the CBD and to fulfil its obligations under the Convention, China has initiated a series of actions and measures. China established the Coordinating Group for Implementation of the CBD with the approval of the State

32 See Li Mingfeng, *supra* note 9, at 29.
33 Kelleher, *supra* note 1, at 4.

Council, which is headed by the NEPA, and composed of the Ministry of Foreign Affairs, the State Planning Commission, the Ministry of Education, the Ministry of Science and Technology, the Ministry of Public Security, the Ministry of Finance, the Ministry of Construction, the Ministry of Agriculture, the Ministry of Forestry, the State Administration of Film, Radio and Television Broadcasting, the State Administration of Industry and Commerce, General Customs Administration, Xinhua News Agency, the Chinese Academy of Sciences, the State Patent Administration, the SOA, the State Traditional Chinese Medicine Administration, *People's Daily* and *Guangming* Daily.

It is recorded that China's marine biodiversity occupies an important position in the world. In China, 20,278 species of marine organisms have been identified, including 14% of the world's total number of fish species, cirripedia 24%, insects 24%, mangrove plants 43%, seabirds 23% and cephapedia 14%.[34] Nature reserves are closely related to the conservation of biodiversity. Their establishment can effectively protect natural ecosystems with representative, prototypical and scientific importance, as well as rare and endangered species. As indicated in a Notice issued by the State Council in 1997 relating to the establishment of 18 national nature reserves in China, the newly established nature reserves are representative and typical of the biodiversity protection in China. Among the 18, there are three marine nature reserves: the Dalian Seals Nature Reserve (Liaoning Province), the Dandong Yalujiang Wetland Nature Reserve (Liaoning Province) and the Zhanjian Mangrove Nature Reserve (Guangdong Province).[35] China's practice in the establishment and management of marine nature reserves is one of the most important aspects of implementing the CBD within China's territory.

Chapter 15 of China's *Agenda 21* deals with the conservation of biodiversity, including the protection of special habitats and ecosystems such as wetlands, coral reefs and mangroves.[36] The *China Ocean Agenda 21* also advocates that China takes a series of actions in this respect including the preparation of the Regulations for the Management of Marine Biodiversity Conservation.[37]

(iii) The Convention on Wetlands of International Importance Especially as Waterfowl Habitat (Ramsar Convention)

This convention was adopted in 1971, and allows State parties to put their designated wetlands on the list provided for under the Convention. Some 48% of the designated Ramsar sites include the coast and so may contain marine components. The Conference of Parties of the Convention has urged countries to give priority to designating new sites from wetland types that are currently under-represented on the Ramsar List so far, including coral reefs, mangroves and sea-grass beds.[38] China

34 SOA, *China Ocean Agenda 21* (Beijing: Ocean Press, 1996), at 50.
35 See "Circular of the State Council on Publishing the List of Luya Mountain and Other State-Level Nature Reserves", *Gazette of the State Council of the People's Republic of China* (in Chinese), No.38 (1997), 4 January 1998, 1649–1651.
36 See *China Agenda 21* (Beijing: China Environmental Sciences Press, 1994) (in Chinese), at 137.
37 See *China Ocean Agenda 21, supra* note 34, 51–52.
38 Kelleher, *supra* note 1, at 4.

ratified this convention on 31 March 1992. In China there are 21 nature reserves listed as wetlands of international importance under the Ramsar Convention with total area of 3.03 million ha, of which nine are marine nature reserves.[39] For example, Dongzhaigang Nature Reserve in Hainan Province (with an area of 3,337 km^2, established in 1980 as a local nature reserve, promoted to the national level in 1986, and accepted in the Ramsar List in 1992) and Mipu in Hong Kong. Other marine nature reserves considered as wetlands are Guangxi Qingzhou Bay Mangrove Wetlands and Xisha East Island Wetlands, which may be put on the Ramsar List at some time in the near future.

(iv) The Convention Concerning the Protection of the World Cultural and Natural Heritage (World Heritage Convention)

This convention was first adopted in 1972 under the sponsorship of the United Nations Educational, Scientific and Cultural Organisation (UNESCO). Under this convention, sites of world heritage are nominated by signatory States and accepted by the World Heritage Committee. By the end of 1998, the World Heritage List contained a total of 582 sites – 445 Cultural, 117 Natural and 20 Mixed – in 114 States. The main marine areas covered are the Belize Barrier Reef and the Great Barrier Reef (Australia), Thbbataha Reef (Philippines), Ujong Kulong (Indonesia), Shark Bay (Australia), Galapagos Islands (Ecuador), Glacier Bay (Canada), Banc d'Arguin (Mauritania), and the Sunderbans (Bangladesh).[40] China acceded to the convention on 12 December 1985. China's four nature reserves (Jiucaigou, Wuyi Mountain, Zhangjiajie, and Lu Mountain) established in the 1990s have been listed as World Heritage,[41] but unfortunately none of them are located in coastal or marine areas. In order to reinforce its protection of the designated World Heritages under the treaty obligation of the Convention, China recently issued a joint document requiring the relevant departments and local governments to avoid over-development of the areas around a World Heritage and to deal with firmly any law-breakers.[42]

(v) International Convention for the Prevention of Pollution from Ships (MARPOL 73/78)

As indicated by its abbreviation, this treaty was first concluded in 1973 and amended substantially in 1978. Under it, special areas have been designated in the Mediterranean Sea, Baltic Sea, Black Sea, Red Sea, the Gulf Area, Gulf of Aden, North Sea, Antarctic Ocean and Caribbean Sea for the purpose of prevention of pollution by oil, noxious liquid substances in bulk, and garbage. The treaty defines the "special area" as "a sea area where for recognised technical reasons in relation

---

39 See *People's Daily* (in Chinese), 3 February 2002, at 2, and 7.
40 See Kelleher, *supra* note 1, at 5.
41 See "Developments of nature reserves during 'nine fifth' period", available in http://www.zhb.gov.cn/nature/index.php3?category (access date: 27 June 2001).
42 See *People's Daily* (in Chinese), 30 April 2002, at 2.

to its oceanographic and ecological condition and to the particular character of its traffic the adoption of special mandatory methods for the prevention of pollution by oil is required".[43] In comparison, it is clear that "special areas" under this treaty are not "marine nature reserves". They are designed for the safety of ship navigation and prevention of vessel-source pollution. However, in the aim of marine environmental protection, they may carry the same purpose as the marine nature reserves. China acceded to this treaty on 1 July 1983. Seas or part of the seas adjacent to China have not been designated as special areas as such. Thus this treaty is the least relevant to China's marine nature reserves. However, with the expansion of marine nature reserves, in particular to the exclusive economic zone,[44] China may ask the IMO for some assistance in order to coordinate the establishment of marine nature reserves and functions of specially protected areas under the MARPOL.

(vi) Other Treaties

China has also ratified other treaties concerning environmental protection. It is recorded that China has ratified about 50 multiple treaties relating to environmental protection, such as the International Convention for the Regulation of Whaling (24 September 1980); the Antarctic Treaty (8 June 1983); the International Convention Relating to Intervention on the High Seas in Case of Oil Pollution (23 February 1990); the Convention on the Prevention of Marine Pollution By Dumping of Wastes and Other Matters (14 November 1985); the Convention on International Trade in Endangered Species of Wild Fauna and Flora (8 January 1981); the Basel Convention on the Control of Transboundary Movements of Hazardous Wastes and Their Disposal (17 December 1991); the Protocol on Environment Protection to the Antarctic Treaty (2 August 1994); and the United Nations Framework Convention on Climate Change (5 January 1993). Although these treaties are not directly related to the management of marine nature reserves, some legal principles or norms are applicable in this respect, and can be borrowed by the East Asian countries, including China, to enhance their management of marine nature reserves. For example, the legal regime for environmental protection in Antarctica has much to recommend it.[45] Under it, protected areas are established in this white continent and its surrounding sea areas, and managed under management plans prepared by the States parties to the Antarctic Treaty.

China pledged to implement sincerely the international conventions to which it has acceded, including the ones addressed above. As officially stated, China should maintain its rights and interests in national environmental protection, undertake international obligation consistent with the level of China's development, and contribute to global environmental protection.[46] If there is a discrepancy between

---

43 Regulation 1, para.10 of Annex I.

44 For reference, see Rainer Lagoni, "Die Errichtung von Schutzgebieten in der ausschließlichen Wirtschaftszone aus völkerrechtlicher Sicht", *Natur und Recht*, Vol. 24 (3), 2002, 121–133.

45 For details, see Zou Keyuan, "Legal Thinking on the Comprehensive Protection for Antarctica", *Peking University Law Journal* (in Chinese), 1991, No. 4, 36–39, 56.

46 "National Ecological Environment Protection Program", *Gazette of the State Council of the People's Republic of China* (in Chinese), No. 3, 30 January 2001, at 18.

China's domestic law and international treaties, China's practice indicates that relevant international treaties prevail, though there is no express stipulation in this regard in China's Constitution.

PROSPECTS

There is a general trend in China to expand its nature reserves throughout the country. It seems that China has realised the importance of the management of marine nature reserves, and the necessity of strengthening it by taking further effective measures. The Programme of the Management of National Marine Environmental Protection adopted in 1998 has listed the strengthening of supervision and management of marine nature reserves and expansion of marine nature reserves as one of the major tasks for the future. In addition, the Programme calls for the preparation and adoption of the Regulations Concerning Marine Biodiversity and Marine Ecological Protection.[47] In July 2001, the government approved 16 new national nature reserves, including one in Liaoning which is located in the coastal area. Meanwhile, in the Notice issued by the Office of the State Council, the governments in the places where nature reserves are located and the relevant governmental departments under the State Council should strengthen the leadership, establish a highly efficient management mechanism, and take favourable measures for the nature reserves by strictly implementing the regulations concerning them.[48] The government has also paid greater attention to protection and reforestation of mangroves. The Guangxi Autonomous Region, a province having the largest area of mangroves in the country, decided in July 2001 to expand the size of the mangrove area from 160,000 *mu*[49] to 600,000 *mu* through a cultivation project. The government of the region also decided to record every location of mangrove forests which have not yet been covered by the marine nature reserves together with the measures to strengthen mangrove cultivation and management in the marine nature reserves.

The National Ecological Environment Protection Programme issued in November 2000 set forth the short-term goal for nature reserves: towards 2000, a new set of nature reserves should be established, and at the same time the construction and management of the existing nature reserves should be strengthened.[50] According to the Programme on Developing China's Marine Nature Reserves, the goal for the time from 2001 to 2010 is the establishment of 110 to 120 marine nature reserves including 30 to 35 at the national level. The total area will reach 12 million ha. There are plans to establish a network of marine nature reserves which should consist of "bay nature reserves", "islands nature reserves", "river mouth nature reserves", "coral reef nature reserves", "mangrove nature reserves", "coastal lagoon nature reserves", "nature reserves for marine historical relics", and

---

47 See "Programme of the Management of National Marine Environmental Protection", *China Ocean News* (in Chinese), 27 October 1998, at 2.

48 See "Approval of 16 new national nature reserves", *People's Daily* (in Chinese), 4 July 2001, at 9.

49 Mu is a unit of area used in China and equivalent to 0.0667 hectares.

50 See "National Ecological Environment Protection Program", *supra* note 46, at 14.

"nature reserves for precious and endangered marine species".[51] In addition, "coastal wetlands nature reserves" should also be included.

Connected with the above is the question whether "marine nature reserves" are identical to "marine specially protected areas". The *China Ocean Agenda 21* put them into two different categories and stated that "the protection measures and development patterns of marine special protected areas are not the same as those of marine protected areas (i.e., marine nature reserves – added by this author) as they aim at the scientific, rational and sustainable use of various ocean resources in the areas for the optimum and integrated benefits". It acknowledged that China had not designated or set up state-level marine special protected areas. However, the differentiation between "marine nature reserves" and "marine special protected areas" is unclear and confusing in China, since there is no such differentiation in the laws and regulations regarding nature reserves, and they only mention "nature reserves". While it is favourable to establish "marine specially protected areas" with stricter management methods, and this term is consistent with the term used internationally, there is some difficulty in practice. At present, what is more important and urgent is how to strengthen the management of marine nature reserves by introducing more effective means so as to realise the protection and conservation goals, rather than creating a new category which may not have significant characteristics vis à vis marine nature reserves.

In order to better manage marine nature reserves, some of the established approaches such as "ecosystem approach" and "integrated approach" are helpful.[52] China has realised their importance in sustainable marine development and environmental protection, as reflected in its *Ocean Agenda 21*, which has attached a project proposal on the sustainability and protection of the Yellow Sea large marine ecosystem, and which regards an integrated management approach as an important way of ensuring sustained, rapid and healthy development.[53] Since sustainable economic and social development in coastal areas cannot be separated from sound environmental planning and management, the above two approaches should be applied to the management of marine nature reserves. In China, the integrated management approach is ever more important due to the fact that the management structure for marine affairs is fragmented and the management authority is distributed to the different government departments concerned.

To summarise, management of marine nature reserves is one of the most important links in the whole chain of comprehensive marine environmental protection. China has enacted various laws and regulations on marine environmental protection, including the prevention of pollution sources from land construction, land manufacturing, vessels, waste-dumping, offshore oil and gas development. All these pollution sources produce negative impacts on the marine nature reserves, thus the sound management of marine nature reserves depends on the effective enforcement of the laws and regulations concerning the prevention of marine pollution at source.

---

51 See Bureau of Comprehensive Marine Management, State Oceanic Administration, *Outline of the Development Programme of China's Marine Protected Areas (1996–2010)* (in Chinese), 23 August 1996, 4–6. (on the file with the author)

52 For details, see Zou Keyuan, "Towards Sustainable Management of China's Marine Fishery Resources: Law and Enforcement", *Asia-Pacific Journal of Environmental Law*, Vol. 2 (3–4), 1997, 310–312.

53 *China Ocean Agenda 21, supra* note 34, 163–167 and 64–65.

Aquaculture and Environmental Regulations: The German Situation within the North Sea

Bela H. Buck, Gesche Krause,** Harald Rosenthal*** and Victor Smetacek*****

ABSTRACT

The use of the North Sea is extremely multi-faceted and highly competitive. Within the vast variety of regulations inside the EU and in Germany, the regulative framework relevant to aquaculture is not yet complete. This chapter provides a short summary of the current legislative framework on international, national, and regional levels, which pertain to the development of aquaculture in Germany. Next, it highlights the question of decision-making in the coastal zone within an integrated coastal zone management (ICZM) approach. It can be shown that there is an ample need for sufficient regulations to optimise the management of marine resources, especially with respect to further ecological and socio-economic sound aquaculture development. Within the ICZM framework for aquaculture management in the North Sea, we propose a scheme for further development and the establishment of an independent regulatory/advisory body, which encompasses all spatial levels. Additionally, we show which tools, such as DSS (e.g. GIS) and active participation, could be used in such a scheme in the decision-making process and what outcomes are to be expected at which stage. The article closes with a call for integrative action in Germany for the further promotion of aquaculture development by endorsing the idea of ICZM in order to sustain the ecological and economic potential of the North Sea while providing an alternative livelihood for coastal communities.

---

* Mr. *Bela Hieronymus* Buck is a Ph.D. candidate at the Foundation Alfred Wegener Institute for Polar and Marine Research, Bremerhaven (Germany). Contact: bbuck@awi-bremerhaven.de.

** Ms. *Gesche Krause* is a Ph.D. candidate at the Systems Ecology Department, Stockholm University (Sweden); Center for Tropical Marine Ecology, Bremen (Germany).

*** Professor Dr. Dr. h.c. mult. *Harald Rosenthal* is professor at the University of Kiel (Germany), Institute for Marine Science, Department of Fishery Biology.

**** Professor Dr. *Victor Smetacek* is Head of the Department Pelagic Ecosystems at the Foundation Alfred Wegener Institute for Polar and Marine Research, Bremerhaven (Germany). Contact: vsmetacek@awi-bremerhaven.de.

A. Kirchner (ed.), International Maritime Environmental Law, 211–229.

1. INTRODUCTION

Aquaculture is presently one of the fastest growing aquatic food production sectors in the world and over the past two decades outputs have substantially increased within European Community (EC) countries. This development has been enhanced by a wide-ranging decline in fisheries yields accompanied by an increase in public demand for aquatic products. Due to limited availability of the conditions required for the development of modern aquaculture, Germany has seen a rather stagnant production level in this food sector.

The overall highly competitive use of the North Sea, for activities such as shipping (trade or private), recreational activities and tourism, extraction or disposal of gravel, marine missions, fisheries, offshore wind farms, cable lines, establishment of nature reserves and other marine and coastal protected areas, has highlighted the need for sufficient regulations to optimise the management of the resources within a multi-use context. In the marine environment, aquaculture production has a very short history and accordingly, regulatory frameworks in countries bordering the North Sea are diverse and still emerging.

The multifunctional sharing of marine waters must be regulated and safeguarded in order to provide all users with adequate user rights, while also protecting the marine environment and the environmental needs of all users. The emerging branch of marine aquaculture faces the same problems of every newcomer for which needs have not previously been considered. So far, a number of regulations are common to all users and are part of the European Union (EU) Directives framework, within which aquaculture will also have to find its place in national regulations.

This article intends to provide a rational summary how various levels of regulations are defined and may be interlinked to lead into recommendations for limited additional reference points within the national and existing international framework to accommodate a functional support system in which marine aquaculture can be integrated in multiple use concepts of the national coastal zone. It shall be demonstrated that an integrative approach to decision-making in the coastal zone would be highly beneficial for the further development of ecological and socio-economic sound aquaculture.

2. AN OVERVIEW OF THE PRESENT LAWS

(a) Historical Background

The principle of the freedom of the Seas (*mare liberum*) can be traced back to Hugo Grotius, who in 1608 claimed the Seas as *res commis* (Grotius, 1916). He asserted that things that cannot be seized or enclosed cannot become property. Grotius noted that use of the oceans for fishing or for navigation by one did not preclude their use by others. The oceans were created by nature in such a state that their usage could not be exclusive but belonged to all humankind (Grotius in Brilmayer and Klein, 2001).

This viewpoint indicated a natural right of mankind to utilise the resources of the Sea. Today the Sea is still generally regarded as commons. However, due to the growing awareness of resource depletion and limitation, the stage that

Hardin (1968) has defined as the "tragedy of the commons" has been reached. The development of the *UNCLOS* (United Nations Conventions on the Law of the Sea) agreement in 1982 can be seen as a move towards a change from this persistent commons perspective to a more regulative, protective rationing of international marine resources in the framework of sustainability.

International as well as national regulations and conventions concerning aquaculture within the EU are quite incomplete. While in some countries regulations for coastal aquaculture are well organised, the terms "aquaculture" and "mariculture" are often vaguely interpreted by regional and local authorities and do not comply with the Food and Agriculture Organisation of the United Nations (FAO) agreed definitions.

While in some countries aquaculture is defined and regulated under the agricultural laws, in others regulations are not centred in one lead agency. Germany is such a case where many regulations of several governmental bodies apply to aquaculture and are confusingly handled (individually and independently), leading to some uncertainty of the license process, not only for the applicants but also for the regulatory authorities themselves (e.g. federal, state, and local laws as well as EU and international regulations need to be addressed). Within the fragmentation of regulation applying to aquaculture there are no regulations concerning aquaculture within the German Exclusive Economic Zone (EEZ) at all (Czybulka and Kersandt, 2000; Buck, 2002). Furthermore, marine aquaculture in German territorial waters is presently very restricted with no hope for expansion, as regulations are stringent, and new licenses are extremely difficult to obtain (Rosenthal and Hilge, 2000). This is the case in particular for the licenses on bottom shellfish culture (Ruth, 1997).

(b) International Laws

Some international conventions, such as UNCLOS, *CBD* (Convention on Biological Diversity), and the *London Convention* (Convention on the Prevention of Marine Pollution by Dumping of Wastes and Other Matter) deal mainly with the protection of the marine environment and the prevention of pollution. Identification and monitoring of human activities that have an impact on the marine environment are included, while adequate environmental impact assessments are required to be carried out for any new development, followed by specific monitoring programmes. However, these regulations do not directly address marine aquaculture and do not therefore include specific aspects needed to fulfil the requirements of all interests. UNCLOS does not even mention the term aquaculture, but postulates measures to prevent, reduce and control pollution which might be originated by aquaculture (UNCLOS Art. 194 § 1, 1982). It also requires measures necessary to protect and preserve rare or fragile ecosystems including the habitat of depleted, threatened or endangered species (UNCLOS Art. 194 § 5, 1982). Like UNCLOS, CBD does not specify the term aquaculture. It primarily deals with impact assessments and avoiding or minimising adverse effects in general (§ 14; CBD, 1992). Within the London Convention an effective control shall individually and collectively promote all sources of pollution of the marine environment, and pledge themselves especially to take all practicable steps to prevent the pollution of the sea by the dumping of waste and other matter that is liable to create hazards to human health, to harm living resources and marine life, to damage amenities or to interfere with other legitimate uses of the sea. Again, aquaculture is not specified in this convention and is attributed to the term "others".

Only the *Agenda 21* explicitly alludes to the term aquaculture. In the Agenda 21, the impacts of aquaculture are discussed in the "Sustainable use and conservation of marine living resources under national jurisdiction" (Section II, Chapter 17, program area D). Coastal states are requested to conduct analysis of the potential of aquaculture and to implement mechanisms to develop mariculture and aquaculture within areas under national jurisdiction where assessments show that marine living resources are potentially available (17.79c, 17.83). Furthermore, coastal states should develop financial and technical co-operation to enhance the capacities of developing countries in coastal aquaculture and mariculture (17.87a). Agenda 21 suggests the following instruments for the implementation. The states should provide for the transfer of environmentally sound technologies to develop aquaculture and mariculture (17.92a) and accord special attention to mechanisms for transferring resource information and improved fishing and aquaculture technologies to fishing communities at the local level (17.92b). In addition, sustainable aquaculture development strategies should be established, including environmental management in support of rural fish-farming communities (17.94c).

(c) Regional Laws

Aquaculture is not mentioned in the *OSPAR*-Convention (*Oslo-Paris* Convention of the Protection of the Marine Environment of the North-East Atlantic), but within the OSPAR contracting parties it is identified as the technology to raise fish, molluscs and crustaceans (Czybulka and Kersandt, 2000). In addition to these convention articles, the Quality Status Report of OSPAR (QSR, 2000) records the actual condition of the impacts of human activities through aquaculture on the environment in terms of the release of metabolic wastes, antifoulants (copper), antibiotics, vaccines and parasites into the water column. Additionally, this report demands further work to assess the effect of implementation of the "ICES Code of Practice on the introductions and transfer of marine organisms" (International Council for the Exploration of the Sea) (ICES, 1984; ICES, 1988 and subsequent updates) and an assessment of the Recommendation 94/6 (PARCOM) concerning "best environmental practice for the reduction of inputs of potentially toxic chemicals from aquaculture use". Besides, the risk of spread of disease and the effect of escaped salmon on the genetic composition of wild stocks should be better documented.

Within the European Community there are several regulations which are relevant to aquaculture. The fisheries industry (including aquaculture) is directly dependent on environmental conditions, the quality of the farmed waters and product handling (in terms of hygiene conditions for the safety of human health) (Theodorou, 2001). However, specific European legislation relevant to limiting the effect of aquaculture on biodiversity is less well established than for capture fisheries. The EU public health provisions are related to the chain of activities involved in the production, harvesting and marketing of marine products for human consumption. EU legislation includes Directives and Council Decisions related to the infrastructure (usually composed of the public agencies of the Member States) capable of assessing water quality (classification), monitoring culture and harvesting activities, and providing adequate surveillance of the chain of supply from the point of production to the point of consumption (Theodorou, 2001). Among the applicable pieces of community legislation, there are (1) Directive 79/923/EEC, which concerns the quality of shellfish waters required to support shellfish life and growth of edible products and which applies to coastal and brackish waters (CEC, 1979; the parameters which are applicable to the designated waters are listed in the Annex) and (2) Council Directive 91/492/EEC and 97/79/EC, which lay down the health conditions and hygiene of live bivalve molluscs (CEC, 1991a; CEC, 1997a). (3) Council Directive 97/11/EEC on the assessment of the effects of certain public and private projects on the environment is also relevant to aquaculture purposes (amending Directive 85/337/EEC). It is mentioned in Annex II 1f concerning intensive fish farming, however, it is not definitely elucidated (CEC, 1997b). (4) The Council Regulation 1181/98/EC amending Regulation 3760/92/EEC, establishing a community system for fisheries and aquaculture, deals with similar regulations, such as the *Common Fisheries Policy* (CFP), which stressed the need for rational, responsible, and sustainable exploitation of fisheries and a more effective control of the whole fishing industry (CEC, 1998). In continuation of the amended Directive 3760/92/EEC, (5) Regulation 2847/93/EEC on control system applicable to the common fisheries policy was created (CEC, 1993). The *Green Paper* on the future of the CFP postulates the development of aquaculture in order to contribute to the supply of fish without increasing pressure on stocks in the marine environment. Aquaculture plays an important role in improving the socio-economic situation of coastal communities by providing alternative employment. The paper ranks priorities concerning the support for aquaculture. Issues addressed concern mainly training and control, research and development, treatment of waste water and the eradication and/or prevention of diseases. All these key issues will be supported by the *Financial Instrument for Fisheries Guidance* (FIFG). Most aquaculture activities are regulated by national legislation of each contracting Party to FIFG, which is influenced by a number of horizontal Community Directives, such as the (6) Water Framework Directive (2455/2001/EC amending Directive 2000/60/EC) (CEC, 2001b). (7) Directive 2001/18/EC (repealing Council Directive 90/220/EEC) on the deliberate release into the environment of genetically modified organisms covers both experimental purposes and the placing of such organisms on the market, which includes release of genetically engineered fish or shellfish (CEC, 2001a). (8) Fish and Shellfish Directive (91/67/EEC) controls animal health and the movement of animals, including infected animals, in order to prevent the spread of disease (CEC, 1991b). Furthermore, there are no regulations concerning aquaculture specifically relevant to the EEZ (Czybulka and Kersandt, 2000).

The International Conference on the Protection of the North Sea (NCS) does not take any position on regulation of aquaculture, but fosters the political impetus for the intensification of the environmental protection work within relevant international conventions, and ensures more efficient implementation schemes for the existing international rules related to the marine environment in all North Sea jurisdictions.

The *Trilateral Wadden Sea Plan* (WSP, 1997), formulated by Germany, Netherlands and Denmark, is aimed at limiting inshore aquaculture areas to the current area extension for mussel culture plots (Chapter 4.1.19). The existing permits specified for oyster culture will remain in force for traditional reasons. According to these permits, importation of seed oysters (whether bottom, rack or longline) is restricted to those from hatcheries that are under veterinary control. New permits will not be granted (Chapter 4.1.20).

(d) Laws in Germany

Within the Federal political structure of Germany, the Government enacts national orders which are mostly completed through the jurisprudence of the Federal States. The Federal States, called "Länder", are in charge and are responsible for the laws which deal with the use of water and with environmental protection. Within the Federal regulative framework, the *Sea Fisheries Law* concerning the open sea regulates the term fisheries, without covering aquaculture.

Concerning fish farm effluents, the *Federal Law on Water* (Wasserhaushaltsgesetz [WHG], 1996) is relevant for the licensing procedure (§ 2 and 7 WHG). However, the WHG does address primarily land-based systems which are considered point source emitters (looking at suspended solid load in terms of BOD [biological oxygen demand] and COD [chemical oxygen demand], oxygen deficit etc.), while water extraction and emission standards depend on numerous regulations. Open systems in coastal areas are dealing without standards being given. However, open waters within the EEZ are not covered. Cage culture systems in water-based marine or freshwater systems represent a matter of use, corresponding to § 3 (1) 4 WHG in connection with § 22 WHG. They need permission, should the situation arise (Schmid, 1993). Whether in freshwater or coastal marine systems, aquaculture regulatory measures under Federal Law (§ 7a [20] WHG and updates) cover land-based systems only.

The *Nature Protection Law* (Bundesnaturschutzgesetz [BNatSchG], 1998) does not include regulations concerning aquaculture in general, but indicates the rearing of fish for scientific purposes (§ 20g (6), 3 BNatSchG) with a restriction on the culture of endangered species (§ 26 (2),1 BNatSchG).

At a Federal State level, all "Länder" bordering coastal waters along the North Sea, such as Bremen, Hamburg, Lower Saxony and Schleswig-Holstein, have their own regulations concerning fisheries and partly on aquaculture within the *State Fisheries Laws* (Bremen: Bremisches Fischereigesetz [BremFiG, 1991]; Hamburg: Hamburgisches Fischereigesetz [1986]; Lower Saxony: Niedersächsisches Fischereigesetz [Nds.FischG, 1978]; Schleswig-Holstein: Landesfischereigesetz [LFischG, 1996]). However, only the State Fisheries Laws of Lower Saxony and Schleswig-Holstein regulate the cultivation of marine organisms, such as oyster farming and the combined mussel fishery-culture (§ 16 and 17 Nds.FischG, § 40 and 41 LFischG). Additionally, Lower Saxony and Schleswig-Holstein have *Coastal Fisheries Regulations* (Nds.KüFischO, 1992; KüFO, 1999), which regulate shellfish culture operations (§ 10 Nds.KüFischO and § 4 and 5 KüFO).

Along the German North Sea coastline a vast area of Natural Parks are designated as the *National Wadden Sea Park* of Lower Saxony, Hamburg and Schleswig-Holstein. Within these nature reserves *National Park Laws* are identified (National Park Law of Lower Saxony [2001], Law of the National Park of Hamburg [Gesetz über den Nationalpark Hamburgisches Wattenmeer, 1990], Nationalparkgesetz of Schleswig-Holstein [NPG, 1999]). These Laws, in combination with the State Fisheries Laws, regulate all aquaculture practices within the parks. While any kind of fisheries (including aquaculture) is prohibited in the nature reserves of Hamburg, the NPG refers to the LFischG to regulate specifically the culture of blue mussels and oysters (§ 6 (2) and (3) NPG) within the area. The cultivation of shellfish is allowed in specifically industrial areas within the park, but shellfish is restricted to blue mussel and oysters (Boysen, 1991). Therefore, raising other species, such as cockles, clams or scallops, is prohibited and therefore any development for shellfish aquaculture is extremely restricted.

Within the National Park Law of Lower Saxony shellfish cultivation is allowed and regulated in § 9 (National Park Law of Lower Saxony) while licences are maintained. When located within the Park area they will undergo changes in operational conditions within the next five years. These include long-range GPS-Satellite monitoring of all operational procedures which are restricted.

Marine fish farming is not specifically regulated in any of these Federal State or Coastal Fisheries Laws. Similarly, the cultivation of macroalgae or crustaceans is not mentioned in the regulations so far identified and described. Any application for a permit will therefore have to be handled as any other industrial application where outputs are limited. The difficulty is that water-based systems such as shellfish farms are incorporated in an ecosystem context in terms of uptake and release of nutrients and food organisms. Thus, conventional emission or immission standards do not apply. Similarly, fish farms operating cage flotillas are dispersed over a larger licence area and are considered as diffuse inputs as compared to point sources (GESAMP, 1996). One of the criteria to be taken as an environmental control aspect is the determination of the "assimilative capacity" (GESAMP, 1996; MARAQUA see below), which will sometimes be in conflict with effluent standards, as larger areas are included in conversion calculations.

Within the EEZ the regulation of marine facilities (Seeanlagenverordnung [SeeAnlV, 2001]) encompasses the erection, operation, and use of facilities which will be used by any offshore industry including mariculture (e.g. floating devices such as net pens and longlines or fixed structures such as cages).

Other laws and acts, such as the *Federal Regional Planning Act*, concerning Environmental Impact Assessments, a Municipal Landscape Plan and the County Landscape Plan, are relevant to both marine and inland waters, but are only defined for the latter (Bridge, 2001).

3. DECISION-MAKING IN COASTAL ZONE MANAGEMENT

Recently, a paradigm shift has taken place from predominantly ecological studies when considering the environmental impact of any activity to a stronger incorporation of socio-economic issues within the decision-making process in coastal areas. This has encouraged cross-sectoral discussions on coastal zone planning and management between different stakeholders, planners and regulators (Underwood, 1995; James, 2000; Kannen, 2000; Lakshmi and Rajagopalan, 2000; Welp, 2001). However, few clear structures on decision process guidance have yet evolved. Few approaches are tested as "virtual trajectories" across coastal systems (from upland to foreshore) with multidisciplinary and transdisciplinary inputs. However, more research efforts are required before evaluation criteria can be identified with sufficient confidence for these to be translated into regulatory measures. It is certainly questionable whether such criteria should result in strongly formulated regulations, as integrated management systems required the optimum resource mix, which requires general regulatory frameworks and objectives that may be adapted from case to case. Socio-economics are gaining importance in the overall assessment criteria (GESAMP, 1996; European Commission, 1999).

Decision-making within Coastal Zones is a complex process, which encompasses ecological, humanistic and economic needs and therefore must be managed jointly. A major role is played by the framework of environmental regulations promoting or limiting certain activities. Decision-making in the face of uncertainty is a common exercise for which skills within management are often as diverse and incomplete as our knowledge on the systems to be managed (Hogarth and McGlade, 1998). Thus, managers depend on good quality science for interpretation of both resource knowledge and uncertainties in a given coastal area.

To incorporate multidisciplinary knowledge requires a platform of communication on which a common denominator for all disciplines and interests involved can be identified (e.g. socio-economic, demographic, ecological, physical, climatic and technological disciplines). Such an approach acknowledges diversity in resource use demand, in views expressed, in terms of environmental and socio-economic interactions, while also opening opportunities for consensus building and/or agreed settlements over controversially debated issues. To implement such approaches, adequate tools are needed that are designed to optimise the benefits of the existing legal framework while identifying gaps to be filled for such optimisation. Although a holistic approach might be seen as one providing the most objective context to solutions (Richter *et al.*, 2001) there is still a need for pragmatic products to attract all stakeholders for the identification of realistic management options.

The limited success of ICZM (Integrated Coastal Zone Management) to date raises the question of why the available scientific information has not been used more effectively to inform the coastal policy, planning and management process (Burbridge, 1997). The development of robust tools to foster the ICZM process depends on a number of conditions within a given coastal region, where agreements and rules are initially based on trust and continuity. These develop over time and need to be amended in accordance with new multi-disciplinary data becoming available. Further such rules, once securely operational, need to be embedded in legal regulations. Thus, regulations are in part a product of the historically evolved functions which are merged with established regulatory procedures.

Richter *et al.* (2001) point to the current dialogue between ICZM managers, politicians, scientists and stakeholders which often suffers from lack of easy flow of relevant information in the right sequence.

So far, several tools have evolved on a test basis for promoting transdisciplinary interchange of information between different stakeholders, managers and the jurisprudence. Some of these that have been of influence on aquaculture development but are not an obligatory procedure and are not yet sufficiently well established at a bureaucratic level are briefly outlined below.

3.1. Decision Support System Analysis as a Tool in the Decision-Making Process

Several computerised Decision Support Systems (DSS) are available (Fabbri, 1998). For the development of a DSS to foster the establishment of sound management guidelines, monitoring programmes are of major importance, as they provide the data needed to install such computerised systems. The main goal of monitoring is to assess whether an activity has an unacceptable impact on the environment, the threshold of acceptability normally being decided on societal grounds. GESAMP (1996) define monitoring in a straightforward manner, as the regular collection, generally under regulatory mandate, of biological, chemical or physical data from predetermined locations, such that ecological changes attributable to, for example, aquaculture can be quantified and evaluated. Reviews, such as Fernandes *et al.* (2001) show how science could provide a monitoring strategy for marine aquaculture operations that is flexible enough to be applicable to a variety of locations, species and situations. They point out that traditionally environmental monitoring has concentrated on a few physical and chemical variables and organisms, somewhat reflecting the current state of the regulations in the coastal zone pertaining to aquaculture. However, there is a trend towards whole-system environment assessments (e.g. OSPAR, 1992; Fernandes *et al.*, 2001), including considerations of the assimilative capacity of specific systems. The current efforts in uniting the coastal zones of the Wadden Sea in the Netherlands, Germany and Denmark through the trilateral National Park agreement can be regarded as a first positive step. For example, the "Common Package" of the TMAP (Trilateral Monitoring and Assessment Program) promotes a unified parameter scheme for data sampling and management which supports recommendations for the development of management strategies on a trilateral basis (Marencic, 2002) and can be incorporated into a regional DSS.

These DSS assist in interpreting complex data sets for improved expert use. For example, SimCoast^{TM} (Simulating the Coast) is one of these systems (Hogarth and McGlade, 1998). These do not affect the regulatory frameworks but often identify interactions of environmental impacts of various resource users and use-methods such as EIA (Environmental Impact Assessment) and EIS (Environmental Impact Statement) as an iterative process rather than a single exercise to determine site-specific limits.

One other commonly employed tool for decision-making in the environmental planning process is Geographic Information Systems (GIS). They are capable of storing vast amounts of data and of representing these in visual format, for example, in maps. Fabbri (1998) suggests that the integration of the GIS spatial information storage in a spatial decision support system would be the ideal way to promote consistent decision-making and to evaluate coastal development alternatives to ensure ecological sustainability in the coastal zone. Such systems support decisions and highlight areas of conflicting spatial demand.

Generally, DSSs are useful for scenario building to aid decision-makers (Warner and Jones, 1998) in their task of weighing the environmental, economic and social values of any one set of conditions against another, thereby presenting sound arguments for several options which are perceived as threads of benefits while identifying optimum solutions (consensus building). The level of certainty (or uncertainty) as well as the precision of data for parts of the scenario produces a negotiation base on which risks can be identified and assessed (through appropriate methods) and proposed solutions rejected or jointly carried. The usefulness of such tools depends on the quality of the data and the representativeness of the identified local or regional stakeholder needs. These are identified in rules and target objectives negotiated between all stakeholders. The level of participation is therefore crucial to success. Despite computerisation, the process is time consuming, complex and difficult to handle, but fosters a highly qualified and better informed decision process.

It has to be realised that such systems are presently under development. They are still in their infancy and require extensive effort in terms of research and further development. One of the advantages of such systems is that they permit a better use of existing vast data sets and the incorporation of other modelling approaches (e.g. numerical models).

3.2. Participation Techniques

The EU demonstration programme (European Commission, 1999) has shown that participation can be crucial. Nonetheless, does this vindicate the temporal, financial and social efforts of participation in terms of "output"? Participation has been perceived as a panacea for many ICZM approaches (Noble, 2000; Van Mulekom, 1999). However, one has to acknowledge that a consensus encompassing all stakeholder groups equally is extremely difficult to achieve and requires a substantial amount of time. Participation can be defined in various ways. Following Govan *et al.* (1998) and Glaser and Krause (2002), we distinguish between 3 different levels of participation:

- The *passive* participation with an exclusive information function, but without participation or informed decision warrants for directly affected groups;
- The *consultative* participation, which involves the stakeholders with limited possibilities and rights of hearing;
- The *active* participation, by which the affected stakeholder is qualified and entitled to make decisions and is liable for actions.

The main success of active participation, apart from the early mediation of emerging conflicts between different stakeholder groups (Warner and Jones, 1998), is in the establishment of rules through consensus-building at local and regional levels. Following the initial joint formulation of the rules by the stakeholders, these can be validated by DSS based on the background data incorporated by the multidisciplinary sciences. Following this validation, by which continuous informing of the participating stakeholders takes place, the rules can be embedded into the existing regulatory framework. This strategy achieves two goals. First, the jurisdiction adapts to the local conditions and needs, and fits the regulatory framework accordingly. Furthermore, as the rules have been initially formulated and agreed by the stakeholders, lower costs for the supervision of compliance with the verbalised regulations can be expected. Thus, policy changes are agreed to by the resource users and thus are more successful than those which are enforced by external entrepreneur activities.

Such approaches have been partially carried out in several countries, for example, in Brazil. Here, the concept of the "*reservas extrativistas*" (RESEX) (extractive reserves) was developed following the intense social clashes in the early 1980s in the Amazon region, between rubber plantation farmers and local traditional communities, which gained international attention through the murder of the community leader Chico Mendes (Allegretti, 1994). One of the ideas of the RESEX is, in brief, resource conservation through self-responsible use by the traditional local communities (Glaser and Krause, 2002). The latter encompasses groups for whom the use of the natural resource comprises economic as well as cultural values.

The process of the RESEX is carried out by *active* participation, by which defined user-rights are assigned to the traditional local communities and stakeholders, these being formulated by and between these groups and the environmental jurisdiction. This approach is led by the knowledge and priorities of the direct resource user. Their improved participatory involvement in the national development process is one of the main goals of the RESEX process. This approach is currently in expansion to the coastal regions of Brazil, but is hampered by a lack of financial resources and poor understanding of active participation in the first place. A more detailed review of the advantages and limitations of this approach is given in Glaser and Krause (2002).

This strategy provides an example of how participation can be carried out in practical terms, and what role the environmental regulations could play. However, one of the major drawbacks within this approach is that outsiders, such as financially strong companies that are common in the aquaculture business, are not included. Often these companies introduce their own value perceptions and economic interests to the coastal areas, and these are not necessarily based on the local conditions. On the contrary, activities of other stakeholder groups, which are likely to affect the proper functioning of an aquaculture farm (e.g. emission of sewage), are commonly not regulated and communicated in order to protect income generation through aquaculture.

4. ICZM FRAMEWORK FOR AQUACULTURE MANAGEMENT IN THE NORTH SEA

What are the lessons learned from the above brief review of the status of tools for decision-making for the environmental jurisprudence? Clearly, there is an ample need to enforce and support good practice in ICZM by the administrations at local, regional and Federal State level. There is an emerging demand for environmental law regulations that move away from the spatial-sectoral disposition of the ecosystem to a more realistic, dynamic and integrative legislation in the coastal zone. Especially in these areas such regulations are necessary, if the authorities wish to keep pace with the current tendency of enforced uses of the marine resources whilst following the constitutional precautionary principle.

To date aquaculture has not generally been considered as having equal rights of access to and use of natural resources in competition for sites in the coastal zone. Existing activities are often protected by legislative systems that are typically based on land laws that are not well suited for aquaculture (Burbrigde *et al.*, 2001). This current legislative state is hampering the further promotion of the aquaculture sector, especially in terms of the gradually increasing resistance to its development, through the non-involvement of other stakeholders during the early consultation and planning phase. As well as emerging conflicts over the control of natural resources, which inevitably arise when *active* participation does not take place between the stakeholders, the groups which retain their traditional access may find them less productive in the long run. There is therefore a need to establish clearer user (property) rights regimes (Burbrigde *et al.*, 2001) but also a well-defined, integrated juridical framework to support active participation and co-management in the coastal areas. Thus, laws concerning the use of marine areas for aquaculture operations have to be modified, or new regulations have to be established, to encompass, amongst others, aquaculture demands.

The above mentioned tools within the ICZM process are only some of the vast array of different approaches. This leads us to the question, at which stage should which tools be used and what would be the expected outcomes? Clearly, there is a need for integrative approaches, co-management, active participation, alternative livelihood scenarios and ecological corridors in order to sustain the Seas as viable ecosystems. In Figure 1, a scheme is proposed for a regulatory framework for aquaculture development in the North Sea.

This scheme shows that the marine management tasks cannot be accomplished by the current authority structure available within the North Sea Federal State communities. We propose the establishment of a multi- and transdisciplinary independent regulative/advisory body, which ties in on different spatial levels and encompasses the affairs of the various Federal State communities in the EU. Over a given timeline, successive activities concerning different topics have to be addressed. Following an interdisciplinary assessment, where we suggest the use of an array of different tools, such as monitoring and establishment of DSSs, an integrated conflict assessment in spatial perspective could be achieved. Following this outcome, the main focus is on the legislation to formulate regulations, from case to case, between the different stakeholders on a transdisciplinary level. Of major importance here

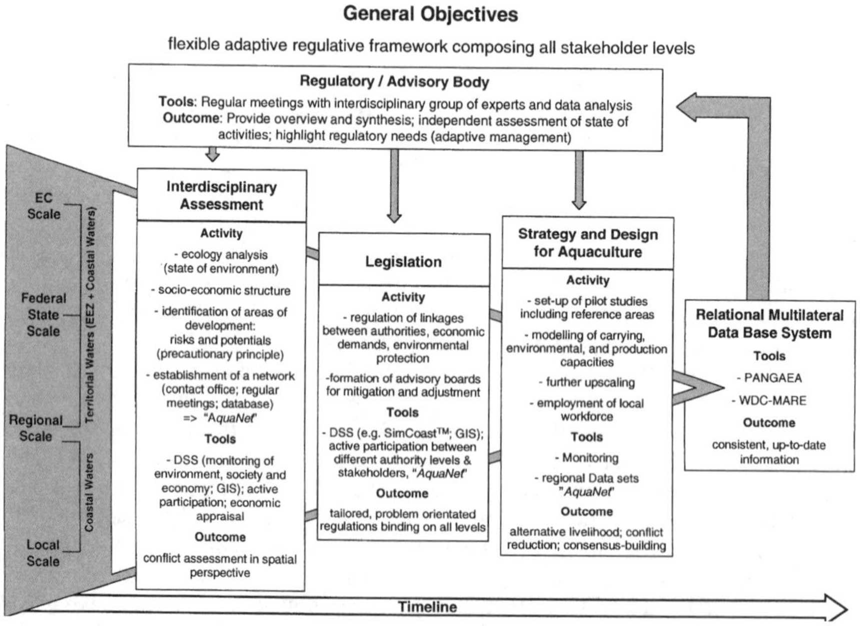

Figure 1. Scheme for the establishment of a flexible adaptive regulative framework comprising all stakeholder levels. The proposed regulatory/advisory body would provide expert knowledge, based on a relational multi-lateral data base, for the sectors "Interdisciplinary Assessment", "Legislation", and "Strategy and Design for Aquaculture" in the regulation and management process on a given timeline. For each of these sectors, several tools are proposed and desired outcomes outlined.

would be the formation of a platform for mitigation and adjustment between all groups involved. As tools for this procedure we suggest, among others, active participation and regular meetings between all stakeholder groups. This approach would lead to a tailored, problem-orientated set of regulations, which need to be binding at all levels. Having defined this framework, we can move on to formulate and test strategies and design of aquaculture at specific, previously assigned, sites. By continuous monitoring of the aquaculture site and reference areas, regional data sets are established, which flow into the relational, multi-lateral data base system. As the approach of the aquaculture is integrated, we expect outcomes to be based on consensus between the stakeholders and to provide alternative livelihoods for local communities. The different steps within the different spatial layers and sectors have to be repeated over time, which thus follows the generation policy cycles 1, 2 and 3 for ICZM proposed by Olsen *et al.* (1997).

5. DISCUSSION

In terms of the constantly increasing demand for marine products, aquaculture is one way out of the food impasse. To satisfy the increased demand for aquaculture products, this sector is currently undergoing a rapid development from a world-wide perspective. In the many considerations of the effects of aquaculture on the environment, the "precautionary principle" is frequently raised. Bengston *et al.* (2001) note that there is a requirement that all activities should be subject to prior review and authorisation. However, this principle should not be used frivolously to stop production if there is no impending environmental degradation. Tools, as outlined above, can be useful for elucidating ecological and socio-economic components and their interlinkages. This is especially timely with regard to the limited spatial resources available in the North Sea for development and extension of aquaculture. Questions pertaining to the number and type of species best suited to a balanced development of aquaculture should be addressed in close collaboration with experts as well as stakeholder groups and need to undergo well-defined decision-making process.

The existing regulations that have been listed above, which deal with aquaculture of marine organisms, have to be tied together or modified in order to provide a basis for straightforward integrative regulation for all stakeholders. First of all, the term aquaculture should be introduced into the regulative framework of all levels of institutions in concordance with the definitions within the Agenda 21, both in international conventions (e.g. OSPAR, 1992; UNCLOS, 1982) and in regional and State laws and directives. Furthermore, a simplification of EEC Directives and regulations should be realised in order to cover all sectors of aquaculture and the "grey areas" within the EEZs.

Regarding the current regulative framework in place for the German Territorial Waters, we suggest the creation of an overlapping comprehensive legislative body which is represented by an advisory board of experts on a multidisciplinary basis (see Figure 1). The cultivation of all potential marine candidates, such as fish, molluscs, crustaceans and macroalgae, has to be defined for all coastal zones of the Federal States as well as within the EU and the EEZ. Additionally, there is a need for regulations to protect and foster aquaculture development as well as to minimise impacts of other users on aquaculture.

A framework for developing new environmental law regulations, especially with respect to the emerging issues within aquaculture development, should incorporate the multi-dimensional interactions and ecosystem functions. It must be clear that for all types of human activities, ecosystems will set the limits as to how large an activity can grow in relation to its resource base. Within this ecosystem framework, the social system with all its institutional and cultural aspects will determine how fast an activity is approaching these limits. Thus, the definition of capacity thresholds on various levels is of importance for arriving at a well-defined scheme for sustainable development.

So far, from an international perspective, Canada has gone furthest in the regulation of aquaculture issues within the coastal areas (Fernandes *et al.*, 2000). Of the other States, the EU has made substantial efforts to establish a general framework of *Scientific Guidelines for Best Environmental Practice* in respect of aquaculture development, which could be widely applicable throughout the EU. The project "MARAQUA" (Monitoring and Regulation of Marine Aquaculture in Europe) is one example of this effort, which has been established and funded under the umbrella of the EU FAIR (Agriculture and Fisheries Programme) program. This two-year project, which commenced in 1999, was a "Concerted Action" and therefore did not involve new research but instead concentrated on a review of existing information and the establishment of agreed guidelines for the monitoring and regulation of marine aquaculture. Three workshops of expert groups, consisting of scientists, producers, regulators and voluntary organisations, took place, each focusing on different aspects of aquaculture development. MARAQUA has produced a critical review of the monitoring and regulation of marine aquaculture in the EU with reference to the implications of national and international regulation, and the role of codes of conduct, codes of practice and management systems in this process. Among other matters, the project analysed the socio-economic basis for approaches to improve the management of marine aquaculture (Fernandes *et al.*, 2000; Rosenthal *et al.*, 2000; Read *et al.*, 2001a; Rosenthal *et al.*, 2001).

The project raised some key issues, which need to be examined further attention in respect of the management and regulation of aquaculture. For example, MARAQUA highlighted aquaculture as an established marine activity which needs to fulfil environmental compatibility criteria in order to achieve sustainability, thereby meeting the social, economic and environmental needs and aspirations of society (Read *et al.*, 2001b). Additionally, the importance of promoting new policies for aquaculture that seek its full integration into an EU common strategy for the promotion of improved integrated planning and management of coastal development was emphasised.

We feel that the outcomes of such projects like MARAQUA provide a sound scientific basis for the further development of new, more integrated and comprehensive environmental regulatory framework to foster the establishment of sustainable aquaculture in the light of active co-management in the coastal zone.

6. CONCLUSIONS AND OUTLOOK

It could be argued that the current regulative framework in place in Germany does not support start-up companies in the aquaculture sector and does not attract potential investors. However, further promotion of aquaculture development should be carried out by the endorsement of the idea of ICZM in order for development to be sustainable and thus maintain the economic potential it holds for alternative livelihoods for coastal communities. This can be achieved by, among other things, considering risk-adverse behaviour and the "precautionary principle" of environmental management (Bodansky, 1991) and the implementation of adaptive management tools, which are suggested in the scheme above. In order to optimise for sustainable development, ICZM should consider both the short- and long-term impacts, which should be reflected in the environmental legislative framework. In this respect, environmental law regulations are of major importance for the promotion of integrated and transdisciplinary management. Legislative issues should encompass not only the direct "problem", for example, regulation of the establishment and maintenance of an aquaculture, but also the participation of the local stakeholders. This could limit the negative effect of external entrepreneur activities, which currently can only be minimally held liable for damages to the ecosystem, as well as to the local socio-economic system. Regulations should also support the establishment of new possibilities and user rights for the local user groups, for example, an imperative for fishermen training for future employment at aquaculture farms which are located on former traditional fishing grounds as a compensation measure. Additionally, a mitigation platform needs to be established where, from case to case, conflicts that arise can be addressed in an unbiased atmosphere and a consensus found. As well as the establishment of an information network, "*AquaNet*", there is a need for a lead agency (e.g. advisory board) in each country to be responsible for cross-sectoral regulatory framework development.

Active participation may influence the success of a sustained aquaculture development in the coastal zone. Herein lies the major role for the development of integrated environmental law regulations in order to minimise biased decision-making within an integrated coastal zone management framework and to support the idea of sustainability.

REFERENCES

Allegretti, M. (1994): Reservas Extrativistas: Parámetros para a política de desenvolvimento sustentável na Amazônia. In: R. Arnt *et al.* (Eds.), *O Desafio da Floresta*, Rio de Janeiro, Relume Dumará: 17–48.

Bengston, D.A., Halvorson, H.O., Pearce, J.B., Rheault, R.B. and Tlusty, M.F. (2001): Lessons learned and challenges. In: Tlusty *et al.* (2001) (Eds.), *Marine Aquaculture and the Environment: A Meeting for Stakeholders in the Northeast*. Cape Cod Press, Falmouth, Massachusetts. 319–324.

BNatschG (1998): Bundesnaturschutzgesetz, Gesetz über Naturschutz und Landespflege.

Bodansky D. (1991): Law: scientific uncertainty and the precautionary principle. *Environment* 33: 43–44.

Boysen, H.-O. (1991): Standpunkt der Fischereiverwaltung Schleswig-Holstein. In: Dethlefsen, V. (Ed.), *SDN-Kolloquium, Probleme der Muschelfischerei im Wattenmeer*. Wilhelmshaven, Schriftenreihe der Schutzgemeinschaft Deutsche Nordseeküste e. V. 50–52.

BremFiG (1991): Bremisches Fischereigesetz vom 17. September 1991, Brem.GBl. S. 309. Geändert durch Art. 1 des Gesetzes vom 1. Juni 1999, Brem.GBl. S. 139 und § 23 Abs. 6 des Gesetzes vom 21. November 2000, Brem.GBl. S. 437.

Bridge, L. (2001): Policy instruments for integrated coastal zone management in selected European countries. Coastlink, Maidstone. 95 pp.

Brilmayer, L. and Klein, N. (2001): Land and Sea: Two Sovereignty Regimes in Search of a Common Denominator. *New York University Journal of International Law and Politics* 33 (3): 703–768.

Buck, B.H. (2002): Open Ocean Aquaculture und Offshore-Windparks: Eine Machbarkeitsstudie über die multifunktionale Nutzung von Offshore-Windparks und Offshore-Marikultur im Raum Nordsee (Open Ocean Aquaculture and Offshore Wind farms: A feasibility study on the multifunctional use of offshore wind farms and offshore mariculture in the North Sea). *Reports on Polar and Marine Research*, Alfred Wegener Institute for Polar and Marine Research, Bremerhaven, 412: 252 pp.

Burbridge, P.R. (1997): A generic framework for measuring success in integrated coastal management. *Ocean & Coastal Management* 37: 175–189.

Burbridge, P.R., Hendrick, V., Roth, E. and Rosenthal, H. (2001): Social and economic policy issues relevant to marine aquaculture. *Journal of Applied Ichthyology* 17(4): 194–206.

CBD (1992): Convention on biological diversity. Rio de Janeiro, 3–14 June, 1992.

CEC (1979): Council Directive 79/923/EEC of 30 October 1979 on the quality required of shellfish waters. *Official Journal*: L 281, 10/11/1979.

CEC (1991a): Council Directive 91/492/EEC of 15 July 1991 laying down the health conditions for the production and the placing on the market of live bivalve molluscs. *Official Journal*: L 268, 24/09/1991.

CEC (1991b): Council Directive 91/67/EEC of 28 January 1991 concerning the animal health conditions governing the placing on the market of aquaculture animals and products. *Official Journal*: L 046, 19/02/1991

CEC (1993): Regulation 2847/93/EEC of 12 October 1993 establishing a control system applicable to the common fisheries policy. *Official Journal*: L 261, 20/10/1993.

CEC (1997a): Council Directive 97/79/EC of 18 December 1997 amending Directives 71/118/EEC, 72/462/EEC, 85/73/EEC, 91/67/EEC, 91/492/EEC, 91/493/EEC, 92/45/EEC and 92/118/EEC as regards the organisation of veterinary checks on products entering the Community from third countries. *Official Journal*: L 024, 30/01/1998.

CEC (1997b): Council Directive 97/11/EC of 3 March 1997 amending Directive 85/337/EEC on the assessment of the effects of certain public and private projects on the environment. *Official Journal*: L 073, 14/03/1997.

CEC (1998): Council Regulation 1181/98/EC of 4 June 1998 amending Regulation 3760/92/EEC establishing a Community system for fisheries and aquaculture. *Official Journal*: L 164, 09/06/1998.

CEC (2001a): Directive 2001/18/EC of the European Parliament and of the Council of 12 March 2001 on the deliberate release into the environment of genetically modified organisms and repealing Council Directive 90/220/EEC – Commission Declaration. *Official Journal*: L 106, 17/04/2001.

CEC (2001b): Decision 2455/2001/EC of the European Parliament and of the Council of 20 November 2001 amending Directive 2000/60/EC establishing the list of priority substances in the field of water policy. *Official Journal*: L 331, 15/12/2001.

Czybulka, D. and Kersandt, P. (2000): Legal regulations, legal instruments and competent authorities with relevance for marine protected areas (MPAs) in the exclusive economic zone (EEZ) and the high seas of the OSPAR maritime area. *BFN-Skripten* 22, Federal Agency for Nature Conservation, Bonn. 84 pp.

European Commission (1999): Lessons from the European Commission's Demonstration Programme on Integrated Coastal Zone Management (ICZM). Luxembourg: *Office for Official Publications of the European Communities*. 1–93.

Fabbri, K.P. (1998): A methodology for supporting decision making in integrated coastal zone management. *Ocean & Coastal Management* 39: 51–62.

Fernandes, T.F., Miller, K.L. and Read, P.A. (2000): Monitoring and regulation of marine aquaculture in Europe. *J. Appl. Ichthyology* 16(4): 138–143.

Fernandes, T.F., Eleftheriou, A., Ackefors, H., Eleftheriou, M., Ervik, A., Sanchez-Mata, A., Scanlon, T., White, P., Cochrane, S., Pearson, T.H. and Read, P.A. (2001): The scientific principles underlying the monitoring of the environmental impacts of aquaculture. *J. Appl. Ichthyology* 17 (4): 181–193.

GESAMP (1996): Joint Group of Experts on the Scientific Aspects of Marine Environmental protection) (IMO/FAO/UNESCO-IOC/WMO/WHO/IAEA/UN/UNEP). *The contributions of science to coastal zone management*. Rep. Study GESAMP 61:1–66.

Gesetz über den Nationalpark Hamburgisches Wattenmeer (1990): *Hamburgisches Gesetz- und Verordnungsblatt*, Nr. 11/1990 of 9 April 1990: 64–66.

Glaser, M. and Krause, G. (2002): Integriertes Küstenmanagement im föderalen Brasilien: Institutionelle, sektorale und legale Strukturen und die Grenzen der partizipativen Planung.- In: Glaeser, B. (Ed.), *Küste, Ökologie und Mensch – haben sie eine Zukunft?* Lit-Verlag (in press).

Govan, H., Inglis, A., Pretty, J., Harrison, M. and Wightman, A. (1998): Best practice in community participation for National Parks in Scotland. Review #107. Scottish Natural Heritage, Edinburgh, Scotland. 88 pp.

Grotius, H. (1916): *The freedom of the seas or the right which belongs to the Dutch to take part in the east Indian trade*. Magoffin, R. (Trans.), Scott, J.B. (Ed.), Oxford Univ. Press 1916 (1633). 22–44.

Hamburgisches Fischereigesetz (1986): Hamburgisches Fischereigesetz vom 22. Mai 1986, Hbg.GVBl. S. 95. Geändert durch Gesetz vom 9. April 1990, Hbg.GVBl. 63.

Hardin, G. (1968): The Tragedy of the Commons. *Science*, 162. Reprinted in Dryzek, J.S. and Schlosberg, D. (1999): *Debating the Earth: the environmental politics reader*. New York: Oxford University Press.

Hogarth, A.N. and McGlade, J. (1998): SimCoast™: Integrating information about the coastal zone. *EC Fisheries Cooperation Bulletin* 11: 29–31.

ICES (1984): Guidelines for Implementing the ICES Code of Practice Concerning Introductions and Transfers of Marine Species. International Council for the Exploration of the Sea: 130.

ICES (1988): Codes of Practice and Manual of Procedures for Consideration of Introductions and Transfers of Marine and Freshwater Organisms. International Council for the Exploration of the Sea: 159.

James, R.J. (2000): From beaches to beach environments: linking the ecology, human-use and management of beaches in Australia. *Ocean & Coastal Management* 43: 495–514.

Kannen, A. (2000): Analyse ausgewählter Ansätze und Instrumente zu Integriertem Küstenzonenmanagement und deren Bewertung. Büsum: Forsch. und Technologiezentrum Westküste d. Univ. Kiel., Bericht Nr. 23: 278 pp.

KüFO (1999): Landesverordnung über die Ausübung der Fischerei in den Küstengewässern, Schleswig-Holsteinische Küstenfischereiordnung vom 23. Juni 1999, GVOBl. Schl.-H: 471.

Lakshmi, A. and Rajagopalan, R. (2000) Socio-economic implications of coastal zone degradation and their mitigation: a case study from coastal villages in India. *Ocean & Coastal Management* 43: 749–762.

LFischG (1996): Fischereigesetz für das Land Schleswig-Holstein (Landesfischereigesetz) vom 10.ö Februar 1996, GVOBl.Schl.-H. S. 211. Geändert durch Gesetz vom 12. Dezember 1997, GVOBl. Schl.-H.: 471.

Marencic, H. (2002): Trilaterales Wattenmonitoring – Status und Ausblick. 1. Tagung "Forschungs-horizonte der Küstenregionen" 13–15 February GKSS Forschungszentrum Geesthacht. 5–7.

National Park Law of Lower Saxony (2001): Gesetz über die Niedersächsischen Nationalparks "Niedersächsisches Wattenmeer" und "Harz" of 11 July 2001. Nds. GVBl. 443

Nds.FischG (1978): Niedersächsisches Fischereigesetz vom 1. Februar 1978, Nieders.GVBl. S. 81. Geändert durch Artikel 34 des Gesetzes vom 22. März 1990, Nieders.GVBl: 101.
Nds.KüFischO (1992): Niedersächsische Küstenfischereiordnung vom 1. Dezember 1992, Nieders.GVBl: 321.
Noble, B.F. (2000): Institutional criteria for co-management. *Marine Policy* 24: 69–77.
NPG (1999): Nationalparkgesetz of Schleswig-Holstein of 17 December 1999. 19 pp.
Olsen, S., Tobey, J. and Kerr, M. (1997): A common framework for learning from ICM experience. *Ocean & Coastal Management* 37: 155–174.
OSPAR (1992): *Oslo-Paris* Convention of the Protection of the Marine Environment of the North-East Atlantic. Paris, 22 September, 1992.
QRS (2000): Quality Status Report of OSPAR Commission, Region II: Greater North Sea. London, 136 pp.
Read, P.A., Fernandes, T.F., Miller, K.L., Eleftheriou, A., Eleftheriou, M., Davies, I.M. and Rodger, G.K. (Eds.) (2001a): The implications of directives, conventions and codes of practice on the monitoring and regulation of marine aquaculture in Europe. Proceedings of the second MARAQUA Workshop held at the Institute of Marine Biology in Crete, 20–22 March 2000. Aberdeen UK: Scottish Executive. 114 pp.
Read, P.A., Fernandes, T.F. and Miller, K.L. (2001b): The derivations of scientific guidelines for best environmental practice for the monitoring and regulation of marine aquaculture in Europe. *J. Appl. Ichthyology* 17 (4): 164–152.
Richter, C., Burbridge, P.R., Gätje, C., Knoppers, B.A., Martins, O., Ngoile, M.A.K., O'Toole, M.J., Ramachandran, S., Salomons, W. and Talaue-McManus, L. (2001): Group Report: Integrated Coastal Management in Developing Countries. In: Bodungen, B.v. and Turner, R.K., (Eds.), *Science and Integrated Coastal Management*. Dahlem University Press. 253–273.
Rosenthal, H. and Hilge, V. (2000): Aquaculture production and environmental regulations in Germany. *J. Appl. Ichthyology* 16: 163–166.
Rosenthal, H., Schnack, D., Hilge, V., Read, P.A., Fernandes, T.F., Miller, K.L., Davies, I.M. and Rodger, G.K. (Eds.) (2000): MARAQUA The monitoring and regulation of marine aquaculture in Europe. Proceedings of the first MARAQUA Workshop held at the University of the Algarve, Faro, Portugal, 6–8 September 1999. *J. Appl. Ichthyology* 16 (4–5): 138–229.
Rosenthal, H., Read, P.A., Fernandes, T.F. and Miller, K.L. (2001): MARAQUA The derivation of scientific guidelines for best environmental practice for the monitoring and regulation of marine aquaculture in Europe. Proceedings of the third MARAQUA Workshop held at Napier University, Edinburgh, Scotland, 28–31 August 2000. *J. Appl. Ichthyology* 17(4): 145–206.
Ruth, M. (1997): Zukunft der Muschelfischerei im Schleswig-Holsteinischen Wattenmeer: Ausgleich zwischen Ökologie und Ökonomie? In: Dethlefsen, V. (Ed.): *SDN-Kolloquium, Zukunft der Muschelfischerei im Schleswig-Holsteinischen Wattenmeer*. Varel, Schriftenreihe der Schutzgemeinschaft Deutsche Nordseeküste e. V. 9–17.
Schmid, R. (1993): Regulating Waste from Aquaculture Production: Federal Republic of Germany. Workshop on Fish Farm Effluents and their Control in EC Countries, Congress Center Hamburg, Nov. 23–25, 1992 – Report. Department of Fishery, IFM Kiel, Kiel. 79 pp.
SeeAnlV (2001): Seeanlagenverordnung, Verordnung über Anlagen seewärts der Begrenzung des deutschen Küstenmeeres.
Theodorou, J.A. (2001): Regulation and Monitoring of Shellfish Aquaculture in Europe. In: The implications of directives, conventions and codes of practice on the monitoring and regulation of marine aquaculture in Europe. Read *et al.* (Eds.). Proceedings of the second MARAQUA Workshop held at the Institute of Marine Biology in Crete, 20–22 March 2000. Aberdeen UK: Scottish Executive. 114 pp.
UNCLOS (1982): United Nations Conventions on the Law of the Sea. Montego Bay, 10 December, 1982.

Underwood A.J. (1995): Ecological research and (and research into) environmental management. *Ecological Applications* 5(1): 232–247.

Van Mulekom, L. (1999): An institutional development process in community based coastal resource management: building the capacity and opportunity for community based co-management in a small-scale fisheries community. *Ocean & Coastal Management* 42: 439–456.

Warner, M. and P. Jones. (1998): Assessing the need to manage conflict in community-based natural resource projects. ODI Natural Resource Perspectives, No. 35. 11 pp.

Welp, M. (2001): Stakeholder Successes in Global Environmental Management. Potsdam: Potsdam -Institut für Klimafolgenforschung. Report-No.70. 49 pp.

WHG (1996): Wasserhaushaltsgesetz, Gesetz zur Ordnung des Wasserhaushalts in der Fassung der Bekanntmachung vom 12. November 1996, (BGBl. I S. 1696).

WSP (1997): Wadden Sea Plan, State Declaration of the Trilateral Wadden Sea Plan, Stade, 22 October 1997.

Compensation for Environmental Damage in Maritime Liability Regimes

*Louise Angélique de La Fayette**

A. INTRODUCTION

1. Environmental Liability

While most international environmental law is found in treaties dealing with the *prevention* of damage to or degradation of the environment, some is also found in treaties dealing with *emergency response* and some in treaties providing for *liability and compensation* where damage has occurred. Most of the regimes established by the liability instruments address either particular sources of damage, such as nuclear activities, or specific areas suffering damage, such as the marine environment, or both. In this paper I shall examine very briefly the compensation for environmental damage in a number of maritime liability regimes, both in existence and under development, and to consider whether those regimes adequately address the problem of damage to the environment *per se*. I shall also mention in passing a number of other liability regimes that may apply to damage to the marine environment or that may serve as useful comparisons, although they have a much broader scope.

Part XII on Protection and Preservation of the Marine Environment of the 1982 United Nations Convention on the Law of the Sea requires states to protect the marine environment from pollution and other forms of environmental degradation from all possible sources, to co-operate to that end on a regional or global basis, to adopt contingency plans for emergency response and to ensure that recourse is available for prompt and adequate compensation for damage to the marine environment. Most pertinently, Article 235 enjoins states to co-operate in the implementation of existing international law and in the further development of international law relating to responsibility and liability for the assessment of and compensation for damage and related disputes, etc.

* Ms. *Louise Angélique de La Fayette* is a Principal Legal Officer at the Division for Ocean Affairs and the Law of the Sea of the United Nations, New York (United States). Contact: delafayette@un.org.

She has been associated with most of the treaties considered in this paper, as a former legal adviser to the Canadian Department of Foreign Affairs and International Trade, and as a representative of the International Union for the Conservation of Nature and Natural Resources (IUCN).

Any opinion expressed is personal and does not necessarily reflect the views of either the Canadian Government, the IUCN or the United Nations.

A. Kirchner (ed.), International Maritime Environmental Law, 231–265.

However, of the several sources of marine pollution addressed in Part XII, only ship-source pollution benefits from an existing and operative liability regime. With respect to land-based activities causing damage to the marine environment, just as there is no global convention to control such activities, so there is no liability regime for any damage caused. Similarly, there is no global convention dealing with environmentally damaging activities on the continental shelf, such as oil and gas exploration and exploitation, and no liability regime in force.[1] While the London Convention 1972 and the 1996 Protocol[2] on the regulation of ocean dumping both provide for the development of a liability regime, states parties have decided that no such instrument is necessary, especially as all dumping of hazardous materials has theoretically been phased out.[3] Finally, while the International Seabed Authority has adopted rules relating to damage caused during deep seabed mining, these are rudimentary and remain to be fleshed out and implemented in practice.

In contrast to the other sources of damage to the marine environment, there is already a fairly comprehensive regime of treaties applicable to pollution caused by ships, including:

1. the International Convention on Civil Liability for Oil Pollution Damage (CLC), 1992
2. the International Convention on the Establishment of an International Fund for Compensation for Oil Pollution Damage, 1992
3. the International Convention on Liability and Compensation for Damage in Connection with the Carriage of Hazardous and Noxious Substances by Sea (HNS Convention), 1996
4. the International Convention on Civil Liability for Bunker Oil Pollution Damage (Bunkers Convention), 2001.

Of these, only the first two are in force. As for the future, a convention on wreck removal now in development will provide for compensation for the cost of removing wrecks posing a hazard to the environment, and one could envisage a convention imposing liability for damage caused by harmful organisms and pathogens in ship's ballast water. In addition, there are conventions on civil liability for nuclear damage and for damage caused by the transboundary movement of hazardous waste that are applicable to damage caused in the course of transport of radioactive material and hazardous waste by sea. The Space Liability Convention could be applied to space objects falling into the sea, and the possible Antarctic liability annex might also be applicable to the marine environment.

---

1 The Convention on Civil Liability for Oil Pollution Damage resulting from Exploration for and Exploitation of Seabed Mineral Resources was adopted in 1977 to provide compensation for damage caused by the exploration for and the exploitation of oil and gas resources on the continental shelf in the North Sea Area. Done at London, 1 May 1977, not in force; Cmnd. 6791. It is not considered in this paper because it is only regional, will never enter into force and uses the outmoded 1969 CLC definition of "pollution damage".

2 Convention on the Prevention of Marine Pollution by Dumping of Wastes and Other Matter, London, 1972; and Protocol to the Convention on the Prevention of Marine Pollution by Dumping of Wastes and Other Matter, London, 1996.

3 Louise Angéligue de La Fayette, "The London Convention 1972: Preparing for the Future", 13 *International Journal of Marine and Coastal Law*, 515–536 (1998).

Somewhat surprisingly, there is no definition of "marine environment" or of "impairment to the environment" in any international regime, except for the one addressing deep seabed mining. Although not all aspects of the liability regime for deep seabed mining are complete, in order to make the following discussion more comprehensible, the terms of this definition might usefully be reproduced here. The "marine environment" comprises:

> the physical, chemical, geological and biological components, conditions and factors which interact and determine the productivity, state, condition and quality of the marine ecosystem, the waters of the seas and oceans and the airspace above those waters, as well as the seabed and ocean floor and subsoil thereof.[4]

At the same time, it should be borne in mind that pollution in the sea is likely to reach the shore, where it will damage the coastal environment. Therefore, a definition of the general environment might also be useful to this study: "environment" includes natural resources, both biotic and abiotic, such as air, water, soil, fauna and flora; the interaction of these in a complete ecosystem; the characteristic features of the landscape; and property which forms part of the cultural heritage, such as historic sites and monuments. Although in the context of prevention, human beings are often included in the concept of "environment" and "environmental damage", in the context of liability and compensation, injury to human beings is usually considered separately. This is because most regimes on liability for damage are based upon traditional tort law concepts of damage to persons and property, with the concept of the environment, both as medium for damage and as an object of damage, being grafted on afterwards, usually not very successfully.

In the only liability regime currently in operation, that concerning oil pollution from ships, the absence of a definition of impairment of the environment has not posed any practical difficulties in most cases. All parties involved accept that oil spilled from a ship constitutes "contamination" that will cause pollution or impairment to marine resources as well as to the coast when washed ashore. In general, the concept of damage to, or impairment of, the environment refers to an adverse change in the components of an ecosystem, their functioning, or their interaction, caused by an external factor of anthropogenic origin. As we shall see, however, the oil pollution regime focuses almost exclusively on damage to property and especially economic loss suffered by individuals, companies and governments, and not on damage to the environment *per se*. Moreover, all the subsequent civil liability treaties have been influenced by the concept of damage in this regime, more specifically the definition established by the 1984 Protocols to the 1969 International Convention on Civil Liability for Oil Pollution Damage (CLC)[5] and the 1971 International Convention on the Establishment of an International Fund for

---

4 For further discussion, see Section D.2, *infra*.

5 International Convention on Civil Liability for Oil Pollution Damage, done at Brussels, 29 November 1969, in force 19 June 1975; 973 UNTS 3. For an account of the background to the conclusion of the CLC, see Balkin, "The Establishment and Work of the IMO Legal Committee", in Nordquist and Moore (eds), *Current Maritime Issues and the International Maritime Organization* (Martinus Nijhoff Publishers, 1999).

Compensation for Oil Pollution Damage (Fund Convention).[6] The only exceptions are the regimes for deep seabed mining and Antarctica.

However, before embarking upon a necessarily cursory survey of the international regimes, especially that for oil pollution damage, a summary of the domestic US law and practice may be instructive. The US legislation and the international regimes appear to have developed in different directions, with the former focusing on damage to natural resources (the environment *per se*), and the latter focusing upon damage to persons and property, while viewing the US regime with suspicion and even hostility. The conclusions to this paper will consider how far these differences are real, rather than apparent, and will tentatively suggest the basic elements of an "ideal" international regime to address the issue of liability and compensation for environmental harm.

2. The US Regime for Compensation for Natural Resource Damage

When the 1984 Protocols to the CLC and Fund Conventions were adopted, the United States was expected to become a party to the international liability regime. However, the 1989 *Exxon Valdez* oil pollution disaster prompted a radical change in course. Because the international regime did not provide sufficient compensation for the level of damage caused by the *Exxon Valdez* and because it did not cover damage to the environment itself, the US decided not to become a party to the revised CLC and Fund Conventions and to adopt instead its own much more stringent legislation in the Oil Pollution Act of 1990 (OPA '90).[7] In addition to stipulating various preventive measures, OPA '90 provides for both higher levels of liability and compensation for damage to the environment *per se*, termed "natural resource damage".

Under OPA '90, the categories of compensable damage are:

1. natural resource damage;
2. damage to real or personal property (injury or economic loss due to destruction);
3. loss of subsistence use of natural resources;
4. loss of revenues, taxes, etc. previously recoverable by government;
5. loss of profits and earning capacity due to injury to property or natural resources;
6. cost to public services, e.g. for removal of oil by government agencies.

"Natural resource damage" is defined as: "Damages for injury to, destruction of, loss of, or loss of use of, natural resources, including the reasonable costs of assessing the

6 International Convention on the Establishment of an International Fund for Compensation for Oil Pollution Damage (Fund Convention), done at Brussels, 18 December 1971, in force 16 October 1978; (1972) 11 ILM 284.

7 US Oil Pollution Act of 1990, 33 U.S.C. #2706. Liability and compensation for natural resource damage were available under a number of earlier statutes, primarily the Comprehensive Environmental Response, Compensation and Liability Act of 1980 (known as CERLA or Superfund), codified at 42 USC #9601 ff.; 33 USC 2701 ff.; and the Federal Water Pollution Act of 1973, 43 USC ##1651–1655. For a recent discussion, see Brighton and Askman, "The Role of Government Trustees in Recovering Compensation for Injury to Natural Resources", in Wetterstein (ed.), *op. cit.*, n 4 at 177.

damage, which shall be recoverable by a United States trustee, a state trustee, an Indian tribe trustee, or a foreign trustee."[8] Under a rule adopted by the National Oceanic and Atmospheric Administration (NOAA) in 1996, the definition of "injury" requires a demonstration of an "observable or measurable adverse change in a natural resource or impairment of a natural resource service".[9]

Finally, the measure of natural resource damages under section 2702(b)(2)(A) is:

(a) the cost of restoring, rehabilitating, replacing, or acquiring the equivalent of, the damaged natural resources;
(b) the diminution of value of those resources pending restoration; plus
(c) the reasonable cost of assessing those damages.[10]

All financial compensation must be used only to pay for restoration and other costs related to the damage to natural resources.[11]

Those who oppose civil liability for natural resource damage usually point to two theoretical problems: the questions of (i) who can claim compensation for damage to elements of the environment that are *res communis* or *res nullia*, and (ii) how to calculate the "cost" of damage to things that have no market price or commercial value such as air, water, or biodiversity, and the loss of "existence value" or aesthetic pleasure. In the US, the question of whom should be compensated was easily resolved by designating federal agencies, state governments or Indian tribes as "trustees" for the natural resources concerned.[12] However, the problem of how to calculate natural resource damage remained, in relation to both the value of the loss of resource use while it is being restored, and the value of damaged resources where they cannot be restored and where the creation of an "equivalent" environment is not possible. It is precisely the question of the valuation of "natural resource damage" and the highly criticised methods for its calculation proposed by economists[13] that have prevented the inclusion of compensation for these aspects of "harm" in the various international treaty regimes.

However, in actual practice, natural resource damage is not compensated in monetary terms in accordance with an economic theory. The usual procedure is for

---

8 In s 2701(20), natural resources are defined as including: "land, fish, wildlife, biota, air, water, drinking water supplies, and other such resources belonging to, managed by, held in trust by, appertaining to, or otherwise controlled by the United States (including the resources of the exclusive economic zone), any state or local government or Indian tribe, or any foreign government."

9 61 Fed. Reg. 504 (5 Jan. 1966).

10 *Ibid.*, s 2706(d).

11 For detailed explanations of how the system actually works, see: (i) a CD ROM produced in August 1996, entitled "Guidance Documents for Natural Resource Damage Assessment Under the Oil Pollution Act of 1990"; (ii) an information package produced by NOAA, which includes a number of explanatory documents, such as "Reversing the Tide: Restoring the Nation's Coastal and Marine Natural Resources" (June 1998), technical documents produced by the Hazardous Materials Response Division in March 2000, and descriptions of actual cases in which restoration has been undertaken; and (iii) the NOAA website, at http://response.restoration.noaa.gov, which also contains legislative texts.

12 For details, see Brighton and Askman, *op. cit.*, n 5.

13 For a comprehensive study, see: "Study on the Valuation and Restoration of Damage to Natural Resources for the Purpose of Environmental Liability", prepared by MacAllister Elliott and Partners Ltd, May 2001, for the European Commission, Document no B4-3040/2000/265781/MAR/B3.

the person(s) liable for the damage either to repair it themselves or to fund the restoration in accordance with a plan approved by the governmental authority. Where restoration of the original site is not possible immediately or at all, the liable person(s) will pay for the creation of a comparable site nearby to provide the same or similar environmental services as those lost due to the oil spill. According to NOAA, most restoration projects are for alternative sites to compensate for "interim losses" while the original site regenerates itself, with or without assistance. As we shall see, up until recently, this kind of restoration has not even been considered in the international liability regime.

B. TREATIES RELATING TO MARINE POLLUTION

The International Maritime Organization (IMO) is the United Nations specialised agency with a mandate to address all aspects of international shipping activities, in particular, ship safety, safety of navigation and protection of the marine environment. Therefore, all the global instruments dealing with damage to the marine environment from ships have been adopted under the *aegis* of IMO. The IMO conventions on liability and compensation have all been prepared in the Legal Committee, a very conservative body most of whose members are either specialists in private (commercial) maritime law, or not lawyers at all, but general diplomats or technical experts, such as engineers. Consequently, it is not surprising that they are not familiar with the law of the sea, with international environmental law or with the ecological services provided by the environment and the need to protect them. When addressing damage caused by pollution from ships, they focus almost exclusively on economic loss suffered by fishermen and businesses reliant on the tourist trade. Even though the livelihoods of these "victims" depends upon the existence of a "clean" environment, paradoxically, the environment itself is viewed as useless and irrelevant.

1. Liability and Compensation for Oil Pollution Damage

After the *Torrey Canyon* oil spill disaster of 1967, IMO adopted a number of treaties dealing with marine pollution, in relation to prevention, emergency response and liability for damage. These included the 1969 International Convention on Civil Liability for Oil Pollution Damage (CLC), providing for the strict liability of the shipowner for "pollution damage" resulting from the escape or discharge of oil from a sea-going vessel actually carrying oil in bulk as cargo. For the purposes of the Convention, "pollution damage" was defined as:

> ... loss or damage caused outside the ship carrying oil by *contamination* resulting from the escape or discharge of oil from the ship, wherever such escape or damage may occur, and includes the costs of preventive measures and further loss or damage caused by preventive measures. (Emphasis added.)

"Preventive measures" were defined as "any reasonable measures taken by any person *after* an accident has occurred to prevent or minimise pollution damage." (Emphasis added.) The terms "environment" and "damage to the environment" are conspicuous by their absence.

At the time of the adoption of the CLC, it was recognised that provision had to be made to supplement compensation under the CLC, should the shipowner not be able to satisfy all the claims or should he be exempted from liability. Furthermore, it was considered to be equitable that the cargo interests contribute to the compensation, for it was the hazardous nature of the cargo that would be responsible for the damage. Therefore, in 1971 IMO adopted the International Convention on the Establishment of an International Fund for Compensation for Oil Pollution Damage (Fund Convention), establishing the International Oil Pollution Compensation Fund (IOPC Fund), funded by payments from companies receiving oil transported by sea into the territories of states parties. The IOPC Fund is an international organisation with headquarters in London, comprising an Assembly, an Executive Committee and a Secretariat headed by a Director.[14] It provides supplementary compensation to claimants who cannot obtain full compensation under the CLC, because the shipowner is not liable, because he does not have sufficient funds, or because the amount of damage exceeds the limitation of his liability.[15]

Although "pollution damage" was defined in the 1969 CLC, "pollution", and "contamination" were not. Lying behind these undefined terms was the scientific practice of referring to the anthropogenic introduction of substances or energy into the sea as *contamination*, while the deleterious effects were considered to be the *pollution*.[16] The CLC and Fund Conventions simply assume that oil is a hazardous substance, which will have deleterious consequences (pollution) if released from a ship. In relation to preventive measures in particular, it is assumed that the escape of oil from the ship and its spreading over the sea and onto the shore must be prevented, and that once it does escape and spread, it must be cleaned up. Both the containment of the oil at sea and its removal on shore are considered to be "preventive measures", because such measures are necessary to prevent further damage to property or to the economic interests of the victims.[17]

While the Director of the Fund may authorise payment of compensation for "normal" cases, the Fund's Executive Committee makes decisions concerning payment in hard cases, interpreting the Convention and determining which claims qualify as "pollution damage". To assist it in this task, the Fund takes the advice of experts, most notably that of the International Tanker Owners Pollution Federation (ITOPF). ITOPF officers travel all over the world at the request of members, their

---

14 For information, see IOPC Fund website at http://www.iopcfund.org.

15 Liability is limited according to the size of the vessel, not the amount of pollution damage.

16 In the 1982 Law of the Sea Convention, pollution of the marine environment is defined as "the introduction by man of substances or energy into the marine environment, which results or is likely to result in certain deleterious effects". This definition was an advance on the work of GESAMP, the IMO/FAO/UNESCO-IOC/WMO/WHO/IAEA/UN/UNEP Joint Group of Experts on the Scientific Aspects of Marine Environmental Protection (formerly Marine Pollution). It has since been modified and expanded in more recent conventions in the light of further scientific research. At a recent meeting attended by the author, GESAMP considered revising its definition of "pollution" in order to bring it up to date and also to formulate definitions of "contamination" and "marine environmental degradation". The latter term includes all forms of impairment of the marine environment, of which pollution is only one.

17 A more accurate term might be "response measures"; however, the initial cleaning up of the oil from sea or land might also be considered as the first stage of reinstatement or restoration of the environment to its pre-spill condition.

insurers and affected states providing advice on the most effective emergency response to oil spills. At the request of the insurers or the IOPC Fund, ITOPF will also assess the reasonableness of preventive measures and the admissibility and amount of claims.[18] Most oil pollution claims are settled by negotiation with the insurer and the Fund, but a few are contested in court, with the possible result of conflicting interpretations of the CLC and Fund Conventions in accordance with different national concepts of pollution damage.

One curious feature of the definition of pollution damage in the 1969 CLC is that it is exceptionally vague and general: it does not indicate exactly what kind of damage is covered. At first sight, it covers *any* loss or damage caused by *contamination* by oil released from a ship carrying oil as cargo.[19] Although damage to the environment was not expressly included, it was not excluded either. In fact, one could argue that almost anything could be included. In the event, in the context of the CLC and Fund Conventions, the precise meaning of "pollution damage" has been determined mainly by the subsequent practice of the Fund Secretariat in paying claims within its discretion, by the Executive Committee in the approval of problematic claims, and in subsequent agreements outlined below.

A challenge to the original, apparently all-inclusive 1969 CLC definition of pollution damage was not long in coming. In 1979, the year following the Convention's entry into force, the USSR submitted a claim for damage to the marine environment by an oil spill from the tanker *Antonio Gramsci*. The amount claimed was based upon a mathematical model prescribed by national legislation providing for compensation to be paid at a rate of two roubles per cubic metre of polluted water, the volume of which was to be estimated by the amount of oil spilled in Soviet waters. Alarmed by the prospect of unlimited claims for damage to the environment *per se*, in 1980 the Fund Assembly adopted Resolution No 3, declaring that:

> ... the assessment of compensation to be paid by the International Oil Pollution Compensation Fund is not to be made on the basis of an abstract quantification of damage calculated in accordance with theoretical models.[20]

The 1984 Definition of Oil Pollution Damage

However, because the resolution was not legally binding, in 1984 the parties adopted amendments to the CLC and Fund Conventions that included a revision of

---

18 For basic information about the work of ITOPF, see the ITOPF website: http://www.itopf.com and The International Tanker Owners Pollution Federation Limited, *ITOPF Handbook 2000/2001*. Consultants and academic experts are also relied upon, including some engaged locally because they are familiar with the area, the oceanography or the state of the fisheries.

19 It might also be noted here that, as the definition of "pollution damage" does not expressly exclude personal injury, the Fund has admitted that claims for personal injury cannot be excluded in principle. However, in practice, the Fund has not admitted claims for injury by inhalation of fumes or for risk to health. In one recent case arising out of the Braer spill, a local landowner claimed for stress and depression resulting from pollution of his property. While admitting that "pollution damage" could include physical injury, the Fund rejected the claims for "stress", asserting that the stress had not been caused by contamination and that it could not pay claims for anxiety or speculative damage.

20 *Report on the Activities of the International Oil Pollution Compensation Fund in the Calendar Year 1979*.

the definition of pollution damage expressly designed to *limit* compensation for impairment of the environment to the costs of reasonable measures of reinstatement. The new definition reads as follows:

"Pollution damage" means:

(a) loss or damage caused outside the ship by contamination resulting from the escape or discharge of the oil from the ship, wherever such escape or discharge may occur, provided that compensation for impairment of the environment other than loss of profit from such impairment shall be limited to costs of reasonable measures of reinstatement actually undertaken or to be undertaken;

(b) the costs of preventive measures and further loss or damage caused by preventive measures.

Even though the 1984 amendments never came into force, the Fund subsequently acted as if the new definition of damage had always been the authoritative interpretation of the 1969 Convention.

The 1984 CLC definition of "pollution damage"[21] is far from ideal. It is awkward and unclear; it mixes a definition of damage with a level of compensation; and it does not state explicitly what kinds of damage will be compensated. Moreover, the definition is not appropriate in all contexts, as "pollution damage" by contamination is not the only possible type of environmental damage, even in the oceans. Despite these deficiencies, the 1984 oil pollution definition has had a substantial influence upon the concept of environmental damage in most subsequent international liability regimes. Similar definitions have been adopted repeatedly, primarily because states feel comfortable with established precedent, but also because they find it difficult to agree on anything else.[22]

The most important feature of the 1984 oil pollution definition is that it is expressly designed to *exclude* compensation for damage to the environment *per se*. Whereas the purpose of treaties to protect the environment is to prevent or to mitigate damage to the environment itself, the purpose of most liability treaties is not to impose liability for damage *to* the environment, but liability for damage to human beings, their property and their economic circumstances *through* damage to the environment. In the liability treaties, damage to the environment itself is usually only relevant in terms of compensation for the cost of removing a hazardous substance and reinstating the environment, where this is possible. Where clean-up and reinstatement is not possible, there is no compensation for damage to the environment itself.

In effect, the 1984 definition was designed to provide compensation to human beings for direct economic loss, including: (i) the cost of cleaning up the oil; (ii) the cost of repairing or replacing property, such as boats, piers or nets, contaminated by oil; (iii) consequential economic loss occasioned by property damage; and (iv) pure economic loss suffered by tourist businesses and fishermen dependent upon a "clean" environment for their livelihood.

---

21 Hereinafter referred to as "the 1984 oil pollution definition".

22 The only instrument with a definition of pollution damage taken from the original 1969 CLC is the 1977 Convention on Civil Liability for Oil Pollution Damage resulting from Exploration for and Exploitation of Seabed Mineral Resources.

Because the 1984 amendments could not come into force without the participation of the US, in 1992 states parties adopted two new Protocols to both the CLC and Fund conventions incorporating the 1984 text, including the new definition of pollution damage, but with different provisions for entry into force.[23] Yet the Fund's problems were not over, because the 1992 Protocols did not come into force until 30 May 1996, and before they did, it faced several claims for damage to the marine environment *per se*, together with a number of other questions regarding the admissibility of claims. In particular, in the 1985 *Patmos* and 1991 *Haven* cases, the Italian government claimed compensation for damage to the marine environment *per se*, as trustee for the national patrimony, which claims were allowed by the Italian courts.[24]

The 1994 Working Group

As a consequence of the Italian cases, as well as a number of questions in other cases regarding pure economic loss, in 1993 the Fund Assembly decided to establish a Working Group to examine several issues relating to the admissibility of claims, including the question of claims for damage to the marine environment. In its report, the Working Group was careful to emphasise that the Fund would only pay for quantifiable economic loss which was verifiable, and for measures that were objectively reasonable at the time they were taken.[25]

With respect to "environmental damage",[26] the Working Group based its work on the 1984 definition of pollution damage in the 1992 Protocols to the CLC and Fund Conventions, taking into account the declaration in Resolution No. 3.

---

23 Protocol to the 1969 CLC, done at London 27 November 1992, in force 30 May 1996; Protocol to the 1971 Fund, done at London, 27 November 1992, in force 30 May 1996. The 1992 Protocols incorporated the unamended text of the earlier conventions to produce two new conventions. Consolidated versions have been published by the Fund. The definition of pollution damage originating in the 1984 protocols and repeated in the 1992 Protocols will hereinafter be referred to as the 1984 oil pollution definition.

24 In the event, in the *Patmos* case, because the claims did not exceed the shipowner's liability, the Fund did not have to pay anything. In the *Haven* case, the Fund and the Italian government agreed to a global settlement of all claims, with the Fund specifically stating that it would not pay anything for compensation for damage to the marine environment *per se*. For a summary of the judgment of the Court of Appeal in the *Patmos Case*, see IOPC Doc. FUND/Exc.30/2, para. 4.15, 29 November 1991. For details, see the account in *Report on the Activities of the International Oil Pollution Compensation Fund in the Calendar Year 1994*, 36–39. For discussion see Maffei, "The Compensation for Ecological Damage in the 'Patmos' Case", in Francioni and Scovazzi (eds), *International Responsibility for Environmental Harm* (Graham and Trotman, 1991); and Bianchi, "Harm to the Environment in Italian Practice: The Interaction of International Law and Domestic Law", in Wetterstein (ed.), *op. cit.*, n 4 at 103. For a report on the settlement in the *Haven* case, see: IOPC Funds, *Annual Report*, 1999 at 42–48.

25 According to *Guidelines on Biological Impacts of Oil Pollution*, published in 1991 by the International Petroleum Industry Conservation Association: "Recovery is marked by the re-establishment of a healthy biological community in which the plants and animals characteristic of that community are present and are functioning normally", quoted in: "Admissibility and Assessment of Claims for Oil Pollution Damage", Report of the Chairman of the International Sub-Committee, *Yearbook 1993*, Comité Maritime International.

26 This is the term used in the report of the Working Group. Apparently, it considered "impairment of the environment" and "environmental damage" to be synonymous.

It considered that the Fund should maintain its position that claims relating to the impairment of the environment should be accepted only if the claimant had suffered a quantifiable economic loss, measurable in monetary terms. In other words, compensation is not payable for damage to the environment *per se*.

Somewhat surprisingly in view of the clear language of the 1984 definition referring to reinstatement, the Working Group then considered whether the Fund should pay for measures to reinstate the environment to its pre-spill condition.[27] On the basis of the 1984 definition of "pollution damage", the Working Group agreed that claims for the cost of reinstatement would only be admissible if they fulfilled the following criteria:

1. the cost of the measures should be reasonable;
2. the cost of the measures should not be disproportionate to the results achieved or the results which could reasonably be expected; and
3. the measures should be appropriate and offer a reasonable prospect of success.

The Working Group emphasised that the test of reasonableness was objective, and should be evaluated in the light of the information available at the time. Moreover, compensation should be paid only for measures actually undertaken or to be undertaken.[28] In fact, the Fund has never paid for anything which it considers to be "reinstatement". By way of explanation, it has asserted that no claim has ever been made for the costs of reinstatement.[29] The Working Group also agreed that the Fund should pay the cost of scientific studies to assess damage to the environment, but only in response to a specific oil spill to assess the precise extent and nature of the damage, and to evaluate whether measures of reinstatement were required.

In endorsing the report of the Working Group in 1994, the Assembly emphasised that the Fund had to maintain its pragmatic approach to the admissibility of claims so as to facilitate out-of-court settlements.[30] The report makes three points perfectly clear. First, the concept of "pollution damage" does not include damage to the environment *per se*. Second, what it does include and what the Fund will pay for is both the reasonable costs of reasonable clean-up measures and "quantifiable economic loss" directly caused by contamination by oil escaping from a ship. This quantifiable economic loss includes both consequential economic loss resulting from damage to property and pure economic loss meeting certain criteria. Third, the Fund wishes to keep its criteria for admissibility relatively vague and subject to its discretionary decision-making power.

---

27 To a certain extent, however, this may be a semantic question, for it would appear reasonable to refer to clean-up activities to remove oil from the coast as the *first* stage of reinstatement or restoration of the environment, while the replacement of any sand or soil removed and the re-introduction of any flora and fauna destroyed could be regarded as the *second* stage. See Conclusions, below.

28 The phrase "to be undertaken" means that Fund will provide funding in advance if the state concerned cannot afford to engage in the reinstatement without first receiving the compensation.

29 Personal communication by IOPC Fund Secretariat. The same assertion has been made by ITOPF in its letter dated 26 June 2000 to the European Commission commenting upon the White paper on Liability; available on the ITOPF website at http://www.itopf.com.

30 *Report on the Activities of the International Oil Pollution Compensation Fund in the Calendar Year 1994*, at 24–29.

The Work of the Comité Maritime International (CMI)

At the same time as the Fund Working Group was meeting to consider the admissibility of claims, the Comité Maritime International (CMI)[31] was working on a study of the same issue, which culminated in the adoption of "Guidelines on Admissibility and Assessment of Claims for Oil Pollution Damage" at its Conference in Sydney in 1994.[32] The CMI study was prompted by the very different approach to the compensation of environmental resource damage under the United States Oil Pollution Act 1990. Among other goals, the CMI wished, first, to investigate whether there could be some rapprochement between the international system and the US system, with the international system perhaps becoming a little more open to environmental claims; and second, to introduce somewhat greater precision into the international system by codifying general principles and the practice of the Fund into a set of guidelines for claimants, legal advisors and judges. Somewhat alarmed by the CMI study, the Fund sought to induce the CMI to align its conclusions with those of the Fund Working Group. However, the CMI maintained its own views. Moreover, while the CMI had hoped that the Fund would endorse its guidelines, the Fund was very careful to ignore them completely.

Current Situation and Future Possibilities

Heretofore, the Fund has been steadfastly opposed not only to clarifying the meaning of "pollution damage" in the CLC and Fund Conventions, but also to codifying its general principles and practice. Instead, it has preferred to retain the old definition of damage, and to keep the criteria for the admissibility of claims and for the assessment of damage vague and uncertain. This disadvantages claimants and has led to inconsistency in the courts.[33] However, as a result of the reconsideration of the oil pollution regime prompted by the *Erika* oil spill disaster in December 1999, the attitude of Fund members has gradually been changing.[34] In a Working Group convened in 2000 to consider possible amendments to the CLC/Fund regime,[35] France suggested that a revision of the definition of pollution damage might be

---

31 The CMI is a private organisation, comprising national maritime law associations from all over the world. It has prepared a number of draft conventions for the IMO, as well as providing expert input on a variety of issues over the years.

32 *Guidelines on Admissibility and Assessment of Claims for Oil Pollution Damage*, Comité Maritime International, *Yearbook 1994*, Sydney Conference.

33 One recent example of this is the recent decision in the Scottish courts in relation to the *Braer* oil spill, in which the Court decision on a question of pure economic loss was much more restrictive than the practice of the Fund. See: "Braer", IOPC Funds, *Annual Report*, 1999, 56 at 57–59, regarding the *Landcatch* case, the salmon price damage claims and the claim by P&O Scottish Ferries Ltd.

34 *Erika* broke up in heavy seas off the western coast of France, spilling around half its cargo of heavy fuel oil. The accident attracted a great deal of attention, because clean-up operations were difficult, expensive, and protracted; because thousands of seabirds were killed; because the vessel had been old and in poor condition; and because the amount of damage far exceeded the capacity of the shipowner and the Fund to pay. For reports on the *Erika* incident, see: IOPC Funds, *Annual Report*, 1999, 118–120; IOPC Fund documents 92FUND/EXC.6/2, 92FUND/EXC.6/2/Add.1; 92FUND/EXC.7/4; 92FUND/EXC.7/4/Add.1.

35 Fund document 92FUND/A/ES.4/7, 6 April 2000, paras 5.3.1 to 5.3.8.

advisable. Although other states disagreed, a number were willing to consider amendements to the section on environmental damage in the Claims Manual. In July 2001 the Working Group agreed upon an amendment to the criteria in the Claims Manual as an interim measure, pending a possible revision of the Conventions. However, at the meeting of the Fund Assembly held in October 2001, a few delegations strongly opposed any such initiatives, which they feared would encourage a flood of expensive claims for environmental damage from governments, environmental groups and individuals. Before reporting on the most recent developments, we shall first consider the remaining instruments in the maritime liability regime, and then other conventions not specifically addressing the marine environment.

2. Other Maritime Conventions

The two subsequent maritime conventions prepared by the IMO Legal Committee follow the basic model of the CLC and Fund and repeat almost exactly the same definition and concept of "pollution damage" as those developed in 1984.

HNS Convention

After an initial failure to agree on a draft at the diplomatic conference held in 1984, several years of further consideration culminated in the adoption of the International Convention on Liability and Compensation for Damage in Connection with the Carriage of Hazardous and Noxious Substances by Sea (HNS Convention) on 3 May 1996.[36] Based upon the text of the 1984 revisions to the CLC and Fund Conventions, the HNS Convention provides compensation for damage caused by the maritime carriage of "hazardous and noxious substances" (mainly toxic chemicals). Unlike the CLC, it covers damage by fire and explosion, as well as by contamination, but it is expected to operate in the same general manner as the CLC. There will be a first tier of compensation provided by the shipowner, up to its liability limits, with a second tier of compensation provided by a fund, much like the IOPC Fund, financed by receivers of hazardous and noxious substances. The HNS Convention contains the same definition of damage as the CLC, except that personal injury and damage to property are expressly included. The limitation on compensation for impairment of the environment is identical: only compensation for reasonable preventive measures and for reasonable measures of reinstatement are admissible. Entry into force has been delayed by a number of technical problems, the resolution of which should not alter the basic scheme of the convention.

Bunker Liability Convention

Damage caused by fuel oil had been deliberately omitted from both the CLC[37] and HNS Conventions, because of the reluctance of cargo interests to pay for such

36 Cm. 3580; also published by IMO in 1997. Not yet in force. The author was involved as a legal advisor in the Canadian Department of Foreign Affairs.

37 Except in the case of tankers in the 1992 CLC and Fund Conventions.

damage, and of shipowners to pay for financial security. However, spills of heavy fuel oil are a serious problem because they are extremely difficult and much more expensive to clean up than other types of oil. Consequently, certain states particularly affected by bunker spills engaged in strenuous efforts over several years to persuade the IMO Legal Committee to elaborate a new International Convention on Civil Liability for Bunker Oil Pollution Damage to cover "pollution damage" caused by oil used to propel the ship and to operate equipment. These efforts came to fruition in the adoption of the new Bunkers Convention at a diplomatic conference held in April 2001. The text follows the model of the CLC, covering only damage by contamination (not fire and explosion), and using the 1984 definition of pollution damage.

At the April 1999 session of the Legal Committee, the representative of IUCN[38] proposed a new definition of pollution damage, spelling out explicitly the types of damage usually compensated by the IOPC Fund,[39] and adding a definition of "reasonable measures of reinstatement".[40] While recognising the merits of the new definition, the proponents of the Bunkers Convention stated that they preferred to retain the old definition, because they viewed the CLC, the HNS Convention and the Bunkers Convention as constituting an integrated regime of liability for ship-source marine pollution, and that they wished all the definitions to be identical, in order to avoid inconsistencies in interpretation.[41]

Draft Wreck Removal Convention

For several years now, IMO Legal Committee has been working somewhat fitfully on a draft Wreck Removal Convention (WRC), the purpose of which would be to assure the right of coastal states to order the removal of wrecks posing a hazard beyond their territorial sea, up to the 200 mile limit. The definition of "hazard" includes both hazards to navigation and threats to the marine environment. Although states have long assumed the right to order the removal of wrecks within their territorial sea, some states were uncertain of their rights with respect to foreign vessels beyond the limits of territorial sovereignty. Furthermore, although the 1969 Intervention Convention and Article 221 of UNCLOS do confirm the right of coastal states to protect the environment from pollution caused by a marine casualty, they do not stipulate that the state most closely affected may order the shipowner to remove a wreck, do not provide for removal in the event of a hazard posed to international navigation, and do not provide for the recovery of costs from the shipowner if the coastal state has to effect the removal itself. Because the draft WRC does provide for compulsory financial security and for the recovery of costs from the shipowner, some states consider it to be a liability convention. However, the instrument might

---

38 The author.

39 The text was similar to that proposed by the author for the Liability Protocol to the Basel Convention, discussed below.

40 IMO Doc. LEG 79/6/3.

41 Report of the Legal Committee on its 79th Session, IMO Doc. LEG 79/11. In addition, many delegations stated privately that they preferred the vagueness of the old definition, as it permitted more scope for interpretation, and for "flexibility" in the determination of the admissibility of claims.

better be characterised as a convention concerning emergency response whose purpose is to *prevent* damage to the environment, not to compensate it.[42]

C. NON-MARINE CONVENTIONS INVOLVING HAZARDOUS MATERIALS

1. Activities Dangerous to the Environment

The Convention on Civil Liability for Damage resulting from Activities Dangerous to the Environment (Lugano Convention) was adopted by the Council of Europe on 21 June 1993[43] in order to provide adequate compensation for damage to human beings, property and the environment from dangerous activities and substances. A dangerous activity is defined as being one involving the production, handling, storage, use, discharge or disposal of substances or preparations posing a significant risk for "man, the environment or property", including substances listed in an annex and genetically modified organisms. The Lugano Convention does not cover the transportation of dangerous substances or goods; its scope extends only to stationary activities, including the disposal of hazardous waste. However, it is relevant to a discussion of liability for damage to the marine environment because the definition of reinstatement is an advance on earlier instruments, including the maritime conventions, and, in my view, should serve as a model for future developments.

As with the maritime conventions, the definition of damage focuses on economic loss or damage, such as loss of profit, occasioned by damage to the environment, with compensation for impairment of the environment itself being limited to the reasonable costs of reinstatement. However, there are some notable differences, most importantly the marked emphasis on the environment *per se* through the definition of "environment" and the novel inclusion of a definition of "measures of reinstatement", both elements not found in previous instruments. In particular, the definition of reinstatement brings to the fore a special concern with restoration of the environment to the condition it would have been in had the damage not occurred:

> "Measures of reinstatement" means any reasonable measures aiming to reinstate or restore damaged or destroyed components of the environment, or to introduce, where reasonable, the equivalent of these components into the environment. Internal law may indicate who will be entitled to take such measures.

Moreover, "measures of reinstatement" are defined to make clear that the operator is liable for the cost of reinstating destroyed components, or of *introducing their equivalent into that environment*. This means not only that the hazardous substance must be removed, but also that positive measures must be taken to restore

---

42 For latest text, see IMO Doc. LEG 84/4 and for discussion in the Legal Committee LEG 84/14, paras 23–53.

43 Done at Lugano, 21 June 1993, not in force; (1993) 32 ILM 1228; see also Council of Europe website at http://www.coe.fr/eng/legaltxt.

the environment to its original condition. Unfortunately, the definition does not explicitly include the cost of assessing the damage, which may be considerable. However, the cost of assessing the damage may have been considered as tacitly included as an element of reinstatement, as in the practice of the CLC regime.

Furthermore, the definition addresses the question of what to do if the original natural resources cannot be restored. The solution is the one adopted in the US legislation. As clarified in the Explanatory Report attached to the Convention, if a certain species of plant or animal has been rendered extinct by the incident in question, an "equivalent" species would have to be introduced into the area, once the clean-up activity had been completed.[44] This is very close to providing compensation for damage to the environment *per se*, for introducing the "equivalent" into the environment is qualitatively different from restoring the environment to its pre-existing state. It is also probably further than the IOPC Fund would be willing to go, at least at present.

While it is regrettable that the Lugano Convention retains the awkwardness of the 1984 CLC definition, the Council of Europe should be commended for having introduced a degree of precision into what the term "environment" comprises and what is meant by "reinstatement". Furthermore, the definition of reinstatement includes a new duty to take measures to restore the environment, including the important possibility of replacing destroyed components. These innovative aspects of the Convention bear a strong resemblance to the equivalent US legislation. All that is missing is liability and compensation for damage to the environment where it cannot be restored, and for loss of use while it is being restored.[45]

2. Hazardous Wastes

After many years of arduous negotiations, in December 1999 the Fifth Conference of the Parties to the Basel Convention finally adopted the long-awaited Protocol on Liability and Compensation.[46] The Basel Convention originated in a call by

---

44 In the words of the Explanatory Report: "40. Measures of reinstatement consist above all and whenever possible in environmental reinstatement or restoration. This concerns the establishment of an environmental situation identical to the one which existed before the damage.

When it is possible to restore or re-establish the environment, the measures of reinstatement may be in the form of the reintroduction of equivalent components into the environment.

This applies for example in the case of the disappearance of an animal species or the irreparable distruction (*sic*) of a biotope. Such damage cannot be evaluated financially and any reinstatement of the environment is in theory impossible. Since such difficulties must not lead to a complete absence of compensation, a specific method of compensation has been introduced. This method of compensation is based on achieving an equivalent instead of an identical environment. This notion relies on the given circumstances of each individual case of damage and is not defined in the Convention itself."

45 At the time of writing, the fate of the Lugano Convention remains uncertain. Therefore, although there is a potential conflict with the Basel Convention Liability Protocol, this conflict may never be realised.

46 Protocol on Liability and Compensation for Damage resulting from Transboundary Movements of Hazardous Wastes and their Disposal, the liability protocol to the 1989 Basel Convention on the Control of Transboundary Movements of Hazardous Wastes and their Disposal. The Basel

developing countries for a prohibition on the "dumping" of hazardous wastes from industrialised states in their territories. Although an immediate prohibition could not be agreed, the Convention did establish a regime (a) to regulate transboundary movements of hazardous wastes on the basis of prior informed consent and (b) to ensure that disposal outside the state of origin would be conducted in an environmentally sound manner. In order to protect themselves still further, developing countries insisted upon the development of a liability regime for damage caused by wastes covered by the Convention being transported internationally and being disposed of outside the state where they were generated. The Basel Convention and its liability Protocol are relevant to the marine environment, as they cover maritime carriage of hazardous wastes and most transportation of such wastes is by sea. Although there is a potential overlap with the HNS Convention, which covers most of the same substances, Article 11 of the Basel Protocol gives precedence to the maritime convention if and when it comes into force.

In 1994, the author[47] chaired a Working Group on Definitions which rejected a definition based upon the 1984 oil pollution text in favour of a more precise wording, proposed by the Chair, setting out exactly what types of damage would be included. Quite daringly, it also decided to include provisions stipulating compensation for damage to the environment *per se*. In May 1997, the new Chairman of the Group of Legal and Technical Experts persuaded the Group to delete the provisions on compensation for damage to the environment *per se*, claiming that they were unique among international instruments.[48] Furthermore, he suggested that inherent problems in the calculation of compensation for damage to the environment would make it difficult, if not impossible, to apply. He therefore proposed the deletion of the elements of the definition relating to compensation for damage to the environment *per se*. The meeting agreed and adopted a definition[49] which was essentially that agreed to in 1994, with damage to the environment *per se* deleted, and with some minor changes in the wording of subparagraph (iii), such as the use of "loss of income" instead of "loss of profit",[50] and the addition of "taking into

Cont.

Convention was adopted at Basel, 22 March 1989, in force 24 May 1992; 28 ILM 657 (1989). The Protocol on Liability and Compensation was adopted at Basel on 10 December 1999 by Decision V/29 and opened for signature in Bern from 6–17 March 2000, as well as at United Nations Headquarters from 1 April to 10 December 2000. The text is on the website of the Basel Convention Secretariat www.basel.int.

47 The author served as head of the Canadian delegation to the negotiations from 1994 to 1996. In 1997 to 1998, she advised the UK government on the conduct of the negotiations. Any opinions expressed are personal and do not reflect the views of either government.

48 This was not accurate, because the 1988 Convention on the Regulation of Antarctic Mineral Resource Activities did provide compensation for such damage, and the 1993 Lugano Convention could be interpreted as doing so. (For the situation in Antarctica, see below.)

49 The official report of the Fifth Session of the Ad Hoc Group of Legal and Technical Experts is found in UNEP Doc. UNEP/CHW.1/WG.1/5/5.

50 This change would enable employees to claim for compensation as well as employers. The IOPC Fund has consistently refused to pay compensation to employees who have been laid off as a consequence of contamination by oil, e.g., those working in a fish processing plant. The owner, of course, may claim compensation for loss of profit. To many, this would appear to be unfair.

account savings and costs".[51] The text reads as follows:

> (c) "Damage" means:
>
> (i) Loss of life or personal injury;
> (ii) Loss of or damage to property other than property held by the person liable in accordance with the present Protocol;
> (iii) Loss of income directly deriving from an economic interest in any use of the environment, incurred as a result of impairment of the environment, taking into account savings and costs;
> (iv) The costs of measures of reinstatement of the impaired environment, limited to the costs of measures actually taken or to be undertaken; and
> (v) The costs of preventive measures, including any loss or damage caused by such measures,
>
> to the extent that damage arises out of or results from hazardous properties of the wastes involved in the transboundary movement and disposal of hazardous wastes and other wastes subject to the Convention;
>
> (d) "Measures of reinstatement" means any reasonable measures aiming to assess, reinstate or restore damaged or destroyed components of the environment. Domestic law may indicate who will be entitled to take such measures;
>
> (e) "Preventive measures" means any reasonable measures taken by any person in response to an incident, to prevent, minimise, or mitigate loss or damage, or to effect environmental clean-up…

In addition to the traditional categories of damage to persons and to property, the definition sets out as separate items: loss of income directly deriving from impairment of the environment, the costs of measures of reinstatement of the environment, and the costs of preventive measures. The listing of separate categories of damage, plus a definition of measures of reinstatement, was intended to clarify exactly what would be compensated, for the benefit of both the victims and the person(s) liable for damage caused by the transboundary movement and disposal of hazardous wastes.

Although clearly taken from the CLC precedent, the definition of preventive measures in the Basel Liability Protocol is an improvement upon earlier formulations in that the use of the phrase "to effect environmental clean-up" makes explicit in the text the practice of the IOPC Fund in referring to cleaning-up or removing the oil as a "preventive measure". The definition of measures of reinstatement is based on the one in the Lugano Convention, but goes one step further by making it explicit in the text that the cost of assessing the damage must be compensated. On the other hand, it also takes a step backward to a more conservative approach by not including "the introduction of equivalent components", where the original fauna and flora cannot be reinstated.

In relation to emergency response, it should be noted that Article 6 of the Protocol requires the person in operational control of the waste at the time of an incident to "take all reasonable measures to mitigate the damage arising therefrom".

---

51 In fact, this had always been done in the assessments by the IOPC Fund, even though not set out in the Convention. When calculating the costs of business disruption as a consequence of oil pollution, the Fund takes into consideration that there will be fewer costs if the business is not functioning.

However, such measures might be inadequate and the state might be required to intervene. This strengthening of concern for damage to the environment *per se* is emphasised still further by Decision V/32, which provides for the use of a trust fund to ensure that both expertise and sufficient funds will be available to protect the environment during emergency response, to assess the damage, and to reinstate the environment to the condition it would have been in had the damage not occurred. Thus, with the Basel Liability Protocol, the concept of environmental damage has now moved definitively to that of damage to the environment *per se*, and the concern is for effective measures for emergency response and restoration of the environment impaired.

Nevertheless, it is regrettable that the negotiators ultimately stopped short in the final definition of reinstatement, by excluding the provision permitting the introduction of equivalent components to replace destroyed components of the environment when the originals cannot be restored. It will be interesting to see in practice how parties will deal with damage to the environment that cannot be repaired.

3. Liability for Damage Caused by Nuclear Activities

There are two international conventions providing for liability and compensation for damage caused by nuclear activities, both adopted in the early 1960s with a view to encouraging the development of the nuclear industry, by providing a specific legal regime concerning liability for nuclear damage. The Paris Convention on Third Party Liability in the Field of Nuclear Energy of 29 July 1960[52] was adopted under the *aegis* of the Organisation for Economic Co-operation and Development (OECD), with participation restricted to members of the OECD.[53] The Vienna Convention on Civil Liability for Nuclear Damage of 21 May 1963, adopted under the *aegis* of the International Atomic Energy Agency (IAEA), was of potentially universal scope.[54] Both conventions apply to damage caused both in stationary installations and in the course of transportation. Furthermore, because all other liability conventions exempt nuclear damage covered by the Paris and Vienna Conventions, these latter will always prevail in respect of damage caused on land or sea, by all kinds of nuclear activities or radioactive materials.

Because the conventions were concluded at a time when almost no one was thinking of environmental issues, and also because of the lack of experience with an actual nuclear accident, neither convention even mentioned damage to the environment. In the Paris Convention, compensation was limited to damage to persons

52 Paris Convention on Third Party Liability in the Field of Nuclear Energy of 29 July 1960, As Amended by the Additional Protocol of 28 January 1964 and by the Protocol of 16 November 1982; text reproduced in Louise Angélique de La Fayette, *Liability and Compensation for Nuclear Damage: An International Overview* (OECD, 1994) 154.

53 Compensation under the Paris Convention is supplemented by funds provided by states under the Brussels Convention of 31 January 1963 Supplementary to the Paris Convention of 29 July 1964 and the Additional Protocol of 28 January 1964 and by the Protocol of 16 November 1982, reproduced in de La Fayette, *ibid.*, 170.

54 See IAEA website at http://www.iaea.org/worldatom/Documents/Legal/liability.html.

and to property. However, while not expressly mentioning the environment, the definition of damage in the Vienna Convention left the door open to other forms of damage by including, in addition to damage to persons and property, "any other loss or damage so arising or resulting if and to the extent that the law of the competent court so provides". Because neither convention has ever been invoked in support of any claim, the precise scope of damage covered has never been established either in practice or through judicial decision. However, the experience of the nuclear accident at Chernobyl in April 1996 made clear that most damage caused by a major nuclear accident would fall within the categories of damage *to* the environment, or damage to persons and property *arising from* damage to the environment.

Almost immediately after Chernobyl, members of the IAEA decided that the Vienna Convention had to be revised,[55] *inter alia*, to increase the amount of compensation available and to expand the definition of nuclear damage. After many years of complicated negotiations, the Protocol to Amend the 1963 Vienna Convention on Civil Liability for Nuclear Damage was adopted on 12 September 1997.[56] Because agreement could not be reached on the details of all types of damage which might be covered under the amendments, the definition of nuclear damage lists damage to persons and to property without qualification, followed by five further categories of damage "to the extent determined by the law of the competent court". Included with this qualification are:

> (iv) the costs of measures of reinstatement of impaired environment, unless such impairment is insignificant, if such measures are actually taken or to be taken, and insofar as not included in sub-paragraph (ii) [damage to property]...
>
> (vi) the costs of preventive measures and further loss or damage caused by such measures...
>
> ...to the extent that the loss or damage arises out of or results from ionizing radiation emitted by any sources of radiation inside a nuclear installation...

Significantly, compensation for damage to the environment *per se* is not included.

Although it is clear that the costs of measures of reinstatement and the costs of preventive measures are eligible for compensation under the revised convention, these costs are recoverable only "to the extent determined by the law of the competent court", which in most cases will be a court in the state where the incident

55 The author was involved in this process as a legal advisor in the Canadian Department of Foreign Affairs. She also worked as a consultant at the OECD Nuclear Energy Agency in 1992–93. Any opinions expressed are purely personal. For further information on the OECD and IAEA nuclear liability regimes, see, by the same author: *International Liability for Damage Arising from Nuclear Accidents* (External Affairs and International Trade Canada, 1988); *Liability and Compensation for Nuclear Damage: An International Overview* (OECD, 1994); "Towards a New Régime of State Responsibility for Nuclear Activities", *Nuclear Law Bulletin*, No 50, December 1992, 7; "Nuclear Liability Revisited" (1993) 1 RECIEL 2443; "International Environmental Law and the Problem of Nuclear Safety" (1993) 5 JEL 3; "The Complex of Issues Involved in the Revision of the Vienna Convention" (Panel), *Proceedings of the Helsinki Symposium on Nuclear Accidents – Liabilities and Guarantees* (OECD/NEA, Paris, 1993) 320; "Nuclear Waste Management" (1993) 4 YbIEL 188; "Nuclear Waste Management" (1995) 5 YbIEL 200.

56 (1997) ILM. Also adopted was the Convention on Supplementary Compensation for Nuclear Damage, establishing a system of intergovernmental supplementary funding for compensating nuclear damage where compensation by the operator is insufficient or unavailable.

occurred, which, except in the case of transportation in another state, will generally be the installation state. This leaves a considerable degree of discretion to the national court in deciding which measures may be compensated and in determining how to assess the costs.[57]

"Measures of reinstatement", "preventive measures" and "reasonable measures" are all defined. Although modelled on the definition in the CLC, the definition of preventive measures in the Vienna Convention adds the proviso that the measures be "subject to the approval of the competent authorities required by the law of the state where the measures are taken". Similarly, the definition of "measures of reinstatement", although modelled on that of the Lugano Convention, adds the condition that the measures be approved by the competent authority where the measures are taken:

> "Measures of reinstatement" means any reasonable measures which have been approved by the competent authorities of the State where the measures were taken, and which aim to reinstate or restore damaged or destroyed components of the environment, or to introduce, where reasonable, the equivalent of these components into the environment. The law of the State where the damage is suffered shall determine who is entitled to take such measures.

Prompted by the contentions of the USSR that preventive measures taken by other states in response to the accident at Chernobyl were excessive or unwarranted, the Convention contains a definition of "reasonable measures" that is unique in the actual texts of treaties already adopted or under negotiation. Nevertheless, it does nothing more than codify the practice of the past 20 years under the IOPC Fund: "Reasonable measures" relating to both preventive measures and measures of reinstatement are defined as meaning:

> (o) . . . measures which are found under the law of the competent court to be appropriate and proportionate having regard to all the circumstances, for example –
> (i) the nature and extent of the damage incurred or, in the case of preventive measures, the nature and extent of the risk of such damage;
> (ii) the extent to which, at the time they are taken, such measures are likely to be effective; and
> (iii) relevant scientific and technical expertise.

Although the costs of scientific studies are not expressly stated to be compensable in the text of the Convention, it is open to national courts to include such costs as an element of the measures eligible for compensation.

To conclude, although the definition of damage in the revised Vienna Convention theoretically encompasses the concept of *environmental* damage, exactly how that is interpreted will depend upon the law of the state whose courts have jurisdiction. Consequently, interpretations may range from the rather narrow approach of the IOPC Fund to the comparatively comprehensive approach of the

57 For a recent discussion of these provisions, see "The New Definition of Nuclear Damage in the 1997 Protocol to Amend the 1963 Vienna Convention on Civil Liability for Nuclear Damage", in *Reform of Civil Nuclear Liability*, Budapest Symposium 1999 (OECD Nuclear Energy Agency, 1999). The Proceedings of the Budapest Symposium contain expert views on the current state of nuclear liability law.

US legislation on CERCLA and OPA '90. In preparation for a similar revision of the Paris Convention, the OECD held a conference to discuss all the issues, including environmental damage, at which one of the main speakers was the Director of the IOPC Fund.[58] Although negotiations for the revision of the Paris Convention are still not concluded, it appears that environmental damage will be covered in much the same way as in the revised Vienna Convention, taking into account the experience of the CLC/Fund regime.[59]

D. ENVIRONMENTAL DAMAGE TO AREAS BEYOND THE LIMITS OF NATIONAL JURISDICTION

1. Liability for Damage Caused by Space Objects

The 1972 Convention on International Liability for Damage caused by Space Objects, 1972 (Space Liability Convention)[60] is the only existing convention dealing with *state*, as opposed to *civil*, liability. It places absolute liability on "launching states", defined as: (i) a state which launches or procures the launching of a space object, and (ii) a state from whose territory a space object is launched, for damage caused by their space objects on the surface of the earth or to aircraft in flight. Significantly, the definition of the term "damage" does not expressly include damage to the environment. For the purposes of the Convention, damage is defined as: loss of life, personal injury or other impairment of health; or loss of or damage to property of states or of persons, natural or juridical, or property of international intergovernmental organisations.

However, in 1978 in the incident involving the dispersal of radioactive fragments of a Soviet satellite over Canadian territory[61] Canada successfully claimed from the USSR the cost of cleaning up the satellite debris and the assessment of the damage. Subsequently, the adoption by the United Nations General Assembly of a Declaration of "Principles Relevant to Nuclear Power Sources in Outer Space"[62]

58 See Proceedings, *op. cit.*, n 63.

59 Private communication from an official of the OECD Nuclear Energy Agency.

60 Convention on International Liability for Damage Caused by Space Objects, 29 March 1972, in force 1 September 1972; 961 UNTS 187.

61 On 24 January 1978, a Soviet satellite powered by a small nuclear reactor disintegrated over the Canadian Northwest Territories. Canada claimed compensation for damage caused by the radioactive fragments of the satellite pursuant to the Space Liability Convention, to the Outer Space Treaty and to the general principles of international law. Although the fragments did not cause any damage by impact, their radioactive properties meant that they could cause radiation harm to persons and animals coming in contact with them. In its claim, Canada explained that the "purpose of these operations was to identify the nature and the extent of the damage caused by the debris, to limit the existing damage and to minimise the risk of further damage and to restore to the extent possible the affected areas to the condition that would have existed if the intrusion of the satellite and the deposit of the debris had not occurred." (Canada, Claim against the USSR for Damage Caused by Soviet Cosmos 954, 23 January 1979, para. 8; (1979) 18 ILM 899 at 904.)

62 "Principles Relevant to the Use of Nuclear Power Sources in Outer Space" adopted by the United Nations General Assembly in 1992 (Resolution 47/68; text at: http://www.un.or.at/OOSA/treat/nps/npstxt.html).

appeared to confirm that there is liability on the launching state to compensate for clean-up costs relating to damage caused by the fall of a space object. Presumably, the principles would apply in the event of such an object falling into the sea.

2. Deep Seabed Mining

The genesis for the negotiation of the 1982 United Nations Convention on the Law of the Sea (LOS Convention) was the discovery of mineral resources in the form of polymetallic nodules on the deep seabed beyond the limits of national jurisdiction. Somewhat ironically, the entry into force of the Convention was delayed by disagreements over the convention regime for the mining of resources in the deep seabed area that had initiated the process. The adoption of the 1994 Agreement[63] modifying the provisions of Part XI of the Convention on the mining regime in "The Area" cleared the way for the entry into force of the Convention, for the establishment of the International Seabed Authority (ISA), and for the development of regulations for the mining of polymetallic nodules under the supervision of the Authority. While the mining regulations themselves are not a liability treaty, they are included in this study because they provide for liability and compensation pursuant to the LOS Convention and the Part XI Agreement. Furthermore, both the requirements for protection of the marine environment and the provisions on responsibility and liability are firmly rooted in provisions of the Convention, primarily in Part XI, but also in Part XII – Protection and Preservation of the Marine Environment, as well as in Annex III.

Although states are responsible for ensuring that activities in the Area are conducted in conformity with Part XI, they are liable for damage caused by their nationals only if they fail to carry out their responsibilities. In turn, the responsibility and liability of contractors (mining companies) is established in Article 22 of Annex III to the Convention, which provides that a contractor is liable "for the actual amount of any damage arising out of wrongful acts in the conduct of its operations". Article 145 of the Convention provides that necessary measures shall be taken with respect to activities in the Area "to ensure effective protection for the marine environment from harmful effects which may arise from such activities". Article 209 of Part XII repeats the requirement for international rules, etc. to protect the marine environment from activities in the Area; Article 215 provides for enforcement in accordance with the provisions of Part XI; and Article 235 provides generally for the development of the law relating to responsibility and liability.

The "Regulations on Prospecting and Exploration for Polymetallic Nodules in the Area" developed pursuant to the provisions of the Convention were approved by the ISA Assembly on 13 July 2000.[64] The regulations contain a surprisingly strong regime for environmental protection. In particular, the regulations for exploration are fairly detailed, providing for baseline studies, environmental assessments,

63 The Agreement relating to the Implementation of Part XI of the United Nations Convention on the Law of the Sea of 10 December 1982, adopted 28 July 1994, in force 28 July 1996; (1994) 33 ILM 1154.

64 Available on the Authority's website http://www.isa.org.jm and in ISA Doc. ISBA/6/A/18.

response to incidents causing serious harm to the marine environment, notification to the Authority of serious harm, and the power of the Authority to take emergency measures. Furthermore, contracts with companies engaging in exploration provide for the responsibility and liability of the contractor for any damage to the marine environment, including after the completion of the exploration. Part V of the Regulations deals specifically with Protection and Preservation of the Marine Environment, setting forth detailed obligations for both the Authority and the contractor. In the event of an incident causing serious harm to the environment, either the contractor must take emergency measures itself or the Secretary-General may do so and recover the costs from the contractor.

The Standard Clauses for Exploration Contracts themselves contain several provisions for the protection of the marine environment, including clause 16, on "Responsibility and Liability". Echoing Article 22 of Annex III of the Convention, paragraph 16.1 of the Standard clauses provides that

> [t]he Contractor shall be liable for the *actual amount of any damage, including damage to the marine environment, arising out of its wrongful acts or omissions*, and those of its employees, subcontractors, agents and all persons engaged in working or acting for them in the conduct of its operations under this contract, including the costs of reasonable measures to prevent or limit damage to the marine environment, account being taken of any contributory acts or omissions by the Authority. (Emphasis added).

Paragraph 16.1 requires the Contractor to maintain appropriate insurance policies.

As to the meaning of the crucial term "serious harm to the marine environment", regulation 1 defines "marine environment" as including:

> the physical, chemical, geological and biological components, conditions and factors which interact and determine the productivity of, state, condition and quality of the marine ecosystem, the waters of the seas and oceans and the airspace above those waters, as well as the seabed and ocean floor and subsoil thereof.[65]

This is a fairly sophisticated definition, which extends beyond anything contemplated in the rather narrow field of the maritime law treaties considered above. However, the definition of "serious harm" is simpler and depends upon further work by the Authority, as well as upon the existence of international standards and practices:

> "serious harm to the environment" means any effect from activities in the Area on the marine environment which represents a *significant adverse change*[66] in the marine environment determined according to the rules, regulations and procedures adopted by the

65 The annotated version of the Draft Regulations prepared by the Secretariat (ISBA/6/C/CRP.2) refers in the notes to the definitions to para. 3.1 of "Guidelines for Marine Environmental Assessments", prepared by GESAMP; the Introduction, para 1 of the Global Programme of Action for the Protection of the Marine Environment from Land-based Activities; Art. 1(3) of the Convention on the Conservation of Antarctic Marine Living Resources; and the definitions reproduced in the Executive Summary of a Workshop on Deep-Seabed Polymetallic Nodule Exploration: Development of Environmental Guidelines, held by the ISA in China, 1–5 June 1998.

66 This is reminiscent of the term "observable or measurable adverse change" in the NOAA definition of "injury to natural resources", in the rules implementing OPA '90 referred to in the Introduction to this paper.

Authority on the basis of internationally recognized standards and practices. (Emphasis added).[67]

While the regulations contain numerous provisions devoted to preventing and responding to any damage to the marine environment and to ensuring that contractors will pay for any damage, including the costs of reasonable preventive measures, there is no mention of restoration or reinstatement. Although restoration might be difficult or even impossible in the deep sea environment, one might have expected at least a stipulation that the environment should be restored "wherever possible".

Moreover, it is not clear whether the contractor will only be liable for the actual costs of any preventive measures, or whether it will also be liable for "the actual amount of any damage", which is undefined. The term "actual amount" is reminiscent of the IOPC Fund requirement that damages be quantifiable in monetary terms and not speculative or based upon theoretical calculations. Since reinstatement of the environment on the deep seabed may not be feasible, it is possible that contractors may not be required to pay for "irremediable damage", with no financial consequences. On the other hand, since so much of the regulations is aimed at protection of the marine environment *per se*, it would be very strange indeed, if the contractor were not required to pay anything, especially in case of fault, as the standard clauses refer to liability for wrongful acts or omissions. The language of the Regulations provides no clear answer to this question. Exactly how it will be interpreted depends upon further work by the Authority.

3. Environmental Damage in Antarctica

In a striking parallel to the expectations for the deep seabed in the 1960s, in the 1980s, the parties to the Antarctic Treaty imagined that vast resources and boundless wealth lay beneath the surface of the frozen continent. They anticipated that commercial mining activities were imminent and inevitable. Hence, in 1988 states parties to the Antarctic Treaty concluded the Convention on the Regulation of Antarctic Mineral Resource Activities (CRAMRA).[68] However, soon thereafter, prompted by concerns about possibly irreparable damage to the fragile Antarctic environment, France and Australia mounted a successful campaign to ban resource exploitation in Antarctica and to replace the CRAMRA by an agreement specifically devoted to environmental protection. The result was the Protocol on Environmental Protection to the Antarctic Treaty adopted in Madrid in 1991.[69] Article 7 of the Protocol prohibits any activity relating to mineral resources, while Article 16 provides for the elaboration of one or more annexes relating to liability for damage arising from activities in Antarctica covered by the Protocol.

Although the CRAMRA has been superseded by the Madrid Protocol, it is relevant to the present study because it contains provisions on response action as

---

67 The annotated version of the Draft Regulations refers to the definition of "pollution" in Art. 1(4) of the LOS Convention, as well as in several of the regional seas conventions.

68 (1988) 27 ILM 859.

69 (1991) 30 ILM 1461; in force 14 January 1998.

well as on liability for "operators" causing damage to the Antarctic environment. As with the other liability conventions, under CRAMRA, the operator is liable for the reimbursement of reasonable costs relating to:

> necessary response action, including prevention, containment, clean up and removal measures, and action taken to restore the *status quo ante* where Antarctic mineral resource activities undertaken by that operator result in or threaten to result in damage to the Antarctic environment or dependent or associated ecosystems.

This provision is unique in the detail of its formulation, which expressly refers to all measures taken in response to a threat of environmental damage, from prevention through to restoration of the *status quo ante*. Yet, the most significant feature of this convention is that it is the only international agreement in which it is clear that an operator would be liable for damage to the environment *per se*. For an operator would have been strictly liable for:

> damage to the Antarctic environment or dependent or associated ecosystems arising from its Antarctic mineral resource activities, *including payment in the event that there has been no restoration to the* status quo ante ... (emphasis added).

Further details on liability and compensation were to be elaborated in a separate protocol, which was never concluded.

Following the adoption of the Madrid Protocol, discussions on an Antarctic liability regime began within the context of an expert group, before moving on to the meetings of the parties. Since the Madrid Protocol covers prevention of damage to the marine environment, it is possible that the liability annex could cover damage to the marine environment around Antarctica. Unfortunately, negotiations for the liability annex have dragged on inconclusively for several years.[70] One controversial issue has been whether damage that was identified and accepted in an environmental assessment could attract liability.[71] The justification for an exemption from liability would be that the operator should not be "blamed" or "punished" for damage that was deemed acceptable in advance by the party having jurisdiction. In my view, this is a false dilemma, for the purpose of the liability should not be to punish the operator, but to make it pay the cost of emergency response and restoration. Indeed, the use of the concept of liability in the Antarctic situation is probably inappropriate, for there is no "victim" of the damage, apart from Antarctica itself. More appropriate and practical would be an approach based on the requirement of the operator to take emergency measures whatever the damage or potential damage, whether it was foreseen or not, as the operator who caused the damage would usually be in the best position to react. The operator should also be required to compensate any other person who took reasonable response action designed to prevent or to limit any damage.

---

70 The author was involved in an earlier phase of the negotiations, while in the Canadian Department of Foreign Affairs. Any opinions expressed are strictly personal.

71 This question has also arisen in relation to national liability laws as well as the draft environmental liability directive of the European Union. In some states, the operator is absolved from liability if it has not exceeded approved levels of discharges, while in others, it is still liable for any damage caused.

At their meeting held in St. Petersburg in July 2001, Parties to the Antarctic Treaty were still unable to agree on the contents of the liability annex. Because of stubborn resistance by some to a comprehensive regime, attention is now focused on a "restricted" annex proposed by the US, covering only the failure to take emergency response measures. Although the US has conceded a broad interpretation of "emergency", it does not include damage caused by gradual or chronic pollution or degradation. However, some parties are insisting that the "restricted" annex would only be a beginning; they wish additional annexes to be developed that will eventually cover all types of damage from all kinds of activities.[72] All that can be said in conclusion is that negotiations are continuing and that the outcome is uncertain. In the interim, we hope that the Parties take all necessary response measures whenever and wherever damage is detected.

E. RECENT DEVELOPMENTS AT THE EUROPEAN UNION AND THE IOPC FUND

The most recent chapter in the story of liability for damage to the marine environment concerns the consequences of the *Erika* disaster for the international regime governing liability and compensation for oil pollution damage. Developments at the European Union (EU) and the IOPC Fund must be considered together, as to a certain extent at least, those at the former influenced the latter. The oil spilled from the *Erika* in December 1999 and January 2000 caused extensive damage to the west coast of France and related interests, resulting in financial loss that would clearly far exceed the compensation available from the shipowner and the IOPC Fund. In consequence, the disaster provoked a number of proposals for action in respect of shipping safety and liability for damage by the European Commission, at IMO and at the IOPC Fund. Because the European Commission responded swiftly with a comprehensive package of measures at the regional level, the two global organisations were prompted to respond with their own proposals in order to protect the integrity of the international system.[73]

First, in April 2000, the 1992 Fund Assembly established an intersessional Working Group (WG3) to assess the adequacy of the international compensation system created by the 1992 CLC and 1992 Fund Convention. At the time of writing, the WG has held four meetings: in July 2000, in March and June 2001[74] and in April/May 2002.[75] At the meetings held in 2001, the WG considered a broad range of issues, most importantly: the levels of compensation, the liability of the shipowner and environmental damage. As a first step, in April 2000, the UK announced that it would submit a proposal to the IMO Legal Committee to raise the limits of liability under the CLC and Fund Conventions as high as possible under

---

72 The Antarctic Project Secretariat for the Antarctic and Southern Ocean Coalition (ASOC) Newsletter, Volume 10, Issue 2, September 2001.

73 For more details, see by the same author: "The Protection of the Marine Environment in 2000", 31 *Environmental Policy and Law* 140–149 (2001).

74 IOPC Fund Doc. 92FUND/A.6/4.

75 Fund Doc. 92FUND/A.7/4, 15 June 2002.

the tacit amendment procedure in the two conventions. This was done in October 2000 by means of two resolutions adopted by the Legal Committee, which raised the compensation amount available under each convention by 50.37%, to a combined total of 203 million SDR (£1,780,000) with effect from 1 November 2003.[76]

However, some states, as well as the European Commission, still believed that the liability limits were too low. The European Commission proposed that the EU establish a special EU oil pollution compensation fund, called the COPE Fund, to provide compensation for oil spills in the waters of EU member states above that provided by the international regime, up to a limit of one billion euros, approximately the same amount as available under the US OPA '90.[77] The COPE Fund would be used only when the cost of pollution damage from an oil spill in European waters exceeded the limit of the IOPC Fund. In order to avoid the problems of delays in payment by the IOPC caused by uncertainty over whether the total would exceed the IOPC limit, the COPE Fund would pay European claimants as soon as their claims had been approved by the IOPC Fund. When the final amount was known there would be a financial settlement as between the IOPC and COPE Funds.

When informed of this initiative at a Fund meeting, some non-EU states expressed concern about regional measures adversely affecting the international regime. In response, several members later proposed the elaboration of a Supplementary Protocol to the IOPC Fund that would serve the same purpose, but would be open to all members of the Fund.[78] Following some discussion, a draft protocol was rapidly prepared during the summer of 2001. By this time, European Ministers had decided that it would be preferable to proceed by improving the international regime, rather than by establishing a European Fund. They adopted a common position supporting the creation of a Supplementary Fund open to all IOPC Fund members. The European Parliament agreed, but proposed adding pollution damage by HNS and Bunker fuels to the draft COPE Fund and insisted upon a review of the international regime after three years to determine whether its operation was satisfactory. If it was not, a European alternative should be adopted.

After being approved by the 92 Fund Assembly in October 2001, the draft Supplementary Protocol was submitted to the IMO Legal Committee with a request for approval for submission to a diplomatic conference. A few weeks later, the Fund requested IMO Assembly to arrange a diplomatic conference to adopt the Protocol in 2003. The approvals were forthcoming and a conference scheduled for May 2003. The Protocol will establish a Supplementary Fund to provide compensation to victims in states parties only when the the amount of compensation owing to the victims exceeds the funds available under the 1992 IOPC Fund. The receivers of oil in states

---

76 Report of the Legal Committee on the Work of of its Eighty-Second Session, IMO Doc. LEG 82/12, 6 November 2000, paras 104–129. The texts of Resolution LEG.1(82) and Resolution LEG.2(82) are in Annexes 2 and 3. Parties to the two conventions not members of IMO were invited to participate in the discussion and vote on this issue.

77 Proposal for a Regulation of the European Parliament and of the Council on the establishment of a fund for the compensation of oil pollution damage in European waters and related measures, 2000/0326(COD); amendment by the European Parliament in Doc. no. A5-0201/2001; both reproduced in Fund Doc. 92FUND/A.6/5, 24 September 2001.

78 Fund Doc. 92FUND/WGR.3/8/4, 1 June 2001.

parties to the Protocol designated under the IOPC Fund would have to pay additional contributions to Supplementary Fund when called upon to do so. Under this scheme, shipowners would not have to pay any additional amounts.[79] Because of a concern about equitable burden sharing between the shipowner and the cargo interests, the International Group of the P & I Clubs, which insure the vast majority of the shipowners, offered to increase the amount paid by small ships on a voluntary basis.[80]

While raising the limits of liability would certainly help to ensure that sufficient funds were available to pay all legitimate claims for pollution damage, the amount of compensation was not the only issue that arose in the wake of the *Erika*. Many other questions remained to be addressed, in particular, that of compensation for environmental damage. Because it suffered from extensive environmental damage from the *Erika* oil spill, France had submitted documents to the Fund examining the concept of environmental damage and proposing to introduce into the Claims Manual the possibility of compensation for environmental damage as a violation of collective property rights, compensation for which would be awarded to the state.[81] While some delegations were sympathetic, most opposed the French proposal, on the grounds that such a radical change would be contrary to existing policy and would require an amendment to the conventions. Subsequently, a group of states submitted as an interim measure a proposal for the amendment of the claims manual, *first* to expand the criteria for the funding of studies to assess the damage from specific oil spills and *second*, to add a number of criteria to clarify what kinds of measures of reinstatement would be eligible for compensation.[82] After preliminary approval by the Working Group, this proposal was considered by the 92 Fund Assembly at its meeting in October 2001. Although a majority of states were in favour of its adoption, a number of delegations expressed concern that the new text might encourage speculative claims. Consequently, the question was returned to the Working Group for further consideration.

Draft European Directive on Environmental Liability

In the interim, the European Commission published a proposal for a Directive on environmental liability providing for compensation for damage to biodiversity, waters and contaminated land.[83] Fund members had already been informed of the EC white paper on environmental liability published in 2000 and had instructed the Director to explain the Fund system to the European Commission.[84] In response

---

79 This is because increasing the liability of shipowners would require an amendment to the CLC and the increase would only apply to ships registered in states parties to the amendment. The consequence is likely to be that shipowners in such states would re-register to another state not party to the amendment to avoid the additional liability.

80 IOPC Fund Docs 92FUND/A.6/4/3, 2 October 2001 and 92FUND/WGR.3/11/1, 20 March 2002.

81 IOPC Fund Doc. 92FUND/WGR.3/8/13.

82 IOPC Fund Doc. 92FUND/A.6/4/5.

83 Proposal for a Directive of the European Parliament and of the Council on environmental liability with regard to the prevention and remedying of environmental damage, COM(2002)17 final, 2002/0021(COD), Brussels, 23.1.2002; reported to the FUND Assembly in IOPC Fund Doc. 92FUND/A/ES.6/6, 15 March 2002.

84 This was a formality only, as a representative of the Commission regularly attends Fund meetings as an observer.

to criticism from industry, which unsurprisingly, did not want to pay for anything, the draft directive differs substantially from the proposal in the white paper. Most importantly, it does not cover "traditional" types of damage to persons and to property and various kinds of economic loss, but only "environmental" damage, comprising the cost of preventive measures, clean-up costs and restoration ("reinstatement" in the CLC/Fund system). Covered are: damage to biodiversity protected at European and national levels; damage to waters as regulated under the Water Framework Directive (2000/60/EC); and contaminated land posing a threat to human health. The basic scheme is that the competent public authority shall require the operator who has caused the damage or the threat of damage to take preventive measures and to restore the environment at its own cost. If the operator cannot be found or will not or cannot act, the public authority will take the necessary measures itself and recover the cost from the operator, as well as the cost of assessing the damage or the imminent threat thereof.

Under Annex II to the Directive, the objective of restoration is stated as being to return damaged habitats, species and associated natural resources, services and waters to baseline conditions. This is to be achieved by rehabilitating, replacing or acquiring the equivalent of damaged natural resources and/or services at the site originally damaged or at a different location. Furthermore, "interim losses" from the date of damage until the return to baseline conditions must be compensated. Both the objectives and the methods resemble closely the United States' regime on liability and compensation for natural resource damage. On the other hand, these provisions of the draft are contrary to the existing policy of the Fund, whose members have been strongly opposed the ideas of replacement by "equivalent components", the compensation of interim losses, and the restoration of an alternative site. Indeed, heretofore the general approach of the Fund has been that one should do nothing to help the environment, as only economic loss was worthy of compensation. This attitude ignores the two crucial facts: first, the economy in question, whether that of the fishery or tourism, depends upon a healthy environment and natural resources; and second, the environment generally provides ecological services upon which natural resources and human life depend.

As for the relationship with international regimes, the Explanatory Memorandum to the Directive acknowledges the existence and importance of international conventions providing for compensation for damage caused during international transport, including the maritime liability conventions. It declares EC policy to be to improve those regimes and it notes the consideration by the IOPC Fund of proposals to amend its functioning in the post-*Erika* era. Hence, under Art. 3.3 the draft Directive does not apply to environmental damage compensated by the CLC, Fund, HNS and Bunker Conventions. However, the Explanatory Memorandum declares that the EC reserves the right to develop its own maritime liability regime if the results of the international negotiations are not "satisfactory". With this draft Directive brought to its attention, in spring 2002 the Fund Working Group turned again to the question of environmental damage.

New Criteria for Compensation for Reinstatement

At the March 2002 meetings of the Fund, a revised proposal for the amendment of the 1992 Fund Claims Manual was submitted to the Working Group by Australia,

Canada, France, Ireland, the Netherlands, New Zealand, Norway, Sweden and the United Kingdom.[85] This included both more liberal criteria for the funding of studies of the effects of oil spills and new criteria for compensation of measures of reinstatement. The proposal was opposed by Japan and South Korea on the basis that the terms used were unclear and that the new text would encourage speculative claims.[86] Most of these fears were allayed in the discussion which followed, during which the proponents pointed out that: (1) the possibility of compensation for re-instatement was already included in the Conventions; (2) there had not yet been any flood of speculative claims; (3) the additional criteria to be fulfilled would make the submission of speculative claims *less* likely; (4) the criteria would not alter the Conventions, but merely clarify some terms; (5) the terms had to be general, as the damage caused by each accident would depend on specific circumstances; (6) the vast majority of any claimants would be states parties to the conventions; and (7) the Executive Committee would decide whether or not the claims fulfilled the criteria and could reject them if they did not. After a few drafting questions had been settled among the states concerned,[87] the Working Group adopted a compromise for submission to the Assembly meeting in October 2002.[88]

The proposal involves a revision of the section of the Claims Manual on Environmental Damage. Beginning with a very strong caveat insisted upon by the Japanese and Koreans stating that in most cases the environment will repair itself, the text does admit that in some cases it is possible to enhance the speed of natural recovery through reasonable reinstatement measures. The aim of such reasonable measures of reinstatement would be to bring the damaged site back to the same ecological state that would have existed had the oil spill not occurred, or at least as close as possible. Rather surprisingly, the text also provides for measures taken at an alternative site, much as in the US and proposed EU regimes, but with an important qualification:

> Reinstatement measures taken at some distance from, but still within the vicinity of, the damaged area may be acceptable, so long as it can be demonstrated that they would actually enhance the recovery of the damaged components of the environment. This link between the measures and the damaged components is essential for consistency with the definition of *pollution damage* in the 1992 Civil Liability and Fund Conventions.

In addition to fulfilling the general criteria for the admissibility of claims, claims for reinstatement have to meet the following special criteria:

- the measures should be likely to accelerate significantly the natural process of recovery
- the measures should seek to prevent further damage as a result of the incident

85 IOPC Fund Doc. 92FUND/WGR.3/11/3, 28 March 2002.

86 IOPC Fund Docs 92FUND/WGR.3/11/4 and 92FUND/WGR.3/11/4/Add.1.

87 Japan and Korea wished to emphasise that in most cases the environment would repair itself, to delete the reference to "innovative approaches" and to remove the term "healthy" in relation to the objective of restoration. They were successful.

88 Text in IOPC Fund Doc. 92FUND//A.7/4, Annex.

- the measures should, as far as possible, not result in the degradation of other habitats or in adverse consequences for other natural or economic resources
- the measures should be technically feasible
- the costs of the measures should not be out of proportion to the extent and duration of the damage and the benefits likely to be achieved.

As for environmental studies, they are to be funded only if they concern damage falling within the definition of "pollution damage" in the CLC and Fund Conventions, including reasonable measures of reinstatement. Furthermore, they must be carried out with scientific rigour and objectivity; they must be proportionate to the extent of contamination and the "predictable effects"; and the Fund should be invited to participate.

This proposal still evinces a rather restrictive attitude to the compensation of environmental damage and a feeling that doing nothing is the best option, or perhaps the least expensive in the short term. For, rather inconsistently, Korea objected to the idea of returning the environment to the state it would have been in had the damage not occurred, because some oil pollution damage in Korea had been so severe that it would take "hundreds of years" for it to return to its original condition. This makes clear that left alone, the environment will not always repair itself, at least not within a reasonable period of time. Moreover, a recent study published by the National Research Council of the United States has revealed that the environmental effects of a major oil spill are longer lasting than previously believed and that even small amounts of petroleum can seriously damage marine life and ecosystems.[89] A specific example of the long-term effects of even minor oil spills is the fact that 62% of the iguanas on Santa Fe Island in the Galapagos Marine Reserve died within a year of the *Jessica* oil spill. Thus, scientific research has shown that restoration measures may be much more important than Fund members realise or are prepared to admit. Nevertheless, if adopted by the Fund Assembly, the new criteria for compensating measures of reinstatement will perhaps be a small step forward. One can only hope that in time, this step will lead to an amendment to the conventions themselves, and also to actual instances of compensation for the restoration of the environment.

F. CONCLUSIONS

1. Damage through the Environment and Damage to the Environment

From this cursory survey of international liability regimes, it appears that definitions of "environmental harm" or "pollution damage" fall into two main categories: (i) those that focus on the traditional categories of damage in national tort law, such as personal injury, property damage and economic loss; and (ii) those that focus on damage to the environment *per se*. Perhaps understandably, because they deal with transnational economic activities where property and human interests predominate,

89 NRC Report available on line at http://www.nap.edu; news report at http://ens-news.com/ens/may2002/2002-05-27-02.asp.

the traditional maritime and nuclear liability regimes and the hazardous waste regime based on them fall into category (i). Conversely, because they deal with unpopulated areas that are not subject to national sovereignty and where concern for the environment is paramount, the innovative regimes for Antarctica and deep seabed mining fall into category (ii). Thus, in the majority of instruments, those in category (i), modelled on the paradigmatic oil pollution regime, the concept of damage does not refer to damage *to* the environment, but to damage *through* the environment to persons, property and economic interests.

Nevertheless, compensation for economic losses in the maritime liability regimes covers damage to the environment *per se* indirectly, because it includes reimbursement of the costs of preventive measures designed to prevent or to mitigate damage to the environment, as well as the costs of restoration or reinstatement of the environment to its pre-damage condition. Thus, although "natural resource damage" or damage to the environment *per se* are not included in the definition of damage, the environment will benefit from the compensation mechanism by the creation of an incentive for the operator to take measures to prevent or limit the damage, and third parties will also benefit, since they will know in advance that they will be compensated for any response action or remedial measures.

Although this method of addressing environmental damage is indirect, it has the advantage of avoiding the difficult problem of devising a definition of environmental damage that would suit all possible sources of damage and all elements and functions of the natural environment and natural resources. Whatever the dangerous substance or material; whatever the component of the environment that has been adversely affected; and whatever the nature of the "adverse change", the "polluter" must pay to have the environment protected and restored to its undamaged condition. The term "polluter" is used advisedly, despite the fact that there are other forms of environmental degradation besides that caused through contamination and hence pollution.[90] "Polluter" is used here both for convenience and to refer to the "polluter pays principle", which is generally accepted as a principle of both municipal and international law.[91]

However, there is one issue that poses a problem and that differs amongst the various regimes. This is the question of the introduction of "equivalent" components into the environment, when the original ones cannot be reinstated. Although the circumstances may be rare, there is a risk that anthropogenic environmental degradation might destroy a unique population of flora or fauna or their habitat. In such a case, the definition of reinstatement in the Lugano Convention and the Vienna nuclear liability convention would permit the introduction of an equivalent species. Unfortunately, because the Basel Convention Liability Protocol lacks the reference to "the equivalent of these components", the cost of such a substitution may not be recoverable under the Basel instrument, even though it has a similar definition of reinstatement. Moreover, it would also not be in the CLC Convention and the succeeding instruments that reproduced its terms. In fact, members of the IOPC

90 There are many other types of damage besides pollution, such as endocrine disruption caused by chemicals, physical damage caused by impact, climate change, destruction of biodiversity by alien species, destruction of habitats, genetic alterations (whether deliberate or accidental), etc.

91 Since space does not permit a full complement of references, we refer only to Principle 15 of the Rio Declaration.

Fund are strongly opposed to the idea of replacement by "equivalent components". This is a gap – perhaps not a large one, but a gap nonetheless – in the protection of the environment by most existing *international* liability regimes.

2. Comparison with the US Regime

At this point, a comparison with the domestic statutory regime in the US may be instructive. As already noted, some commentators have criticised the US regime for its reliance on economic valuation techniques for calculating monetary damages in cases where compensation is awarded either for loss of "interim use" and non-user values (termed "complementary restoration"), while restoration is underway, or in cases where restoration of the original site is not possible. However, a focus on such situations and even on monetary damages to be awarded in "normal" cases would be misleading, because in practice, the US authorities concentrate their efforts not on collecting monetary damages, but on facilitating the restoration of the damaged environment. Moreover, they prefer the polluter to effect the restoration itself, or to pay expert contractors to do so, with the government agency exercising only an oversight function. Even in cases where complementary restoration is deemed necessary, or the original site cannot be restored, the preferred option is not monetary damages calculated in some dubious abstract manner, but the acquisition or creation of an equivalent site nearby.

Hence, the difference between the US and the international regimes is not so large as is commonly perceived. In their practical effects, there would appear to be clear similarities between the two in their focus on clean-up and restoration, which is likely to cover the vast bulk of damage to the environment *per se*, or "natural resource damage" in American terminology. Both regimes provide compensation for clean-up costs, for assessment of the damage (understood rather than stated in the international regimes), and for restoration or reinstatement of damaged resources (environment). The main difference is the focus on damage to property and to economic interests in the oil pollution regime and treaties derived from it, and their relative neglect of damage to the environment *per se*, which is the main focus of the US regime.

This fundamental difference in focus leads to three specific differences in relation to natural resource damage. First, contrary to the provisions of US legislation, in the international maritime liability regime, the introduction of equivalent components is not covered. Second, while the US legislation covers compensation for loss of use of natural resources and for non-use values (such as "existence value") during the period of rehabilitation or restoration (so-called "interim loss"), the international regime does not. Third, where the original site is so badly damaged that it cannot be restored, the US regime provides for the creation or acquisition of an "equivalent" site in a nearby area. In contrast, in the international regime, where the original environment cannot be restored, there is no compensation, nor any alternative remedy.[92]

---

92 This will not be changed by the new text on environmental liability in the Claims Manual, as it only allows measures on a nearby site if they enhance recovery at the site of damage.

This lack of compensation for irreparable damage has aroused considerable concern amongst environmentalists, for it appears to be unjust, to say the least, for polluters to have to pay for clean-up costs in the case of minor damage, but to pay nothing at all if the damage is so severe that the environment cannot be restored. The obvious solution is for the international regimes to adopt the US practice of the introduction of reinstatement through the introduction of equivalent components at the same site or the creation of an equivalent site nearby. Where this is not possible, the alternative would be to make the polluter pay, and pay heavily, outside the civil liability regime, by means of administrative or criminal penalties, including imprisonment, for the most extreme cases.

3. Recent Developments

Up until recently, the international regime for maritime liability and compensation demonstrated scant concern for damage to the environment. While focused almost exclusively on economic loss and injury to persons and property, it strongly resisted any attempts to provide compensation for damage to the environment *per se*, strictly limited funding for assessment of environmental damage and and never paid compensation for environmental reinstatement. In contrast, other liability regimes that apply to the marine environment, such as the Basel Convention Liability Protocol, the nuclear liability conventions, and especially the regime for deep seabed mining, have taken a much more liberal and progressive approach, more in line with domestic US legislation. The *Erika* disaster prompted a reconsideration of the traditional maritime approach and a working group established by the IOPC Fund is examining whether the oil pollution liability conventions should be revised. A similar review has not been undertaken of the HNS and Bunkers Convention, which are not yet in force.

Because the review of the international regime for maritime liability is far from complete, it is still too early for a final assessment. However, it appears that members of the IOPC Fund are moving slowly towards an acceptance that more might be done to repair damage to the environment itself, as well as compensating economic losses suffered by human beings as a consequence of that damage. Still more remains to be done, as an amendment to the Claims Manual is but a first step. Because the manual is not legally binding, what will eventually be required is an amendment to the conventions themselves to clarify the meaning of pollution damage and of reasonable measures of reinstatement and to add assessment costs to the list of compensable items. While at present IOPC members are extremely reluctant to change anything, pressure from the European Union in the form of a regional regulation aimed specifically at the marine environment and/or a directive in environmental liability generally may compel it to take more radical action. Those concerned about the protection of the marine environment can only hope that attitudes may change fairly rapidly.

Index

A complete list of titles in the series is available on out website at www.wkap.nl.

55. *New Technologies Justice and Law of the Marine Environment/Nouvelles technologies et droit de l'environnement marin*
Jean-Pierre Beurier, Alexandre Kiss, Said Mahmoudi (eds)
(ISBN 90-411-9756-7)

56. *The Peaceful Settlement of International Environmental Disputes: A Pragmatic Approach*
Cesare P.R. Romano
(ISBN 90-411-9808-3)

57. *International Fisheries Management*
Stuart M. Kaye
(ISBN 90-411-9820-2)

58. *Multilateral Development Banking: Environmental Principles and Concepts Reflecting General International Law and Public Policy*
Günther Handl
(ISBN 90-411-9807-5)

59. *Implementing International Environmental Law in Germany and China*
Tao Zhenghua and Rüdiger Wolfrum (eds)
(ISBN 90-411-9843-1)

60. *Kyoto: From Principles to Practice*
Peter D. Cameron and Donald Zillman (eds)
(ISBN 90-411-1689-3)

61. *Liability for Damage to Public Natural Resources: Standing, Damage and Damage Assessment*
Edward H.P. Brans
(ISBN 90-411-1724-5)

62. *Evolution and Status of the Precautionary Principle in International Law*
Arie Trouwborst
(ISBN 90-411-1785-7)

63. *Economic Globalization and Compliance with International Environmental Agreements*
Alexandre Kiss, Dinah Shelton and Kanami Ishibashi (eds)
(ISBN 90-411-1995-7)

64. *International Marine Environmental Law: Institutions, Implementation and Innovations*
Andree Kirchner (ed)
(ISBN 90-411-2065-3)

65. *The Antarctic Environmental Protocol and its Domestic Legal Implementation*
Kees Bastmeijer
(ISBN 90-411-2064-5)

European Environmental Law (Looseleaf Service)
J. Salter
(Basic work ISBN 1-85966-050-9)